THE PRACTICE
OF PREACHING

THE PRACTICE OF PREACHING

Copyright © 1995 by Abingdon Press

This book is printed on acid-free, recycled paper.

Library of Congress Cataloging-in-Publication Data

Wilson, Paul Scott, 1949–
    The practice of preaching / Paul Scott Wilson.
      p. cm.
    Includes bibliographical references and indexes.
    ISBN 0-687-19506-3 (alk. paper)
    1. Preaching. I. Title.
  BV4211.2.W56 1995
  251—dc20   94-24126
                                              CIP

Grateful acknowledgment is made for the use of excerpts from the New Revised Standard Version Bible, copyright © 1989, by the Division of Christian Education of the National Council of the Churches of Christ in the United States of America. Used by permission.

"Ars Poetica" (p. 6) is from COLLECTED POEMS 1917–1982 by Archibald MacLeish. Copyright © 1985 by The Estate of Archibald MacLeish. Reprinted by permission of Houghton Mifflin Co. All rights reserved.

Methods of preaching on pp. 163, 216-17 are from PREACHING THE TOPICAL SERMON by Ronald J. Allen. © 1992 Ronald J. Allen. Used by permission of Westminster John Knox Press.

Sequence (p. 181) and other excerpts are reprinted from HOMILETIC by David Buttrick, copyright © 1987 Fortress Press, SCM Press. Used by permission of Augsburg Fortress, SCM Press.

Sermon outline (p. 203) is reprinted from DESIGN FOR PREACHING by H. Grady Davis, copyright © 1958 Muhlenberg Press. Used by permission of Augsburg Fortress.

Questions (p. 216) are reprinted from PREACHING AND THE LITERARY FORMS OF THE BIBLE by Thomas G. Long, copyright © 1989 Fortress Press. Used by permission of Augsburg Fortress.

95 96 97 98 99 00 01 02 03 04—10 9 8 7 6 5 4 3 2 1

MANUFACTURED IN THE UNITED STATES OF AMERICA

THE PRACTICE
OF PREACHING

PAUL SCOTT WILSON

ABINGDON PRESS
Nashville

A poem should be palpable and mute
As a globed fruit

Dumb
As old medallions to the thumb

Silent as the sleeve-worn stone
Of casement ledges where the moss has grown—

A poem should be wordless
As the flight of birds

    *   *   *

A poem should be motionless in time
As the moon climbs

Leaving, as the moon releases
Twig by twig the night-entangled trees,

Leaving, as the moon behind the winter leaves,
Memory by memory the mind—

A poem should be motionless in time
As the moon climbs

    *   *   *

A poem should be equal to:
Not true

For all the history of grief
An empty doorway and a maple leaf

For love
The leaning grasses and two lights above the sea—

A poem should not mean
But be

                   —Archibald Macleish, "Ars Poetica," 1926

ACKNOWLEDGMENTS

To many people thanks are due. Without help this book might not have appeared, at least in its present shape. My first thanks are to my family. I offer special thanks to Paul Franklyn, Steven W. Cox, and their colleagues at Abingdon Press for their input throughout the process; to John M. Rottman my teaching assistant and wise consultant through much of this time; to Ronald J. Allen, Jana Childers, Joan Delaplane; Craig Loscalzo, Stephen Farris, Charles L. Rice, Laurence H. Stookey, Richard L. Thulin, Michael E. Williams, Deanna Lee Wilson, Donald C. Wilson; and to several additional members of the Academy of Homiletics for reading the manuscript in various drafts and whose identities are known to themselves. Finally, thanks are due to my students, to Principal John Hoffman of Emmanuel College, and to the President and Board of Regents of Victoria University in the University of Toronto, for their support of this project.

To our sons (Adam, Dave, and Rob)
and to their cousins next door (Jeff, Kim, and Niki).

CONTENTS

CONTENTS

CONTENTS

CONTENTS

PREFACE

Seminary students anxiously making their way down the hall to their first preaching class may ask questions like, "How long can I delay preaching before my peers?" or "Why not just submit written sermons?" or even "Why did I ever consider ministry?" This anxiety can be a good sign. Preaching is important. Our entire vocation may seem to come into focus, or question, when we sign up for our first preaching assignment. Though we know that Christ is the focus, not the preacher, and that Christ speaks through us, these troubling thoughts nag and tug. What if I cannot preach? Should I even be considering ministry? Am I wasting my time? Will I disappoint all of those who have encouraged me to be here? There are few other courses in seminary that evoke such questions about call to ministry.

On the other hand, as students, we may find some comfort in knowing that preaching classes are designed to provide the knowledge and skills that we may be lacking. In the preaching class we are not like Cain and Abel, competing to bring the best offering to God. We compete only with ourselves to improve our potential as God's servant. Excellent preaching develops over many years in the pulpit, and only then with care, after building on a solid foundation.

Other reasons are behind our initial anxiety. Anyone hiking through theological country in any part of the globe will know that it has been affected by the same forces that have affected society, culture, and politics in the last hundred years. We have changed the way we think about how institutions and structures function in their effective operation and management.

Power and authority also are key issues in evaluating the anxiety of the preacher. At least two sources for our ideas of the nature of ministry have changed. No longer is the preacher automatically granted authority by virtue of the office. The church itself is no longer necessarily seen as a positive thread in the social fabric, much less in the "good life" of the individual. We can name few "princes of the pulpit." They have been replaced by individuals in ordered ministry with a variety of strengths or specialties. In some models of vocational ministry (e.g., facilitator-enabler), the ministry of the laity becomes the primary focus. One gift of such models can be the increased role of congregational contribution to the sermon.

Taken to its extreme, however, this tendency is at odds with preaching. Different voices arise: "No one person should have the authority to speak for everyone." "Everyone should share in the preaching." "Let us do away with preaching altogether." How can the preacher speak authoritatively in that sort of relativizing climate? Moreover, if new role models are sought, few are available for women, who, along with many men, may feel uncomfortable with traditional models of preaching.

A prospective preacher, therefore, may feel torn in this cultural and ecclesial climate when learning to preach. Preaching presumes authority. Most congregations list preaching at the top, or near the top, of desired ministry skills. Ministry depends on it. Churches want it. We all need it. Christ mandated it. Yet who are we through preaching to place demands upon others? Still, our traditional claim nonetheless remains, that preaching is God's work and one of the best means for us to exercise Christian instruction, pastoral care, and prophetic challenge. There is simply no substitute for it, and without it, the church would cease to exist. To be fine preachers we need a positive image and understanding of what we are doing, one that is suited to helping us meet the needs of churches in the twenty-first century.

Consider one further reason for possible anxiety. Students may have heard that not since the Middle Ages or the Reformation have such mighty winds swept the homiletical highlands. If we ask some of the oldest preachers, we can be told how, in just one century, the average length of sermon in many denominations has gone from nearly an hour to perhaps a quarter of that. Theorists now speak of propositional and narrative preaching; of deductive and inductive sermons; of different cultural understandings of preaching; of the role of parable in Jesus' teaching; of the pericope and various kinds of criticism (historical, redaction, form, sociological, literary, canonical, rhetorical, etc.); of the role of a reader's experience in interpreting texts; of greater ecumenical cooperation and sharing of scholarly resources; of the influence of the Roman, Lutheran, Episcopal, and Revised Common lectionaries; of changes in worship; of ways of thought being altered by mass media and computer technology; and of a host of other changes. What is at the heart of these changes? What are we leaving behind? What are we moving toward?

Of course many of these changes have connections to other changes in society at large. Many scholars now point to the difference between the modern, which has been a dominant paradigm since the Enlightenment, and the postmodern, elements of which have been copresent but have gradually become dominant ways of describing current society. The modern-postmodern social contrast can be quickly and loosely sketched using a variety of terms.[1] As preachers we are right to be critical of each column.

The Modern Age	The Postmodern Age
centered	decentered and dispersing
theistic	polytheistic
product and goal	process and service
vertical ideas of authority	horizontal ideas of authority
focus on separate disciplines	interdisciplinary focus
focus on the individual	focus on the social system
machine	community
unity of item	unity of system
independence/autonomy	interdependence/relationship
objective/subjective	relative
authority of fact	authorities of interpretation
information	communication
singleness of meaning	plurality of meanings
meaning "in" and "behind" the text	meaning "in front of" the text

If we scan preaching books at the library, we quickly get a sense of change. Many of the titles identify varieties of sermon form, from expository and doctrinal to sermons that adopt the form, function, or mode of expression of the biblical text. We also see changes in thematic concerns: for instance the number of preaching books devoted to feminist, liberation, cultural, and social-justice preaching. Important as these formal and thematic matters are, they constitute but one part of a larger movement of long-term significance for the homiletical climate.

Fundamental to many of the changes we are seeing around us in theology as a whole is the increased importance given to experience, in particular the experience of those who have been silent or

13

oppressed or otherwise excluded from participation in decisions that affect individual and communal life. It was the experience of injustice by workers that led to the social gospel movement; of poverty in Latin America that led to liberation theology; of white, male, middle-class bias in traditional theology that led to feminist theology; of racial, cultural, and economic bias that led to black and womanist theology; and, within the limited sphere of worship in some denominations, the experience of exclusion among laity that led to theology of liturgical revision.

Many, though not all, of the changes in homiletics today are also related to various claims of experience (e.g., of the preacher and listener), even beyond these theological movements. Toward the beginning of this shift to experience, four claims were made for the renewal of preaching that have since proved to be foundational for contemporary homiletics:

1) The sermon . . . proceeds from the Bible as God's Word to us and connects with the situation of the hearers; it does not arise from religion in general and address the universe.
2) The sermon moves fundamentally to confirmation from affirmation, rather than to evidence from axiom.
3) The sermon seeks concretion by bringing the meaning of the text to expression in the situation of the hearers, rather than abstraction by merely exhibiting the text against its own background.
4) The sermon seeks forms of construction and communication which are consistent with the message it intends to convey, not necessarily those which are most traditional, most readily available, or most "successful."[2]

Of course the call for preaching to relate to the experience or situation of the hearers is at one level simply a call for relevance, and this is demanded in every age. However, in recent decades it has also become a call for new sermon forms, content that reflects human experience, and form that enhances content and function, such that what is spoken and what is effected are one, as in Archibald Macleish's prescription for poetry in the epigraph.

This textbook introduces students to the breadth and depth of the homiletical field, much in the manner that we might expect of an introductory textbook in any other field. As in other fields, use of the term "introductory" need not imply anything about its readers (i.e. whether they are undergraduate or graduate theological students, or experienced preachers). It is addressed directly to students engaged in theological education, and tries to speak to the concerns and ques-

14

tions that they have as they begin studying homiletics. It is written to challenge students in helpful ways, without the expectation that they will have finished with their learnings when their preaching course is done. Excellent preaching is, after all, a lifelong goal for all of us. Attention is given to all stages in the development of a sermon, to important trends in homiletics, as well as to the relationship of preaching to other key courses in the theological curriculum.

At the same time, this book is written to enable preachers already serving churches to overhear what is being said in the classrooms; Fred Craddock helped us understand the importance of overhearing in the preaching and learning process *(Overhearing the Gospel)*. Assistance is provided here for ministers, pastors, and priests to apply learnings in their own situations. Much more needs to be said about preaching and its relationship to worship than was possible to say here, (1) for reasons of length, and (2) for reasons of diverse denominational backgrounds and worship practice of readers. I have chosen simply to use the word "sermon" rather than a dual reference to sermon and homily, hoping that readers who prefer homily will forgive this attempt at being less clumsy.

Several assumptions were at work in the writing of this introduction. A textbook in preaching should: (1) foster a love of preaching and a love of language; (2) draw on the history of preaching; (3) fairly represent a variety of approaches; (4) present preaching as a theological task; (5) be practical; (6) be challenging; (7) present a coherent vision of future homiletical directions; (8) contribute new insights; (9) assist readers and instructors with examples, exercises, and guidelines along with theoretical understanding; and, (10) meet the needs of students in helping them actually to prepare a sermon. The approach here is rooted in the structure of theological language, in an attempt to avoid the necessary limitations of a thematic approach.

This book is divided into four sections. Each section develops from a current perspective one of the four great historical traditions from which homiletics has sprung: I. Oral Tradition (oral cultures and ways of thought), II. Rhetoric (the art of persuasion, here particularly as it relates to theology),[3] III. Hermeneutics (the art of interpretation), and IV. Poetics (literary theory and issues of form and content). Each chapter makes use of an initial abstract, numerous sidebars, sermon examples, concluding multiple-choice review questions, and questions for small group or class discussion to help make the material as accessible as possible. In addition, specific exercises are offered throughout for the student to use in working toward a completed sermon.

The section on hermeneutics, at the heart of the book, is divided into four chapters. Readers desiring to work on a sermon in an orderly manner while reading this book (or preachers on a week of independent study leave) are encouraged to read the Oral Tradition section alongside "Monday" in the Hermeneutics section; the Rhetorical Tradition with "Tuesday"; "Wednesday" of the Hermeneutics section on its own; and "Thursday-Friday" of the Hermeneutics section alongside the Tradition of Poetics. (See appendix 2.)

In organizing this project, it was tempting to stay with the canons or sets of rules of classical rhetoric. Aristotelian rhetoric had three canons to assist the public speaker: *invention* (ways of discovering what there is to say about a topic); *arrangement* (ordering thought in correct ways); and *style* (making language and material suitable to its purpose). Roman rhetoricians added another two to bring the classical canon to five: *memory* (making material memorable both for delivery and reception); and *delivery*. Early in the project it became apparent that this would not work, in part because the Aristotelian categories ended up dominating much of the material here; and because faithfulness to classical rhetoric is never the goal of a preacher.

The primary purpose here is not to identify leading traditions informing preaching, or even to identify changes affecting the contemporary homiletics, or to point to new or emergent directions. It is rather to provide a preaching manual that will assist preaching today, and to encourage us all to think how we may better assist God, who meets us all, especially in proclamation of the Word.

Emmanuel College
University of Toronto
Easter, 1994

SECTION

I

The Oral Tradition

The Scriptures are God's voice. The God who spoke in human history to the chosen people of Israel, and whose events of self-revelation are recorded by the scriptural witnesses, is the same God who speaks to us today through those same biblical texts and in our lives. As preachers, we boldly claim that God uses our voices to speak God's Word in the lives of people today, through the correct reading and interpretation of Scripture. While voice and speech need not be our exclusive metaphors for discussing this means of grace (God finds other ways of "speaking" to people, whether or not they are able or willing to hear), these are nonetheless our dominant metaphors and God's most explicit means. They underline that while preaching uses ordinary voice to speak to ordinary matters of life, it is no ordinary speech.

Preaching may be helpfully compared and contrasted with poetry, which also is no ordinary speech. For instance, preaching, like most poetry, is composed to be spoken. Archibald Macleish wrote the poem epigraph of this book for sound. For instance, only in speaking aloud the third couplet of his poem do we hear, in the repeated sibilant "s," the faint sounds of sleeves on stone, or the softness of the moss: "Silent as the sleeve-worn stone / Of casement ledges where the moss has grown." In a similar manner in worship, we hear the voice of God speaking to us in the sound of preaching.

17

Moreover, Macleish's poetry, in a small way like God's speech in the Genesis creation account, creates the subject of its speech. The poet can speak about the rising moon and because of his attentiveness to words, we see the moon and experience it rising twig by twig beyond the branches of the trees. Thus Macleish claims that a poem should be wordless, creating the event such that we no longer notice the words but encounter their subjects: "A poem should not mean / But be."

In an even more vibrant sense, the same is true of preaching, particularly if we, like the poet, are attentive to use of words. We no longer listen only to the words, but participate in an event. We encounter God in Christ who speaks to us. The people who are named in the sermon from around the world, portrayed in various circumstances, become again our brothers and sisters, who like us are under the Word and can no longer remain faceless, nameless, or beyond our concern or celebration. In this limited sense we might echo Macleish in saying, A sermon should not mean / But be. Yet it is not passive.

Dietrich Bonhoeffer instructed his students to listen to sermons with the expectation of encountering Christ.[1] This did not mean listening to sermons the way we must learn to listen to them in homiletics classes, which is necessarily in a critical manner with a view to strengths and weaknesses of the preacher's theology, craft, and art. In actual worship we seek in some ways to suspend critique, as much as this is wise or possible, seeking the discernment of the Spirit to hear the sermon as though Christ is speaking it to us, which in good measure is in fact the case. God uses the preacher's faithful interpretation of Scripture to offer a saving message in power to us. This can mean more than listening to see if we agree with what is said and identifying that with Christ speaking to us. It can mean that in an act of personal and corporate discipline, we imagine or otherwise conceive of Christ actually doing the preaching.

Many artists, poets, and preachers today are like prophets of old, boldly naming social and spiritual wrongs. Archibald Macleish, for instance, also wrote a Pulitzer Prize–winning play about Job, *J.B.*, to highlight suffering and injustice in our time.[2] Walter Brueggemann sees poets as prophets in his identification of Christ as the final poet:

Those whom the ancient Israelites called prophets, the equally ancient Greeks called poets. The poet/prophet is a voice that shatters settled reality and evokes new possibility in the listening assembly. Preaching continues that dangerous, indispensable habit of speech. The poetic speech of the text and of sermon is a prophetic construal of a world beyond the one taken for granted.[3]

It is through the oral event of preaching that this world beyond our assumed world is revealed as trustworthy and true. It is through preaching that we lay all our fears, cares, sins, hopes, and needs upon the Word.

Preaching is no ordinary speech. However, preaching is no ordinary poetry either. It is the sound of God speaking, and as such, it is the intelligible sound of our salvation taking place. It is oral speech of a unique sort, rooted in Scripture and the oral traditions that gave it birth. It remains part of oral traditions we can no longer hear and for which historical records of sermon manuscripts are poor substitutes. In preaching we also perpetuate oral traditions we have heard for those who follow.

At least two important aspects of inherited oral tradition can help give foundation and shape to preaching in the present. One of these is preaching as God's event, the subject of chapter 1. The other is the oral language and thought we find in the Bible that contribute to making preaching an oral event, the subject of chapter 2.

PREACHING AS GOD'S EVENT

The central purpose of preaching is the disclosure of God, an encounter with God through the Word, more than information about God. Two relationships characterize the preaching event for the congregation, a relationship with God and a relationship with the preacher. Each of these is explored theologically in part to highlight the difference between teaching and preaching, and in part to explore the manner in which God uses who we are as preachers to communicate the Word. A concluding sermon extract demonstrates practical lessons from the two relationships.

The recent revolution in homiletics has encouraged reexamination of most aspects of preaching. One perspective has suffered for lack of specialized focus: the purpose of preaching. A recommitment to purpose has the potential for helping us to understand what needs to be preserved and what needs to be created afresh in performing familiar tasks as preachers.

In exploring the purpose of preaching, we do not start with questions of form or content, working forward to the finished sermon. Nor do we start by asking what it means to preach. Instead, we start at the end of the sermon, as listeners meditating on the purpose of what we have heard. If we recall even now our best experiences of preaching, we may ask, What stands out? What happened? What did that sermon achieve? What did it effect? What was set in motion?

In the finest sermons we feel renewed hope, stronger faith, and recommitment to mission. More simply stated, we experience God. For this reason we claim that preaching is an event in which the congregation meets the living God. When we use the word *event* in this way, we mean an action, an occurrence, something that happens in a moment of time in the lives of the hearers. When we say that this is a divine event, we acknowledge that through preaching, God chooses to be encountered. Since this encounter effects a new relationship with God of reconciliation and empowerment, we may also acknowledge preaching as a salvation event. All of this is part of the purpose of preaching.

Once we begin to take the purpose of preaching seriously, and begin conceiving of it as an event in these dynamic ways, it does not take us long to realize that we have made a departure from our more common ways of thinking about sermons. These prior ways often fall somewhat short of meeting God in an event, of embodying an active relationship or communication with God.

> *Preaching is an event of encounter with God that leaves the congregation with stronger faith and deeper commitment to doing God's work.*

By dreaming what preaching can be, we may find better ways to communicate God's love. Thus our aim here on the one hand is conservative: to portray homiletics in sufficient detail so as to clarify key issues and point readers to other sources. On the other hand our aim may sound somewhat bold: It is to provide guidance to those who want to assist God in making their preaching more of an event of divine encounter, something that happens in our lives and the lives of our people. Feminist theology has alerted us to the importance of conceiving of what we do in terms of relationships. Postmodern criticism similarly elevates relationship such that "the authentic phenomenon in any event is not *fact*, but *relationship*."[1]

With this in mind we turn to two relationships that are central to the congregation's experience of the sermon: a relationship with God and a relationship with the preacher.[2]

A Relationship with God

When we speak of God, much less of a relationship with God, our language is inadequate. Though God's identity is revealed to us in the Scriptures, theologians have reminded us that the essentially mysterious God does not lose mystery upon being revealed.[3] Our knowledge of God is imperfect. In addition, this relationship is not between equals; our love, in contrast to that of God, is imperfect. Moreover, this relationship is with God in the three persons of the Trinity, and it is this triune relationship that is fostered by the preaching and sacraments of the church.

God uses the sermon for self-revelation, for it is in the reading and correct interpretation of Scripture (a safeguard provided by our traditions) that God chooses most to be revealed. The nature of this identity, we say as Christians, is not different or separable from what is revealed in the Christ event, which occurred at a particular time and place in history, yet is nonetheless the same event which encounters us in and through preaching in our present time. Thus we may speak of the sermon as God's continuing self-giving, through which human sin is both called to account and condemned, and in which we are encountered by a reconciling love which is stronger even than death itself.

What we may rightly expect of this relationship is witnessed through the ages: God is unconditionally for us, desiring fullness of all human life with a love that is without end. It is God who sustains and empowers us for ministry, each day according to our needs. It is God who uses our words to reconciling purposes in the shaping of community. And it is God who bestows on preacher and congregation alike our identity in Christ through sacraments of the church and proclamation.

It is a temptation for preachers to think of the sermon as an object or a thing like an essay or lecture, rather than as a vehicle that God uses to establish a relationship with God's people. Salvation is communicated and authentic life is bestowed: God comes to us through preaching.

What we may not expect of this relationship is also clear: We are not in control; God's ways are not our ways, nor are they determined by our ways; and God will play no favorites, for all people are loved, as the rain falls equally on the just and unjust.

It is common for many of us to conceive of the sermon as something less than an event of encounter with God. In the pastoral life we tend to conceive of the sermon as a thing: It is an object that we construct, or an essay that is written, or a task to be done, or a paper that is due, or a theological lecture, or biblical interpretation, or discussion of issues for our time. These are all relevant activities in themselves, but they are not normally events of divine encounter.

How we think of a task affects how we do it. Phillips Brooks (1835–1893), the great Episcopalian preacher of Trinity Church in Boston, spoke of one difference between preaching as lecturing and preaching as he thought it should be:

Much of our preaching is like delivering lectures upon medicine to sick people. The lecture is true. The lecture is interesting. Nay, the truth of the lecture is important, and if the sick man could learn the truth of the lecture he would be a better patient, he would take his medicine more responsibly and regulate his diet more intelligently. But still the fact remains that the lecture is not medicine, and that to give the medicine, not to deliver the lecture, is the preacher's duty.[4]

Something should happen in preaching that reflects the relationship it effects. God initiates relationship and restores identity through preaching. The sermon offers love for the unloved, and justice for the downtrodden—in other words, God acts in and through preaching. We begin to conceive of the sermon as an intimate and personal event in a communal context with community-shaping power. It is God's salvation breaking into the world.

Consequently our thinking must shift. For instance, we must see that a relationship with God is begun and maintained, not just a relationship with ideas about God. When the sermon goes well, information concerning God is not the purpose of the event so much as God's formation of us in Christ's image. The sermon we listen to is less an intellectual exercise than it is our being reclaimed by Christ as God's own. We do not hear witness about Christ, so much as we experience Christ's love encountering us. We do not receive a summons to authentic life, so much as we experience its bestowal as God's gift.

We may be led to several claims about preaching. Good preaching is less instruction about community than community happening: the Holy Spirit constituting the assembled community as the Body of Christ in and through the proclamation of the Word and celebration of the sacrament. Preaching then can be less a discussion of the things wrong with this world than it is Christ's beginning a new world as people gather around the Word. The sermon can be less an object than it is an action of divine encounter by which a relationship is renewed. While God comes to us in many ways, we affirm not least that God comes to us through preaching.

This idea of God reaching out to embrace us through preaching is not original or innovative, nor should it be, though it has languished in the life of our churches, sometimes because we ourselves are not embracing an intimate God. Preaching cannot be conceived as just another functional task that we do in the course of a busy week, if we keep struggling with this idea that the sermon is God's event, that God is the one doing the acting, that God has called the preacher and the community of the church to this place and time, that God is the one who is empowering the preacher to preach, that God is the one who is empowering the listeners through the hearing, that the sermon itself is a manifestation of God and God's grace, and that God will again be manifest in the lives of the people going out to the world. While the preacher obviously composes the sermon, and the listener is actively engaged in interpreting it,[5] it is appropriate to speak of God's work in even these roles: We cannot testify to Christ, nor comprehend such testimony, separate from God's action in and through the Holy Spirit (I John 4:2, 15).

It is from a relationship with Jesus Christ that all other important aspects of the sermon flow, however we might name them: the contributions of the congregation and preacher; biblical and contemporary interpretation; teaching; judgment; correction; conversion; prophecy; pastoral care; witness; grace; justice; and various kinds of mission activities.

The sermon at one level is God's doing from beginning to end. It is God's action through the preacher, during the past week and in the pulpit, and particularly through the listeners, in the pews and throughout the coming week. In itself it is a manifestation of God.

David James Randolph, drawing on Barth and others and seeking to bring fruit of the school of interpretation then called the New Hermeneutic into the pulpit, spoke of preaching as event: "The key to this approach is that its emphasis falls on what the sermon does, rather than what it is." He identified what it does by quoting John Wesley: "To invite. To convince. To offer Christ. To build up; and do this in some measure in every sermon."[6]

The idea has grown in acceptance and implication in recent years.[7] Eugene L. Lowry notes that "while philosophers may be centering on the question of truth, the preacher's goals focus on *experienced truth*."[8] Sallie McFague said of Jesus' preaching in the parables, "They are not primarily concerned with knowing but with doing."[9] Fred B. Craddock speaks of the sermon needing "realization not information," and adds, "Preaching both proclaims an event and participates in that event, both reports on revelation and participates in that revelation . . . here and now."[10] Don M. Wardlaw says, "The Word of God happens; it becomes a proclamation event in the lives of the people experiencing the sermon."[11] Eduard Riegert notes, "We receive too much information as it is. People are hungry for an encounter with God; they do not merely want to know about God, they want to know God."[12] Finally, David J. Schlafer notes that

in catholic tradition, the sacraments of the church, through word and gesture, achieve what they symbolically announce. . . . All of these perfectly natural elements, touched by grace, are transformed and do transform. Similarly, the words of preaching are merely, fully, human words. Yet, engraced by the Word, they actually accomplish the salvation they announce.[13]

24

The idea of divine encounter in preaching is appropriately as old as the church, and derives from our understanding of the sermon as a breaking open of God's Word. Justin Martyr wrote (c. 150) concerning the hearing of Scripture,

When you hear the words of the prophets spoken as in a particular character, do not think of them as spoken by the inspired men themselves, but by the divine Word that moved them. For sometimes he speaks . . . as in the character of God the Master and Father of all, sometimes as in the character of Christ, sometimes in the character of the people answering the Lord or his Father.[14]

We may even now sound a note of caution, however. We do not make Christ present by preaching. Christ is already present in the church, not least through Baptism, and surely it is only through this presence of Christ that preaching is made possible.[15] However, we must balance this claim with another. Christ's historic presence in the church is active, not static, as though it were a quality the church might contain. We cannot take Christ's presence in the church for granted, as though Christ were at our disposal. The event of Christ's continuing self-giving through Word and Sacrament is essential for the life of the church, not least because by this the sinful church becomes the true church.[16] Holding in tension these two perspectives of continuing presence and continuing self-giving, we begin to understand the precise nature of this event. Thomas G. Long echoes Luther and Calvin in noting that "to speak in Christ's name is to claim Christ's own promise, 'The one who hears you, hears me' (Luke 10:16)."[17] Our task, then, is not to bring Christ to the church, but to find Christ there and to bring our people before God's throne of judgment and grace.

Alternatives

Of course there are other views of preaching we could legitimately hold—indeed, other ways in which we could use the term *event*—that are feasible alternatives to preaching as an event of divine encounter. We do not need to discard these various important alternatives in naming what can be an additional goal for our preaching.

For instance, preaching is also **teaching.** The New Testament uses separate words for preaching *(kerygma)* and teaching *(didache). Kerygma* means to herald or proclaim the coming of God's Realm in Jesus Christ. *Didache* is teaching about the consequences of Christ's coming.

Distinction between these words in Greek (and related terms in Hebrew) is not absolute; the tasks are related. This lack of distinction is hardly surprising, since preaching in the infant church was notoriously fluid. It took a variety of shapes and contents, both within and outside the setting of worship, and included martyrdom.[18] Even in the Middle Ages preaching remained broadly understood, when Alan of Lille (1128–1202) identified it as what is spoken, what is written in a letter, and what is done by deed.[19] Teaching is a part of preaching, for we can never separate the proclamation of God in Jesus Christ from instruction about what this means. Nonetheless, preaching has rarely been considered identical to teaching, lecturing, or instructing. One way we make a distinction is to say that teaching may be about God, while preaching may be an encounter with God.

Another possible alternative is to think of preaching as an event of **divine remembrance.** In this we may conceive of the sermon as a recital of redemptive and formative events through which God is revealed. G. Ernest Wright thinks of biblical theology in this manner, in *God Who Acts: Biblical Theology as Recital.* This remembrance of events makes important claims on us today.

Still other legitimate alternatives include conceiving of the sermon as an event of **prophecy,** in which the consequences of our own actions, or the actions of God, are laid out before us as a warning or to increase our current awareness of God. Similarly, preaching can be an event of **praise** to God (in the manner of Romans 10:8-17); or an event of biblically based **storytelling** that enables us to dream of new possibilities for this world; or an event of evangelism and **conversion** in sharing the gospel and attracting new members; or an event of **pastoral care;** or an event to help support the **institutional life** of the church; or an event to galvanize the congregation to a particular action or **protest;** or an eschatological event that is a necessary **prelude to the end times** (see Matt. 24:14).

These are all acceptable ways of thinking of the event of preaching. However, each of these contains the potential for something more: an experience of God's encounter in and through the proclamation of the Word. When we give priority to thinking of the sermon in this way, whatever other ways we employ, we are less likely to lose sight of the centrality of God's action in our midst. Without this purpose in

> *Other ways of conceiving of preaching as an event may supplement our primary understanding of preaching as God's event:*
> • *teaching*
> • *divine remembrance*
> • *prophecy*
> • *praise*
> • *biblical storytelling*
> • *pastoral care*
> • *evangelism*
> • *conversion*
> • *institutional support*
> • *social action, and*
> • *heralding the end times.*

mind, it is easy for our language to imply that God is remote and abstract, indifferent, impersonal, passive, functionally—or apparently—irrelevant.

If we keep this high goal of preaching before us, we may think of the sermon primarily as a vehicle God uses to reestablish a relationship with us. God comes to us, we may say, in the preaching, through the Holy Spirit, to make atonement for our sins, once more to lay claim to our lives, once more to bring us face-to-face with our salvation. We may conceive of the sermon as something God is using now, even as we listen, to judge, nurture, and reshape our gnarled and twisted lives, and to bring forth God's purposes for the world.

How we speak says something about God's Word. Thus in talking about God's love, we can conceive of God's love actually going forth, and we speak in a manner that allows our people to experience that love. Obviously this means, at minimum, matching tone and gesture. Thus if we are issuing an invitation, we do not become reserved and hold back; our language and manner become warm and invitational. Or if we are proclaiming the Good News, we will not speak as though we have just bitten a pickle; there is something joyful in our words and demeanor.

However, preaching as God's event means more than this. It means creating in words the kinds of experiences and relationships that embody what is spoken. Both what and how we communicate will be altered.

A Relationship with the Preacher

Even as God initiates a relationship through the sermon with God's people, the congregation experiences a relationship with us as preachers. This relationship can help or hinder what God is accomplishing through the sermon. Ancient tutors in classical Greece named this essential dimension of any communication process "ethos"—the ethics or character of the speaker. If a community is not convinced of the integrity of a preacher, if they do not trust the relationship, no matter what is said, or how well it is said, they may not listen. On the other hand, if a congregation senses that as preachers we believe what we are preaching, that we care about them, that we stand with them under the Word not against them and over the Word, then communication is enhanced.

Of course everything that we say or do communicates an impression of our identity. As an analogy, it is common knowledge in employment interviews that within the first thirty seconds, interviewers have made their decision about the candidate, and it rarely changes after that time. An argument can be made, therefore, that since similar quick decisions are made about the preacher, there is little we can do in preaching to alter how we are received. We are who we are. We cannot help communicating this. Besides, most people in the congregation already know who we are, not least by the quality of our pastoral care. Thus we might say that the most authentic relationship is the one that happens most naturally, with least attention.

Beyond this, we might argue that the preacher should stay out of the sermon by avoiding first-person pronouns. Karl Barth believed that any attention to ethos was interference with the Word: "The preacher does not have to speak 'on' but 'from' *(ex)*, drawing from Scriptures whatever [is said. The preacher] does not have to invent but rather to repeat something. No thesis, no purpose derived from [the preacher's] own resources must be allowed to intervene."[20]

We might consider, however, that it is inaccurate, or at least wishful thinking, to define the preacher's role as nothing more than a conduit. Whether we are writing history, or preaching God's Word, we always speak from the limitations of our own time and culture. God's message changes us, and we also change it for those who receive it from us. Mere instrumentality does not exist in preaching.

Furthermore, God never intended the Word to be handled with sterile gloves, kept free from contact with anything human. If this had been the intention, Christ would not have come among us in human form. We may hope to be translucent, allowing God's light to shine through our words and actions. But we can never be transparent, as though we do not speak from our humanity. God alone makes perfect the communication of the Word, in the heart and soul of the willing hearer. In this process, God uses who we are in all our humanity to bear the Word.

Taking our countering argument one step farther, we know that our best relationships flourish only with care and attention. Ethos in preaching is never simply to be conceived as communication of information about who we are as preachers. Ethos is not about satisfying one's own ego needs, or turning the sermon to focus on oneself. Rather it is the nurturing of relationship between the congregation and preacher. This happens in the course of the preaching, in and through what is being said, as part of the actual message. Classical rhetoricians would claim that ethos is of such importance that it is the main element that determines listener response. Today's rhetoricians call this *identity:* When listeners make a positive judgment about the ethos of a speaker, they identify with the speaker and what the speaker is saying and give that person authority.

Such claims about the primary importance of ethos need careful nuancing in relation to the church and worship, however, for at least two reasons. First, the authority to preach is an office given by the entire church, in accordance with Scripture, usually through laying on of hands at ordination, only after the candidate has been thoroughly tested with regard to call, character, theological knowledge, and ability to interpret Scripture correctly. Authority to preach is not something listeners individually determine for themselves whether or not to bestow each Sunday. Second, as an act of spiritual discipline and out of an understanding of the nature of Christian community, listeners overlook aspects of personality in order to listen for God's Word. We are, after all, listening to the Word in the prayer that we may encounter the living Christ. Nonetheless, good pulpit ethos is essential in enabling God's Word to be heard.

Ethos in a sermon has some fluidity. Pulpit ethos is not a quality that the preacher possesses, nor is it secured because a listener likes the person of the preacher.

Who you are is not the issue, but who your hearers perceive you to be. We may not like the sound of that, but it is radically true. If people perceive you as a compassionate, caring person, they hear your words of compassion and care with their heads and hearts. But if your congregation considers you aloof and unapproachable, they will have trouble hearing and experiencing your message of compassion. Even if you feel you are warm and caring, the congregation's perception may be quite different.[21]

Moreover, ethos has to do with what the preacher is discussing, and it changes during the sermon, in accordance with what is being said and who is doing the listening.[22]

Preachers cannot leave ethos simply to chance, because ethos (positive or negative) is interpreted by listeners to be a result of decisions the preacher has made or is making. Everything that the preacher says or does in preaching reflects choice in the process of communication. Ethos is thus a response the preacher causes. Nonetheless it is the listener who finally evaluates and thus individually determines the preacher's ethos. In fact, as Aristotle said, "It is [the person addressed], the hearer, that determines the speech's end and

The preacher's character, as portrayed in the sermon, should be an intended aspect of preaching, reflecting choices the preacher has made to build trust. Ethos is reflected in the preacher's moral, intellectual, spiritual, emotional, and personal habits, in and behind what is said.

object."[23] Ethos is commonly assessed through what listeners know of the preacher's moral, intellectual, spiritual, emotional, and personal habits, largely through what is learned or signaled of these in the sermon itself.[24]

We may list a few of the obvious ways in which these habits are signaled in the sermon. **Moral** habits are evident through the preacher's character, trustworthiness, ability to make the right kinds of decision in difficult circumstances, and respect of others with different opinions. **Intellectual** habits are demonstrated by the emphasis that the preacher places on being informed and getting the correct facts; the preacher's curiosity and interest in both people and political, social, and cultural events; and the preacher's dedication to a disciplined life of study (including study leave), the fruits of which are clear. **Spiritual** habits are signaled for example by the preacher's knowledge of Scripture, willingness to talk about God, ability to talk about all manner of human situations in appropriate theological ways, depth of faith, and reliance upon God. **Emotional** habits are communicated through the preacher's concern for the congregation, through the preacher's demonstration of emotion appropriate to the subject matter, and by the preacher's ability to enter into the suffering and joy of others. **Personal** habits are evident through grooming, dress, manners, and mannerisms.

These general truths about ethos translate into four practical guidelines for the preacher. First, while ethos is of concern from the beginning to the end of the sermon, it is of particular importance in the opening minutes, when a relationship with the hearers must be reestablished. This means that the introductory material to the sermon should not be too demanding, for listeners are still trying to adjust to the preacher as a person.

Second, while as preachers we are usually the only ones actually speaking during the sermon, we need not monopolize the conversation, and our tone need not be authoritarian. The congregation contributes to the sermon in various ways, through conversations, educational events, situations of pastoral care, and through individual and communal sharing of talents and life in the church and its mission. Our words can reflect conversations, actions, and concerns that we have seen or heard during the week, voiced in a loving manner that allows the congregation to identify with what we say.[25]

Third, ethos is determined not just by what information the preacher chooses to communicate, but also by whether or not listeners agree or disagree with the preacher's claims. It is thus important that the preacher

30

try to reflect accurately a variety of viewpoints, not just his or her own. This is especially the case if we are speaking to controversial issues; we can reflect on positions counter to the one we are taking, positions that members of the congregation might hold. These multiple viewpoints that anticipate objections are what David Buttrick calls "contrapuntals."[26]

Fourth, ethos presumes that we speak to the congregation about things that matter to them. We could call this preaching to the needs of the congregation, not just to our own needs as preachers. In other words, preaching presumes pastoral care. Harry Emerson Fosdick (1878–1969) of Riverside Church in New York was a great proponent of preaching to need. He said that lectures had "a subject to be elucidated" in contrast to preaching, which had "an object to be achieved."[27] Thus if he was preaching on the need for joy, he would explore the subject of joy theologically and then move actually to create it in the sermon.

In preaching to need, we may generally look first to Scripture, for we often do not independently know what best we need and we determine the agenda of preaching in relation to Christ. It is therefore helpful for us to distinguish between the expressed need of the congregation, the congregation's actual need, and the preacher's need. The expressed need is what the congregation might say or has said that it needs, in its own words. A parallel situation exists in counseling situations, where parishioners often identify a presenting issue, or ostensible reason for the visit, which may be different from the actual issue. For instance, a teenager might complain of having no friends, when the real issue is lack of parental expression of love. In the congregation also, the expressed need might differ from the actual need.

The actual need is the need of the congregation as it is discerned scripturally and theologically and stated using Christian vocabulary. For example, the expressed need might be: We need fewer meetings. The actual need might be: We need to know God; or, We long for community.

The actual need of a congregation is not determined apart from Scripture, for as Christians we speak of the human situation in relationship to God. Normally the actual need may be determined as we study the biblical text, listening for what God is saying to our particular situation. For instance a text might say, "God seeks to be known"; or, "God establishes relationship." Once this central idea of the biblical text has been established, we can move back to the actual need to be met in the con-

- **Expressed need**—The need the congregation identifies for itself, in its own words.
- **Actual need**—The need of the congregation as discerned scripturally and theologically and stated using Christian vocabulary.
- **Preacher's need**—The agenda of the preacher that may be unrelated to the needs of the congregation.

gregation (i.e., We need to know God; or, We long for community; or, We desire peace and justice). We might also try to get back beyond even this actual need to the expressed need, so that we are using the congregation's own words as part of the sermon (i.e., Why does God seem far away?; or, It does not seem like many people care about us). It is often helpful to move from the expressed need to the actual need in the course of the sermon itself.

Good preachers will be attentive to the expressed and actual needs of the congregation each week as part of the sermon process. When the preacher avoids these, the preacher is prone to act out of the preacher's need, which may have little to do with a relationship with the congregation. The preacher's need is the preacher's agenda, what the preacher thinks the congregation ought to know, though it is unrelated to their lives. The preacher's need is not necessarily negative: It may even be prophetic. It is the task of the preacher, however, to find some legitimate connection, some relationship between his or her material and the congregation, such that the preacher's need becomes an expression of the congregation's actual need.

> Homiletical Method and Ethos
> 1) Pay attention to ethos throughout the sermon and particularly in the opening minutes.
> 2) Reflect conversations or attitudes of the congregation in preaching.
> 3) Present viewpoints counter to your own, particularly on controversial subjects.
> 4) Recognize in the sermon the difference between the expressed need and the actual need of the congregation. Avoid preaching something that is only the preacher's need.

We anticipate and articulate perceived needs, attitudes, and possible responses. We take a deliberate approach to ethos in the sermon. We assume that everything that we do and say has the potential to engender trust; thus, we choose words, stories, issues, and experiences with appropriate anticipation both of what they say and what they do, especially in terms of trust and love.

Fostering Relationship in a Sermon

How do we foster the congregation's relationship with ourselves and with God? What do these look like in a sermon? They are an aspect of everything that is said when we preach. They can be present in important ways even when we are presenting the biblical text or telling a story from our experience.

Consider the last third of this sermon on Matthew 4:1-11, the temptation of Christ. I was struck by the fact that Jesus' temptations were his own, and that ours might be similar or quite different. One of our temptations as Christians today is not to be involved, to go with the privacy and isolation offered by a massive society where it is easy to hide and only to do those things that help us feel closer to God. It is a temptation because, like many temptations, it appears satisfying or even good but upon closer inspection is not. It is self-destructive to remain detached, giving only to those who can give in return. Seen in this light, even the desire to be closer to God, to be innocent, under certain circumstances can be a sin. We do not gain innocence from detachment, or by our own actions, but by faith in Christ.

Innocence comes from Jesus Christ. It has already come for us. Our innocence dawned on that first Easter morning, in all its radiant splendor, when God in Christ announced to the world: The power of death is not ultimate. My love is ultimate. Our innocence washed over us in the waters of our baptism. Our innocence is the person of Jesus Christ, who meets us in the stranger, from out of the midst of struggle, and pain, and temptation, and the grime and grit of daily life. Do not seek innocence by retreating from the world and thus retreating from Christ. He stands with his arms already enclosing you, when the temptation seems greatest to give up serving others. Even now, there is not one of you here who is outside of God's love. No matter what you have done or has been done to you, Christ even now gives you the power to walk the right path.

[The words chosen here are as intimate, personal, and loving as possible. Even their use may help the preacher establish trust with the congregation. The next story was chosen because there was a large number of youth in the congregation.]

Eric Clapton is an extraordinary musician who was honored this week in the Grammy Awards. He has known tragedy. His only child Conner was barely four years old when he fell 52 stories to his death from a condominium window in New York, two years ago. *[I tell this quickly to get it out of the way, since I do not want the tragedy to be my continuing focus.]* Until his son was born, he said, he had little reason for living, and little reason for loving. It was after his son's birth that a change happened. He swore off alcohol, became a recovering alcoholic, and for the first time in his life started to love. He was just starting to know his son, and he wrote for him. "My songs came to me from my demons, but it was an angel I liked to play for." *[The imagery here may help recall the biblical text.]* "The day before the accident," his estranged partner said, "Eric and Conner had gone to the circus where they had spent the most wonderful day of their lives." Recovering alcoholics know what temptation is, every day of their lives. Members of Alcoholics Anonymous begin by saying, I cannot do it on my own, I need the help of God.

After Conner died, both parents could have given up. But they did not. Instead, Clapton wrote a beautiful ballad to his son. His partner returned to

Milan to begin rebuilding her life, where, one day, in a shopping mall she first heard the song. She sat down where she was and wept. The song was so powerful and healing. You may have heard him singing it this week on television when he received his Grammy Award for his song "Tears in Heaven." Knowing his story, and hearing his song, was like having an angel come to minister, as in our text: Clapton is singing to his absent son: "Would you know my name, if I saw you in heaven? Would you hold my hand, if I saw you in heaven?" [How these words are said is almost as important as what they say.] When Clapton received his award, he thanked his son for bringing love into his life, for bringing him back to life.

We may say that Clapton and his partner had a lot of strength, and it is true. We also know, whether or not they know it, that the only source of such strength is the only One who can bring good out of evil, purpose out of a meaningless life. [Note the manner in which God is identified as the actor here.] This is the One, Jesus Christ, who touches us in glorious love, and allows us to enter in love, even with tears, to the pain of others.

This one example may help us to identify several things concerning the relationship with God and the relationship with the preacher in sermons:

1) Nearly everything that we say can have implications for both our relationship with God and our relationship with our listeners. Conversation about God can say something about our attitude toward the congregation. Similarly, conversation about people like Eric Clapton can say something about both God and our own attitude toward other people.
2) The love that preachers require to maintain effective ministry comes from God, and yet God uses the congregation and the preacher to administer that love among them and to the world. Preachers can enable the congregation to be loving to all people, by preaching in a manner that communicates love for the congregation, and by modeling loving actions in the world that the sermon presents. Love begins as we are gathered around Word and Table, receiving God's love. People are often most loving when they experience themselves being loved.
3) Some of the trust that preachers must earn comes from faithful representation of the Bible and tradition. Speaking from the Bible, the vast history of tradition, as well as local heritage, gives hearers confidence in the preacher and what is being said.
4) Preachers should uphold evenhandedly various mission activities in the church and speak to the interests of different age groups. If we rarely include aspects of teen or rock culture in preaching, we need not expect much interest from that age group in church or preaching.

5) Stories like the one about Eric Clapton can have appeal beyond the group that knows who he is (i.e., a rock guitarist who came to fame first in the 1960s and whose career has had a remarkable resurgence). He is first of all a human being, someone for whom God cares. In this case many members of various ages would have watched the Grammy Awards on television that week, or read about them in newspapers.

6) We may tell stories about various people in our sermons to show God acting in the world in the same way we have seen God acting in the biblical text. I do not know for certain if Clapton would name God in his own story. Although I do not present his life as a model for Christians, I nonetheless interpret his story from a Christian perspective. The primary concern, however, is the congregation's relationship not with the preacher or with Clapton but with the person of Christ.

Exercise 1:1 Write a paragraph or more about someone whose action you admire or whose situation concerns you, without mentioning yourself. Suggest how God is acting in or through that person or situation.

Exercise 1:2 After you have finished the paragraph, read what you have written imagining that it was written by someone else, or as though you were hearing it in a sermon. Identify several adjectives or phrases you would use to describe the author of those words, as if those words were the only clue you had to that person's character. Now make another short list of adjectives or phrases, this time to identify the qualities of God's character that have been communicated through your words.

Review Questions for Chapter One

Select the best answer for each of the following questions.

1) In the sermon as God's event, the role of the preacher is
   a) to make the sermon seem like God's event
   b) to enhance God's event
   c) to get human concerns out of the way of God's Word
   d) all of the above   [b]

2) The sermon is
   a) what God does
   b) what the listener does
   c) what the preacher does
   d) all of the above   [d]

3) The best sermon, first and foremost
   a) teaches us about the Bible
   b) teaches us about our theological tradition
   c) leads us to God
   d) leads us to deeper commitment   [c]

4) Ethos in the pulpit means the
   a) character of the preacher
   b) ability of the preacher to speak persuasively
   c) preacher's need
   d) preacher talking about himself or herself   [a]

5) In a sermon, ethos is ultimately determined by
   a) what is said at the beginning of the sermon
   b) the manner in which the sermon is preached
   c) what the preacher says about himself or herself
   d) the listener   [d]

6) The term "preacher's need" in this chapter refers to
   a) an agenda that does not relate to the congregation
   b) a need of the preacher, similar to the actual need
   c) something that is negative by nature
   d) a shared agenda of the congregation and preacher   [a]

Questions for Discussion

1) Since in any case the sermon is God's word, is it presumptuous to assume that we can assist what God will accomplish through our preaching?
2) If we could not hear, it would be appropriate to change our language concerning preaching as an oral event. What new language might we need? Does the Bible offer alternatives? What understandings are important to preserve? What would have to change?

PREACHING AS AN ORAL EVENT

Preaching is an oral event. The passive words we use for God may in fact stand as barriers to God's coming to us. How the biblical writers understood God's Word is distinct from our orientation toward the printed page. Both the Bible and oral cultures suggest practical guidelines for using concrete language and action statements about God.

We may think of the sermon as a relationship with God. We probably conceive of preaching as a relationship with the congregation. We may even come into the pulpit with a sense of expectation and excitement concerning the wonderful things God will do today. However, our words often still work against us, even if we are wanting to facilitate an encounter with God.

Words as Barriers to God's Event

Why should we care about words when we are trying to communicate God? Why not merely speak and leave the rest to the Holy Spirit? These are fair questions. In answering them we remember that our work assists that of the Holy Spirit (even as our lack of work can be a hindrance) and that the Holy Spirit uses us to accomplish God's purposes. Our words are tools we put into God's service. Words affect understanding.

Consider some conflicting ways in which we use words: We talk about the Bible as a book, when the Word of God is in fact a living

Word. We talk about preaching as "the message of Good News" when it is Christ who is the Good News and who speaks it to us. We preach that "Christ is our example," placing priority on our action, when it is in fact Christ who is giving us power to walk in his footsteps. We say, "The text says . . . ," "The gospel says . . . ," or "The story of our faith tells us . . . ," perhaps rightly hesitant to proclaim, "God says." We say that "the Gospel story has the power to save us," when it is God who saves. Many of the words we use to discuss preaching are nouns (e.g., proclamation, sermon, homily, homiletics, the Word, interpretation) rather than verbs stressing action and personal relationship. Words we use for God's encounter (e.g., sacrament, salvation, grace) further lead us to conceive of God in nominal, abstract, or remote ways.

The language that we use to speak about God not only affects how we think about God; it affects how the congregation thinks. Faith can be strengthened or diminished by the language we use to understand it. Unfortunately, some of the words, especially nouns and adjectives, that are indispensable for our understanding of God are at the same time communicating something we do not intend, that God is distant and passive. Think here of obvious and good words such as *eternal, immortal, immutable, omniscient, perfect, powerful,* and a host of others that in varying degrees speak one important truth and yet inadvertently undermine another by implying that God is impersonal and remote. More often we are simply unaware of the words and images of God we actually use in our preaching.

The consequence of this kind of language for our faith is clear. If we take objectification of God into the pulpit, abstraction smothers our preaching. We may say, "God's immutable and eternal will may be discerned to oppose injustice in the world," instead of merely saying, "God fights injustice." There is an urgent need for us to learn to speak with deep simplicity and concrete clarity about God's action in our lives.

> The preacher's words can hinder the event of God's encounter by portraying God in nominal, distant, abstract, passive, or impersonal ways.

Such vibrant speech is hard to retain in educational systems that are largely geared to the page, the essay, and the written exam. Already by the late 1800s, educational examinations in schools and universities had largely switched from oral to written form, a development that would ultimately help erode the oral skills not least of preachers in training. By then as well, rhetoric (the classical oral art of persuasion) was in such decline that T. S. Eliot later noted that it had become "merely a vague term of abuse for any style that is bad."[1] Unfortunately, the pendulum has swung so far that some schools do not offer courses in speech, even within a culture that now reads less and watches television more.

Luther said that sermons should speak to the heart of the people: "Don't consider those who claim to be learned but be a preacher to unschooled youth and sucklings."[2] Karl Barth echoed him: "Let [preachers] be simple . . . follow the path on which the Bible leads them [and] see things as they are and as they unfold in actual experience. This will preserve them from displays of doctrinal erudition which are of no great importance."[3] Knowing the truth of these remarks does not in itself enable us to meet the demand, however. Additional knowledge about words is needed, particularly knowledge of how our choice of words can actually assist God.

Words in Aid of God's Event

Even as our words can hinder the event of God's encounter in the sermon, our words can also assist this event. We may start by considering the language we use to discuss God. We can try to minimize abstract academic speech in favor of concrete speech rooted in experience. How might we do this? We can use the Bible as our model. Gerhard von Rad was not the first to observe that "we cannot assume that our conception of 'the word of God' or of the function of words in general is identical with that held by the prophets."[4] Important insights such as this have sometimes been swept out of the theological house along with much of the biblical theology movement in recent times. It is wrong to separate biblical doctrines from their cultures, or to impose a rigidly uniform theology on the Bible. For instance, we cannot speak of merely one biblical understanding of Word. Nevertheless, one truth about biblical languages has doctrinal implications: The many biblical understandings of God's Word, and of word in general, are different from our own, in part because Hebrew and Koine Greek are not languages of abstraction.

All language, of course, is abstract. What do we mean then when we speak of abstract words? They are words that are abstracted from experience. Sallie McFague calls this type of language conceptual and secondary, in that it arises out of reflections on experience and sometimes develops abstractions from abstractions.[5] We know abstract language, for it is the sort that dominates theological education, yet concrete language, rooted in the world we see and touch, is necessary for the pulpit. McFague designates this language imagistic and primary, for it builds directly on the world around us. The distinction is very important in the pulpit.

The difference can be illustrated. The following discussion of the inspiration of Scripture by Owen Thomas is abstract in a manner appropriate for some systematic theology:

This theory of verbal inspiration and of revelation as the communication of propositional truths from God to humanity does not fit the facts of the Bible. It makes the words of the Bible the locus of revelation rather than the events described in the Bible. The words of the Bible are the record of events and the interpretation of them as events in which God is acting. Faith or the reception of revelation in the Bible is clearly not the acceptance of supernaturally communicated propositions but rather trust in and obedience to the living God who confronts humanity in the events of the Bible.[6]

While this use of language is effective for its argumentative and written purpose, if used from the pulpit it will not be effective in most congregations. For preaching, we might try something more concrete:

When the Bible was written, God did not decide to lie down in lines on a page and squeeze into particular words lined up on that page, that we could then dust off and lift up and have them turn back into God's truth. God always has been found where the action is happening, in the midst of human affairs, particularly where people are in despair and needing a help that is beyond themselves. The Bible records crucial events, but it is the living God who speaks through them illumining the events of all times. It is God who in this manner shows us who God is, and it is this God who meets us now and gives us all the faith to carry on.

Concrete language such as this (you may be able to provide a better example) enables clear communication with the hearer.

Abstract language is important in shaping our understanding, and we cannot, and need not, eliminate it from preaching. A problem arises only if too much of our pulpit language about God is abstract: God is thus perceived as remote from experience. Our purpose therefore can be to encourage balance, by promoting words that portray a present, committed, and loving God who gets involved and acts in human history and in individual lives.

Exercises in Concrete Language About God

Although we find many examples of it in the Bible, the college educated often find it difficult to use concrete rather than abstract language. It is so important for preaching that it merits time not usually afforded it. Not all biblical models may be useful, but here are the principal ones I have identified in surveying the Scriptures. They offer some possibilities for us to make God's action more immediate in our preaching.

Exercises 2:1-9C I suggest that students try to imitate each exercise (without trying to remember all the categories). Do not be discouraged if at first you struggle to come up with examples similar to the ones provided. The ability to speak concretely with images can be a lifelong goal, much like practicing a swimming stroke. Preachers in congregations might try over several weeks to incorporate an example of one of these exercises in each sermon preached.

2:1 We may speak of God's Word as Event. Here we might model our speech on one of the Hebrew renderings of *word (dabar)*. Instead of speaking of God's word as an abstract thing (like our idea of word), we could speak of God's word as action, doing what God speaks. Isaiah spoke this way: "So shall my word be that goes out from my mouth; / it shall not return to me empty, / but it shall accomplish that which I purpose, / and succeed in the thing for which I sent it" (Isa. 55:11). Or we could do as the psalmist, and look to actions in the natural world. God's word is like a messenger or like weather: "He sends out his command to the earth; / his word runs swiftly. / He gives snow like wool. . . . / He sends out his word, and melts them; / he makes his wind blow, and the waters flow" (Ps. 147:15ff.).

Example: God's Word is misunderstood if we think of it as last month's unopened mail. It is not something we can push to one side or trample underfoot. It is more like a fax on line, a phone call coming through, a speeding train in a tunnel, a plane taking off, a planet spinning into a new day that will not be stopped.

2:2 We may speak of the Word as Speaking. The most important Hebrew and Greek words for word (including *dabar* and *logos*) share a common root, meaning "say," "speak," "tell," "utter," "narrate," "consider," or "explain." Instead of using phrases like, "the gospel tells us," or "the text says" (phrases that we need not entirely eliminate), we can create our own variations of the prophetic, "Hear the word of the Lord" or "Thus says the Lord."

Example: "Do you not hear God's voice right now, whispering in your ear?" or, "Listen for what God is saying to us now," or, "Christ is calling each of you by name, Mary, Bill, Tom, Sarah. . . . Put in your own name. You can hear it."

2:3 *We may speak of the Word as Creating.* By occasional references in our preaching over months and years, we can eventually communicate that a current sermon is not just something being preached and heard, it is about something that God is creating right now. Here we remember both the Genesis creation account and Psalm 33:6, in which God's word is the agent of creation: "By the word of the LORD the heavens were made, / and all their host by the breath of his mouth."

Example: We may be sitting here thinking, "This is all good and well, but when I leave this place, everything is just going to be the same as it was." Well that isn't true. While we have been here listening to God, God has been busy with the clay of our lives, molding a new future filled with new possibility and promise. With God creating our future, how can we dwell on our past?

2:4 *We may speak of the Word as Torah or instruction.* Often we think of God's law as a written ordinance or document. In fact it is often closer to a military command, something which, once issued, will be carried out. As such God's law carries God's continuing promise of fulfillment. It is a living trust, a binding word. It is also a gift, showing us the way, freeing us to focus in the right directions, without having to second-guess every decision. We may speak of this instruction affectionately, warmly, intimately, as though in addressing the law we make no distinction between it and God who uttered it, or between it and our relationship to God. The psalmist spoke in this manner: "I treasure your word in my heart, / so that I may not sin against you. / Blessed are you, O LORD; / teach me your statutes. / With my lips I declare / all the ordinances of your mouth. / I delight in the way of your decrees, / as much as in all riches" (Ps. 119:11ff.).

Example: How certain are the words God utters, for they fly to their destination without delay or detour, arriving at the same moment they are sent, making straight the crooked ways, healing those who are wounded, feeding those who are hungry, visiting those who are alone.

2:5 *We may speak of attributes of the Word using personification.* Personification of the attributes of God (e.g., wisdom, love, power) in the manner of Proverbs, can help communicate a personal God whose actions may be readily seen in this world: "Does not wisdom call, / and does not understanding raise her voice? / On the heights, beside the way, / at the crossroads she takes her stand; / beside the gates in front of the town, / at the entrance of the portals she cries out . . ." (Prov. 8:1ff.).

Example: God's love does not mope around the apartment, moving from fridge to TV and TV to fridge, occasionally looking out to see if anything is happening. God's love does not know too many places to go, and cannot get to them all soon enough.

2:6 *We may speak of the Word as objects in action.* Our model here can be some of the startling imagery of the Bible, which pictures God's Word in surprising ways. Thus in Zechariah, the words of God's curse upon the thief materialize as a "flying scroll," measuring thirty feet by fifteen feet: "It shall enter the house of the thief . . . and it shall abide in that house and consume it, both timber and stones" (5:1ff.). Elsewhere God's word becomes a substance to eat: "Your words were found, and I ate them, / and your words became to me a joy / and the delight of my heart" (Jer. 15:16); and, " . . . eat this scroll, and go, speak to the house of Israel. . . . Then I ate it; and in my mouth it was as sweet as honey" (Ezek. 3:1ff.); and, "So I went to the angel and told him to give me the little scroll; and he said to me, 'Take it, and eat; it will be bitter to your stomach, but sweet as honey in your mouth'" (Rev. 10:9).

Example: Take this word of hope which you have been given this morning, climb in it, and drive it home. Let everyone see you driving it, and wave to all you see. Go up and down Main Boulevard honking all the way along, so that everyone will hear. Park it outside your place in some conspicuous spot, maybe with a yellow line, and to everyone who asks, "Whose is that?" just say, "It belongs to Christ."

2:7 *We may speak of the Word as Power Given to Us.* The dreams we have been given of God's Realm as it should be are not empty dreams. When we share them they have already started to happen because they are God's dreams, and we have them in the power of God. It was this way for the prophets. God tells Jeremiah, "Now I have put my words in your mouth. / See, today I appoint you over nations . . . / to pluck up and to pull down, / to destroy

43

and to overthrow, / to build and to plant" (1:9-10). This was the way with Paul: "My speech *[logos]* and my proclamation *[kerygma]* were not with plausible words of wisdom, but with a demonstration of the Spirit and of power, so that your faith might rest not on human wisdom but on the power of God" (I Cor. 2:4-5). This was the way with the exorcisms of the disciples. This is the way with us, for Christ commissioned us with his power (Mark 16:15ff.; Matt. 26:18ff.).

> *God's Word may be variously portrayed as:*
> • *event*
> • *speaking*
> • *creating*
> • *command*
> • *personified action;*
> • *objects in action;*
> • *power given to us; and*
> • *one of the three persons of the Trinity.*

Example: These words flow ahead of us this morning. A great tide of mercy has been poured freely upon the land. Wherever you see it needed, just say the word, and you will see it, trickling at first, making a tiny rivulet on the hardened earth, then soaking the soil, and rising to cover even the hard-to-reach places. There can be no despair in a land that is awash with mercy.

2:8 *We may speak of the Word in relation to the Trinity.* Of course there is not a more personal, concrete, or active way for Christians to speak about God than to speak of the Persons of the Trinity. The Trinity, as a concept in language in addition to a reality about God, affords opportunities to speak of God in many ways in any moment. Without these ways, our ability to speak about God would be severely constrained. These ways speak of the Trinity as both transcendent and immanent, and infer God's intimate involvement in human affairs. Three affirmations about the triune God will help us here. Perhaps no better lessons can be learned by the starting preacher than these three:

A. The triune God is acting. If preaching is desired to be an event of divine encounter, God needs to be communicated as doing something. God is not passive. We may make God (or Jesus Christ, or the Holy Spirit) the subject of sentences. We may use active verbs. We can watch particularly for opportunities to cut out words like "that," "there is," "there are," and "can," or "could be _____," as in the following:

Poor: It is true what has been testified through the ages that God is love.
Better: God loves each created person, and will until the end of time as so many people continue to testify.

Poor: There are many signs of God's presence in our midst.
Better: God is moving mightily in our midst.
Poor: The ways in which prayers are answered by God can be listed.
Better: God answers prayer in many ways too numerous to count.

- B. God in the Trinity is present now. Some of our customary language lacks immediacy by placing God's action somewhere in the future, only as a possibility, and modified with conditions (e.g., "If we will do this, then we may expect . . ."). Jesus was continually pointing to God's activity right now by speaking of "the Realm of God," especially in his parables. He told, demonstrated, and embodied what this Realm looks like in the present: love, peace, forgiveness, mercy, justice, disruption (at times), righteousness, compassion (= entry into another's suffering), freedom, equality, and the like. Thus if we are dealing with forgiveness, we may proclaim God forgiving in the present:

Right now in your silent confession, God is receiving your confession and is reaching to you in forgiveness.

Or, prior to our asking:

Even before you dared to turn again to God, God had already granted your forgiveness that you might get on with loving others in the present and not be preoccupied with unloving in the past.

- C. God's mercy is wide. All too often in our preaching we mention people near us, but do not go on to mention people on the other side of the world in dire situations of need. If we can speak specifically of God's actions toward them in one of the persons of the Trinity, we may eventually communicate that no one is beyond God's care and that in any place we go we can expect to encounter the God we proclaim:

What a difference it would make to how we and others view the world if we were to identify God around us. Strolling through the flower gardens at the park, a mother stops the stroller and goes over to the fountain where her two children are fighting over whose turn it is to have a drink. The ice cream of one falls on the shirt of the other. Both start to cry. "Peace," she says to them as they start in again, blaming each other. She tells them a story of when she was a girl as she cleans off the T-shirt of the one with fountain water and a tissue. Then she lifts them, one at a time, to the fountain. The action of God is like this.

45

When we pray "Peace," it does not always happen quickly. But it always begins and it will happen. It happens as surely as seed planted in the ground and watered will sprout. As surely as we prayed all those years for peace between the West and the East, those prayers eventually blossomed, and their blooming had more power than all the guns and corrupt governments. The sound of the blossoming prayers in the lives of the people of the East drowned out the din of a tearing iron curtain. The action of God. Even the newspapers caught at least the signs of the God who made it all happen.

Spoken Words

One further dimension of our language used in the service of God is essential in framing our approach. God's Word is spoken. Preaching is an oral event. Such an obvious point may seem scarcely worth stating again, yet there is more here than meets the eye (or ear).

Suppose we were to attend a church service where the preacher was well-prepared, but became ill. Copies of a full, written manuscript of the sermon that was to have been preached are distributed, to be read silently during the service. While the unusual exercise might be of benefit, we would not ascribe it the same status we would a personal, spoken address by the preacher who composed it. A sermon depends upon personal expression, tone, gesture, emphasis, and pace to communicate the preacher's intent. In written form these features are absent.

Suppose the unfortunate preacher is able to send a videotape of the sermon to be played in the service. Would that suffice? Is the solution to insufficient numbers of preachers the videocassette? or telephone link-ups? or satellite TV? or even three-dimensional holograms of virtual-reality technology? Whatever value these may have, the nature of preaching as an event still suffers. Preaching is personal communication that uses eye contact and is based in this time and place, in the personal and social needs of this hour, as preacher and congregation experience God's Word together. Though preaching needs extensive preparation, there is nonetheless an element of spontaneity to it. We are open to the moving of the Holy Spirit to make certain emphases, or proceed in a different direction, even as we preach. The preacher is a person of the gathered community and trust is essential. Even in business major deals are rarely consummated over fax or video-telephone.

Most important for preaching as an oral event, is the office of preacher. As preachers, we are set apart by the church for the particular office of Word, sacrament, and pastoral care. This office is a symbol, not a sign; symbols participate in the reality they represent. The preacher both represents the authority of the church, and is the one whom Christ uses in a particular way to speak Christ's authority to our lives.

In becoming preachers, we have agreed to place the congregation's welfare ahead of our own personal wants. This covenantal relationship of trust and love is embodied in the preacher, and for this there is no disembodied technological substitute. One of the problems of religion in America, says Charles L. Rice, is the "disembodiment of the Word," for instance through television.[7] The fact that the minister, pastor, or priest preaches is important for how preaching is heard.

Sermons are spoken: This is essential to their nature, not incidental. The church has always insisted that the sermon is a spoken word.[8] The Word is not silent. Although most of our theological libraries have large collections of sermons, these documents gained that name by having first been preached. We might even say that a written document becomes a sermon only through its having been spoken. Sermons are events in time, God's Word addressed to particular congregations in particular circumstances. For this reason Luther claimed that the gospel "should not be written but shouted" and that "the church is not a pen-house but a mouth-house."[9]

Herein lies part of the problem for those of us who preach. In Luther's day (and in some local communities and regions today such as parts of the Appalachians, or parts of Newfoundland, or in tribal cultures around the world) writing imitates speech. We can see this even in ancient Hebrew, Greek, and Latin manuscripts. There, as in actual speech, individual words and sentences run together, without punctuation or even capitalization to mark sentences. Preference was given to recording sounds that could be reproduced and understood when spoken, not to words that could themselves communicate directly from the page independent of sound. Moreover, punctuation evolved as an encoded form of voice inflection. In English, "?" means the pitch rises at the end of the sentence and "." means the pitch falls. We could say that even a good manuscript struggles to be heard.

With the tremendous influence of radio, television, and the music and film industries, much of our conversation imitates speech and topics that we hear. However, when studying theology this is generally not the case. After often eighteen years of academic training for ministry, most of it for the page, our theological writing tends not to imitate speech; rather, our theological speech normally imitates writing. Speech that imitates academic writing often sounds like a lecture, or an essay being read. When using it, we will repeat the theological language and jargon of articles we have read; we will probably stay in our "heads" and not move also into our "hearts"; and we will keep experience at arm's length. Once we conceive of preaching as an oral event, we begin to shift our ways of thinking. Instead of composing with the eye for the page, we begin to compose with the ear for oral delivery and aural reception, attentive to various needs of the listeners.

Words Heard

How may we compose sermons for the ear? Numerous teachers have been suggesting for years that this is not just a matter of composing aloud, and using words that sound good to the ear. A different way of thinking is involved. The differences are similar to those between a highly literate culture and a highly oral one.

We can get a sense of this by looking at the Bible. The biblical world was predominantly an oral culture. While our biblical records obviously come to us from skilled ancient writers, the writer's world was a specialized world, not the typical world of most people. Writers were saturated with oral ways of thought.[10] We often assume incorrectly that rural biblical communities were literate in our sense of literacy. We assume incorrectly that the biblical writers thought of writing the way we do. Writing was a skilled technology, and markings on the page were notes that needed to be sounded in order to be understood.[11] Thus we miss the significance of much of what we read. For example, we would be closer to authentic biblical understandings of God's Word if we said instead: the Sound of God, the Speaking of God, God's Voice, the Action of God, or the Event of God's Encounter.

It would be easy for us, along with many thinkers, to judge such ways of thought negatively, as bordering on magic, or as unlearned, prelogical, or prerational, belonging to "primitive" societies that lived by myths that no longer correspond to a reasonable worldview (e.g., in the judgment of Rudolf Bultmann and his followers). However, tutored by less elitist scholars of anthropology, teachers more wisely avoid comparisons that lead to calling such societies "primitive" and in fact appreciate their sophistication. Only with struggle do we recover their more vibrant ways of thinking and speaking for the pulpit.

One feature of language in oral cultures is worth imitating in preaching: This language was "attentive to the sensory (the concrete) and was more disposed to describing actions than to creating abstractions because people hearing what was said or sung could feel and follow concrete actions."[12]

New Perspectives on Oral Ways of Thought

"An arranged mind is resistant to seeing,"[13] says Eduard R. Riegert about the need for imagination: "The preacher is constantly at work trying to unarrange minds and lives."[14] The fascinating research results of Russian scholar Aleksandr Luria into peasant culture may serve to awaken the imagination of the preacher to new ways of thought.[15]

First, although we might consider our times to be quite different from Luria's, many of the people in our own congregations and towns may not have much education, or even with education may think in ways similar to the people among whom he did his research without necessarily being like them. In fact, the electronic media may be resensitizing us to oral and imagistic ways, although we ought not simply to equate our "second stage" orality and the primary stage orality that Luria studied. Second, much of the biblical literature we preach demonstrates oral thinking. Third, Luria's subjects display a consciousness that is shaped by the ear, not the page. Their concrete mode of expression is more easily received and remembered, particularly in light of its oral delivery. Fourth, simple respect for ways of thought different from our own (oral or not!) is an essential part of any ministry.

Luria's research was done after the Bolshevik Revolution in Russia, and just prior to the introduction of literacy programs in the former U.S.S.R. He studied orally educated (illiterate and semiliterate) peasants. His book was not published in Russian or English until the 1970s. Among his more dramatic findings are the following:

—People who were without formal education and innocent of reading and writing were confused when asked to group similar colors. They named individual colors not with abstract terms but according to objects of the same color: tobacco, liver, wine, lake, sky, decayed teeth, and so on.[16] (Note how few colors are named in the Bible. Colors are vivid for us, yet even our color names are abstractions. If we want to see color in the Bible we must see the objects.)
—When shown cards with geometric shapes, the peasants identified objects with those shapes: a circle was identified as a bucket, sieve,

moon, or watch; a triangle was an amulet; a square was a door, house, or mirror.[17] (We do not tend to notice that our geometric shapes are themselves abstractions.)

—When shown two triangles, one with one apex not joined, the other with none of the apexes joined, Luria was told that they were both unfinished and were placed in that manner in order to be completed.[18] (Many situations we discuss in preaching could legitimately be viewed in other ways than the manner we present them, if only we could be open to seeing things as others see them.) Analogical thinking of this sort, that seeks referents in experience, is important in theology (see McFague and Tracy[19]) and preaching.

—There was a picture of three adults and one child. Which one did not belong? They all belonged. They were all working and the child was needed to fetch things.[20] (In oral cultures, things exist for practical purposes. If we apply this practical demand to theology, as Horace Bushnell argued we should,[21] we will picture the practical consequences, in moral or spiritual life, of any of the doctrines that we preach.)

—The same question about "not belonging" was asked of a grouping of a glass, a saucepan, spectacles, and a bottle, with a similar result. "You can't cook in the glass, you have to fill it. For cooking, you need the saucepan, and to see better, you need the spectacles. We need all four things. That's why they were put there."[22] Differentiation is made using functional logic. (Often in preaching we need to acknowledge the connections people make, for example, "everything is for a purpose," in order to help them move to a more mature Christian perspective.)

—Participants resisted defining objects. Since objects could be seen, what was the point? When pushed they defined by comparing with other objects, naming features and how they function.[23] (Some of us probably resort to definitions too readily, when we could simply demonstrate what we mean.)

—Syllogisms were not used to infer new understanding. For example: Precious metals do not rust. Gold is a precious metal. Does it rust? Respondents to this type of question would say they did not know. It had not been part of their experience.[24] (Often the logical forms of argument we have learned in school carry less weight in the parish or congregation.)

—When asked to describe who they were, they responded in terms of physical characteristics, and appealed to what others might say about them.[25] (There was no abstract sense of self. Instead, people are what they do and say, although this is disputed in ethics today.

Character, as in movies today, is defined more by action than by motive. The same principle is excellent for preachers to follow in telling stories of contemporary experience.)

These responses did not indicate lack of intelligence. They indicated a different use of intelligence, an alternate way of thinking. We can use them to awaken us to possibilities of thinking different from our own.

Exercises in Oral Ways of Expression

Luria's discoveries are relevant for our preaching because our preaching is oral. Our sermons are heard aurally. Our rhetoric must reflect our medium. Write for the ear, not for the eye, is the frequent homiletical maxim. This is no small task. It requires more than a shift in our language about God. If we take seriously the work of people like Luria, Marshall McLuhan, Levi-Strauss, and other anthropologists,[26] a fundamental shift in our thinking and expression, in other words our consciousness, is needed. To some students, it may not seem possible.

The only way to effect this important shift is to practice it. Walter J. Ong's foundational book, *Orality and Literacy: Technologizing the Word*, identified features of oral thought from his research into oral cultures.[27] Some of them are adapted here to provide exercises to help us move from writing for the page to writing for the ear. Again, I suggest that students write exercises in imitation of the examples provided.

2:9 *Accumulating thought*—To present Christian doctrine or teaching in a sermon, we need some linear progression of thought. However, if we are presenting material from experience, we may allow some of it simply to accumulate, without much commentary. Thought in oral cultures tends to be added or accumulated rather than analyzed, sorted, and subordinated. (Ong cites the use of nine introductory "ands" in the creation account of Genesis 1:1-5.)

For instance, if we want to establish in preaching that people today are afraid, we do not turn the sermon into a research paper fit for sociology or psychology seminars. Rather we accumulate a few quick simple situations, representing the breadth of the congregation's experience, including women and men, citing instances from the news media or elsewhere. We need not try to prove or define something that is common sense, but we do need to make it concrete, able to be visualized.

Here is a short example of accumulation on the subject "People are afraid today." By the end of the series, the idea is forming in the minds of the congregation:

A young mother comes home with her preschool child, closes the door, turns the lock, pushes the dead-bolt and sets the chain, secure at last. *[pause]* A man in midforties with a family and mortgage eases off on the gas pedal of his pickup as the factory comes into view, and he wonders, "Will this be the day I get my notice?" *[pause]* A new resident in the home sees the sunlit newspaper in the lounge lying open to the obituaries page and picks it up fearfully. *[pause]* We all live in fear of one thing or another.

2:10 *Repeating for emphasis*—Excellent preachers will help the listeners hear what is being said through artful use of repetition. Ancient storytellers used this to ensure that the listeners stay on track. Rhetoricians encouraged the device and called it *copia* (i.e. "copious").

If we say something in a written essay, it is counted as having been said; often a teacher will judge it negatively if it is said again. In preaching, by contrast, we have not said it until it is heard, and often it is not heard until we have said it several times. Clearly we are not talking about repeating trivial ideas, or repeating entire arguments, or encouraging sermons that go nowhere, like a record with a stuck needle.

Repetition of key ideas is not only helpful, it is essential if people are to understand our meaning. In an oral message we must compensate for people not being able to go back with their eyes over words, rereading what they have read. This is why we make the surprising claim that the preacher is responsible not only for what is said, but to a large extent for what is heard as well.

Various types of repetition may be used. It may be repetition of the central idea of the sermon, the same way each time. It may be the kind of repetition necessary for oral "paragraphs," where one idea is the subject of the paragraph, and is simply rephrased many times, moving ahead only slightly with each sentence.

Laura Sinclair demonstrates how repetition of one simple idea, over and over, can be done without its seeming clumsy. Such care in speaking forms an excellent paragraph of oral thought. The idea that gradually takes shape as we listen is "We once had compassion," an idea that is hinted in the first line, and restated in different words in each subsequent sentence. She is preaching from Ezekiel:

As a community, we lack compassion for one another. Years ago, we as a Black race did not have orphanages, shelter homes, and foster homes filled with our children. We had what are called today "extended families." If a relative died and left children, we took them into our homes and raised them as our own. If there was no family, close friends took them into their homes and raised them. We cared about one another's children. We were interested in their growth. Our parents and grandparents didn't find themselves in nursing homes. We provided for them and cared for them in the warmth of our homes, where they knew that they were being loved and cared for. We didn't leave our responsibilities to the state or the federal government. The church and community took care of their own. I wonder, Can our community's bones live?[28]

2:11 *Building trust*—Establish a good relationship with the people before asking them to entertain new ideas. Hearers are conservative by nature. They favor the familiar. They need trust (ethos) to be developed. The preacher may thus first strive to reflect who they are, represent their views, speak on their behalf, and name their concerns in bringing them before the Word.

Consider how quickly Fred B. Craddock wins our interest and respect in the following example. He does so primarily by naming one of our own possible responses to Romans 16:1-16 as his own response. Here is the opening paragraph of his Thanksgiving sermon "When the Roll Is Called Down Here":

I hope you will not feel guilty if your heart was not all aflutter during the reading of the text. It's not very interesting. It's a list of names, a list of strange names. I always tell my students in preaching class, "When you're preaching from biblical texts, avoid the lists. They're deadly. Don't preach from the lists." It seems that Paul is calling the roll. That's a strange thing in itself. I have never worshiped in a church in which anyone got up and called the roll. It could be very dull. Well, it could . . . it could be interesting in a way.
Calling the roll sometimes is not all that bad. Last December . . .[29]

2:12 *Connecting to real-life experience*—Theological thought can connect to the lives of people. We do this best by speaking of relationships. God is relational. Our interests are relational, having to do with people. The stories that we seek are primarily those dealing with people interacting: real-life events, not fantasies; actual experiences, not the preacher's sleeping dreams; actual conversations between people, not interior monologues; purposeful thought and action, not the preacher's freely associated train of thought; and stories about humans in preference to animals or sunsets.

53

For instance, in this brief example, Ronald J. Allen quickly and vividly paints a picture (complete with sound) about a genuine human dilemma. He lets us meet a person who is an alcoholic, rather than talk in abstract ways about alcoholism, or faith's response to it (note how he arranges his words on the page to facilitate oral speech):

> The woman wakes up in the morning,
>   her life as shattered as the bottle
>   she threw against the wall before she passed out.
> But the name of Jesus
>   is above the name *alcoholic*
>   and those who are in him
>   know that booze does not have the final word.[30]

2:13 Emphasizing the present—We may speak with an emphasis on the present. In oral societies stories of the past are told, often with historical facts adjusted to describe the current state of affairs. The significance of things is determined by present habitat and usefulness.

As students, we tend to treat biblical events as we would history in a written essay, because they happened more than two thousand years ago. We reduce the stories to facts rather than relate those stories as events by creating with our words vivid scenes as from a movie. Audiences and congregations are still more captured by events being told as though they are in the present than as distillations and abstractions from past experience.

Poor—Emphasis on the past as history:

The Gospel of John tells us that on the night of Jesus' appearance to Mary in the garden, the disciples were afraid of the religious authorities who might be looking for them. The commentaries suggest that the house where they hid belonged to a rich person: It had doors that could be locked. The fact that Jesus appeared to the disciples in spite of the locked doors tells us that Jesus appeared in a manner other than his earthly body, which was fully human and suffered the limitations of our bodies.

Better—Emphasis on the past as present:

The disciples tried to shut out hope. After Mary Magdalene told them she had seen Jesus alive in the garden, and talked with him, the disciples went to a rich person's house where there were doors, doors they could lock, and be alone in their fear of the police. The Risen Christ would have none of it. He comes to them as he comes to us. As they are gathered on that first Easter Sunday night, he appears in their midst and says to them, "Peace be with you." He shows them his hands and side, in the same manner that he would have us know that he is the same one as was put to death. He would not have his followers focus on the past.

2:14 Using action words—We can be attentive to words that do things. In oral cultures, words are not things, the way they are for us, but acts that accomplish their purposes. Words have power, like the utterance of "peace" in Luke 10:5-6. God creates by sound in Genesis. Naming things in any culture gives some powers over them, as when Adam names the creatures in Genesis 2:20.

We know not least from parenting that affirmation is more important than criticism in changing behavior. In preaching we can use words that empower the community and affirm the individual (e.g.,"It is not possible for you to know how much God loves you, just as you are, at this moment"). We may also picture words in action, that is, people doing the actions that through God's Word we would wish them to be doing.

Consider all the action words that Ola Irene Harrison uses in this poignant reflection on her own attempts to minister and the bitter-sweet scroll that John ate in Revelation 10:9 (note how she also writes for sound):

> But I hold in my file a letter saying
>   "Yes, they felt you were better qualified,
>   But they believe the pastor should really be a man"?
> John's sweet but bitter scroll
> Is common food for many in ministry
> (And not only women)
> But for all those who have been called to speak
> A difficult word on behalf of Jesus Christ
> All pastors who struggle to speak both the comfort
>   and challenge of the gospel
> All those who champion causes that conflict with
>   "the way things have always been"
> Called to preach for the sake of
> Christ's church and for the sake of creation
> Not only ministers but all Christians seeking to witness
>   to God's presence in this world
> Speaking hope where there is no hope
>   peace when there is no peace
>   light when all you can see is utter darkness.[31]

2:15 *Composing for clarity and feeling*—Charles G. Adams of Detroit, rated by some as one of the top preachers in the United States, is a master of balanced phrasing to devise a simple idea with passion.[32] Consider two consecutive samples from a sermon on prayer that I line out for easy viewing:

When we reach up, God reaches down.		We live in God's life.	
" reach out	" reaches in	" love "	love
pray	hears	stand	strength
call	answers	breathe	spirit
trust	blesses	eat at	Table
work	strengthens	drink from	Cup
serve	inspires	feast in	bounty
study	instructs	see in	light
listen	speaks	think in	truth
stray	pursues	We are God's children.	
fail	forgives		
fall	picks us up		
And when we die God lifts us up where we belong.			

2:16 *Composing for memory*—Speak in ways that help your memory, so that you do not have to rely heavily on a written manuscript. One way is to line out thought, as Allen and Harrison have each done, above. Some people use felt-tip pens to color thought units in the manuscript, so they can find the next unit of thought immediately upon looking down. Some take only notes from the completed manuscript into the pulpit. Whatever route we follow, it is wise to go over the sermon manuscript as many as eight to ten times aloud, alone, and perhaps looking in a mirror to establish eye contact and to test gestures. Some preachers, those who learn best by hearing, prepare for preaching by speaking into a cassette recorder, listening to the entire sermon played back, then trying the process again and revising, as often as is necessary to gain confidence and emphasis for delivery.

With these and similar exercises, some preachers gain entire freedom from manuscripts, although that need not be our all-consuming goal. Nonetheless, only when we are overfamiliar with our material, with its location on the page, and with its sound and rhythm, can we be sufficiently free of our manuscript to be more fully present, talking to our people not the page, and thinking what we are saying, not reading it.

The easiest and most reliable way of remembering lengthy material, in addition to what we have been saying, involves use of regular rhythm in language, formulas, proverbs, repeated phrases, and other similar patterns of thought. Try composing sentences aloud. Memorization is not simply a mental exercise. It involves the senses and movement of the body, such as may be seen in the rocking movement of Orthodox Jews reciting prayers at the Wailing Wall in Jerusalem. One reason the King James Version of the Bible is beautiful to the ear is that it was composed for the ear, designed to employ the natural rhythms of voice, even though its English was intended to be slightly archaic, even for Jacobean ears. (For reason of its imitation of natural speech rhythms, a colleague in drama uses it as the best tool for helping students to discover the natural power of their voices.) Pamela Moeller's experimental kinesthetic homiletic is designed to help preachers involve their bodies in sermon preparation and delivery.[33] Henry H. Mitchell uses sensory, emotional, intuitive, and logical data in encouraging what he calls a "holistic encounter" with the biblical text.[34]

Writing for the ear includes:
- *accumulation of thought;*
- *repeating for emphasis;*
- *building trust;*
- *connection to real-life experience;*
- *emphasis on the present;*
- *use of action words;*
- *composition for clarity and feeling; and*
- *composition for memory*

Experiment for yourself to discover what devices can be built into your sermons to help you remember: Is it senses (i.e. sensory material included in your sermon)? images? ideas? patterns of thought? sound? rhythm? Material to be preserved can be placed in memory patterns and systems that help us to remember. Of course, memory patterns that assist our delivery will also assist the comprehension of the congregation.

Preaching as an oral event is of course a natural place to start in our consideration of preaching, for the purpose and medium of preaching should be in our mind from the start. We conceive the sermon in particular ways to focus on God's action, and we shape our language both to emphasize that action and to enable an experience of the God of whom we speak.

Review Questions for Chapter Two

For each line indicate true or false:

1) The words of the preacher
   a) make God present in the sermon   [F]
   b) can hinder the event of God's encounter   [T]
   c) can help the event of God's encounter   [T]
   d) are important vehicles for what God is accomplishing   [T]

2) Abstract language in the sermon
   a) is unavoidable   [T]
   b) is to be maximized   [F]
   c) should be eliminated   [F]
   d) should be used with care   [T]

3) Luria's work found that people without formal education are
   a) intelligent   [T]
   b) imaginative   [F]
   c) sensory   [T]
   d) concrete   [T]
   e) naive   [F]

4) Writing for the ear includes:
   a) accumulation of thought   [T]
   b) avoiding repetition   [F]
   c) emphasis on the present   [T]
   d) use of active words   [T]
   e) making sounds of all objects mentioned   [F]

Questions for Discussion

1) In advocating concrete language of the sort found in the Bible, are we in danger of losing for the pulpit insights from the traditional language of systematic theology?
2) Can language for preaching itself become an idol? How as preachers can we discern if or when focus on language (or other areas of

study) causes us to lose sight of Jesus Christ at the heart of our procla-mation?

Sermon Exercises for Section I

2:17 Check one of your past sermons (or an essay if you have never preached) and circle every abstract word (e.g., "love," "hope," "sanc-tification," "revelation"). Try expressing the thought more simply, or pictorially. Oral speech is sensory, relating to the material world and the senses. From the start, we might begin by:

—speaking what can be seen (e.g., His lip trembled as he spoke).
—speaking what can be heard (e.g., Her voice grated against the night).
—speaking what can be tasted (e.g., Some of these ideas have soured).
—speaking what can be smelled (e.g., There is an odor of Lazarus here).
—speaking what can be touched (e.g., These are prickly remarks).

If sensory images do not come to mind easily in writing a sermon, focus on them in a final revision of the sermon manuscript. For fur-ther examples see, for instance, Charles L. Bartow, *The Preaching Moment: A Guide to Sermon Delivery* (Nashville: Abingdon, 1980), esp. pp. 33-46.

2:18 Make a list of all the words and images you use for God in your private devotional life. Now read through one of your sermons and make a list of all the words and images you have actually used for God. What conclusions do you draw?

2:19 Pick a biblical text upon which to preach. Read it carefully and determine what God is doing, either directly in the text itself, or behind the text, considered in the context of the Bible book. Write two paragraphs as you might for a biblical or theological essay, one about God's action in the text itself, and one about some doctrine or teaching of the church that relates to this action. Now rewrite those paragraphs in a less abstract manner, in a way appropriate for a sermon. You might compare what you have written with samples from this chapter.

2:20 Write an introduction to a sermon, something that will capture attention. It might be a story of someone whose experience does not seem to bear out the truth we are seeking to proclaim about God (thereby establishing creative tension in the sermon). It might be some image or story that leads into an image or the story in your biblical text. It might be a lively discussion of the importance of today's topic, again employing concrete and active speech. Remember that, particularly in the introduction, people will be listening for clues to discover who you are and will not yet be ready to grasp any important or difficult ideas.

Before going directly on to the next chapter, students wanting to prepare a sermon may wish now to turn to section III, chapter 6, "Monday—What the Text Says."

SECTION

II

Rhetorical Tradition

At first glance it might seem that rhetoric and theology are poles apart. Rhetoric in its classical sense is the art of determining what will be persuasive for listeners. It identifies principles of effective communication that were initially devised in ancient Greece to help individuals defend themselves before peers in court, and was modified by successive ages to the present.

Theology in the broad sense is faith seeking understanding, God-talk that provides a foundation for the church's worship, preaching, teaching, and mission. Based in revelation as received and recorded in Scripture (not in the first instance in reason or observations of society or nature), theology concerns the reality of God and God's relationship to the world. Thus rhetoric and theology are perhaps rightly kept apart, their purpose and function being widely different. Our focus is appropriately theological.

On the other hand, many of us have visited churches where the preacher, widely judged to be an excellent theologian and a devoted scholar, could not communicate. Sermon ideas were well conceived, shaped by Scripture, and informed by tradition, but few of those present actually understood what was said in terms of their own lives, and the preacher consequently seemed aloof and remote.

We have also been to churches where the preacher had a "gift of the gab," an ability to animate and hold the attention of the congregation. Listeners had a sense that they were seen and recognized as though each one were being addressed, even though what was said of the Bible or theology was minimal, and the effect of the sermon seemed over when the sermon was over.

For preachers, neither theology nor rhetoric can stand on its own, and each is ignored only at great peril. Augustine, himself a teacher of rhetoric prior to his religious conversion, recognized this requirement to unite the two. He did not devise an extensive rhetoric because, as he noted, it could be found elsewhere: In his age rhetoric (usually as developed by Quintilian) formed the basic education of students. Augustine wrote the first homiletical textbook of the church, in which he addressed rhetoric in the Bible. He recommended that preachers imitate what they found there (*On Christian Doctrine*, Book IV). Throughout the history of preaching, largely because of Augustine, rhetoric and theology have gone hand in hand.

Revelation needs both to be given by God and received. Thus we say that Scripture, as the reception of God's revelation, participates in revelation. In the same manner the Word must be both preached and received. Reception is not just a matter between God and the individual, in the manner that we have commonly assumed in theology for many decades. Reception also concerns the preacher's experience, language, theology, rhetorical skills, in fact entire life, in service. In other words, as preachers we come to see our theology and our rhetoric as inseparable: We have not done good theology until it has been communicated to our people.

CHAPTER THREE

THEOLOGY AND RHETORIC

Our own attitudes, and those inherent in aspects of theological education, can pose barriers to preaching. We fail to recognize rhetoric in theology and the distinctiveness of theology for the pulpit. How we do homiletical theology is altered if preaching is conceived as God's event. First, theology is conceived as relational, and returns to the rhetorical roots of preaching in conversation that is aimed at persuasion. Second, persuasion results not just from reason (logos), but also from character (ethos) and emotions (pathos), elements that have been present, though largely ignored, in theology through the ages.

We conceive of preaching as the event of God meeting us. A sermon, conceived in this manner, is not merely words. Our words do things. God uses them and acts through them to bring forth God's purposes. Within the sermon, theology becomes part of this event, and adopts some of its character.

An understanding of preaching as God's event affects not only the words we choose and oral ways of thought, but also how we communicate theology in the pulpit. Two things happen. First, we conceive of theology increasingly as a vehicle to facilitate relationship between God and God's people, and less as a platform to communicate objective information or to explain ideas. In other words, we return to the classical roots of preaching, and join with others in approaching it in part as rhetoric. While preaching is unique, not least by being God's word, it is closely related to rhetoric as conversation or dialogue

63

whose aim is persuasion or identification that seeks to enroll people in a way of life.

Second, when preaching can be an event of encounter with God, we must also conceive of something that ought to happen in the theological movement of the sermon. However, certain prejudices exist in the attitudes we ourselves bring to preaching. They work against our conceiving of the sermon in this exciting manner.

Barriers to Homiletical Theology

In preaching classrooms there are students, men and women, from a variety of backgrounds. While not all intend to be ordained, they all value preaching. If asked, "Where do we learn to do theology in the pulpit? How do we become competent theologians?" most would respond, "In the systematic theology classroom."

The answer is partly true. No one can be well-prepared for the pulpit without a solid background in systematics. Many systematic theologians see the entire enterprise of their discipline to be in service to preaching, though this motivation has declined with the fragmentation of systematic theology in seminary faculties.

Consider the positive contributions of systematic theology to our task. It provides a comprehensive account of Christian faith, teaching the manner in which the various beliefs and doctrines of the church are related as a system. It ensures that our knowledge forms a kind of cohesive whole. It enables us to relate to many different theological texts instead of a collection of complementary or contradictory passages. It informs us of what scholars have said and are saying and equips us to speak with the authority of the church. It devises new doctrines and tests the faithfulness of the church's preaching. It instructs us how to use words in ways that honor what God has accomplished in Jesus Christ. It is closely related to the pulpit (most of the theology books and biblical commentaries written through the centuries, at least until the 1900s, started as collections of sermons; for example, Augustine's commentary on the Psalms and Calvin's *Institutes*). It traces for us the evolution of the church's doctrine, helping us to understand how we have arrived at the present, that we may honor what needs honoring in our traditions, and avoid repeating errors of the past, even as it plots future directions.

Nonetheless, on its own, systematic theology provides inadequate preparation for doing theology in the pulpit. There are several obvious reasons that may be quickly cited before exploring the subject in greater depth: It is written for the page, not composed for oral delivery. It is addressed to scholars, not the average person in the pew. It has its own particular technical language, referring to schools of thought and arguments of others, that is not readily accessible to the layperson. It addresses topics not always having practical application. It may attempt to exclude experience. It usually seeks to establish its truths through propositions. It may refer less to Scripture than to the work of other scholars. It is commonly more concerned with examining and explaining the faith, than with proclaiming it; indeed, it sees itself arising out of preaching in a mediating position between the teaching of the church and the sermon itself. All of this is natural and to be expected. Each theological discipline (including homiletics) conforms to its own established norms, in response to issues that are part of its continuing history, issues that may be unique to it.

When we name these issues—issues concerning audience, language, style, goals, form, and so forth—we are speaking about matters of classical rhetoric. Rhetoric in its classical sense is the art of persuasion. However, we are so far removed from classical education, with rhetoric at its core, that we commonly dismiss rhetoric as mere empty words, as phrases lacking substance that are meant to impress by their cleverness. Because of this misconception, many of us naturally think of systematic theology outside the realm of rhetoric.

However, within this century, rhetoric has been repropriated, not as a study of ornamental language, but as language geared to communicate a message in particular ways. Literary critic I. A. Richards said in his landmark *Philosophy of Rhetoric* in 1936, "We have to renounce . . . the view that words just have their meanings and that what a discourse does is to be explained as a composition of these meanings—as a wall can be represented as a composition of its bricks."[1] Rather, he said, we have to search for an "interdependence of meanings" that acknowledges that words have many meanings and many ways of achieving their purpose.[2] In other words, the modern search to understand how meanings happen and what texts mean (a discipline we call hermeneutics) originates from rhetoric's concern with the purpose of discourse, the form it takes, a consideration of what is persuasive, and understandings of how persuasion happens. The importance of rhetoric is increasingly

The modern search to understand how meanings happen and what texts mean (a discipline we call hermeneutics) originates from rhetoric's concern with the purpose of discourse, the form it takes, a consideration of what is persuasive, and understandings of how persuasion happens.

recognized within philosophy (the respected journal *Philosophy and Rhetoric* was started in 1968 to meet growing interest), literary criticism, and the Bible itself—hence the rise of rhetorical criticism in the late 1960s.

Amos N. Wilder was a participant in this discussion with his *Early Christian Rhetoric: The Language of the Gospel* (1964). He was keen to acknowledge the unity of form and content in the Bible. He claimed the right of biblical texts to stand on their own, apart from extraneous considerations brought to them having to do with the author or with matter or content separated from form. He argued the need to move away from the reduction of biblical texts to a particular moral, doctrine, principle, or ideal. He wanted the New Testament to be considered within its own oral and written setting in ways that acknowledge "various genres, voices and images," as the text comes to speech in our setting.[3]

Some theologians now see theology as rhetoric. We have all been taught to avoid argument ad hominem, that is, argument not based in pure reason and directed for instance to personality rather than the issue at hand. David S. Cunningham, a systematic theologian steeped in rhetoric, persuasively argues (he is a rhetorician!) that it is the very nature of speech that prompts, in complex ways, readers or hearers to construct the character (i.e. ethos) of the speaker, and make their response to what is said partly on the basis of that character. Thus he says, "Given our account of the relevance of character in assessing an argument, it seems that, not just for philosophical arguments, but for any act of persuasion whatsoever, we may justifiably claim that all arguments are *ad hominem*—directed toward the person."[4] Moreover, since the claims of theology are not scientifically or logically demonstrable, hence not objective, and since we are dealing with faith not science, he maintains:

Theologians are involved not in the exchange of propositions, nor even in edifying "conversations," but in debates, disputes, and arguments. Theologians are always seeking to persuade others—and to persuade themselves—of a particular understanding of the Christian faith. The goal of Christian theology, then, is *faithful persuasion.*[5]

We could reasonably respond, of course, that God's claims are as demonstrable as those of science, and as objective too. In faith and through revelation we have a confidence in our central theological claims that surpasses the confidence of empirical scientists.[6] Moreover, many scientists are now seeing their knowledge based in certain theories as akin to faith. All noetic structures contain improvable assumptions: Proof is rarely absolute. We could add that with regard to the sermon, it is ultimately the work of the Holy Spirit to take what we offer and to convince the listener.

The fact remains, however, that we still speak not just to the converted, or to Christians with identical understandings. We therefore gear our speech to be persuasive in logical and other ways, without the satisfaction of complete control or an absolute logical proof, recognizing that in the minds of the listeners, there are other competing opinions, understandings, and beliefs.

Of course as soon as we admit the reality of persuasion that is based not just in fact, ideas, and logic, the notion of objectivity and impartiality is undermined. We must modify some of our assumptions in the church and academic enterprise. At minimum we admit to the presence of bias, and we commit ourselves to working against biases that contradict our faith. More broadly, we might recognize that impersonal, objective speech is impossible (though some speech is more personal and some is more just than others).

Furthermore, much theology can be affirmed as making less than objective or absolute claims in propositional exchange. It is often a form of "faithful persuasion" that in the minds and hearts of hearers does compete with other interpretations, worldviews, and philosophies. For Cunningham and others who typify postmodern attitudes, such as Rebecca Chopp and Don S. Browning, theology is a dialogical, open-ended, organic process of communication that resists closure and cannot achieve the certainty for which many of us long.[7] Rather than claim that truth is our possession, Cunningham would have us rely on truth that is akin to the event of revelation: "In other words, truth can once again become something that *comes to us*—rather than something that we grasp and manipulate how we will."[8]

In recognizing that even systematic theology has its own rhetoric, its own audiences and means of persuasion, we are saying something quite simple. We are saying that systematic theology and preaching for the most part have different audiences and purposes, and therefore different rhetorical goals and strategies for achieving those goals. Consequently, systematic theologians writing in their discipline are generally an indirect resource for preaching rather than direct. Some preachers, longing for immediate applications and in need of a sermon for Sunday, unfortunately confuse the sometimes indirect contribution of systematics with irrelevance. Nothing could be farther from the truth.

Excellent preachers keep reading systematic theology throughout their ministries, to sharpen thought and deepen understanding. Even just a few pages a week, thoughtfully considered, or the reading of a page or more each day until we discover a fresh understanding, will make an enormous contribution to our sermons over the years. We do not have to be able to trace the direct and immediate benefit to a particular sermon, although we may be able to do this. The writing of systematic theologians should inform what we say, even if they perhaps may rarely be invited to say it directly for us. We are acknowledging here that homiletical theology[9] has a different identity from its systematic cousin, and hand-me-downs in either direction frequently make an uncomfortable fit.[10]

We have all sensed the difference between good systematic theology in a book or essay and good homiletical theology in the pulpit. Failure to speak about these differences as openly as we might has led to three assumptions that function as barriers in the past to students desiring to become excellent preachers:

1) We have assumed that systematic theology can move directly into the sermon. Form and literary criticism have shown us that the original form of a biblical passage—oral or written, song or letter, law or prophecy, saying or parable—is part of its meaning. It should thus be clear that systematic theology, for instance, is not simply a content wandering through the seminary lecture halls looking for a form. It has a form already that helps determine, and is determined by, its content and function. For systematic theology to find a home in the sermon, both form and content must be modified.

Systematic theology is not simply a content wandering through the seminary lecture halls looking for a form. The sermon similarly is not simply a form looking for content, an empty genre waiting to be filled. Each has its own form and content.

Conversely, a sermon is not simply a form looking for content, an empty genre waiting to be filled. (We say this recognizing that the problem of some preaching today is precisely its lack of theological content.) The content of theology—systematic or homiletical—is related to its organization, structure, style, aspects of oral expression and delivery, as well as aspects of its anticipated reception and appropriation by the hearer. The medium is the message. The form is content. The rhetorical method is meaning. The relationship is relevance.

Even beyond this, we claim ideally that everything

68

we say in a sermon has theological implications. Theology cannot be narrowly conceived as a portion of the sermon, as phrases to be added to or taken away from the whole. The parts relate to the whole and should be composed or considered in the context of the whole, even as the whole would be altered by the loss or alteration of any of its parts. While parts may vary in theological strength and their testimony to Christ crucified and risen, there are no portions of the finished sermon that are appropriately conceived as being more God's Word than others. It is through the entire event of the sermon that God speaks.

2) We have assumed a minimal distance between the pulpit and systematics class. The rhetorical gap between classroom and pulpit is no small furrow in a wheatfield that students might hop. When we get close, we discover a sizable fissure, deep and wide. Too often in the past, the gap that students need to jump has been underestimated, with unfortunate consequences.

As students, we move from the systematics and Bible classes, down the hall to the homiletics class, perhaps in the mistaken assumption that we are looking for a sermon outline and homiletical application for our theology. Instead, we are expected to comment on the Bible, tradition, and all the various demands of daily faith and life. Moreover, we are to do so in ways that strengthen faith and nurture community. We are to use a style that is caring, without cynicism or mockery, that demonstrates love for our people. We are to avoid both the defensiveness and offensiveness that sometimes can be fostered in classrooms where competition is encouraged. Often we end up scrounging for rhetorical tools that can compensate for lack of integration (a) between congregational and seminary needs in some classes, and (b) between an educational training geared toward written essays and vocational demands for skillful oral speech. Past students have frequently been expected to negotiate these differences more by intuition and common sense than by instruction.

3) We have assumed that preaching needs minimal foundation in seminary. Courses like systematic theology, church history, and biblical studies make essential contributions to preaching, of the sort already named concerning systematics. Many seminaries do not require as compulsory a course in homiletics and those that do may require only one course out of thirty. As a result, we are encouraged by our educational institutions, often inadvertently, to see these for-

mer courses as occupying the high ground of theological education. Their connection to the sermon is assumed; but not purposely stated, explored, and tested on a continuing basis in the classrooms. Moreover, sermons are rarely assigned in classes outside of homiletics, and individual sermons or books of sermons are rarely assigned as readings. In view of this situation, it might be appropriate in theology, Bible, or history classes to offer sermons as assignments and to be more mindful in other ways of the needs of those preparing to preach. By the same token, we are often encouraged to see the sermon itself as representing the necessary dilution of these subjects, or popularization, or translation into common terms. In some seminaries preaching is functionally seen as a form of technology or "public speaking" rather than theology.

A century ago it was common that homiletics and speech were each a yearlong course in the three years of divinity training. In addition, students were required to preach to the school prior to graduation. Most courses discussed preaching. As students today, we are affected on many levels by the current lack of attention to homiletics: The underlying, subtle message in some institutions is that pursuit of graduate research and teaching is more important than the pulpit. The fact remains that preaching is essential, and most churches seeking new ministers, pastors, or priests list strong preaching as one of their greatest needs.

The sermon is not the dilution, popularization, or translation of theology. It is rather the completion of theology, and is made complete through Christ speaking it and constituting the church through it.

Since proclamation of the gospel (in both word and deed) is our highest calling as Christians, it would seem wise as students of homiletics to shift these deep-seated assumptions in what may be a bold manner. I believe that the sermon is not the dilution of theology; it is rather the completion of theology, made complete through Christ speaking it and constituting the church through it. We might even say that the church is most truly the church when it is preaching in worship, for it is through the Word and sacrament that salvation comes to the world, and it is through our lives being transformed in the cruciform image that our acts of justice, mercy, peace, and love are begun once more in power. Homiletical theology should be among our best theology (although not our most systematic), deserving our keenest attention, calling our best candidates, for it is not simply about God, it is God speaking to the world, speaking us into creation, speaking us into reconciliation, speaking us into new life over which Christ presides in glory.

Homiletical Theology as a Relational Event

Homiletical theology functions as a relational event in two ways. One concerns Christ and the other concerns our neighbors and the function of rhetoric.

Theology and Christ

In the opening chapter we said that the highest purpose of preaching is the event of God establishing a relationship with us. We repeat that here because we are calling homiletical theology into service for that relationship. As such, the theology we do in the pulpit is centered in God's saving action in Jesus Christ.

This means that we have nothing to proclaim if we do not have Christ, crucified and risen. We join with those who first confessed him as Lord and Savior and with the women who were his first preachers in saying not just, "He is risen!" but also, "He is the Christ! We have met him! The one who was dead is alive!"

If we lose sight of this as our message, that it is at the heart of whatever we say, our sermons easily become literary, historical, theological, exegetical, cultural, or thematic exercises. People come to church, however, to learn about and to rediscover God, alive and active in their midst. They yearn to experience once more Christ making a difference to their lives, in terms of both demand and hope. The Good News that constitutes "gospel" cannot be proclaimed with effect if as preachers we breezily take our people on an expressway that bypasses the cross and empty tomb at the center of our faith.

Why is this focus so necessary? No matter what Christian truth we are trying to communicate, listeners are always appropriately asking of the preacher, "Why should I believe this?" For example, "Why should I believe that the Bible is true, or that Jesus did miracles? Why believe that love will win out in the end? Or that we should live good lives? Or that God strives for the end of all suffering and injustice? Or that there is a heaven?"

We should not be surprised. These are similar to the questions that we as preachers must ask ourselves when we preach on biblical texts dealing with any of these issues. Each time we prepare a sermon, we must ask, "So what? Why should the congregation believe what I am saying? What reasons can I provide to assist the work of the Holy Spirit?"

In an introductory preaching class, we paused for some time while individual students ventured answers to why we preach the miracles of Jesus. The answers they gave were good and showed depth of theological reflection, but seemed to come up short as a homiletical view of God. One student did not understand the point of the question since the Gospels are expressions of theology that are rooted in history; thus, the miracles are making a point about who Jesus is. Another noted that we have the miracles on authority of the witnesses in the communities of faith that recorded them. Another spoke about Scripture as the inspired Word of God that we accept on faith. Someone else said that Jesus was the Son of God, thus all power was his. Another spoke of the miracles we continue to experience today, including our own individual faith. Then someone offered the strongest answer and greatest reason for preaching.

The strongest motive for preaching can also be the simplest: "Because of the resurrection. I have encountered the Risen Christ in my life and thus know firsthand the power of God's love." The resurrection is the foremost miracle at the heart of our faith. It is a barrier and a stumbling block (to ourselves as well as to others), and yet remains the only door to the Christian faith.

We preach the miracles of Jesus not merely because they are recorded in Scripture, but because the miracle of salvation that God has worked in Jesus Christ is our firsthand experience. We preach the miracles because the One who was put to death, as testified in Scripture, the same One who is alive now, has encountered us in the depth of our sin and claimed us as God's own through the community of divine love. Upon knowing Christ in this manner, no miracle seems deniable in Jesus' earthly ministry. Is there any power in this world or the next of which we need continue to harbor fear?

Or to take another example, why do we preach life after death? The nature of Christ's encounter with us is love, as testified in Scripture, tradition, and our experience, and we affirm that God's love is without end. Thus we necessarily conclude that what awaits us after death can be none other than the same love already shown to us by Christ, that we participate in around the communion table. Even beyond this, we have already experienced the power of Christ in overcoming death in our lives and the lives of others, be this in terms of overcoming injustice, oppression, self-centeredness, or in facing mortal limitation in a variety of ways.

It is fair to expect that not every student may feel comfortable when speaking about the cross and resurrection in such a direct manner, and there are a variety of reasons why such a position can be faithful and have integrity, particularly in a time of vocational discernment.

Moreover, witness to the cross and resurrection is not a formula that magically transforms any discourse into a Christian sermon. Nor do we have to turn each sermon into an intellectual treatise on the subject—often we may simply point.

The fact remains that we could read for several hours on any number of theological questions and themes (like miracles, virgin birth, or heaven), but they are secondary motives when compared with the cross and resurrection. Until we take people to the central event of the faith, where they must again make a commitment of faith in confessing Jesus of Nazareth as the Christ, the anointed One of God, we are without the firmest foundation possible for what we are saying, and they are without the firmest foundation possible for believing us. They can remain at a safe distance, without making a leap of faith, safely debating such intellectual issues as, "Are miracles possible?" or, "Can a virgin give birth?" The leap of faith is made not within the boundaries of reason but at a place near the border where we face head-on the contradiction of the cross. This is the place to which reason can lead, yet it can only point beyond to faith. At this place of decision, we might still choose to deny a risen Christ, even though Christ might be standing before us. If the people before the preacher are to hesitate or stumble, as may be appropriate, it is best that they do so in the right place, which is at the foot of the cross, where the stakes are considerably higher than the outcome of an intellectual debate.

This may seem too difficult. As preachers we may try to avoid the cross and resurrection, thinking perhaps that the subject, however briefly addressed, is too difficult for our people (or ourselves) to struggle with this week. Ironically, in avoiding it, we make our message more difficult to accept. The hymns, prayers, Scriptures, symbols, banners, and windows that surround us in worship all speak of Jesus as the Christ. Until this profound mystery is addressed in some manner, however succinctly, even through mere pointing, until it becomes a conscious focus in our minds as listeners, the cross and resurrection effectively stand as a great unanswered and perhaps subconscious question for us in worship: What does this mean? or, Who is this One we call Jesus Christ?

Until we take people to the central event of the faith, where they must again make a commitment of faith in confessing Jesus of Nazareth as the Christ, the anointed One of God, we are without the firmest foundation possible for what we are saying, and they are without the firmest foundation possible for believing us. In avoiding the difficulties of the cross and resurrection, ironically we make our message more difficult to accept.

Perhaps none of the reasons we may offer to persuade others can be experienced as fully satisfying if we avoid this one. For instance, we might tell people that Jesus was a great moral teacher whose teachings are to be trusted; yet we might not tell them that we follow his teachings because of who he is as the Son of God, and that his identity is decisively revealed for us through the cross and resurrection. The reasons we may give will be like many life preservers cast on the surface of the water. They can give the illusion that we are providing the help that is needed, and many in the congregation may even depart thinking they have received it, but not one of these reasons has sufficient buoyancy in itself to keep afloat for long those who are in need.

We are simply trying to give our people good reasons for believing what we are saying. Take people back to the basis (even if they have not named it as such) of their own belief, to the heart of what the church teaches, and have them recall or identify their own experience of the risen Christ, which is the true starting place of faith. Give them the language that they themselves may need and are entitled to—the same language that we need and struggle adequately to find—to help them understand their experience.

Surprisingly enough, when members of the congregation have again made the move to confess Jesus as the Messiah, in one manner or another, they begin truly working with the preacher in the course of the sermon in naming for themselves reasons to believe.[11] Only at the point where the nonsense of the cross makes sense of our troubled world, do we nurture true conviction. Without proclaiming the cross, we can never be sure that we have done what we could to enable the work of the Holy Spirit.

Of course this poses difficult questions for us. What about preaching the Old Testament? Certainly, we avoid doing what some early Christians did: We avoid crudely reading Christ back into the Scriptures, as though they were about Jesus all along and the Jews had it wrong. There is prophecy in the Old Testament. Yet even those passages that we read in church as prophecies of Christ (e.g., the servant will be a light to the nations—Isaiah 42), Gardner C. Taylor has preached, are "not clear and conscious prophecies of Christ . . . but conclusions from gazing in the direction of the everlasting God."[12]

It was unnuanced preaching of the other sort that contributed to the rise of anti-Semitism and the Holocaust. Some of its roots may be found in the New Testament Scriptures themselves, and Clark M. Williamson and Ronald J. Allen give preachers helpful pointers to

74

avoid it.[13] It is the same God who speaks in both Scriptures, and, I believe, who speaks in other major faiths as well: There is only one God, though I can know God through only my own faith experience. We find the message of God's salvation in the Old Testament text before us and develop it within its own historical context. Richard Lischer, for example, points to a sampling of salvation paradigms in the Old Testament: "The covenant, the new covenant, deliverance from Egypt, God's love for the lowly, the messianic promise, return from exile, the reign of God, the Day of the Lord."[14] Then we move to proclaim the resonance and concurrence of that message with the truth we know in Jesus Christ. Denying a christologi-cal center to the Old Testament, we still affirm a chris-tological center to our preaching. We do not suddenly become "unitarian" when we preach the Old Testament.

> *Denying a christological center to the Old Testament, we still affirm a christological center to our preaching.*

As an example, a sermon on Moses and the burning bush might fail if the discussion of holy ground is weak, (a) because the action of God, who alone makes ground holy, is ignored, (b) because our experience of places made holy by our encounters with the risen Christ are ignored, and (c) because we are not led to anticipate events where we may expect to be encountered again in the future. Christian experience with holy ground cannot effectively be separated from Christ. Preaching is strengthened by being solidly rooted in the depth and breadth of the listener's experience.

Of course the same approach can be taken with New Testament texts, since individual texts or pericopes have their own contexts and histories that often do not directly speak of the cross and resurrection. Thus we seek a central idea in the text at hand, and then explore, however briefly or indirectly, connections with the Easter event.

> *Homiletical Method*
> *a) Discern a central idea of the biblical text.*
> *b) Develop the biblical text in the sermon in relation to that idea.*
> *c) Explore what the cross and resurrection says to that idea. (See Chapters 4, 6, and 7.)*

Theology and Rhetoric

Homiletical theology concerns a relationship begun with us in Jesus Christ. In addition, it concerns a relationship begun with the congregation. Thus a second way in which we identify homiletical theology as a relational event is to speak of it as rhetoric. Rhetoric we have defined in its classical sense, as the art of persuasion—giving good reasons for people to believe what we are saying. Our homiletical theology presumes a relationship with our people even as it anticipates their needs and nurtures that relationship.

Already we may howl in protest: Even when many systematic theologians may not want to consider theology as employing rhetoric, or might admit rhetoric but deny relevance in paying attention to it, we ourselves could insist that rhetoric in the pulpit is wrong. We could say, "Rhetoric is persuasion. Persuasion is manipulation. Christians have no business manipulating others." We could add, with Luther and Calvin, that it is our business to proclaim, not to persuade; only the Holy Spirit can do that. Finally, we might note that the logical appeal or logos of Christian preaching, in a strict and limited sense, is Christ (the Logos or Word in John 1:1), and we need only attend to Christ. Certainly any preacher is on firm ground when following the advice of Cyprian (200–258), who said we are to use "not clever but weighty words, not decked up to charm a popular audience with cultivated rhetoric, but simple and fitted by their unvarnished truthfulness for the proclamation of divine mercy" (*Letter to Donatus*, 2). Of course in saying this, he used rhetorical devices, as has every critic of rhetoric from the time of the church fathers.

Another howl of protest may come from another direction. Metaphors, symbols, and biblical texts have many possible meanings that cannot be boiled down just to single meanings. The task of postmodern rhetoric, some might say, is not to persuade of one point of view, but to deconstruct reality and to emphasize plurality, ambiguity, and choice. Disruption of settled cultural presumptions about reality is after all an essential function of the gospel.

> Homiletical theology presumes a relationship with our people, even as it anticipates their needs and nurtures that relationship. In other words, homiletical theology presumes rhetoric: We need to have reasons if we are to persuade others of the truth of Jesus Christ.

Anything can be taken to extremes, however, and without the balance of the gospel, this approach can lead to relativism, or an attempt to deconstruct even Jesus Christ. As preachers we do not preach a text in the first instance, deconstructed or reconstructed; we preach Jesus Christ, crucified and risen, as he encounters us through the Holy Spirit and in the church. Our rhetoric is in Christ's service.

In spite of our protests, however, every time we speak we unavoidably influence what happens. What is avoidable and should be avoided is bad manipulation, unfaithful persuasion, that which takes advantage of our hearers. Moreover, the Holy Spirit needs our offering with which to work. Whether in a rural or a downtown church, varieties of persuasion will be at work every time we speak, planned or not, working for or against us, whether we like it or not. Ignoring this truth does not make it go away. We simply have the choice of whether or not to be purposeful in our use of it. It comes down to this: We need to have reasons if we are to persuade others of the truth of Jesus Christ. This is why Gerard A. Hauser has claimed, "In speaking and writing, you can use marvelous language, tell great stories, provide exciting metaphors, speak in enthralling tones, and even use your reputation to advantage, but what it comes down to is that you must speak to your audience with reasons they understand."[15]

Pulpit theology, like systematic theology, is not identical to rhetoric yet involves rhetoric. Preaching is never simply the exchange of information from the preacher to the congregation, in a manner analogous to the transmission of data from one computer to another using a modem. If it were, relationship could be left out of it. When we do theology in the pulpit, we are always mindful of those to whom we are speaking.

Obviously, we are speaking to people, not data banks; what we are doing involves head, heart, and soul; mind, body, and spirit. It is natural that people respond to the Word of God in their full humanity, even though we follow Paul, for instance in his instruction concerning speaking in tongues (I Cor. 14:2ff.), in giving priority in worship to that which is intelligible and builds up the church. Problems arise as soon as we deny full response: in denying movement in worship, or when only intellectually affirming truths that should make a difference in our lifestyle, or in being overguided by our emotions to the exclusion of factual evidence. Nonintegration can imply disintegration. Thus it would be appropriate for us to think of our theology broadly, as addressing not just the mind, but the breadth of integrated human experience.

Teachers of rhetoric in the ancient Greek and Roman Empires (including Cyprian and Augustine, who taught rhetoric prior to becoming preachers) seem wiser than we are. We seem to think, after years of formal education based in reason, that if sufficient rational reasons are supplied for doing something, people will do it. We also tend to think that the politician who gives the best-reasoned speech is the one who will win the election, though we have seen that frequently this is not the case. We similarly assume that if a sermon gives enough facts about an ecological issue or sufficient arguments about social justice that people will be convinced.

The ancient rhetoricians knew, however, that we do not do things just because they make sense, even as we sometimes do things that make no sense. Paul knew the same truth: "For I do not do the good I want, but the evil I do not want is what I do" (Rom. 7:19). These teachers wisely spoke not of one way but of three ways in which we may be persuaded by a speech. Any one of them might primarily account for someone's particular response:

—reasons of *logos* or logical appeal of arguments and facts
—reasons of *ethos* or ethical appeal (i.e. character and
   integrity of the speaker)
—causes of *pathos* or emotional appeal

Aristotle said that "[ethos] depends on the personal character of the speaker; [pathos] on putting the audience into a certain frame of mind; [logos] on the proof, or apparent proof, provided by the words of the speech itself."[16]

Without naming logos, we have tended to concentrate on it in preaching, largely ignoring the other modes of persuasion. We nonetheless also tend to think that because of the importance of knowledge and doctrine, logos is the most important. Clearly, in a sermon, a kaleidoscope of imagery and feelings (pathos) is no substitute for the gospel, and similarly, an enthusiastic presence of the speaker (ethos) is no substitute for lack of preparation. However, the influence of logos in our theological community has been too great, particularly when we have thought of logos narrowly as logic: We have been encouraged to believe that theological truth is logically verifiable (when it is in fact rooted in revelation) and adequately captured in objective or propositional ways (when it depends on the narrative and poetic as well).

> Three Ways to Persuade
> 1) logos—logical reasons
> 2) ethos—ethical reasons
> 3) pathos—emotional causes/reasons

Furthermore, so little attention has been paid to pathos and ethos that we may not yet be able fully to assess their power. Some of us might say that we liked a particular sermon, for example, thinking that we liked its intellectual content, when in fact it was its emotional power that most persuaded us. Episcopalian bishop Phillips Brooks (1832–1893) believed the ethos of the preacher was so important that he made it part of the central feature of his homiletic. Ethos is more than our personal ethics: It has to do with the personality of the preacher and the character of relationship with the hearers. Brooks said, "Preaching is the bringing of truth through personality" in stating the theme of his 1877 Lyman Beecher Lectures.[17]

Recently, Henry H. Mitchell and Robin R. Meyers have been among the boldest of a variety of people who claim the necessity of persuasion in preaching.[18] Mitchell advocates that we choose material for an "affective purpose" as opposed to solely a "cognitive" purpose. "Emotional logic" must prevail, for the sermon must happen as celebration in the lives of the people.[19]

Meyers advances the idea of "self-persuasion" as a goal for preachers. He is implying that understanding a sermon is not the end of the interpretation process for the listener. Rather, the end is the listener being persuaded by reasons the self provides (not the sermon)—yet as a response to the sermon—in accepting what the sermon is saying. Thus self-persuasive preaching, in contrast to message-centered preaching, is "about getting [people] to talk to themselves in specific ways about specific things."[20] We do this in large part by what he calls vicarious identification with the emotional states of others: "We do not necessarily need a rhetorical strategy to arouse emotion in others so much as we need a rhetorical strategy to exhibit the authentic emotions in ourselves."[21]

Intended rhetoric is essential for the pulpit, yet as preachers we must also stand at some distance from it. Preaching is God's event, not ours. While this large truth can never be an excuse for casual sermon preparation, we employ this truth in our devotional attitude. We put forward our best efforts toward faithful persuasion, and pray that in doing so we facilitate the clarity with which God's voice is heard. Nonetheless, Meyers' basic advice is important: Do not preach a sermon that does not first persuade you.

> *Homiletical Method:*
> *In writing your sermon, learn to vary your primary means of persuasion, such that, through what you are saying:*
> - *at times you are conscious of appealing primarily to logical argument.*
> - *at other times you are deliberately fostering your relationship with the congregation.*
> - *at yet other times your main thrust is emotional.*

Since persuasion depends in part upon us, our preaching should appeal on all three levels of logos, pathos, and ethos. In order for this to happen, theology should be relational, inviting response rather than shutting it down. Several things must be in place: (1) The congregation must experience that what we say arises out of our own vital relationship with God. (2) What we say must be experienced as arising out of relationships with the people to whom we are speaking, addressing their relationships with God and others, voicing their understandings, and anticipating their needs, concerns, and responses.[22] (3) Our preaching must be experienced as integrating head, heart, and soul (or loosely: logos, pathos, and ethos). Homiletical theology is not an intellectual exercise that results in a cool dispensing of knowledge over a prescription counter; it involves our entire lives in devotional purpose. Homiletical wisdom suggests that to achieve these goals today, our approach will be conversational and dialogical in tone and style, rather than assertive or authoritarian.

Review Questions for Chapter Three

1) According to this chapter, which answer is wrong? The sermon is the
   a) completion of theology
   b) dilution of theology
   c) complement of theology
   d) end of theology
   e) beginning of theology   [b]

2) Preachers should pay attention to rhetoric because
   a) many claims compete for listener loyalty
   b) all communication involves rhetoric
   c) the Scriptures were first spoken
   d) all of the above   [d]

3) Which has been argued as the best response? We preach the miracles of Jesus because
   a) they are recorded in Scripture
   b) they point to Jesus' identity
   c) Christ is risen
   d) we experience miracles   [c]

4) In preaching an Old Testament text we
   a) deny a christological center to the text
   b) find God's message of salvation in the text at hand
   c) affirm a christological center to preaching
   d) all of the above   [d]

5) Pathos is persuasion rooted in:
   a) appeal to psychology
   b) appeal to emotion
   c) appeal to character
   d) all of the above   [b]

Questions for Discussion

1) What benefits and drawbacks would there be, and in what seminary courses, to including sermons as assignments?

2) Biblical pericopes (units) have their own form, unity, and integrity, arising out of specific historical situations. Do you think it appropriate to relate each text we preach to the cross and resurrection? Might we equally stress, for example, the need for repentance? Should texts be allowed independence from larger theological concerns?

THEOLOGY IN
THE SERMON

Something needs to happen theologically in the sermon if preaching is to reach its potential as God's event. This chapter identifies ways we may strengthen our theology in the sermon and its persuasive effect. Numerous lessons are drawn from systematic theology as well as from homiletical theology. Suggestions are made for theological intervention with a text.

If theology were simply a content looking for a form, we could attach our theology to any form or structure at hand. In spite of postmodernist assertions however, we assert that, for the sermon at least, form, content, and function are inseparable. Thus, for instance, we claim that a sermon may create in its words the hospitable conditions for the relationship with God that its words actually initiate. In other words, talk of justice can become an experience of justice. Discussion of hope can create the reality of hope in our midst. What we want to say affects how and where we say it.

Miscommunication occurs when form, content, and function do not relate (for example, a preacher reads an impersonal essay on death at a funeral; a "sermon" is preached in a comedy club; something sad is spoken with a smile). The relationship of these elements allows us to assess the speaker's intent, the character of the speaker, and ultimately thereby, the quality of what is said.

When the sermon is a theological event, we may look to theology to influence basic form or structure, regardless of what other structures we may also employ. To allow theology this foundational role need not significantly reduce the variety of sermon forms available to us. We merely mean that good theological reasons exist for the choice and arrangement of what we say. How we do theology, therefore, becomes an issue. What method or methods do we follow to achieve our desired results? We suggest two approaches that will stand preachers in excellent stead. One comes from systematic theology. The other comes from homiletical theology.

> *If the sermon is a theological event, we may look to theology to influence basic form or structure, without significantly reducing the variety of sermon forms available to us.*

Method in Systematic Theology

Long before any of us actually set foot in seminary we were doing theology. We reflected on our experience in light of our faith life and teachings of the church. What we began when we came to seminary was simply the formal and often systematic study of theology. One of the hardest learnings we face as students is how to preach theological issues persuasively. What skills can we build to become competent? Four lessons recommend themselves for the pulpit, each having to do with method.

The first lesson from systematic theology is that we keep God near the center of our discussions, instead of affording occasional glimpses of God at the periphery. Too often as preachers we are tempted to think that we are preaching about a doctrine, or a truth, or a story, or a text, and we forget the more basic focus, that we are preaching God. Systematic theologians often agree that their appropriate focus is first on God, God's self-disclosure in the life, death, and resurrection of Jesus Christ, in particular, and in human history in general. In addition, the focus is on human response to God, both actual and potential.

With a view to keeping the focus on God, several theological steps have been identified that preachers can use:

1) Ensure that the issue, question, or subject is in fact theological (i.e., not psychological, sociological, historical, empirical, etc.) and separate the theological element if necessary (i.e., anxiety is a theological issue when it concerns lack of meaning in life).
2) Clarify and interpret key terms.
3) Indicate several possible responses (e.g., cause, relationships, identity, complement, opposite, etc.).

4) Identify a theological standard or norm that is commonly used as a source of authority (i.e., from Scripture or tradition).

5) Make an argument in light of that norm, for instance by indicating what Scripture says, what tradition says (a theological dictionary may be of help), and what theologians say.[1]

The second lesson from systematic theology can be to imitate the theology of those who stand as models for the church, including great preachers. We need not think of imitation as something that robs us of our creativity or our own ability to think. Rather, imitation awakens us to patterns of thought or expression that can be transformed into our own style, personality, and theology. Even by copying into a notebook an argument or paragraph, we can learn how someone thinks, and thus learn how to employ principles for ourselves.

Systematic theologians often focus primarily on God; God's self-disclosure in the life, death, and resurrection of Jesus Christ, in particular; God's self-disclosure in human history in general; as well as on human response to God.

For centuries art students have learned by imitation in copying the works of great artists. Through the Middle Ages, theological method was primarily imitation and citation of the church fathers, their quoted words standing as automatic, semiautonomous, divine proofs. Still today, most of us formally learn theology by imitation in writing essays in which we quote others, and by learning the doctrines, propositions, and creedal affirmations and stories of the church. These serve both as substance for our understanding as well as limits or boundaries for those in the community of faith.

Of course if we rely on imitation, if we do not understand what we are doing, if we cannot think through doctrines and ideas for ourselves and be clear on our own thoughts, we are not really doing theology.

Few of us will actually receive direct formal instruction on the most basic features of theological method: how to discover what there is to be said about a particular subject (i.e., the ancient rhetorical canon of invention); how to structure theological thought; how theological language works; what is theological process (not just content); the relationships between method and meaning, and form and meaning, and other issues.[2] These matters only recently are emerging as central to the theological task, in part because of issues arising from rhetoric, hermeneutics, and poetics.

Part of the difficulty in our getting beyond simple imitation is that there is no standard theological method comparable to the scientific method. We can listen at the open doorways of a few classrooms to overhear theologians wrestling with this problem: David Kelsey is dismissing the possibility of a normative approach: "There is no special theological 'way' to argue or 'think,' if that is taken to imply a peculiarly theological structure to argument. Accordingly, analysis and criticism of theological 'systems' are not likely to be illuminating."[3] Richard Grigg is saying, "It is bad enough, a critic might say, that theologians cannot agree upon the specifics of the *how* of theological thinking. But there is no general agreement among theologians even about theology's *what!*"[4] George Lindbeck notes that a universal norm is impossible because all cultural and linguistic expression is conditioned by the symbols of that culture.[5] Thomas Oden, in his deep suspicion of all that is modern, would have us return to classical theologians and the early church, "because of its close adherence to apostolic faith and because a more complete ecumenical consensus was achieved in that period than any period since."[6] David Tracy would have us return to the classics for another reason, to discover new tools of interpretation with which we might make a new beginning.[7]

Even in classrooms most influenced by liberation theology, in which method receives much attention, there are wide differences. James Cone insists on a new starting point for theology in the needs of the oppressed: "God is black," he says, in an attempt to get away from pervasive racist assumptions that God is white.[8] Rebecca Chopp speaks as a feminist: "There is no one method or theory that can accomplish the needed transformation. There are, instead, insights and strategies that arise out of the margins that may allow for new possibilities and visions."[9] Even amongst feminists there are differences, some seeing women's experience as the only norm, and others seeing both women's experience and Christian tradition as contributing to what is normative.[10]

We have been talking about the importance of imitation of models in systematic theology. Part of the difficulty in using our second principle concerns our own postmodern world. With so many competing theological positions, whom do we look to today as a model? This much should be clear: To be effective preachers we must look to imitating those theologians whose writing shows a sensitivity to the realities of congregational life, needs, and consciousness. Some theologians are prophetic in arguing for positions that most congregations would find radical yet impossible to hear. They play an important role in the life of the church at large, challenging us to new claims of the gospel as well as reminding us that our own perspectives are always partial and limited. However, students training for ordained ministry are training to speak, in the first instance, with and on behalf of the congregation and the wider church before the Word of God, not over and against the congregation, or regarding the congregation as the opposition. It is out of the ability to do this that the possibility of prophetic utterance of the preacher arises.

Common to all systematic theology is our third methodological principle: Test the logical consequences of any doctrinal position taken. Ask, for instance, What is at stake for the church if this position is held? For example, if we lose sight of the fact that in confessing Jesus Christ we confess both the historical Jesus and the Christ of faith, we call into question the whole idea of the church.

Or to take another example, a student might have difficulty with the doctrine of the virgin birth, in spite of the fact that it is attested in Scripture and is part of our classical creeds. By asking what is at stake in this doctrine, we discover that its denial could be interpreted many ways: (1) that Jesus is less than divine, (2) that Jesus was just another person, or (3) that Jesus was not born at all and only appeared to be human. Each of these positions has been taken in history and been judged heretical. So rich is the intellectual tradition of the church that most doctrines can be analyzed both by what they actually say, and by what, if we turn them over, they avoid saying. In other words, in denying any doctrine (an action we take in conjunction with our church) we need to decide whether its flip side is a statement we wish to defend.

This kind of dialectical (question-and-answer) thinking is essential for the preacher. We need to be cautious in our use of it, however. It can limit our ability to perceive a wide range of possible alternatives. Were such an approach our only tool, we would close doctrinal understanding to new insight by merely accepting the status quo, as feminist and other theologians have observed.

By testing the logical consequences of positions, schools of theological thought are developed. We come, then, to our fourth principle:

> Methodological Helps from Systematic Theology
>
> 1) Keep God at the center of your discussions.
> 2) Imitate the theology of those who stand as models for the church.
> 3) Test the logical consequences of any doctrinal position you might take.
> 4) Identify your own (and your church board's) theological method.

Identify as clearly as possible your own theological method or approach. Sometime early in your ministry to a congregation, sit down with your church board and have them do this as well. Most congregations have both defined and assumed theological limits and boundaries that the preacher should know. While the excellent preacher will keep pushing at a congregation's limits and boundaries, calling people afresh to new claims of the gospel message, this can be done only within a relationship of mutual respect and trust. The preacher must never consider the congregation as the enemy and may never use the sermon as an opportunity to vent personal frustration or anger in ministry. Preachers should seek a counselor for such expression (even as pastors seeking to counsel do well to submit to the same).

Theologies may vary on a wide variety of issues: the sources of theology (Bible, tradition, experience, or some combination); interpretation of Scripture; openness to other disciplines of knowledge; focus beyond the church (i.e. the church's role in society and culture), and the like.[11] For example, here are the broad and simplified outlines of four theological methods. Most of us would not find ourselves in complete agreement with one or another of these methods:[12]

Orthodox	*Neoorthodox*
starts with Christian tradition	starts with God's total otherness
reacts against the modern	reacts against cultural religion
historical and mystical	revelational and catastrophic
assumes conformity is normal	assumes experience is deceptive
truth is contained in established forms	truth is transcendent, not contained in human forms
theology "from established authority"	theology "from above, and beyond culture"
sin as corruption of the will and disobedience of God's will	sin as separation from God and rejection of human limitation
preacher relies on the authority of the institution or office	preacher claims the authority of revelation over experience
listeners accept the authority of the church to instruct	listeners affirm the sufficiency and absolute necessity of grace

Liberal	Liberation/Feminist/Black
empirical starting points	starts with marginalized people
responds to the nonbeliever	responds to the oppressed
philosophical and metaphysical	sociological and political
assumes harmony and progress	assumes injustice as normal
searches for truth in premises and propositions	truth emerges out of theory and praxis using narrative
theology "from above"	theology "from below"
sin as egoism, lack of love, and failure of human potential	sin as injustice and covetousness in human systems
preacher draws on contemporary culture and Christian tradition	preacher is political and speaks for the oppressed
listeners test their own experience with tradition	listeners claim their own authority

Whatever method we may use in our theology will inform our preaching, which is one reason why preacher and congregation should have at least a broadly compatible theology. It is too simple to say that the preacher's role is not to convert people to a particular theology, ideology, or political position, for we preach from a particular theological perspective and seek to foster actions and beliefs that conform to that perspective. Nonetheless, our common purpose and priority is to convert people once more to living a relationship with Jesus Christ.

Method in Homiletical Theology

Three methodological ideas leap at us from the pages of preaching history with the highest recommendation.[13] The first is limitation; that is, concentrate on only a few core doctrines. The preacher, in always speaking to the life of the congregation, avoids climbing aboard novel doctrines that take off without having to land for refueling. Of course there are other occasions, for instance in church education, when the widest variety of doctrines may find expression. But in the pulpit, several doctrines hold sway.

What are these central doctrines? They are identified for us by our faith tradition. They are the doctrines the church has identified as core doctrines. For example, John Broadus in the 1800s echoed the priorities of his church in his time by teaching preachers to concentrate on the "great" doctrines, identified by him as sin, providence, redemption, repentance, and atonement.[14]

The great Scottish preacher of the 1900s, James S. Stewart, reflected the chief concern of his church when he insisted on a paradox: We will discover the greatest variety of sermons if we focus on Christ. Stewart advocated four dimensions of this: Christ's death and resurrection; the inbreaking of the Realm of God with power; God's intervention in individual human lives; and in history.[15] This idea of focusing on Christ became the organizing principle of his Lyman Beecher Lectures on Preaching at Yale, and the Lectures give proof of the variety that Stewart advocates.[16] Stewart also contended that Christ-centered preaching is assisted if we preach the Christian year (see the facing chart), although it is not followed in all denominations.[17]

Samuel D. Proctor reflects his own particular African American tradition when he identifies key doctrines, or what he calls "four themes that drive my preaching like strong, moving pistons":

1) God is present and active in human affairs and intervenes in our behalf [i.e., immanence and transcendence].
2) Spiritual renewal and moral wholeness are available to us all [i.e., conversion and transformation by the Holy Spirit].
3) Genuine community is a realizable goal for the human family [i.e., church and the inbreaking of the Realm of God]
4) Eternity moves through time, and immortality is an ever-present potential. We have already passed from death unto life when we love [i.e., incarnation and eschatology].

Proctor adds to these a fascinating dynamic. He asks himself, "What is the opposite of this doctrine in the lives of my congregation?" Once found, he includes it in his sermon: "When I canvass the antitheses to these four main theses, I cannot find enough time or places to preach the sermons that are generated."[18]

Fred B. Craddock calls for preachers to stay focused on such doctrines as "creation, evil, grace, covenant, forgiveness, judgment, suffering, care of the earth and all God's creatures, justice, love, and the reconciliation of the world to God." He puts the matter of core doctrines into appropriate perspective: "Theology prompts preaching to treat subjects of importance and avoid trivia."[19]

How might we preach doctrines for the seasons of the church year?

Doctrines to Preach in the Christian Year

ADVENT: The four weeks prior to Christmas are designated Advent (= approach). They anticipate God's approach in three ways: Christ's Second Coming at the end of time (eschatology); Christ's approaching birth in history; and Christ's approaching birth in our own lives. As nights (in the northern hemisphere) move to greatest length and human troubles threaten to overwhelm, the anticipation of God's saving action mounts. In preaching we may heighten the despair even as we accentuate the hope. We do not forget Easter in Advent: the One who comes is the Redeemer who died on the cross. Any preaching emphasis on Advent as the beginning of a new year (where the lectionary year begins) may be misplaced: Theologically the Christian year begins with Easter.

CHRISTMAS: December 25, the Western date, and the Sundays following, mark God's becoming flesh in the Incarnation. God acts decisively on our behalf that through Christ we may know God, and God's purpose for us. God's way is the way of weakness and vulnerability of a child, accepting the limitations of humanity. Christ is fully God and fully human. God has the final word on human affairs.

EPIPHANY: The Western date is January 6, followed by Sundays after Epiphany in Ordinary Time, leading in the ecumenical calendar to Transfiguration Sunday. Epiphany literally means appearance or manifestation of God. The preaching focus on Epiphany is upon the appearance of God in Christ in his earthly ministry. Traditional readings on Epiphany and Sundays following regularly include the following manifestations of God: the descent of the Spirit at Jesus' baptism, God's revelation to the Gentiles (i.e. the Magi), and Jesus' first miracle at Cana.

LENT: Beginning with Ash Wednesday, these forty days (excluding Sundays, i.e. six weeks), traditionally were a time of penitence in preparation for Christ's giving himself upon the Cross on our behalf. Sundays are excluded; they reflect the season while they remain celebrations, though somewhat muted, of the resurrection. We preach the reality of sin and evil, and our own complicity in them, never underestimating their power or our capacity for being deceived. Against these we place Christ's refusal to give in to temptation, that is, his determination to accomplish our salvation for us. This is the traditional season of training for membership and is a good one in which to reexamine Christology, since the cross and resurrection are drawing near and are continually before us.

The Season ends with Palm/Passion Sunday and Holy Week (including Good Friday). Preaching focus remains on the work of the Savior, with secondary emphasis upon human failure to recognize who Jesus was and is, our incomprehension of his mission, and our inability to reconcile ourselves with God. The way of the world is death, especially death of the innocent, even Jesus Christ. Yet the way of God is to suffer even death for our salvation.

EASTER: The dating of the entire Great Fifty Days of Easter varies from year to year since Easter Day itself is the first Sunday after the first full moon after the spring equinox. Since without Easter we would have nothing to preach, this can be interpreted to be the most important Sunday of the year. Death has had its say and God's power is greater. Christ overturns the powers of the world. A new age has dawned in which Christ rules in power and glory. Through most of this season the Gospel lessons feature resurrection appearances of Christ. (Note: Preachers are well advised to prepare a draft of the Easter sermon, the most celebrative of the year, well before becoming immersed in the penitential mood of Lent and the demanding pressures of Holy Week. Too many Easter sermons are in fact Good Friday sermons.)

Every Sunday celebrates the resurrection, thus every Sunday of the Christian year reflects Easter joy. God has accomplished in Christ what we could not accomplish for ourselves. Forty days after Easter is Ascension Day, marking Christ's ascent into heaven to sit at the right hand of God. This is seen not as a cosmological problem but as an affirmation that (a) what was begun in the incarnation is brought to completion, and (b) the limitations of the incarnation are overcome: By the power of the resurrection, Jesus is known to us in every time and place.

THE DAY OF PENTECOST: The fifty days (hence "pente") of Easter end with the descent of the Holy Spirit on the disciples, the birth of the church.

ORDINARY TIME: Ordinary Time or Latin "counted time" is the time outside of the seasons of Advent, Christmas, Lent, and Easter and includes Trinity Sunday (the first Sunday after Pentecost) and the

Reign of Christ (the last Sunday before Advent). Whereas in one half of the year we look for God's revelation in the great events of salvation history, during Ordinary Time we look for God at work in the ordinariness of human life. We are not alone and powerless. Christ is in the church and may be encountered in the world. We are empowered by the Holy Spirit to act in concert with God's will. The end of the human story is not in doubt for Christ reigns over all (even over our waiting that marks Advent).[20]

In addition to the principle of limitation to core doctrines, we have a second principle from homiletical theology. A sermon must have movement, through developing stages. Find movement within theology to provide direction for the sermon. We may commonly do this in one of two ways:

a) Find a natural logical movement within a doctrine (i.e., a theological concept or teaching of the church). The doctrine might come from the biblical text, the church year, or some topic. For instance, if we were preaching on the Incarnation, we might move from the human need that God perceived, to the meeting of that need by God becoming flesh. If we were preaching on suffering, we might move from the reality of human suffering, to typical human response (i.e., the apparent absence of God in those situations), to God's actual response (i.e., the manner in which God in Christ has already entered into that suffering and taken it upon Godself).
b) Find a theological movement within your biblical text. Theological focus has become an important area of biblical and homiletical study. We correctly assume that the biblical writers are making theological points even as they witness to God's self-revelation through the events that are being reported; that is, the writers are not simply reciting history.

Our third methodological principle from homiletical theology is this: Use theological intervention with your biblical text. This important subject is one of the least discussed in biblical criticism today, partly because we are appropriately wanting to safeguard the text in its historical setting and context.[21] We therefore strive to employ exegesis "to bring out" meaning from a text rather than eisegesis "to bring in" meaning to a text. However, when we read a biblical text, we read it through the canon, our tradition, and faith. In other words, we never read any biblical text just on its own terms, in isolation from our Christian interpretative tradition, as though it were any other nonscriptural text. From the time of the early church a dominant principle of interpretation has been the analogy of Scripture: Obscure scriptural passages are interpreted by other passages of Scripture that are clearer. (Augustine encouraged us to look for the loving interpretation of Scripture when literal meaning is in doubt.) There are several situations in which reaching beyond our particular preaching text might be useful and important: when a biblical text has no apparent or explicit (a) theological theme, (b) focus on God, or (c) Christology.

> *Methodological Helps from Homiletical Theology*
>
> *1) Concentrate on only the core doctrines.*
> *2) Find movement within theology to provide direction for the sermon, (a) in a doctrine, or (b) in a biblical text.*
> *3) Use theological intervention with your biblical text when there is no apparent or explicit (a) theological theme, (b) focus on God, or (c) Christology.*

a) No apparent theological theme. A biblical text may not demonstrate sufficient theological focus in itself. For instance, many of the proverbs might seem to display a wisdom and common truth one scarcely needs to come to church to hear. Nonetheless, in one proverb we might legitimately discern a doctrine we could develop (e.g., talk of money might imply stewardship); in yet another proverb we might find a structure or movement that matches the structure or movement of a doctrine (e.g., "if . . . then" is the basic structure of covenant); in yet another we might find our theological focus in the context of the verse, or the religious and social situation of the text, or the function of proverbs as wisdom literature (e.g., God gives us reason in order that we may respond appropriately to the world); in yet another, for instance a proverb about a widow, we might purposely amplify the truth that is disclosed in the text through the lens of our theological tradition (e.g., God is acting when justice is being done).

b) No explicit focus on God. A second instance in which theological intervention is important concerns focus on God. Of every text we legitimately ask, What is God doing in, through, or behind this text? We should be able to answer this question. For example, if we are preparing to preach on Mark 1, concerning John the Baptist's preaching in the wilderness, it would be important not to be enticed into proclaiming John the Baptist. The same point could be made concerning any of the disciples, apostles, prophets, or saints. Who is John the Baptist to us? We do not pray to him. He is not our source of hope. He is pointing to someone else, and it is to this One that we also point.

Even more important, however, is God's action through John. His message is Isaiah's message: "Prepare the way of the Lord, make straight his paths." The same message had been proclaimed for hundreds of years. If it had been possible for Israel to achieve, it would have been done. This is exactly the point. Try though we might, we are unable of our own resources to make straight our crooked ways. Thus this story is in fact the beginning of God's making straight our ways in Jesus Christ. It is God who is acting in John, it is God who is acting in our preparations, it is God who enables us to do what John, on behalf of God, commands.

> *Theological intervention concerns focus on God. Of every text we legitimately ask, What is God doing in, through, or behind this text? We should be able to answer this question.*

c) No explicit focus on Christ. A third instance in which theological intervention may be helpful or necessary concerns Christology. This important kind of interpretation may be helpful with any text as a way of helping to connect our preaching to the cross and resurrection. It is used in conjunction with careful historical-critical exegesis, ensuring that we have allowed the text to correct and reform our own attitudes, behaviors, and doctrinal convictions. We come under the text in bringing additional interpretative material to it. Thus, as was mentioned in chapter 3, we use Christology to discover, amplify, or reinforce the Good News we have proclaimed from the biblical lesson. The cross and resurrection are not an "easy out" for the preacher, a quick or pious escape device from a tough text in which hope is hard to find, or from a sermon that is drawing to a close with yet no hope on the horizon.

There are two very important ways of employing Christology. The first is a movement to the cross. We look for some hint in the biblical text's imagery or words of the cross or resurrection. The parable of the rich man and Lazarus (Luke 16:19ff.) becomes a fuller expression of the Christian faith if we follow the hints Jesus gives us. He implies that no one will be raised from the dead to give warning to the rich man's five brothers. Yet even in using this language Jesus is pointing to the cross. In other words, the text is whispering, "Preach the resurrection." Thus, over and against the message of the text at one level (i.e., "It is too late") we might hold another theological truth (i.e., "In Christ it is not too late"). In other words, in Christ we have one who has come to us from the dead and it is not too late to hear, or to act upon, the life that is offered to us.

Similarly, in the parable of the wedding banquet (Matt. 22:2ff.) we may affirm the stark consequences of unpreparedness for the pre-pared banquet. Yet that is not the fullness of the Christian message we proclaim. We may set this against what our faith also affirms; namely, that in our baptism, Christ put on us a garment of high cost that makes us worthy to enter the eternal banquet in the Realm of God.

A second means of justifiable theological intervention in a biblical text goes in the other direction, from the cross to our biblical text. Having said in the sermon what we can about the text at hand, we now say, What does this text mean in light of the cross and resurrec-tion? Consider, for instance, the great commandment to love God and your neighbor as yourself. It leaves us finally cast upon our own resources to do this loving. Theologically we affirm that we are only able to love in this manner because we have first been loved by Christ. In other words, it is because Christ was able to love God and neighbor as self, that it becomes possible, through the Holy Spirit, for us to do the same. When we fulfill the great commandment, it is because God is acting through us.

In using this sort of theological interpretation, or resurrection hermeneutic, as I call it, many biblical texts that have been interpreted only to convict us, can also serve as instruments to nurture God's community of love.[22] (By reverse strategy, texts that seem to imply an absence of judgment can be interpreted to convict us.) We use this hermeneutic with caution, however. For example, we avoid reading the Old Testament typologically, as though the stories there are types of the Christian story, and exist only to serve it. Authen-tic Good News arises from the biblical text at hand: If it is not seen to arise first from this text, and God's action in and through it, theological intervention in the sermon is likely to seem too easy, unconvincing, disconnected and shallow, quite the opposite of God's Word.

> *We use Chris-tology only to amplify or rein-force the Good News we have proclaimed from the bibli-cal text at hand. In mov-ing to the cross, we look for some hint in the biblical text's imagery or words of the cross or resur-rection. In moving from the cross to our biblical text, we ask, What does this text mean in light of the cross and res-urrection?*

Are we justified in using theological intervention with a biblical text? Such intervention was merely assumed throughout history, prior to the recent impact of historical-critical methods. The ques-tion may be put in another way: Was it the intent of the New Testa-ment communities, or has it been the purpose of the church, to isolate New Testament passages from the larger Christian story? We preach the truth of one pericope (i.e. a unit of Scripture) not on its own, but within the saving message of the gospel of Jesus Christ. Far from distorting biblical texts in reading them in this intertextual manner, we are becoming more faithful to the scriptural setting and context. The cross and resurrection is a legitimate concern of every New Testament text for Christians. We as Christians can never do more than pretend to read a biblical text as though the cross and resurrection is not our lens. All of this simply means that we use theological intervention purposely, with the utmost care and sensitivity, in order that we not distort God's Word while proclaiming it boldly.

Review Questions for Chapter Four

1) The core doctrines for preachers are those that
   a) we as preachers decide are core
   b) the congregation decides are core
   c) the church at large decides are core
   d) all of the above   [c]

2) Which of the following was not a lesson from systematic theology for preaching:
   a) identify your own theology
   b) imitate the theology of those with whom you disagree
   c) keep the focus on God
   d) identify what is at stake in any doctrine   [b]

3) Pick the best answer: In the Christian year we celebrate the resurrection of Christ
   a) at Easter
   b) every Sunday
   c) every Sunday except during Advent and Lent
   d) in the Easter season   [b]

4) Which is least likely? Theological movement in a sermon might come from
   a) inside the biblical text
   b) outside the biblical text
   c) within a Christian doctrine
   d) outside a Christian doctrine   [d]

5) We use christological intervention with a biblical text when
   a) we can find no Good News in the lesson
   b) preaching the New Testament
   c) amplifying hope in that text
   d) we need to end the sermon   [c]

Questions for Discussion

1) Through theological education we may be exposed to ideas that might seem new or even radical to many of the churches we will serve. Identify what some of those might be in your own experience. Keeping in mind an appropriate tension between pastor and prophet, and between the preacher's need and the congregation's need, how might you handle these issues responsibly (or would you handle them) when you are preaching?

2) As preachers we must occasionally use theological intervention with a biblical text. Is there any difference between theological intervention, as it was advocated in this chapter, and eisegesis, and if so, what is the difference?

3) Identify core doctrines in your own tradition. What specific theological question does each raise? (For example, a key question for salvation can be, Why did God create the world such that salvation was necessary?)

PREACHING AS AN EVENT OF HOPE

Hope has been assumed to be the nature of preaching. However, in our age we cannot presume to exclude implications of experience from preaching. Both judgment and grace are needed. The homiletical order for these, if we are preaching sermons of moderate length, is from judgment to grace. They may be conceived as two parts of the sermon, whatever form we might choose. Two kinds of judgment and grace correspond to each other. A concluding sermon is offered in demonstration.

At the heart of the Christian faith is the Easter hope. Jesus Christ is risen. The power of death has been broken. This stands as a future promise, for the living and the dead, and as the character of hope that already breaks into our present. God meets us not least in the sermon, confronting the reality of our sin, breaking and negating the future that we deserve as sin's consequence. Of course we cease to follow Christ's way if we abandon hope, and thereby look away from God. We put our trust elsewhere, for instance, in possibilities of human accomplishment or human measurements of success. Cast on our own resources, there is no hope, for as Jesus said, "Apart from me you can do nothing" (John 15:5). However, by trusting in God's grace, all things are possible. We are a people of hope, as the word "gospel" or "Good News" indicates.

Such clear truths have obvious implication for preaching. Since God's Word comes to us and constitutes us as a gathered community, preaching is inseparable from hope. Nonetheless the need arises for a chapter on preaching as an event of hope: The regular preaching diet in many churches is one of sermons that are less than hopeful. While hope may be uttered, it is often not sufficiently developed for listeners to apprehend its import. Preaching hope is not simple or straightforward. It involves rhetoric put in service of communicating the faith. Hope comes, not from what we can do on our own, but from the knowledge and appropriation of what God has done in Christ and continues to do through the Holy Spirit and us.

We use hope in the widest sense here to include that family of terms closely related to the cross and resurrection, that speak to the overall tenor of life as God intends it to be lived. Thus, for example, hope used in this manner includes two immediately related terms, faith and love, in Paul's triad of I Corinthians 13:13; and other terms like "joy" and "courage." Each term requires the Christ event in order to be fully understood and appropriated theologically.

Preachers have always affirmed that preaching is hopeful, at least from an intellectual perspective. The nature of preaching as God's Word makes it hopeful. Clearly there are many possibilities for the theological thrust of a sermon. For instance John Calvin, seeking to enable regeneration through preaching, cited II Timothy 3:16 and thus emphasized edification, reproof, correction, and instruction. We may similarly preach: condemnation, fear of God, repentance, spiritual discipline, moral rectitude, endurance, acceptance, obedience, submission, self-denial, forgiveness, justification by faith, liberation, protest, justice, peace, nonviolence, praise, thanksgiving, reconciliation, and a long list of other possibilities. There are many biblical texts we will preach that have exactly these kinds of thrust. None of these emphases is antithetical to what is meant here by hope, although not all are sufficiently strong on their own to give adequate expression to hope. This claim needs further exploration.

The theological emphasis we choose for many sermons is not sufficiently hopeful to give adequate expression to our faith.

In theology we commonly understand hope in a particular way.[1] Hope is rooted in the love of God in Jesus Christ, who both reconciles us to God's saving purpose and decisively discloses the ultimate end of human history to be that love. The One in whom we put our faith is the object of our hope, for this anointed One of God is now glorified with God. Thus at one level, Christian hope has the intellectual status of a fact that is testified by Scripture and affirmed in faith.

At another level, hope is also an experience. The cultural use of the word "hope," which identifies hope as an emotional feeling, attitude, or experience, cannot be the whole Christian story. Genuine hope comes, we say, only in relationship to God. God uses preaching to establish this relationship. What we experience as a feeling of hope, properly rooted in faith and justice, is a gift from God.

Hope is also the nature of God's law. We affirm that law or instruction from God (torah) is a gift, both a yoke and a joy: It is hopeful, for the instructions God gives us to correct our lives are a guide for the redeemed.[2] Such a positive view of instruction is more common in everyday experience than we might assume. For example, a colleague told how he had been trying to assemble a new barbecue that came without instructions. His father-in-law and a friend, neither of whom was mechanically gifted, gave humble assistance. He experienced the grace of instruction (and of his spouse) very clearly when, as tempers were near fraying, his wife came, noted the trouble, and reached into the discarded packaging to discover the instructions for assembly.[3] Instructions can be a means of blessing. Since God has created us, we delight in receiving God's instruction. In classic Reformed theology, to listen to God's Word with joy and to respond in thankful obedience is a gift.

This understanding of the inherent hopefulness of preaching, is essential for our task. It helps to clarify that when we speak of matters of hope, grace, blessing, and the like, the theological or intellectual truth we affirm cannot be reduced to mere feeling or experience. For example the grace we receive in a sacrament does not depend upon our feeling that we are graced. By the same token, our hope (who is Christ) remains constant though at times we may be overcome with doubt or experience despair in the course of carrying out our mission. For this reason an essential function of the Word in worship is the upbuilding of the community in faith (Eph. 4:12).

This foundational understanding that preaching is hopeful has also been a source of numerous problems for the pulpit, one that curiously diminishes the hope we find there. Preachers assume the hopeful nature of preaching, and thus often also assume that we need not attend rhetorically to hope in our sermons. The following problems commonly arise:

1) *Anthropocentric Preaching*—The Good News of Christ's resurrection of course means dire consequences for us if we do not change our ways. Thus the emphasis of the sermon needs to lie on what is required of us, in light of the promise that is ours. As soon as we make this step, however, we have moved from focus on what God

has graciously accomplished for us in Jesus Christ, toward what we might accomplish for ourselves, albeit in the form of obedience to God.[4] An important balance is needed between our best attempts at faithful lives of service, on the one hand, and faithful dependence upon God on the other. Without sufficiently giving voice to what God is accomplishing in the sermon, we may end up like a cyclist who loses balance and careers off the path into the rocks and bushes. Human potential and human tasks are not our primary focus. Our hope rests in God, not ourselves.

2) Moralizing—A related issue is moralizing, turning every biblical text into something that we must do, or that God tells us to do, when many texts are not concerned primarily with instruction or rules for right living. Unwarranted moralizing not only distorts the biblical text by importing a foreign message, it works against hope by failing to communicate and mediate the saving action of Jesus Christ.

For example, in preaching the cleansing of the Temple (John 2:13ff.) we would be moralizing if we said that the text means we are to clean up our churches. Of course, that the church needs cleansing may be true. However, that is not the specific thrust of this text. Jesus is not portrayed here primarily as our example. He is our Lord and Savior who acts and speaks with authority, in this case teaching us concerning true worship. As Savior, he invites us into faith, where we must make responsible decisions by trusting in God. Moralism tends to reduce Jesus to an example, and preaching of this sort reduces faith to a matter of mere obedience to rules, or worse, to a laundry list of things to do.

3) Excessive Reverence of the Biblical Pericope—Prior to modern histori-cal criticism, preachers commonly preached on individual Bible vers-es extracted from passages without concern for their contexts and his-torical settings.[5] The history of preaching sometimes shows evidence of sermons in which verses were bent to the purposes of the preacher, and priority to God's message was lost. It is essential that we first lis-ten to what Scripture is saying, such that God may correct us, for the Word presides over the church and must be upheld in that position by preaching.

However, we may now be guilty at times of allowing the Bible to become too much the university's book at the expense of recognizing the church's ownership. We may inadvertently distort the biblical text, even while we are faithfully employing scholarly exegesis, praying for guidance, and preaching the pericopes (units of Scripture usually larger than verses) of the New Testament—if in doing so we forget about their overall purpose, as Scripture, which testifies to the risen Christ. Thus we might be tempted to expound a particular biblical text even as we neglect the broader hope to which it moves.

> *Preaching by its nature as God's Word is hopeful. Yet if we are not careful to develop this hope, our preaching can become: (1) anthropocentric, (2) moralistic, (3) unduly focused on the biblical pericope, or (4) insensitive to what listeners need in appropriating hope.*

4) Failure to Consider Sermonic Reception—The gradual loss of rhetorical studies in theological and other programs occurred a century ago. The possibility of delivering objective knowledge was culturally assumed. Moreover, the delivery of a speech was assumed to be largely identical to its reception. If something was said by a preacher in authority, it was safe to assume that it was received, commonly accepted, and believed. Such preacher-at-the-center models, reflecting other male social roles, to a considerable degree could virtually ignore the experience of the congregation. Experience was not given the same high profile it is today in educational and other circles. Informed by refined theological understandings of the word *hope*, which often removed hope from the level of experience, preachers in former eras knew more readily than we do that sermons are hopeful—even if their central message was, "Do not do this!" or, "Cut this out!"

Of course, even as the authority of preachers is sometimes not assumed, the experience of listeners cannot be ignored altogether today. If you are about to burn your hand, it is essential to receive a warning shout. To be hopeful, however, preaching needs to be more than a warning shout or admonishment. We begin to recognize this once we consider communication as a two-way street, involving both speaker and hearer. The child who is given sharp parental instruction also needs a warm embrace and words of assurance and love.

Adults have similar needs in relation to God: We need more than instruction in the sermon. God has met this need above all in the manner of God's personal self-giving in Jesus Christ. God does not come to us simply as information but in flesh and blood. To encounter Christ is to encounter more than hopeful information. In preaching, then, we normally offer the hope that is Christ in a manner that can be properly received and appropriated by the congregation.

Some individuals will experience such an encounter as shame and utter condemnation of their manner of life. They will recognize in

Christ the recollected faces of those they have injured. Even this conviction is the first step toward authentic hope, for hope without conviction of sin is unlikely to be genuine. Of course there are others who will recognize the voice of the One they came seeking, or who comes seeking them, because the familiar hope that unites Good Friday and Easter is clearly developed in the sermon. This hope is what they need and have come to depend upon. It is to be as audible as the bread and wine at the Table are visible, and is to be clearly offered by Christ for acceptance by all.

Many sermons give muted hope that is simply not as loud as we might expect, given what God has accomplished for us in Jesus Christ. Hope requires articulation in the sermon and identification in our experience of the world.

We can never proclaim the fullness of the gospel. This does not explain why many past and present sermons give such muted hope; it is simply not as loud as we might reasonably expect, considering the nature of what God accomplished for us in Jesus Christ. Thus we recast some theology and preaching practice in light of our learnings: We cannot be content to plead the hopefulness of preaching if we (1) avoid articulating genuine hope, or (2) avoid facilitating some experience of it which embodies an encounter with the risen Christ. The preacher has responsibility, then, for making Christ's presence in preaching as fully audible and intelligible as possible. Thus some responsibility for reception of the Word lies with the preacher and the preacher's skill with rhetoric.

Issues of Form, Content, and Function

Preaching hope is not to preclude what subjects we discuss, nor what theological perspectives we bring to them in the sermon. What it does preclude, as a norm, is sermons that take no account of what God has accomplished for us on our behalf, proceeding as though the events of the cross and resurrection make no difference in the broader world in which we worship and live.

Similarly, preaching hope is not to adopt cultural optimism, accentuating the positive and believing that things will turn out all right in the end. As Donna Schaper notes, "Hope is not based in the evidence, and is not damaged when the evidence disappears."[6] At the same time, the reality of God always persists as evidence. We are positive only because we look to God. By faith we are positive even as we look on the tragic suffering in the world and enter into its pain. We are a people who cannot deny the hope that proclamation helps to impart, as a number of scriptural texts affirm: As Paul said, "We proclaim Christ crucified . . . Christ the power of God and the wisdom of God. For God's foolishness is wiser than human wisdom and God's weakness is stronger than human strength."[7] Yet preaching does look at the world with its masks removed and in being what God is speaking actually perpetuates the overthrow of the world's powers that stand against God. Thus preaching is far removed from public optimism.

Moreover, preaching hope should not try to force all biblical texts into the same mold. Of course, many passages we preach do not end in hope. Since the 1960s biblical studies and theology have taken great pains to avoid finding any center or core theology in the Bible. However, the debate that presided over the demise of the biblical theology movement did not remove the simple fact of the cross and resurrection from the heart of biblical witness.[8] We may honor the rich variety of biblical witness without ignoring that event which stamps our proclamation with its particular character. While the cross and resurrection is not always our direct or only subject of address, our words "have the *form* of the cross, presuppose it, drive inexorably to it, and flow from it . . . cut[ting] in upon our lives to end the old and begin the new."[9]

What have homileticians said about this? Perhaps because the current revolution in preaching gathered momentum after the biblical theology movement had peaked, there has been surprisingly little discussion about a theological center of preaching. Richard Lischer emphasizes law and gospel, underlining that preaching moves "through one or more of the following sets of antitheses: chaos to order, bondage to deliverance, rebellion to obedience, accusation to vindication, despair to hope, guilt to justification, debt to forgiveness, separation to reconciliation, wrath to love, judgment to righteousness, defeat to victory, [and] death to life";[10] Justo and Catherine González emphasize liberation;[11] David Buttrick announces God's new age that has begun in Christ.[12]

Generally, however, homileticians have sidestepped the issue, preferring to analyze homiletical structure rather than name a theological center of proclamation. If we consider possible sermon structures, many choices are available to us, from deductive to inductive (see chapter 10). Thomas G. Long has helped recall for us that preaching should reflect the wide variety of rhetorical forms of the biblical materials themselves: These in fact represent "the many ways in which faithful people respond to and live their way into that basic story."[13] Whereas the larger gospel story is "in the background," it is the form and function, for instance of biblical parables, psalms, and proverbs, that are "in the sermonic foreground."[14] In other words, the shape and rhetorical purpose of individual Bible pericopes provide the dominant rhetorical strategy for sermonic discourse.

With regard to the rhetoric of the biblical text, we ask this: Is it to the rhetorical strategy of a particular biblical text in its historical setting that we give final sermonic priority? Or is it to the sermonic purpose guided by the purpose of the faith community in receiving those texts as canon, in witness to the larger faith story?[15] From a homiletical perspective both strategies are required, with the Christian community's shaping story and understanding of that story at the heart of our message each time, not pushed into the background, or separated from the preacher's insights or purposes.

Discussions of sermon structure do not avoid the burden of choice concerning the theological issue at the heart of preaching. Whether or not we agree that hope is at the core of preaching, we all come to a biblical text with some theological perspective. Theological presuppositions help us to determine, for instance, even where a particular reading should begin or end. They help us to determine priority of meaning in a text. They shape what we say about a text. It is also true that many preachers cannot find hope in a text because they are not trained to see it, or they have not asked themselves what God is doing in, through, or behind the text (see chapter 7).

Furthermore, when we choose a sermon form we also often choose a theology without being aware of it. For instance, if we decide on a sermon that moves from exegesis of the biblical text to an application of that text today, we have already tilted toward a theology of judgment, knowingly or not.[16] Expository sermons, for example, move once from exegesis to application and frequently express explicit hope only in the closing minute (e.g., "Nonetheless, our hope rests in Jesus Christ, who died that we might have life, and have it abundantly"). If we deal only once with the Bible text, we usually emerge from it with a message of instruction and judgment (since we can preach grace most fully only in relation to judgment). Thus a single movement into the biblical text will commonly leave the congregation dealing mainly with what we must do. Such grace as there is will normally be the muted grace that undergirds instruction and teaching, not the echoing grace that comes when we proclaim from the empty tomb. Often these sermons do not allow an opportunity for the congregation (1) to discover grace in or through the biblical text at hand, (2) to experience God's grace meeting them in the sermon, or (3) to visualize what God's acts of grace look like in this world. In this sense, there is no theological neutrality with regard to sermon form and function.

Furthermore, there never has been such neutrality. The early church read Scripture through Platonic lenses; the Middle Ages used Aristotelian; the modern church used Enlightenment lenses of various sorts and shades (e.g. Hegel); in the postmodern era, we struggle to know which lenses to use. For example, Stanley Hauerwas names this as his textual lens: "No account of any text is truthful that is not about God's care of God's creation through Israel and the Church. A sermon is scriptural when it inscribes a community into an ongoing Christian narrative [i.e., acting as the church in the world]."[17] It is important to name our approach whether it is hope or something else. It is a risk not to name it, for then we are subject to all manner of influence that cannot be addressed by the community of faith.

Perhaps this observation can simply be a call for us to be more deliberate in talking about how theology influences the form and function of the sermon itself. In other words, form and function are not mere tools to help in understanding the biblical text. They are matters that concern the theology that we preach. If we or our teachers choose different theologies from hope to guide the sermon, our proclamation will be informed of these theological purposes. We may each ask ourselves, If Christian hope is not the core movement in homiletical theology, then what is it for me and my tradition? and, How may I implement this more fully in my preaching?

Homiletical Implications of Hope

Whether or not we accept hope as a normative movement for proclamation, it is sufficiently important to require that we understand what is at stake and gain facility in employing hope homiletically. How may we assist the hope which is Christ in our sermons?

Our hope springs from the historical events of the cross and resurrection. The traditional theology that allows us to preserve their important relationship speaks about authentic hope using the language of judgment and grace.

Judgment points out our wrongdoing. Clearly judgment that culminates only in the crucifixion of Christ cannot in itself be our hope. Similarly, contemplation only of the resurrection, forgetting about the events that led to and culminated in Good Friday, cannot be our hope. We make a mistake if we equate either judgment or grace, on its own, with hope. Grace belongs in the context of the price God paid for our salvation. Grace without high cost, that also judges the listener, is a fiction; Dietrich Bonhoeffer called it "cheap grace." Thus to have the correct equation we must write: hope = judgment + grace.

hope ≠ judgment (though judgment is part of hope)

At the simplest level, judgment places upon us the burden of responsibility to act. We may define this judgment in two ways: (1) as God's word against us and the sin that separates us from God, and (2) as continuing social responsibility in the world around us, that we bring on ourselves as a society, for continuing to say no to God (i.e., the consequences of our sin, for instance in cycles of violence, oppression, or poverty).

hope ≠ grace (though grace is part of hope)

At the simplest level, grace is God's acceptance of the burden that is ours to act. Grace may also be

hope = judgment + grace

defined in two ways: (1) as the action of God in Jesus Christ to reconcile us to God's purpose (i.e. atonement), taking on the burden of judgment, that we might live fully to God and one another, and (2) as God's continuing intervention in history and human affairs to bring down whatever stands against God and to restore the world to God's purpose. No matter how far we have strayed, or how severe the judgment upon us, God never leaves us without signs that point to God's realm as living, real, and active.

Since we cannot preach hope by simply preaching grace, the hopeful sermon necessarily contains both judgment and grace in tension with each other. Each needs the other to complete its expression. Grace gains its relevance as hope in relation to judgment. John Wesley called the preaching of both judgment and grace in every sermon "the scriptural way, the Methodist way, the true way."[18] Charles H. Spurgeon (1834–1892), the famous Baptist preacher of Southwark, London, taught his preaching students:

Judgment, while it can be a gift, puts the burden on us, emphasizing what we must do. Grace, while it can judge us, puts the burden on God, emphasizing what God has already done in accepting the burden that is ours.

The grandest discourse ever delivered is an ostentatious failure if the doctrine of the grace of God be absent from it; it sweeps over [our] heads like a cloud, but it distributes no rain upon the thirsty earth; and therefore the remembrance of it to souls taught wisdom by an experience of pressing need is one of disappointment, or worse.[19]

Many Protestants use the alternate terms "law" and "gospel," although these pose a host of confusing

107

problems, not least because of their history.[20] Some preachers influenced by Reformation ideas misused this approach. Gospel or grace became a device of convenience that was tacked to the end of a sermon without any connection to what went before:

[In this pattern of misuse the] gospel is not the end of the law, not the advent of the new, not the act of liberation making its way into our lives, it is just the ratification of the law, which is probably the real reason why there is resistance to the old law/gospel method. Since there is no end, no real gospel, it becomes a species of psychological gimmickery. One tries to scare the Old Adam into becoming Christian.[21]

If we are going to preach hope, a number of additional comments may be made.

Further Comments for Preaching Hope

1) Moving from Judgment to Grace—Preachers, as a norm, are wise when structuring sermons theologically to move from judgment to grace.

In making this claim, we cannot appeal to any consensus found amongst biblical texts. A sermon can be written in the manner of many biblical texts, for example in apparently ignoring judgment and grace (e.g., the boy Jesus found in the temple, Luke 2:41ff.); or in moving from grace to judgment (e.g., the Ten Commandments in Deut. 5:1ff.); or in moving back and forth (e.g., the Epistle to the Romans);[22] or in moving from judgment to grace (e.g., the story of Zacchaeus in Luke 19). But we recall that the overall Bible story is itself filled with hope as it moves from promise to fulfillment. It moves from expulsion from Eden to the New Jerusalem; from the Exodus to the promised land; and from the cross to the resurrection, and not in the reverse order.

Moreover, we will find no consensus if we turn to theologians. Luther argued that it is only when we are awakened to our sin that we may find safety and security in Christ. Wesley said that judgment and grace may be preached, "in their turns," or "both at once," as is the case with all of the "conditional promises" of the faith.[23] Karl Barth affirmed that the homiletical order is important, but could not decide what it was, for he contradicted himself. Still, judgment to grace, he said, reflects the preacher's spiritual discipline throughout the week in preparation for Sunday:

The preacher . . . comes before [the] congregation . . . pierced by the Word of God and has been led to repentance in the face of divine judgement; but also as a [person] who has received with thankfulness the Gospel of forgiveness and is able to rejoice in it. Only in this progression through judgement and grace can preaching become genuinely original.[24]

Many preachers and teachers of preaching do not identify a position on this theological issue, though in practice many still employ this judgment-grace dynamic. The sermon moves to what Henry H. Mitchell calls "celebration" and "contagion" of joy in many African American churches.[25] Frederick Buechner (in his Lyman Beecher lectures that theologically are much more sophisticated than his terms) says that "the gospel is bad news before it is good news"; it is "tragedy" before it is "comedy and fairy tale."[26] Eugene Lowry's "homiletical plot" moves to "experiencing the gospel" and "anticipating the consequences."[27] Fred B. Craddock charges readers to preach hope:

Proclaim from the housetops what was, with great difficulty, struggle, and risk, heard and received with faith. . . . It is a shout of recognition of the Good News of God's grace. . . . [T]he shout symbolizes the intensity and the tenacity of the love that not only is the message but impels the message. . . . an alert to all forces of evil: there is another voice to be heard, another claim for human life.[28]

A similar understanding may be at the heart of David Buttrick's homiletic in the understanding that our preaching, as a continuation of Christ's preaching, is to shape the consciousness of hearers to what God has accomplished in a new social order.[29]

We cannot finally decide on the order of judgment to grace on the basis of any particular biblical texts or theologians, however. The extraordinary fact we profess is that God, who demands our obedience, also provides it in the gift of Jesus Christ. We are most fully human when we are most fully reliant upon God in faith. Our decision about order comes down to something very basic and practical, having to do with the stuff of homiletics, that is, with rhetoric and communication of the gospel. Normally we seek to send our people away from church with more hope, joy, courage, love, and faith than they had when they entered, not less. We ask: What theological movement in the sermon will be most persuasive in engendering hopeful, faith-filled lives? The experience of listeners, while never our ultimate determination in preaching, is nevertheless an essential aspect of our proclamation. Homiletics, like other disciplines in our times, has been significantly swayed by the legitimate claims of experience. How, then, may we best communicate Christ's hope in responsible ways?

When we anticipate how preaching will be received, we remember two things: (1) that it is ultimately not up to us how the Word will be received, but to God and the individual, and (2) that Scripture primarily directs the Word we preach. Judgment before the Word results in something that we must do, dependent upon our own resources. Generally, time is required in the sermon to move the congregation to a place of sufficient trust and awareness that they can admit sin, need of God, fearful living, or whatever, not to mention understand the sin more deeply. To move back and forth between judgment and grace allows neither to be actually experienced.

Grace, by contrast, results in an awareness of what God has done and is doing in Jesus Christ and through the Holy Spirit. Like any idea in an oral presentation, this awareness of God's action also takes time to form in our minds and hearts. A simple propositional declaration of the Good News found in Jesus Christ does not normally allow that Good News to be appropriated by the hearers. To appropriate what we hear we need sufficient time and focus to visualize and experience what is said, both emotionally and spiritually. Only an exceptional preacher or an unusual sermon can end by detailing our responsibilities and what we must do, and in so doing also end with a powerful sense of what God is doing. Thus we may recommend a theological norm for the movement of the sermon: from judgment to grace, each with substantial, balanced focus.

2) Two Kinds of Judgment, Two Kinds of Grace—We tend to think of judgment along a vertical (or transcendent) axis, with God above and us down below, being judged for our failure to keep God's commandments. Judgment in this sense awakens the guilty conscience, for as Herman G. Stuempfle has said, it hits us like a hammer and brings us to our knees when asking for forgiveness. This is a very important understanding of judgment, reflected in large portions of the Bible.

However, for practical purposes there is another biblical understanding that Stuempfle has developed.[30] We may use judgment on a horizontal (or immanent) axis that is even more important for preachers. It can free us from moral finger-wagging and pulpit-thumping of the sort that, used to excess, communicates not least an understanding of ministry which has the preacher at the center as the one in authority and control.

Using this second kind of judgment, we hold a mirror up to the world as it truly is, not as we like to pretend it is, and we find ourselves badly needing God. Stuempfle called this second understanding of judgment a "mirror of existence." This mirror reflects conditions after the biblical fall: accidents, illness, and natural disasters. (Theologians, such as Paul Tillich, have named lack of meaning, anxiety, despair, disease, as theological issues here.) This mirror also reflects our communal and individual responsibility in relation to systemic evil (evil that resides in human systems): We become conscious of living in wealth while millions are dying in poverty; or of failing to root out what breeds violence; or of misusing the earth's resources. (Theologians, for example, Juan Luis Segundo, James Cone, Beverly Harrison, and Dorothee Soelle, have joined many throughout the centuries in naming poverty, injustice, inequality, and oppression as theological concerns.)

Another implication is this: We employ Good News appropriate to the judgment. If we use the vertical, transcendent understanding of judgment (the "hammer" variety, which finds us at fault, with a guilty conscience, before God's throne), we will proclaim grace as forgiveness, new life, and fresh opportunity to begin again.

By contrast, if we use the horizontal, immanent understanding of judgment (which mirrors life as we know it in a fallen world, in its injustice, lack of meaning, oppression), we will proclaim grace as that which overturns the powers of this world and reveals God's saving work in our midst (e.g., justice, purpose, liberation). Stuempfle called this function of grace "antiphon [i.e. sounding back] to existence."

	Two Kinds of Judgment and Grace	
	Vertical Axis/ Transcendent	Horizontal Axis/ Immanent
	1. JUDGMENT (hammer)	1. JUDGMENT (mirror)
experience:	a guilty conscience	consciousness of others' suffering
result:	request forgiveness	desire for action
	2. GRACE (forgiveness)	2. GRACE (overturning)
experience:	forgiveness	overturning the world
result:	a new beginning	justice, peace, etc.

The right kind of grace must match the right kind of judgment. The primary word of grace to the lonely person is not, You are forgiven. Rather, where we encounter loneliness we will proclaim companionship. Where we perceive despair we will proclaim new hope. Where we find hunger we will proclaim nurture. Where we wage war we will proclaim peace.

In all instances of grace, the Good News is God's action, not ours, although we may picture God working through us. We seek to discover God's action first in the biblical text. Then we seek to find that action in our world. Thus we identify God as the One who enables good acts. We proclaim the Good News knowing that even as we speak it, it is happening, both by virtue of God's nature, and because it is already becoming a reality in our lives. In point of fact, "The present moment, the sermons, the sacrament, *is* what God has decided to do!"[31]

3) The Sermon in Two Theological Parts—A judgment-to-grace paradigm can be a theological norm, regardless of what other sermonic forms and theological emphases we might wish to employ. Thus the sermon may be conceived in two roughly equal parts, each of which gains its strength from the presence of the other. The first serves to make us aware of our sin. It puts the burden on humanity to change. Imperative words in the sermon like "should," "must," and "have to" belong here.

The second part proclaims that God accepts the burden for that change in and through Jesus Christ. It insists that the Christ event (from Bethlehem to the empty tomb) has made and continues to make all the difference in human history. By the end of the sermon, judgment is not erased. Rather, even as it may anticipate grace, it exists in tension with grace, and grace is the dominant note because it is God's (and our) final word. Invitational words like "may," "we are empowered," and "there is now nothing that can prevent you," are appropriate to this section.

Let us take John 15:1-8 as an example, in which the dominant theme concerns Jesus as the vine and his Father as the vinedresser. One word of judgment is that branches bearing no fruit will be cut off and burned. To find enough to say about this textual idea for several minutes, in a manner that will engage our listeners, we become like movie directors. In addition to using material from the commentaries, allow the text to come to life for instance by creating a hillside vineyard through which Jesus and his disciples are walking. (For example, one could count the thin plumes of several fires burning and smell smoke on the faint breeze that blew in from the sea. A keen eye could spot the vinedressers near their fires, pruning and cutting, the sun occasionally glinting off their knives. They were preparing the vines in hope of another season of bounteous harvest. Jesus said, "I am the true vine, and my Father is the vinedresser . . ."). Such discussion will help enable listeners to picture what Jesus is saying and experience what it means. We can speak of the discomfort we feel at Jesus' portrait of God carrying a knife.

Now come to today. We could speak of this judgment in vertical ways: If we do not follow God's way, God will cut us off and throw us on a scrap heap for burning. Alternatively, and perhaps of more interest, we could speak of this judgment in horizontal ways: We live in fear that we are not good enough for God, or that friends, or our children may be cut off from God, or that whole nations at civil war seem to suffer the absence of God. Remembering that this text is not independent of the larger Christian story, we could move to the cross to affirm the sad familiar truth that our sins separate us from God, for God does not abide sin, and we are cut off from God, as a knife cuts a branch from its vine.

In a similar manner (after taking a writing break for a few hours) we might now turn to the grace section. Keeping the resurrection before us we could say, God in Christ became the branch that was cut off that we might be spared (or we could take a more obvious idea: Jesus has already cleansed us by the Word—v. 3). Jesus is the true vine who claims us as his own. Again we would need to find enough to say in the text and elsewhere to keep the focus on this developing idea for several minutes. Stay with the one thought or image that expressed an action of God. Do not be sidetracked by other images.

Finally, we would apply the textual idea of grace to our situation: In Christ we cannot help bearing much fruit (that is, if apart from Christ we can do nothing, then with Christ, all things are possible). We could tell the stories, for instance of God's working through Nelson Mandela or South African parliamentarian Helen Suzman (the only voice of opposition to apartheid in parliament and the only woman member of parliament) for all those years, eventually bringing the collapse of apartheid. And we could suggest how God is using even the small acts of good we do.

In terms of our actual practice, we may already signal a few things: (1) The Bible text, as the normal source for what we say, should be treated at least twice in the sermon. (Beginning students are advised to stick to only two substantial developments of the text, including comments from theology, commentaries, and sensory details that will help to create pictures, making each textual development around 200 to 375

Homiletical Method for Preaching Hope

1) *Generally treat the Bible text at least twice in the sermon (first as judgment, then as grace).*
2) *Apply the text twice to our situation (judgment + grace).*
3) *Maintain the integrity of each section.*
4) *Maintain the continuity of the whole by matching the appropriate kinds of judgment and grace.*
5) *Split an illustrative story if necessary, between the sections.*
6) *At roughly the midway point (a 50/50 or 60/40 split is good), develop the main idea of grace from the biblical text.*

words—a few minutes of focus on one thought [a rough guide for preaching is 100-125 words per minute].) The first encounter with the text develops judgment and the second develops grace. As Gerhard O. Forde has said:

> In moving from text to sermon, one would do well to look first for the offense, the killing letter of the text, the hard saying, the uncompromising word. . . . Then one can subsequently turn it over as life-giving Spirit. . . . In the parable of laborers in the vineyard, the keeper's retort, "Can I not do what I want with what is my own?" is tremendously offensive. But it must be so preached precisely as offense to kill the old so that it can be turned over into life-giving spirit. For our only chance is that God can do what God wants with what is [God's] own.[32]

(2) After each biblical treatment, which needs to be at least a paragraph of sustained focus if it is to take shape in our minds, make some form of application to our time, such that we fully understand the scriptural truth in our time. (3) Maintain the integrity of each section, by keeping judgment in the judgment section and grace in the grace section. (4) Maintain the continuity of the whole sermon by having the dominant form of judgment (hammer or mirror) in the first half correspond to the dominant form of grace in the second half. (5) If you are illustrating with a story of today's experience that implies both judgment and grace, split the story (in the same manner that we did the biblical text). Tell the judgment part in the judgment section and the grace part in the grace section. When returning in the grace section to an earlier story, this should occur near the end of the sermon, for it almost always signals closure to the listeners. (6) At roughly the midway point (a 50/50 or 60/40 split is good), develop the main idea of grace from the biblical text, with God as the actor. Having brought us to an awareness of our profound need for God in the first half, both through discussion of the biblical text and application of the text to today, simply move back to the text for the hope we are needing. The movement is natural. We look for what God is doing in or behind the text.

114

These matters should become clearer in studying the following chart. It concerns the two theological parts of the sermon. Items in the left column are paired with items in the right. This chart can be used by students in the composition of the sermon, for the same matching of function should happen there. I suggest that students, after writing the first half of the sermon, check to see which of these versions of judgment most match what they have written. Then check to see what versions of grace are the appropriate partners for roughly the second half.

Possible Movement of the Sermon

Judgment (or law) may be broadly conceived in various ways, all of which find us, the church, our neighborhood, or our world, falling short of God's plan. The emphasis here is upon what we must do or fail to do at God's urging.

Grace (or Good News) may be conceived in various ways, all of which depend upon a portrayal of God doing the acting, taking responsibility for our sin. The evidence that we offer, in addition to the biblical text and tradition, is found in the cross and resurrection, the true source of Christian hope.

From:

To:

—condemnation

—forgiveness

—our view

—God's view

—the opposite of the hope we will proclaim from the biblical text

—Christian hope as found first in the biblical text (and larger gospel story)

—situations in which we would have wanted (or not wanted) the gospel message to be true

—situations in which we see the truth of the gospel message

—a true reflection of who we are in the brokenness of our life before God, our masks removed, our sins exposed

—a description of the manner in which God has already met us, embraced us, and given the strength to continue

—a development of the judgment in the biblical text and its application to our lives

—a development of the grace in the biblical text and its application to our lives, complete with mission possibilities

115

—a focus upon the manner in which Christ continues to be crucified today, or in which the exodus is today's story

—a focus upon Christ's resurrection power today, and the inbreaking of the Realm of God in our midst

—our doubts concerning God (or God's actions in the biblical text)

—the certainty that is ours in faith that takes account of doubt

—identification of our real needs, as opposed to our conceived needs

—God's meeting of our real needs

—a problem in the world boldly confronted (e.g., poverty, violence)

—a portrait of God's action in meeting the needs of this world (e.g., for hopelessness there is now hope; for despair there is faith; for anxiety there is comfort; for war there is a God who is acting for peace; for homelessness there is a mighty God, willing that a home be found)

—the world's values (e.g., the manner in which what passes for love or success lets us down)

—Christ's overturning of the world's values (e.g., strength is found in weakness)

—our "no" to God (and God's "no" to us)

—God's "yes" to us

—our "no" to the world

—God's "yes" through us

—a deepening sense of our distance from God

—a mounting sense of God's having closed the distance between us

—the ways in which the burden of responsibility for what is wrong lies with us

—the ways in which God in Christ has accepted the burden and acted to enable us to meet the demands

—dependence upon our own resources

—dependence upon God

—the apparent absence, unfaithfulness, fickleness of God

—the steadfast presence, faithfulness, and certainty of God

—"should," "must," "have to"

—"may," "we are empowered," "nothing can prevent us . . ."

—it is too late

—it is not too late

4) *Judgment and Grace as Homiletical Events*—It is not just information about judgment and grace that we are communicating. The hearers may

encounter Christ and may actually experience judgment and grace, particularly if each is given time for development in the sermon.

Again, however, for judgment and grace each to be experienced, sufficient time needs to be allowed. Charles H. Spurgeon in the late 1800s already knew time limits to squeeze the contemporary sermon: Instead of an hour, he was advocating sermons of "forty minutes, or, say, three-quarters of an hour," for "if a fellow cannot say all he has to say in that time, when will he say it?"[33] When sermons were an hour, or three-quarters of an hour long, perhaps a single movement from judgment to grace was less important than now, when sermons are frequently fifteen to twenty minutes. Generally, time limits dictate that we can move from judgment to grace only once.

Several reasons in addition to limits on sermon time discourage moving back and forth many times between judgment and grace. David Buttrick has suggested that it takes three to four minutes for an idea to take shape in our minds as listeners.[34] Again, were we to attempt repeated movement back and forth between judgment and grace, neither one could come into proper focus. Listeners only starting to experience judgment, for instance, would find themselves being moved to grace; thus, the full implications of judgment in relation to the cross and this world would be lost. Conversely, listeners only starting to glimpse the implications of grace for their lives, would find themselves shifted back to their sins. Both judgment and grace would become diluted.

Instead, we should be looking for ways to heighten judgment and grace. When Jesus said that anyone who looks at a neighbor in lust has already committed adultery, or that anyone who is angry with another has already committed murder, he was not just using hyperbole (a convenient interpretation that allows us to escape from condemnation). Jesus disrupted his culture's understanding of sin, and in so doing expanded the reality of God's grace.

If a congregation finds the Christian message irrelevant, it may be that God is hard to find in the sermon, such that hope is not created. Too frequently we (preacher and people) are the subject of the sermon, and our actions are the focus. God is either left out or portrayed as a remote or feckless onlooker.

5) Mission as Good News—The sermon ends with our vision appropriately focused toward mission and living lives of service. What does God require that we do? Mission is a duty and obligation of Christians, the reason for which we are constituted as the body of Christ, and appropriate sermonic exhortation to mission places the burden upon us, not God. Thus service, sometimes ritualized as a call to discipleship, is an imperative of faith and a judgment upon us if we avoid it.

If we take seriously that preaching effects a transformation of the world by the Word, we may reconceive even the nature of exhortation to mission. Obedience is required, yet God gives us everything to meet the demand, each day sufficient unto itself. Mission, rather than a burden, becomes our wholehearted response to an overwhelming awareness of God's love. Mission itself is transformed from an onerous, even impossible task in light of the cross. Now we reach for it, want it, need it as the essential and full expression of our response to God's encounter ("For my yoke is easy, and my burden is light"—Matt. 11:30). Mission situations thus become a form of both invitation and assurance. They are places of labor but also promises of places up ahead in which we will encounter the risen Christ. Response becomes a delight and privilege, even though the call to service may be something that we instinctively resist, often feeling incompetent to handle the task.[35]

Finally, we come again to the importance of anticipating and reflecting in the sermon what God is accomplishing through our words. In order for grace to be perceived as grace, it must be portrayed in the sermon as the action of God. We therefore use speech that pictures God acting in the midst of human affairs. We use phrases that allow others to hear Christ's approaching footstep, or to feel the wetness of his saliva on our eyes, or to experience the firmness of his healing touch.

We might say something like this, concerning mission: "It is true that that woman, lying in her hospital bed, drew great comfort in hearing her daughter's distinct footsteps approaching from down the hall. But it is also true that those same footsteps reminded her of footsteps she had heard many times in her life, the footsteps of Christ drawing near." Far from being a question of mere style, this is part of the gospel message. It is the content taking shape.

A Sermon on Christian Unity

The following sermon is an example of how we might put some of the learnings from this chapter into practice. We look for the ways in which a relationship with God is encouraged, and for appeal to *logos, pathos,* and *ethos.* In addition we experience one expression of the judgment and grace movement. I preached this sermon in an ecumenical setting to start the Week of Prayer for Christian Unity in 1993. The assigned text was John 15:12-17. Here is the sermon as it was preached, with my commentary, primarily on judgment and grace, placed in brackets.

Strangers to Love No More

I am honored to be asked to speak on this occasion of several area churches coming together to mark the Week of Prayer for Christian Unity. We are all particularly grateful to our hosts for making the arrangement whereby we might gather as Christians from diverse backgrounds, together to give God thanks and praise in song, silence, word, and prayer, and to pray in particular for Christian unity. *[I include these prefatory remarks here because they are opening courtesies. However dull in this instance, they are used to establish the topic (logos) and the foundation for a relationship with the speaker (ethos). If I had been preaching in my own congregation, the sermon might have begun with the next paragraph.]*

Some people anticipate this topic of Christian unity with very high expectations. "Honey, we can't possibly go to Florida that week. It's the Week of Prayer for Christian Unity." Some people look forward to this week more than the Super Bowl. *[It was being played as we worshiped. In this section I am lightheartedly acknowledging the way life is, for instance the fallenness that is ours, in perhaps preferring football to worship. I have chosen in this instance more horizontal emphasis than vertical, for example, the hammer of judgment if I had stressed that Jesus demanded unity.]* If that person is here I would like to meet you at the close of the service. You may be more devout than many of us taking leadership in this service.

You don't need to become involved in many of these services for Christian unity before you realize that we are in this for the long haul. *[This is a second horizontal dimension of the judgment or law arising from this particular occasion.]* We need not be like the sect in Korea a couple of months ago whose leader convinced members to hand over their life savings because the end of the world was at hand. If, as a result of our service tonight, and in anticipation of Christian unity coming tomorrow, we were to put up our church buildings for sale, give some of our clergy notice that their services are required no longer, at one level it might be an expression of faith. At another it would be foolishness. This is the constant dilemma of the Christian who is bold and daring in Christ's love, risking again and again: are we faithful or are we foolish? Given the practical implications of what Christian unity might mean—the hours of meetings, the endless debates—there is a part of us that may hope that what we are doing tonight is foolishness. We should be careful what we pray for, for all prayers are heard, and all are answered, and some are answered just the way they are asked. *[This last sentence is an example of judgment on a vertical axis. In both of these previous paragraphs, ethos and pathos are given priority.]*

119

Most of us sense no trouble when we hear Jesus' words in our gospel text and think of those from neighboring churches sitting next to us in our pews: "This is my commandment, that you love one another as I have loved you. No one has greater love than this, to lay down one's life for one's friends. You are my friends if you do what I command you." No trouble here. Most of us live in the same neighborhood. We may work with one another, go to the same parks, shops, and restaurants. It goes without question that we will help each other as much as possible. We love one another, we call one another friends, as Jesus called us friends, we hear stories of people risking lives for others, we are even willing to pray for unity. Yet, whenever we hear a Bible passage like this that does not give us problem, we should pause. We may not be hearing it rightly. *[Priority has shifted to logos. The opposite of the Bible message here provides us with the developing judgment upon us: we do not love one another as Jesus loved us. The flip side of a text's message may occasionally be used to reinforce homiletical judgment or grace.]*

A few weeks ago our youngest child, who is twelve, took to walking the dog at night. On his own. With his cousin from next door. Without being asked. We should have known something was up. It seemed to take awhile for the spark to catch, but one night recently was suddenly lit up in the knowledge that they were smoking: our son and our niece—not the dog. The night exploded with visions of what else might be hidden, or what other drugs might be tried in the future. When we get right down to it, most of us are more concerned with family unity, with just getting through, than we are with the apparent luxury of dreaming how all Christians might be united. *[This story (used with permission) and the next, are two recent stories that mirror life as we know it and thereby identify the judgment under which we live. They also will serve to articulate our emotional resistance (pathos) to Christian unity, for which we are judged on a vertical axis.]*

A beloved seventy-seven-year-old grocer in the West End, near where we live, was murdered last week. His name was Osyp Kawun. He was called Mr. Thankyou because that is what he was always saying—although the thanks should have gone the other way. He gave free candy to the schoolchildren and would open late in the night for neighbors—to lay down one's life for one's friends. A shocking death like that reminds us that we are more appropriately concerned with fighting against crime and poverty, than we are with fighting for Christian unity. In light of the current horrors of former Yugoslavia, we are more rightly concerned with unity among groups in our own land, than we are with whether we are Baptist, Christian Reformed,

Lutheran, Pentecostal, Presbyterian, Roman Catholic, or United Church, or any of the other thirty-one flavors from which we may choose. *[This represents the climax of the judgment section of the sermon. In this there is an equal measure of logos, pathos, and ethos. We turn immediately to logos in the development of grace. In the first instance in the sermon, grace arises from the biblical text.]*

But isn't that just the point? Family unity, neighborhood welfare, national unity, international peace are far more important than our denominational differences. This is why we should set them aside. When Jesus commands us to love one another, as I have loved you, he did not mean, love other Christians, as I have loved you. He did not command us to love those who are like ourselves, differing from us in relatively minor ways in the hymns that we sing, the ways we worship and understand Jesus as our Lord and Savior. Rather, the eyes-wide-open command was for us to love those it is hard to love, lay down our lives not just for our friends, but for our enemies—because in Christ even our enemy we now call friend. *[Here the church's teachings about love and friendship are brought to the biblical text.]*

Love one another as I have loved you, no one has greater love than this, to lay down one's life for one's friends.

If praying for Christian unity means anything, it means praying that God will help us put aside our differences, that God's love may flow through us, that suffering may cease. *[Here there is an increasing attempt to identify grace as the action of God, using active verbs tied to specific events. Grace here is predominantly horizontal to correspond with the predominantly horizontal judgment of the first half. Note how the next sentence will struggle to keep the focus on God's action.]* As Christians we are, with one universal accord, to be united in common pursuit of that coming day, for which God yearns and mightily empowers, when all will be one and there will be war no more. It is a day that is already dawning, for more than the first rays of its glorious light have been seen. They were cracked loose from the tomb of night on that first Easter morning. They were cracked loose in our own lives, even before we first recognized, each one of us on our own, that the risen Christ had died not just for our neighbor, not just for our friend, not just for the good person, but for you, and you, and me that we would be strangers to love no more, a friend to Christ, a friend to all in this world. *[The quickened pace here and the rhythm of speech add an additional dimension of pathos to complement the gospel.]*

An irony is found in these words: love one another. *[The message of Good News from the text is again briefly set within the context of the relevant Christian doctrine, drawing on other biblical texts where appropriate.]* God is love. All love comes from God. Therefore the love that we give is God's love. It is God who is doing the giving through us. The yoke is heavy but the burden is light. Love one another means simply saying "yes" to God.

[I believe that the Good News here is not yet sufficiently specific in our lives for the congregation to be able to identify in life around them. A story is needed of someone who embodies the truth of Christ's love. This story must also accomplish two other objectives: It must provide us with some vision of our own mission and it must stand as a counter to the two judgment stories told earlier.]

I was "channel surfing" on the television and caught the end of an interview with a woman on screen. She was saying how she had been victim of an act of violence as a child and had lost her ability to speak. She was mute for five years. Some people called her mentally retarded. One day, during this time, her grandma said to her, "Honey, I'm not worried about you. I know that when you are ready, and when God is ready, you are going to talk." "Well," the woman went on, "if my nanny could see me now, on the same platform as the president of the United States, and me, speaking, to the whole nation . . ." and her face broke into the most wonderful smile. I thought she must have been someone who had spoken at a Clinton rally on his way to Washington. I wished I had heard her name. And then the next day, while I was watching Clinton's inauguration, there she was, the same woman. Her name was Maya Angelou, Clinton's favorite poet, and she was giving the inaugural poem. "History," she said, "despite its wrenching pain, / Cannot be unlived, but if faced, / With courage, need not be lived again." Whenever we hear someone dreaming of unity and reconciliation, we hear Christ speaking today.

[There was an end to one of the earlier stories that I return to here because it further embodies grace. Splitting a story in this way between judgment and grace, and thus between the early and later parts of the sermon, does not seem unnatural to the congregation and helps to bring the sermon to an appropriate close. Preachers should be cautious to return to a story from the first half only at the ending because it almost always signals closure; we may keep on speaking, but the congregation may not keep on listening.]

Her words were in my mind last weekend, when I drove by Mr. Thankyou's store, who had died a few days before. It was a cold day. The wind was blowing a fine snow, hard. Sometimes you see something and you can hardly believe what you are seeing. On the steps of his store, and on the icy stretch of sidewalk out in front, there were fresh bouquets of flowers laid down everywhere. I do not know how many teenagers, or parents and their mittened children, had said, "We must do something," and they did it with tears and daffodils, chrysanthemums, roses, tiger lilies, and love. That cold and snowy place seemed to become human again. Such is the power of God's love that sets our differences aside and makes us united, as one. *[This conclusion brings us full circle—the appeal is primarily to pathos.]*

(A Note to Readers: Before going directly on to the next chapter, those using this book as a textbook may wish now to turn and read the second part of the chapter on hermeneutics—chapter 7, "Tuesday—What the Text Means.")

Review Questions for Chapter Five

Choose the best one of the available answers:

1) We preach hope because
   a) things turn out all right in the end
   b) gospel means Good News
   c) Christian hope awaits us in the future
   d) the power of death will be broken   [b]

2) Hope as a focus becomes important for preachers
   a) in the last minute of the sermon
   b) after the sermon
   c) when we stick with hope as an intellectual construct
   d) when experience of the listener is considered   [d]

3) The movement of the sermon from judgment to grace
   a) is the only available option
   b) eliminates most other sermon form possibilities
   c) offers an experience of hope predominant
   d) none of the above   [c]

4) Which is not a predominant description of grace?
   a) God's acceptance of the burden of judgment
   b) our Christian duties
   c) our lives used by God
   d) God's intervention in human history   [b]

5) Which of these fits judgment on a horizontal axis?
   a) transcendent
   b) systemic evil
   c) hammer of judgment
   d) need for forgiveness   [b]

Questions for Discussion

1) With what type of judgment and grace do you more readily embrace: hammer of judgment and the grace of forgiveness or mirror of existence and grace that overturns the world? why? What memories do you have of each?

2) We have seen that the words we use have much to do with the proclamation of hope. How would you explain the relationship between faith and language?

Sermon Exercises for Section II

5:1 In the preface it is suggested that readers read section 2 together with chapter 7. If you have done this, take the Bible text you have been working on and identify from it one idea to develop for the central theme of your sermon. Write it as a complete short sentence. I suggest that it focus on an action of God. Name a key doctrine in that statement. Write a paragraph on that doctrine for a congregation, keeping in mind the need for clarity, simplicity, and what you learned earlier about oral speech for aural reception. You might even try to say it in a manner that someone who is twelve or thirteen could understand and find interesting and persuasive. Check what you have written to see if it contains elements of all three modes of persuasion: logos, pathos, and ethos. If any of these elements are missing, see if you can now add them.

5:2 Using the chart on judgment and grace, identify whether the doctrine or passage you have now written is predominantly judgment or grace (e.g., does it put the burden on us or on God in Christ?). Continuing to use the chart, now write a similar passage in the other theological function.

5:3 Using the chart, list in two columns, one for judgment and one for grace, all the ideas you see in the biblical text as you go through it phrase by phrase, verse by verse. Keep these ideas as very short sentences. If in doubt about which column to choose, decide according to what you might say about the idea if you were asked to elaborate on it. (For now ignore ideas that seem neutral.) Still on the basis of what you might say about each, go through once again, marking each judgment idea as seeming to function on either a vertical axis (e.g., They disobeyed God; or, God commanded them) or a horizontal axis (e.g., Many were hungry, without hope, etc.; or, They were unloving). Do the same for ideas concerning grace (e.g., vertical: God forgave; horizontal: God gave them food; or, The man was opened [i.e. by God] to love; or, Jesus healed the woman).

SECTION
III

Hermeneutical Tradition

As Christians we are a people of the Book. We center our lives on God in Jesus Christ, as revealed to us in Scripture. This truth, however, does not in itself account for why we preach from the Bible. It is, after all, a secondary truth. The poorest reason we could give to anyone for preaching from the Bible is to say that this is just the way it is done. The primary truth without which none of us can be a true preacher is that we have been encountered by Christ in our lives. Thus we make claims of Scripture in a circular fashion, which is inescapable with a doctrine of revelation: We know that the One we have met is Christ because of the testimony of Scripture, which confirms that this is the same Jesus who died and is risen. And we believe Scripture because through it we are led to Christ and to God's love.

Of course, being a people of the Book immediately poses problems. Written texts require interpretation. We ask who has authority to interpret, what is a correct interpretation, and what are the roles of contemporary experience and the Holy Spirit? Origen comments that it is Christ who reads Scripture to us, which may be true at one level, but it is satisfying only as a devotional comfort. Such comfort will not aid the preacher for long in the rigors of creating sermons.

This section is devoted to helping us explore these essential issues, by taking us step-by-step through the task of interpretation, one day at a time in what could be a typical week of the preacher's life. We move in four steps from Monday through to the completed sermon at the end of the week, with tasks specific to each day. Taken together, these four steps are intended to offer a complete picture of the hermeneutical (interpretative) process, which is often assigned to the biblical studies department in seminaries.

If the church's preaching is to improve continuously, it may require a heightened value, and this starts with the words and attitudes we bring to it. How we currently understand the hermeneutical process is part of the problem: It is incompletely portrayed in the halls of seminary because historically, preaching (along with other text-producing activities) has been left out of the discussion of knotty theological or textual problems. We assume that a preacher arrives at an interpretation of a biblical text, and that the sermon follows as the fruit of some additional process instead of recognizing that the sermon itself is the interpretation.

Hermeneutics is incompletely portrayed in the halls of seminary because preaching (along with other text-producing activities) is often left out of the discussion.

We may think of sermonic interpretation merely as a form of "how to" (that is, how to write a sermon or how to plan your week), instead of claiming preaching as the chief purpose of interpretation and as a primary motive for biblical studies. The long-term consequence can be erosion of preaching. For example, as a result of deep ferment in the 1960s, an erosion was experienced when many people questioned the value of the Bible and preaching, and thus many preachers received inadequate foundations.

The full picture of the interpretation process includes preaching. Reluctantly, because such discussions often require spatial analogies (circles, spirals, and so on), I picture this process as a "hermeneutical square," distinct from the "hermeneutical circle." The hermeneutical circle refers to the back-and-forth movement we make between the biblical text and our world as we come to understand what is said. It also refers to the same movement in any other act of interpretation (e.g., in a conversation). Within education, it refers to the necessary interchange between theory and practice. Theory strengthens practice and practice strengthens theory. When Schleiermacher suggested the idea of this circle two centuries ago, it was adequate to portray the hermeneutical process as it was then understood. It still accurately describes the back-and-forth interchange between any of the four stages of the interpretative process, but it no longer, in itself, captures the whole.[1]

We use the spatial idea of the hermeneutical square to describe the four-stage progression we make: from receiving a (biblical) text to providing finally an interpretation of it in the form of another text (which in the case of homiletics is the sermon). The stages then repeat for the next interpreter (in this case, the congregation).

A sketch of the square, prior to discussion of it, may help us. The stages are more interdependent (i.e., they rely upon the hermeneutical circle) than is at first apparent.

The Hermeneutical Square

Monday: **1) What the text says.** Understanding the biblical text (translation plus initial literary and theological readings)	Tuesday: **2) What the text means.** Analysis and explanation of what others have said (study of commentaries, tradition, and theology)
Thursday/Friday: **4) What the preacher says.** The purpose of the interpreter concerning the listeners shapes a new text (e.g. sermon) in response to the biblical text	Wednesday: **3) What experience says.** Discovery of the relevance or application of the text for today, anticipating the responses of other listeners in different situations

MONDAY: WHAT THE TEXT SAYS

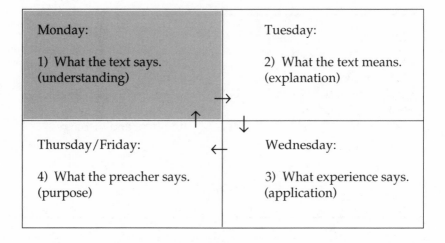

Monday:	Tuesday:
1) What the text says. (understanding)	2) What the text means. (explanation)
Thursday/Friday:	Wednesday:
4) What the preacher says. (purpose)	3) What experience says. (application)

The first of two traditional stages of hermeneutics, understanding the text, is developed here. Students are shown how to use literary and theological exegesis to understand the text. The first step of a historical expansion of the biblical text is introduced.

Nothing is more important for the quality of the finished sermon than the quality of time we allot to it over the greatest number of days. Some of our best thoughts initially form subconsciously while we are doing other things. Sixteen hours of rushed preparation on Saturday are not worth eight or ten quality hours spread through the week (and eight or ten still might be minimal preparation!).

For this reason, on Monday, though it may be your day off, take a few minutes to choose a biblical text for next Sunday's sermon and learn its details. It may be chosen with the assistance of a Sunday lectionary (i.e., a book of prescribed biblical lessons) although the lectionary has both assets and liabilities for the preacher.[1] The ecumenical lectionary (published as *The Revised Common Lectionary*, Abingdon Press, 1992) is similar to the Lutheran and Episcopalian lectionaries, deriving from the Roman Catholic lectionary produced out of Vatican II. Its three-year cycle of readings rotates through the Gospels (year A, Matthew; year B, Mark; year C, Luke; with readings from John in each year) and a wide range of other biblical texts.

Generally we should choose only one of the Sunday texts to preach (lectionaries offer three lessons and a psalm), the frequent norm being the Gospel lesson. Alternatively, we may find one common focus to preach among the various readings when there is close thematic linking (in the lectionary, thematic linking is particularly strong during Advent through to the Baptism of the Lord, and Lent; during ordinary time no thematic unity was intended). Harry Emerson Fosdick, who held the congrega-

> *Choose one biblical text and make reference to the others, only if necessary and helpful, using obvious images, ideas, or story lines.*

tion's needs in high regard, once criticized use of historical criticism in the pulpit, saying that a congregation rarely came to church "desperately anxious to discover what happened to the Jebusites."[2] We might say the same thing concerning the biblical texts that are read on Sunday: The congregation rarely comes to church with a desperate need to know how the psalm relates to the epistle. This may be the preacher's need. The congregation needs to know God. Normally, choose one text, therefore, and make reference to the others, only if necessary and helpful, using an obvious image, idea, or story line.

On special days of the church, because there is both the biblical text and the meaning of the day to expound in relation to the needs of the congregation, we are under even tighter constraint to choose primarily one text and to keep our focus in that text clear and simple. Our struggle on any of these Sundays is to keep the focus on God.

Choose a text, therefore, for which you have some passion, one that initially either excites or annoys you. We ought only very rarely to preach against texts.[3] Some texts will seem so obscure we may set them aside with others to await more insight. Nonetheless, initial negative response to any text is energy that can often be turned into positive, collective purpose through study and prayer during the week. Texts that initially disturb us can produce excellent preaching. Of course all texts, at some level, must disturb us, for God's Word is not complacent.

The purpose of this first stage of encounter with the biblical text is simply to understand what it says. What it says, however, is often not self-evident. The careful reader will continue reading a text until things previously unnoticed in it begin to appear. Thomas Troeger described this process of being "attentive to what is" as imagination.[4] With a text we know well, we are seeking to penetrate the barrier of familiarity so that we may see it afresh.

It is helpful for us to adopt, in turn, two different roles as we determine what the biblical text says. The first role is that of the preacher as a literary student. This role encourages a basic, human response to the text, without any specific theological agenda, and allows us to see simply "what is." The second role is that of the theology student in the seminary. In this role we take seriously what is meant by the authority of Scripture. Each role provides important insights.

The Preacher as Literary Student

Nearly until his death, Northrop Frye, the great literary critic whose study of the Bible was entitled *The Great Code,* himself an ordained minister, would walk by our gray limestone college of theology to the building next door named in his honor, to teach the Bible as literature. In his classes, students with no background in biblical study would read the stories in remarkable ways. They did not necessarily favor the people that God favored. Some could not overlook the fact that the land given to Israel was stolen from the Canaanites. Many felt Jesus was foolish to die as he did, and that he in fact committed suicide by entering Jerusalem. Their interpretations were among a variety of legitimate possibilities, if one were reading the Bible only as literature. They were honest, human responses to the text of the sort that many in our congregation might share. We should seek this kind of honest, human response for ourselves as a starting place with any biblical text.

Obviously the church has established a range of normative readings for biblical texts, because the Scriptures as canon are meant to nourish a community of faith. These norms, at this stage, are not yet our concern.

In fact, if we are seeking norms within literary criticism, they are hard to find. In the last hundred years we have seen a surprising range of literary models that claim that a literary text means: (a) what it was intended to mean (later called "intentional fallacy"); (b) what it alone says it means (New Criticism); (c) what it says in relation to history and means of production (Marxist criticism); (d) what it addresses in society (sociological criticism); (e) what its structure says it means (structuralist criticism); (f) what it claims it does not mean (deconstructionist criticism); (g) what the elements of narrative disclose (e.g., character and plot, narrative criticism); (h) what patterned responses it effects in readers (reader response criticism); (i) what is persuasive or compelling to its readers (rhetorical criticism); and, most recently among others, (j) what the text says as a relationship between the writer and reader, with most expected norms overthrown (e.g., texts do not have meaning, postmodern criticism).

It is helpful for preachers to be aware of the degree of decentering that has occurred in society that these various kinds of criticism reflect. Each of these separate literary perspectives has something to teach us. However, at this introductory level, when we are in the role of "the preacher as literary student," we may stick to some basic, conservative principles of literary criticism. The first is that each literary text stands as its own best source of interpretative data. A poem's meaning, for instance, can be said to be independent of any meanings it does not itself support, and separate in important ways even from what its author somewhere else might say was her intent. A naive first reading of a biblical text will offer us some initial understanding of that text. Subsequent rereadings will seek evidence to support or correct this understanding.

A second principle of literary criticism is this: Many possible correct understandings exist for any work of literature, and some contradict one another. We have seen this among friends when discussing a poem or movie. Each interpretation offers new understanding. Clearly, some interpretations are stronger than others.

A third principle I add is that persuasive interpretations generally require three separate pieces of information pointing to the same truth. "Why three?" we may ask. "Is this not arbitrary?" In some ways it is. For instance, we do not always have three pieces of evidence, so we must go with what we do have. Nonetheless, the strongest case is still made with three or more pieces of evidence. The reason is that literary criticism often looks for repeating patterns. For example, one episode in someone's behavior may strike us as strange and raise questions in our minds; two similar incidents suggest a pat-

131

tern that may still be dismissed as coincidence; but three or more similar incidents suggest a pattern or theory in which we may have some confidence, perhaps enabling us to anticipate future behavior or to identify a personality trait.

Or, to take another approach, we can discuss the psychological motives that Ruth had for staying with Naomi only if the text itself states them plainly, or gives us three solid clues pointing to the same motive. If these are not provided, motive is not a focus of the text and we have no strong textual basis for discussing it. We end up psychologizing the text; that is, attributing motives to a character, which the text does not actually support. As a rule, psychologize us, imagining why we would do something, rather than project this onto the text.

Of course, to some degree this kind of textual distortion may be inescapable, particularly if we are trying to create the character of Ruth in narrative ways in a sermon, such that listeners have a chance to meet her, and not just hear about her. In a way, preachers often think like movie directors, needing to make decisions about details the text does not mention if we want to end up with a film. Textual accuracy sometimes can be sacrificed for realism, but only if we do not stray too far from the biblical text, and if what we determine through study to be the central meaning of the text is already secured in the sermon.

Concerning Ruth, the biblical text offers at least four pieces of information that allow us to draw some conclusions about her motives: She loved Naomi. She did not choose to return to her own mother. She wanted to stay with Naomi past death (Ruth 1:17). She was loyal (3:10).

Literary interpretations may have a wide range of possible foci, each with its own questions. Only some of the following questions will be answered on Monday. Some of these await the second stage of our process for answers. Before going to biblical commentaries and other resources—activities we may delay until Tuesday—we do well to work through on our own both a translation of the biblical text (if we have the biblical language) and some of the following questions. In this manner we begin to discover not only the biblical text, but also what there is to say about it.

In this case we will use the call of Isaiah, in Isaiah 6:1-13 (NRSV), to provide an example of the kind of responses that are possible.

Exercise 6:1 Students might try to answer these questions with their own biblical text. In time, and with patience and experience, the process will become easier and more automatic. Initially it may be easier to answer these if working in a small group.

132

MONDAY: WHAT THE TEXT SAYS

An Initial Literary Reading of a Biblical Text

focus	questions
1) character	Who are the main characters? What are they like? How can they be described?
2) plot	What happens in this text? Why does it happen? What is the sequence of events?
3) context	What happened before this section? after? How does context affect the meaning here?
4) conflict	What is the main conflict here? What caused it?
5) resolution	What is needed for resolution? Who must do it? Or, if conflict is resolved, will resolution last?
6) author	What can be said about the human author or writer? Why was it written?
7) audience	For whom is it written? What effect was intended?
8) reader identification	With whom in the text do I identify? Why have I made that choice?
9) form	What is the form (or genre) of this passage? Is it a song? letter? law? epic? parable? saying?
10) function	What is the function of this passage in terms of the entire work?
11) structure	How could the structure be sketched? Does it build to a climax? Does it have separate parts?
12) style	What is distinctive about the author's style? Are there distinctive phrases or key words?

133

13) power	Who has money? power? Who is poor? powerless?
14) patterns	Are there unusual patterns? (e.g., three times of questioning? two acts that fail? four journeys?)
15) connections	Do any of the above connect with similar things elsewhere in the Bible?
16) translations	How do several English versions compare? What does the original Greek or Hebrew say?
17) parallels	Do parallel accounts differ (e.g., between the Gospels, or Samuel, Kings, and Chronicles)?
18) puzzles	What is surprising or does not fit? What questions do I take to the commentaries?
19) emotions	Do I like this text? dislike it? Why? With what feelings am I left?

Applications for a Biblical Text (Isaiah 6:1-13)

We now turn to the call of Isaiah to see what literary criticism can yield for the preacher.

1) Character—King Uzziah is dead. Isaiah is afraid and considers himself and his people unworthy. One of the six-winged flying seraphs has a powerful voice. The Lord is not pleased with the people of Judah.
2) Plot—In a vision of a heavenly temple, Isaiah sees God sitting on high. Thinking he will die for looking on God, he finds his lips purified by a coal. God chooses him to condemn the people of Judah to exile.
3) Context—The vision is preceded by oracles of destruction, in particular by a foreign power destroying Israel at God's command. Following the vision is a confrontation with King Ahaz, who is slow to hear.

4) Conflict—The main conflict is between God and Judah for its sin. There are minor conflicts within Isaiah for he is unclean and looking on God, and he must deliver a harsh message to his people.

5) Resolution—A messenger must be sent to pronounce God's judgment and to prevent Judah from turning to be healed. They must be exiled and their land destroyed leaving only a burned "stump." The stump will be the hope.

6) Author—Isaiah gives an account of his call and hence of his own authority to prophesy, which suggests that he is facing opposition. He does not want to give the harsh message (i.e., "How long, O Lord?").

7) Audience—Without yet checking commentaries, we may guess this is written for the people of Judah, for the king of Judah, and perhaps also for a future time when Isaiah's opposition is removed.

8) Reader identification—I identify with Isaiah, since he is the only human, and perhaps also because he is portrayed as being good. However, I fear I am more like the unclean people of Judah.

9) Form—The passage is an autobiographical oracle, one in a series of oracles. Verse 3b seems to be a hymn and verses 9-11 are poetic, while the rest is narrative prose.

10) Function—The oracle seems to function in at least two ways: to establish the divine authority of Isaiah, and to indicate divine purpose behind the destruction of Judah.

11) Structure—There are two parts: the first focuses on Isaiah in the heavenly court, at first unworthy and then purified. The second is dominated by the Lord's speech. At the center is Isaiah's, "Here am I; send me!"

12) Style—The call is distinctive in itself, as are the six-winged seraphs and the coal that purifies but does not burn.

13) Power—Even though God is all-powerful, Isaiah nonetheless is left with the decision as to whom God sends.

14) Patterns—A high earthly king is brought low by death. A vision of the high heavenly King brings Isaiah low in confession. The Lord purifies and raises Isaiah to pronounce that Judah will be brought low.

15) Connections—The burning bush, like this coal, burns without burning. Other calls come to mind: Moses, David, Jeremiah, and the disciples of Jesus.

16) Translations—One of the things that struck me here was the frequency of unusual three-part constructions: "Holy, holy, holy";

sets of wings; references to himself (v. 5); actions of the seraphs; threefold destruction of cities, houses, and land.

17) Parallels—Make a note to check these in going to commentaries (commentaries in fact tell us of a parallel with I Kings 22:19-23). Parallels are especially important when studying the Gospels.

18) Puzzles—Why does the Lord want Isaiah to prevent the people of Judah from turning and being healed? How does what will happen to Judah relate to Israel? Is this written before or after the exile it predicts?

19) Emotions—Personally, I like the care given Isaiah in the heavenly court. I do not like the harshness of the judgment upon Judah. The Lord seems to be playing games in hardening hearts, yet I like the implication that if Judah could turn, they would be healed.

Any preacher needs to determine how much of a biblical text to consider. A Gospel reading might include several short parables, or an Epistle selection might contain several pithy sayings. There may be many background details that are important. We must decide for ourselves what to cover, often largely on the basis of the projected unity of the imagined sermon. Remember that we seek to preach mainly one clear, simple, God-focused complete thought, not just an image or picture. Moreover, we cannot preach everything there is to say.

> We must decide for ourselves how much of a particular biblical text to preach upon, or how many of the details to cover, often largely on the basis of the projected unity of the imagined sermon.

Alternatively, in a situation noted by Eugene L. Lowry, the *Revised Common Lectionary* provides only Genesis 9:8-17 of the Noah story. There is no judgment on humanity, no building of the ark, no gathering of the animals, no storm—"What we have is the rainbow (in a redundant passage)."[5] It is the preacher who will decide the section to be preached by remembering two things: (1) An assigned reading may be extended or shortened if the preacher deems it appropriate and (2) an entire story need not be read in church in order for that story in its fullness to be preached.

The Preacher as Theology Student

Literary students of the Bible help us to see that when we Christians read the Bible as Scripture, we read from a particular slant. God is the focus. We read for what is said about God and us. We seek to understand why any particular text is preserved as Scripture. For the preacher as theology student, the text does not stand fully on its own, independent of the Christian traditions that provide interpretative angles we take to be correct.

This perspective may seem to contradict the Protestant Reformers, who were in agreement that Scripture could be interpreted by the authority of Scripture alone *(sola Scriptura)* and not by unwritten oral traditions. Yet they were already standing in a tradition that employed the hermeneutical circle or spiral in interpretation, even if it had not been named. Reformers were protesting interpretations and principles for interpretation that had no basis in Scripture and reason. They nonetheless said that it is the continuing community of faith that judges the adequacy of interpretations of Scripture. They agreed with Augustinian tradition, for instance, in giving primacy to the literal interpretation, and in figurative passages to the interpretation that fosters love.[6]

We ascribe to the Bible an authority over life. When we think of the authority of Scripture, we may tend to think of it as something static—yet as long as there has been Scripture there has been preaching (see Neh. 8:5ff.), a frank admission that interpretation is necessary. An alternative understanding of the authority of Scripture is that it is dynamic. The authority of Scripture is its power to convict, to slay sin, to bring us into God's grace, and to establish a new world order. This takes place through preaching. In other words, if we accept this view, the authority of Scripture derives from the nature of preaching as divine event. David Buttrick helpfully develops this important understanding of authority for our time:

God's authority in Christ locates us, with all our contending claims and counterclaims, before the cross as judged/forgiven people. So, instead of having a locus of authority, for example, Bible, experience, or tradition, we are located by God's authority in the presence of Christ crucified where we may know who we are—frightened, inept, unsmart, but assuredly called disciples who live by grace in God's wide mercy. Jesus Christ crucified is authority in the church.[7]

Theological questions, unlike those of the literary student, are not anthropocentric, putting us at the center. Rather, they are theocentric, putting God at the center. Human identity, needs, and wants are seen in relationship to God.

Perhaps late on Monday night, before bedtime, once the text as literature is clearly in focus, the preacher begins asking the questions of the theology student. These questions, unlike those of the literary student, are not anthropocentric, putting us at the center. Rather, they are theocentric,

137

putting God at the center. Human identity, needs, and wants are found in relationship to God. Here we might limit focal questions to a few, some of which depend upon a prior literary reading. We continue with Isaiah 6:1-13 as a sample text.

Exercise 6:2 Students might continue working with their own biblical text for preaching. Remember that answers at this first stage should still be tested with further study beyond the text itself. Moreover, there will be other possible responses than those given below, precisely because this is a process of interpretation.

An Initial Theological Reading of a Biblical Text

1) God in the text: What is God doing in the text itself? God is appointing a messenger to carry God's Word to God's people.
2) God behind the text: What is God doing behind the text, in the larger events? God is calling a halt to the apostasy of Judah and Israel and is acting to bring forth righteousness.
3) Judgment—What is God's judgment (i.e., law, condemnation, identification of human failing)? The people have ceased to distinguish good from evil, so God will banish them and destroy their lands.
4) Change—What change is demanded of humanity? The people are to return to God, but it seems too late for change here, for the Lord will harden their hearts.
5) Hope—What is the hope (i.e., grace, Good News, empowerment)? The hope is not for this generation, but for those to come, that there will be a "holy seed" in the "stump" that remains. Nonetheless, God is the only source of hope, and the implication is that God could not help healing the people if they do turn, and that is why their hearts are needing to be hardened.
6) Empowerment in the text—Does the text itself indicate what God does to enable change? God sends Isaiah in order that the people may at least understand what is happening.
7) Empowerment beyond the text—What is God doing in the larger story to which this text belongs? God does restore God's people and Jerusalem in Isaiah 40–66.
8) Identity—What does this tell us about who we are? who God is? We are a people liable to self-deception of the sort God will not tolerate.
9) Belief—What are we asked to believe? God will take action even against God's loved ones to achieve God's purposes.

10) Action—What is God instructing and therefore enabling us to do? We are to repent of our evil and to remain open to God's purposes, living our lives in grateful obedience.

11) Christology—What does the cross and resurrection say to Christians concerning themes raised in this text? In Christ we have an advocate who has taken upon himself our hardened hearts. The "holy seed" has come to fruition and we partake of the judgment and of the righteousness offered us in Christ.

A Brief History of Stages One and Two

We have been discussing Stage One of the hermeneutical process, "What the text says," and we have been considering it from the perspective of a literary and theological reading, an initial reading using the preacher's own resources. Before we move on to the next stage of interpretation, and in order to understand it, a summary of learnings that have emerged from research into hermeneutics may be helpful.

Our current stage of understanding "what the text says" is similar to the early stage of hermeneutics itself. Translation and interpretation was originally thought to be a linear exercise. Even at this stage, it could be argued that the original text had expanded to include the newly translated version. Words were substituted for other words according to rules of grammar and syntax in order to support, clarify, and secure the text's meaning.[8] In fact, for much of history translation was mere substitution. It was possible to hold the doctrine that the content of Scripture is univocal and clear. Thus the Reformers claimed that their doctrines were simply the content of the New Testament in a different form. Most preachers, prior to higher criticism, would identify a doctrine in their scriptural verse and move, in the body of the sermon, to discussing that doctrine (not their biblical text) anywhere it was found in Scripture.

Friedrich Schleiermacher (1768–1834) upset this notion for preachers when he began asking troubling questions, such as, "What views of the ancient world did the biblical writers have? What did they think? How did their language and culture affect how they thought? How did these various factors affect what they wrote?" He recognized that there was a distance (1) between the biblical text and the events it described, and (2) between the biblical text and the later scholar or preacher. He therefore visualized interpretation as a circular exercise (hence the "hermeneutical circle"), or more accurately a spiral of continuing dialogue between the text, its background, and the language and times of the interpreter.

With Schleiermacher, two things happened. First, the understanding of text again expanded: New bodies of material were seen as relevant to the text that had not been recognized before.[9] To translate a biblical text meant going beyond the Bible itself. Other texts had to be considered that gave access to biblical cultures and worldviews. Thus modern history and historical-critical approaches to the Bible arose.

Second, two stages in interpretation were conceived. The first stage became referred to as "understanding" a text *(Verstehen)*,[10] or what we are calling "what the text says." Alongside it there appeared an interrelated, second stage. This second stage, which has been called "explaining" a text *(Erklaren)*, we designate "what the text means."

It is to this second stage that we now move, as we trace how the notion of *text* continued to expand.

Review Questions for Chapter Six and Section III Introduction

1) Hermeneutics is often incompletely portrayed in seminary because
   a) history is omitted
   b) no distinction is made between text and commentary
   c) text production is ignored
   d) people do not care about preaching   [c]

2) The preacher as a literary student examining a biblical text
   a) should avoid emotional response
   b) should go directly to the commentaries
   c) asks questions
   d) seeks God in the text   [c]

3) The preacher as theological student wants to know of the biblical text
   a) what human action is required
   b) what God is doing to enable human response
   c) what Christology has to say
   d) all of the above   [d]

4) The hermeneutical circle
   a) describes translation as a four-stage process
   b) is an image for dialogue between the text and today
   c) describes what is known as circular thought
   d) all of the above   [b]

Questions for Discussion

1) Given the bewildering array of literary-critical approaches to a text, and the decentering of postmodern society in general, is there anything that safeguards against anyone's saying, "Scripture means whatever I say it means"?
2) A theological reading of the biblical text puts God at the center. How do we do this in our discussions of the text, and even more broadly in our ministries, without seeming always to speak about God at the expense of seeing the people in front of us?

TUESDAY: WHAT THE TEXT MEANS

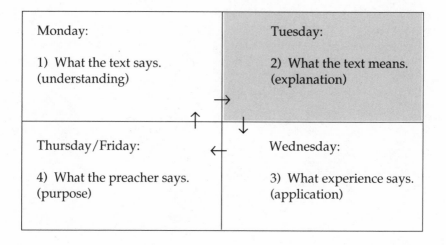

Monday:	Tuesday:
1) What the text says. (understanding)	2) What the text means. (explanation)
Thursday/Friday:	Wednesday:
4) What the preacher says. (purpose)	3) What experience says. (application)

Biblical criticism for the sermon is discussed. Students are shown how to develop and test ideas. Moves, concerns of the text, and the central idea for the sermon are explained and demonstrated. A preacher's practice worksheet demonstrates key ideas. An explanation is offered as to why the idea of text within hermeneutics is expanded yet again.

We already have a good sense of what the text says. We do not now abandon our literary and theological questions. Rather, today is the day to pull from the shelves or the database some books that will help answer our earlier literary and theological questions.

TUESDAY: WHAT THE TEXT MEANS

What a text says does not always clarify what it means. Witness Jesus' disciples in Matthew who heard what he said, yet frequently asked what he meant by his parables. Explanation, or clarification, is the key idea here, and the community of faith and scholarship is the focus. We want trusted commentaries on the chosen biblical text that explain its meaning and its relationship to its larger book and to the entire canon; theological books that explain a key doctrine, including theological dictionaries;[1] general reference books like a Bible dictionary and atlas of the Bible that explain key terms, places, and social practices; Greek and Hebrew lexicons and as many versions of the text as one has available that help explain the original text; books of sermons to clarify how to use ideas; and journals as appropriate. We have seen that in both literary criticism and theology, there is much discussion about what a text does mean. For our purposes as preachers, what a biblical text means relates to its historical and cultural background.

Origen handled the problem of a broad potential field of meanings in Scripture by throwing the door wide open: He assumed that since Scripture was dictated by God, every jot and tittle was pregnant with meaning for those who were spiritually discerning; his unbridled allegorical interpretations often had little textual support. Augustine took a more sensible route, adopted by tradition, in favoring the literal, particularly on passages of faith and morals; in cases of dispute, Scripture meant what the church said it meant (this was known as the rule of faith). In our times we continue to struggle for additional ways of both (a) uncovering what the text says and (b) limiting the problem of abundant meaning for preaching. In this task biblical criticism plays an essential role, although it poses liabilities as well.

The Role of Biblical Criticism

Preachers are the first to celebrate when study of the biblical texts has been assisted by modern historical criticism. We can scarcely conceive of preaching without using the fruits of this criticism to explain what a text means. We know immensely more than our ancestors about how Scripture was written, the historical background of the writers, their biases, the role of editors in reshaping material, and the like. This understanding has helped preachers in addressing many issues that have stained the fabric of Christian history (e.g., anti-Semitism, racism, sexism) and other situations of injustice in our communities and beyond.

Still, some today are seeking a correction in biblical studies. Recovery of early forms of the biblical texts (e.g., the project of the Jesus Seminar in which scholars vote on the likelihood of the historical Jesus having made the various statements attributed to him)[2] does not result in texts that are more foundational for preaching, nor does it bring us closer to the Jesus whom we attest in faith through the Scriptures. Thus we do not preach the version of the parable of the wedding guests found in the Gospel of Thomas just because it may be closer to the original version Jesus told. Nor do we start speaking of the church as having, with "Q," five gospels not four.

> Recovery of early forms of the biblical texts does not result in texts that are more foundational for preaching, nor does it bring us closer to the Jesus whom we attest in faith through the Scriptures. God's Word is contained in and revealed most clearly through Scripture, not historical method.

Nor do we give higher faith value to words that Jesus is voted most likely to have said. Gerald T. Sheppard notes about Isaiah that "one should not confuse the recovery of a more 'reliable' historical portrait of the eighth-century B.C. prophet with the discovery of a more reliable 'Scripture,' since ancient traditions do not become Scripture through their fidelity to principles of modern historiography."[3] Said another way, God's Word is contained in and most clearly revealed through Scripture, not historical method. To go one more step, to the degree that the Holy Spirit speaks Scripture, we say for purposes of the faith that there are no words of Jesus that Christ does not speak, and no teachings that are more preachable than others.

Perhaps the most acerbic critic of modern directions is Thomas C. Oden, who is critical of "the bone-dry valley into which [Bultmann's] form criticism has lately shepherded preaching."[4] He calls historical biblical criticism a "broken promise": "Have the texts been made more understandable? . . . Have the texts been made more accessible? . . . Has critical method elicited or inhibited moral decision?"[5] He cites Walter Wink, with whom he agrees: "The outcome of biblical studies in the academy is a trained incapacity to deal with the real problems of actual living persons in their daily lives."[6]

These barbed criticisms are perhaps better put to preaching than to the students of biblical studies. They can serve as a caution to us, first, that essays and lectures on biblical passages have their own value and rhetorical purpose, but they do not themselves normally constitute preaching. Second, historical criticism yields far more information about biblical texts than is helpfully communicated in a sermon. It can be misused by preachers with a shortage of things to say. The correction needed for preaching might be found in preaching that keeps the focus on God in relation to humanity, and that frequently, if not normally, develops hope in theologically responsible ways.

We relentlessly suggest that preaching can be the event of God's encounter with us, resulting not least in a renewed relationship of faith and action. This can mean four things in relation to the biblical text:

1) Approach the biblical text foremost as a document of faith. Thus we bring our conceptions and needs, and the needs of our world, to submission before the text in a scholarly manner. Yet we give priority to the text not merely as a lesson in history, but as a document of faith. After we have taken care to be academically and intellectually responsible with the biblical text, understanding its background, context, and the theology of our tradition, we do well to recall the poetic words of Martin Luther: "This [Bible] lesson is just like the sun: in a placid pond it can be seen clearly and warms the water powerfully, but in a rushing current it cannot be seen as well nor can it warm up the water as much. So if you wish to be illumined and warmed . . . then go to where you may be still and impress the picture deep into your hearts."[7]

2) Continue to ask of every biblical text, "What is God doing in or behind the events of this passage?" Warren H. Stewart is only one of several preachers who note how important it is that the starting place for biblical interpretation for preachers is with God: "Hermeneutics in preaching does not begin with the text but with the Author of the text."[8]

3) Identify the implications of the biblical text for your own life. If we expect the text to come alive in the lives of our people, it must first have happened in our own life as we pursue the leading of the Holy Spirit. What did God say to us through it? We should be able to identify the difference this has made or could make to our lives. We may not include the personal impact of this text in the finished sermon, but we can use it in all cases to inform our composition.

4) Name the idea or ideas from the biblical text to develop. One purpose of biblical studies can be the starting point of the sermon, that is, the naming and selection of biblical ideas to develop in the sermon.

Tuesday is the latest day in the week for this if we are to allow enough time to mull the sermon as a whole.

Moves, Concerns of the Text, and Central Ideas

As preachers, what are we looking for when we exegete a biblical text? This important question should be asked more frequently. One of the problems confronting theological education today, and thereby preachers, arises from the separation of hermeneutics and homiletics. Most biblical scholars (many of whom also preach) remain fixed in the rhetorical world of their commentaries, uncertain about what to suggest as a way of moving the text into our world. By the same token, many homileticians (many of whom are biblical specialists) often remain located in the modern world in writing about preaching, silent about the most basic elements of the process that led them from the Bible.

The difficulty of switching between worlds is illustrated in one of the most detailed studies in homiletics, David Buttrick's *Homiletic: Moves and Structures.* An enormous strength of his project is to make preachers attentive to how ideas become conscious in the minds of listeners: He indicates how often a new idea may be ventured (e.g., every three to four minutes), how many diverse thoughts may be entertained at once (he says at most three), and what is needed before a new subject is ventured (i.e., the current idea or topic must be repeated, as a way of closure, followed by a pause). Perhaps borrowing from Vladimir Propp's classic study of fairy tales,[9] Buttrick calls a unit of thought centered on a single meaning in consciousness a "move" (it may help to think of these as a lengthy paragraph or two, for in written form they usually are). Each "move" initially arises from the biblical text and then shifts to our own situation.[10]

Move: a unit (or paragraph or two) of thought centered on a single meaning initially arising from a biblical text and then shifting to our situation.

What is to happen in the minds of the hearers? They are to be led through individual moves to discover the field of meaning that the biblical text discloses. Buttrick recommends that we develop moves located in sequenced "structures." We may still need help, however, in knowing how these moves initially take shape in the consciousness of the preacher. (He suggests that they might emerge out of the plot or logic of the biblical text.)[11]

Other writers speak to the origin of sermonic ideas. They speak of a single idea arising from the biblical text around which the sermon is developed. How does this idea arise from the biblical text in front of us? The process is at the heart of the preacher's task and is important to understand. It involves first discovering the possibilities and concerns that the text makes available, and then selecting from them.

We can go through a biblical text verse by verse to state in very short sentences as many ideas as we can find. I believe that the text becomes conscious to the preacher only through this kind of process. We may think that an idea for preaching just "happens" in our minds. However, when it does, it is only because the mind, at a subconscious level, has broken down the text to find some unit of meaning. A form of deconstruction of the text has occurred. In fact, as long as this process is only subconscious, preachers will probably struggle to find enough ideas in a text to preach, or will not readily discover fresh insight to a passage. That is why it is essential that we bring this naturally subconscious hermeneutical act to consciousness, and thereby start to make of it a deliberate preaching tool.

Concerns of the text are short sentences. They are any ideas with which a biblical text is legitimately concerned. They need to be confirmed by our studies. Concerns of the text are normally discovered in three places: the biblical text itself (often in the process of literary or theological criticism); biblical commentaries; and our own background knowledge relevant to the culture and times. In fact, when we go to biblical commentaries as preachers, we go specifically looking for these concerns of the text, for they are the germinal ideas of proclamation. In other words, right from this early deconstructive stage, we are gearing our approach to the text toward proclamation. As we will see, concerns of the text vary in homiletical strength. In theory at least, each concern of the text represents a single idea that has the potential to become a central idea of the entire sermon, or the subject of one of the sermon "moves." Moreover, we may analyze any sermon and determine what concern or concerns of the text it used. If we couple the process of identifying concerns of the text with the process of literary and theological criticism, we will have a firm base for our preaching.

Concerns of the text: ideas with which a biblical text is legitimately concerned, expressed in short sentences. Normally these may be discovered in three places: the biblical text itself, biblical commentaries, and our own background knowledge relevant to the culture and times.

As preachers dedicated to the clearest possible communication, it is important to appreciate just how small an idea is. One short sentence contains many ideas, enough for a paragraph if we learn how to explain or expand it. The shift of one word in a sentence presents new ideas. Equally important, the same process of deconstruction of our own complex thought can make it more clear if we learn to identify separate ideas, developing them one at a time in a chosen form of sequence or progression.

Exercise 7:1 Students working on a biblical text in preparation for a sermon may now list as many concerns as they can find. Students who wish to begin work on preaching hope (see chapter 5) may designate the concerns of their text as judgment or grace, according to how they choose to develop them in preaching. At this point merely listen for a note, a faint sound on the breeze. Remember that generally an idea is judgment if it "sounds" like judgment, if it depicts human failure to do God's will, or puts the burden of responsibility to do something upon us. And generally something is grace if it sounds hopeful, at least hinting at God's action and the responsibility God takes, or has taken, to enable change. Some ideas may seem neutral and may simply be noted as supportive details. Use this list and your own scholarship to do a similar exercise with your chosen biblical text, line by line.

Concerns of the Text

j = judgment   g = grace   n = neutral

Text—Isaiah 6:1-13 (NRSV): Isaiah's Call

Samples from the biblical text itself:

King Uzziah died. (j, if one accepts that death is often experienced as
                 a judgment)
The country was in mourning. (j)
Isaiah had a vision. (g)
The Lord appeared to Isaiah. (g)
Six-winged seraphs praised the Lord. (g)
All earth is full of the Lord's glory. (g)
Isaiah fears for his life. (j)
He is unclean. (j)
He has seen God. (j)
The angel brings an altar coal. (j/g)
The coal touches Isaiah's lips. (g)

The coal does not burn his lips. (g)
His sin is blotted out. (g)
God needed a messenger. (j/g)
Isaiah offers to go. (n)
God calls Isaiah forth. (g)
God gives Isaiah what he will need. (g)
Isaiah's word will dull the people's minds. (j)
God will prevent some from understanding God's Word. (j)
They will not be healed. (j)
They will be made desolate. (j)
The Lord will send them away. (j)
Not one tenth will remain. (j)
A remnant will survive. (g)
The remnant will be a holy seed. (g)

Samples from commentaries:

Uzziah died around 735 B.C. (n)
Judah is threatened with war from the north. (j)
Isaiah sees heaven's holy courts. (g)
The holy realm is dangerous to the profane world. (j)
God creates a new identity for Isaiah. (g)
God will not tolerate disobedience. (j)
Isaiah pleads for God's people (i.e., "How long?") (g)
The desolation is like the destruction of the vineyard (Isa. 5). (j)
The seed will sprout a light for all nations (Isa. 9:2). (g)
God's purpose is larger than any one group of people. (j/g)
God's purpose of salvation will not be thwarted. (g)

Samples from background knowledge:

Isaiah 1–39 anticipates the Babylonian exodus (Isaiah 40–55). (n)
Ability to understand God's Word is a gift of God. (j/g)
This text influenced New Testament and Reformation attitudes about those who fail to understand. (j)
Isaiah as a whole stands as a text of strong judgment and also abundant promise. (j/g)

Note that none of these concerns of the text is phrased as a question; questions fall short of the meanings to which they point. Similarly, these sentences are not statements about general themes that merely announce a topic, but tell us nothing about it (e.g., "This is about the meaning of call").

The importance of concerns of the text can easily be missed. In order to preach any text well, we must first be able to see what ideas it contains: We must deconstruct a text before we can construct what we wish to say. To force judgments on the text in this manner, far from being artificial, is both natural and essential. Every time we speak about a biblical text we have done this kind of exercise at some level of thought. Moreover, as we have said, any sermon can be deconstructed to identify what "concerns of the text" have served as organizing instruments. An exercise such as ours simply makes the process more purposeful and controlled. The full value, however, will be apparent only in using these statements to make bridges to our world (see chapter 8).

From a list such as this, a number of preaching possibilities begin to emerge for the preacher, not all of which need be, or can be, used in one sermon. Readers seeking to go beyond these suggestions to full sermons on Isaiah 6 may find three quite different examples in two readily available sources, Paul Tillich's *The Shaking of the Foundations*,[12] and James W. Cox, ed., *The Twentieth Century Pulpit*, volume 2.[13]

Focusing on an Action of God

There are many ways in which preachers speak of the key biblical or theological idea in the sermon. It is generally accepted that if the preacher cannot say in a sentence what the sermon is about, then the preacher may not know, and the hearers probably will also not know. Fred B. Craddock refers to this key sentence as "what the text says";[14] and Thomas G. Long calls the same thing a "focus statement," one that focuses the sermon around a unifying theme.[15] Ronald J. Allen speaks of the "sermon-in-a-sentence": "(a) The subject is normally God. (b) The verb is usually an activity of God. (c) The predicate is normally a benefit or other outflow of God's love and justice (as indicated in the verb). (d) The sermon-in-a-sentence is usually positive and offers the community hope and encouragement."[16] Henry H. Mitchell advocates a "controlling idea" from a "succinct, positive, biblical verse."[17]

Homiletical synonyms: focus statement, unifying theme, sermon-in-a-sentence, central idea, controlling idea, major concern of the text, what the text says

Similarly, I speak of the major concern of the text— the one concern of the text we make into our central idea or focus statement. This major concern is important in further helping to identify the actual source of the central idea for the sermon (and this source has been elusive in homiletics). The source is the list of concerns of the text that have already begun to render more preachable the biblical text in its historical and cultural setting. From all of the various concerns of the text listed, we choose one to be the major one. It is major for two reasons: (1) It is one of perhaps several possible ideas that we determine as central to the biblical text, and (2) we make it major in the sermon because of the manner in which we focus on it and all other ideas serve it. Our goal in composing the sermon will be to focus on and with it, to see the biblical text and our world through its lens.

David Buttrick, by contrast, writes that the purpose of a sermon "cannot be stated in some clear single sentence"; rather, we discover in the text "an intending of," a field of meaning that, like film in a camera, will eventually allow us to "see what we are seeing."[18] He encourages us to think of a structure of meanings that we want to bring forth through the subject matter; thus, we would sketch a series of "moves" and work through them. Both Buttrick's phenomenological approach and Craddock's inductive approach describe accurately the homiletical process from the perspective of reception: The field of meaning intended by the preacher is gradually narrowed and brought into sharp focus by the end of the sermon. The preacher is moving listeners not to one specific thought so much as to a range of legitimate possible meanings in their lives.

Buttrick's objection to communicating one idea rather than leading the listener to a field of meanings is appropriate. The process nevertheless starts with a central idea that has taken shape in our own consciousness as preachers, one that will open the gate to this field. Ideas need words. We should think clearly about our own purposes. In other words, in seeking to escape static "points" in a sermon, or sermons that only try to communicate an idea (i.e., sermons addressed almost exclusively to logos, ignoring how we hear and form consciousness), we do not escape the need for clearly stated ideas.

What we identify as our focus will depend on our purpose:

1) If we are writing a sermon from one of the variety of possible purposes of preaching, any strong theological idea or topic may stand as our theme. The idea should be kept short so that it can be repeated, and so that we can eventually both hear and remember it, exactly as it was said.

2) Alternatively, if we are wanting to do more than this and have our people meet God through the preaching, then we will preach in a manner that helps to effect or bring about what we proclaim. We will focus on an action of God (or an action of one of the Persons of the Trinity) for the sentence around which we develop the sermon. This action might be judgment.

3) However, if we are wanting to do even more than this and preach hope, the idea we choose should focus on God's action of grace. As Ron Allen says, "Even when the community falls under indictment, the sermon-in-a-sentence seeks to show how the gospel empowers the congregation to move beyond its limitations."[19]

Exercise 7:2 Here are some possible major concerns of the text. These have God as the subject and focus on acts of grace. Identify a few potential major concerns from your own biblical text.

Biblical text	*Possible major concerns*
Gen. 9—Noah and the rainbow	God initiates the covenant.
Exod. 20—Ten Commandments	God gives us the way to life.
Ruth 4—Ruth and Boaz	God restores the outcast.
Isa. 6—Isaiah's call	God accomplishes God's will.
Luke 11:33f.—Letting light shine	Christ lights our lives.
John 4—The woman at the well	Christ bestows true identity.
Acts 13—The Holy Spirit and Paul	The Holy Spirit directs the church.
Phil. 2—Christ's self-emptying	God exalts the lowly.
Rev. 21—God's wiping away tears	God in Christ comforts the suffering.

If the sentence around which we develop the sermon focuses on an action of God, we are more likely to avoid the problem of sermons that marginalize God or leave God out. If this sentence also focuses on an action of grace, we are more likely to avoid the problem of sermons that leave out hope.

Either way, we can speak of God in active ways, thereby avoiding that other problem, sermons that portray a passive or ineffective God. Luther proposed that the problem was avoided by the very act of preaching. His "God not preached" was precisely of this nature: abstract, hidden, remote, passive, majestic, refusing to become known, reluctant to act, unwilling to save. By contrast,

"God preached" reveals God's true nature, and makes atonement for our sins.[20]

Luther did not take account of rhetorical strategy, so he did not notice that even the language we commonly use in preaching may inadvertently portray God in the manner he sought to avoid. Consider common phrases that we often use: God knows what we suffer; God understands our pain; God hears our cries. On closer examination we find that these verbs are passive, and through them, God is unintentionally portrayed as an observer who is content to understand, know, hear, or love without doing anything to help. God is a couch potato ready to change the channel when viewing becomes unpleasant. If we are suffering pain or loss, it is crucial to know that God is actively doing something.

Such claims do not avoid the problem of evil (theodicy) for the sermon; rather, they bring it to the fore for homiletical comment. A process theologian might say that God is helpless to intervene in situations that have been wrought by nature or human hands. Or in cases such as the Holocaust, some people might say that the silence of God is without answer. These may be legitimate approaches, yet as preachers we may take our lead more directly from any number of biblical texts. We may boldly assert the action we find there as descriptive of God's action today. God does not always prevent the trouble that comes our way, but God always accompanies us in it. The power of evil may temporarily thwart God's purposes, but it cannot do so ultimately or with decisive power, for that power rests with Christ alone, and the outcome is assured.

Even as Jesus continually pointed to the inbreaking of the Realm of God, we keep pointing to the same inbreaking around the world. The God we preach is active in human history, indeed is inseparable from history, though often hidden within it. This is true not just in previous ages, but in events around us: God is discernible even in the midst of tragedy and war, and not least in preaching itself. God does not avoid getting messed up in our lives, even to the point of death on a cross. Thus we join with Paul in affirming that the Spirit intercedes for us (Rom. 8:26) and in proclaiming, "We know that all things work together for good for those who love God" (Rom. 8:28). By portraying God's action, and eventually depicting what this might look like in the midst of particular local and global situations, we facilitate the event of God in our midst.[21]

Tuesday in the preacher's week concludes with five methodological suggestions for using "concerns" identified for the text:

Homiletical Method for Concerns of the Text

1) Keep concerns of the text as short, complete sentences. Avoid a question format; instead, say exactly what you mean.

2) Choose one of these ideas to become the subject of the sermon, or what we are calling the major concern of the text or focus statement.

3) A few other ideas may become the focus of individual "moves" within the sermon. (Buttrick suggests up to five or six moves in a sermon of twenty minutes. I suggest longer moves for beginning students, of up to five minutes in a short ten-minute sermon for class.) Should you choose to preach hope, choose a judgment move for the first half and a grace move for the second half.

4) Many of the concerns of the text that are not chosen as theme statements for individual moves can still be used to develop and support those that we do choose.

5) Often a theological progression of ideas (for instance from judgment to grace) may be chosen, in preference to following the actual chronology of the biblical text.

Exercise 7:3 Here is an important supplementary exercise to try with any biblical text to ensure that the full range of ideas from the text is being considered. Whether or not the sermon will focus purposely on judgment and grace, list as many concerns of the text as possible, using one column for judgment and one for grace. Now go through each column, one item at a time, and invert it for the opposite column. Thus if you have a judgment concern, it becomes a gospel statement that makes theological sense. Then check to see if that new statement might also be a legitimate concern of the text that was invisible before. Or if you have a gospel concern, inverted it can become a judgment statement that makes theological sense.

Let us be very clear that this exercise is not a way of forcing a text to adopt a predetermined theology. It is a way of determining, however, whether the limitations of our own particular circumstances are preventing us from seeing legitimate interpretations within the text itself. Furthermore, in doing such an exercise on a regular basis we gain theological facility and agility: If we are not producing authentic concerns of the text, we are at least venturing theological possibilities that find support and verification in our tradition.[22]

154

Example using Luke 13:31-35:

Judgment	*Inversion to grace*
Herod seeks to kill Jesus.	Jesus seeks to save Herod.
Jerusalem will kill Jesus.	Jesus will die for Jerusalem.
Jerusalem will not see Jesus until they recognize him.	Jesus will be present though he is not recognized.

Grace	*Inversion to judgment*
Jesus is casting out demons.	Demons would cast out Christ.
Jesus will finish his work.	Humans cannot finish what is required of them.
Jesus would be as a mother hen.	We do not choose nurture.
Jerusalem will name Jesus blessed.	Without Christ we may feel cursed.

Example using our world:

Judgment	*Inversion to grace*
We must trust in God and use our faith to help others.	God gives us our faith that God may work through us.
We have to follow God and do what God instructs.	God empowers us for encounters of love and justice.

A Brief History of Stages Two and Three

We have been considering our second hermeneutical step, explaining "what the text means." Explaining a biblical text is a process of dialogue with the text itself and with the wider Christian scholarly community through the ages, up to the present day.

It became apparent to interpreters that there was another dimension of the hermeneutical process that should be considered beyond understanding and explaining. It was the dimension of experience, and it was a factor present from the beginning of the interpretation process. Rudolf Bultmann's idea of "preunderstanding" has found general scholarly acceptance: "No exegesis is without presuppositions." He meant that we approach the text with "a certain idea of the subject matter with which the text is concerned."[23] The reader's experience, which played a key role early in the interpretation process, was important also in a reader's final interpretation. Within limits, he concluded that the product of hermeneutics is neither fixed nor final: "The understanding of the text is never a definitive one; but rather remains open because the meaning of the Scriptures discloses itself anew in every future."[24] In other words, the understanding that we have of Scripture is always conditioned by our own social and cultural setting and events.

The role of a reader's or listener's experience has become the key hermeneutical issue of our time. Hans Georg Gadamer, for instance, speaks about arriving at the text's meaning through a process originating in the experience of human language. His process is understood through philosophical description, rather than by an empirical, scientific method.[25] He speaks about the purpose of hermeneutics as a "fusion of horizons" between the text and the interpreter, yet experience is largely invisible in his discussion of hermeneutics.[26] For both Gadamer and Paul Ricoeur, the first two steps of hermeneutics (understanding and explanation) remain the only primary axes of hermeneutics.[27]

We nonetheless claim that the ineffective preacher will always be the one who tries to eliminate or curb the importance of experience in the sermon. Said another way, the misguided preacher is the one who never gets beyond explaining the text.

Review Questions for Chapter Seven

1) The focus of the second stage of the hermeneutical square is
   a) application
   b) understanding
   c) preaching purpose
   d) explanation   [d]

2) A concern of the text is
   a) a concern we bring to the text
   b) any idea with which the text is concerned
   c) what the text is trying to say
   d) the central idea of a text   [b]

3) What is not true of a major concern of the text?
   a) it will be the subject of a "move"
   b) it may normally focus on God's action
   c) it can be a synonym of focus statement and central idea
   d) there is only one in any text   [d]

4) If we wish to preach hope, we do best to focus on
   a) any strong theological idea
   b) an action of God
   c) an action of grace
   d) any of the above   [c]

5) The first two stages of hermeneutics were inadequate because
   a) the interpreter's experience was ignored
   b) the biblical writer's experience was ignored
   c) the biblical character's experience was ignored
   d) all of the above   [a]

Questions for Discussion

1) If Bible texts do in fact have many meanings, what gives us confidence in the interpretation we choose to offer in a sermon?
2) In preparing to preach, two legitimate yet conflicting interpretations present themselves. What do you do and why: (a) Preach both in the same sermon, (b) preach one this time and the other in the future, or (c) choose one and stick with it on any future occasion so as not to contradict yourself?

WEDNESDAY: WHAT EXPERIENCE SAYS

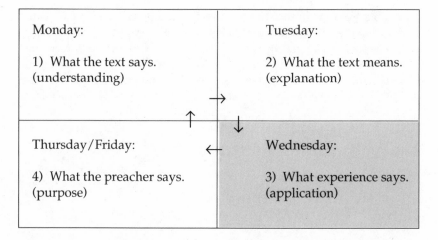

Monday:	Tuesday:
1) What the text says. (understanding)	2) What the text means. (explanation)
Thursday/Friday:	Wednesday:
4) What the preacher says. (purpose)	3) What experience says. (application)

The third stage of hermeneutics arose in theology during the 1900s out of political awareness of the reader's background and culture influencing the text's interpretation. Strategies are developed to be critical of contemporary culture. Concerns of the sermon flow from the text to address our world in six categories of experience. The central idea that we preach can be found in a systematic fashion.

In the foregoing chapters the preacher (a) completed a homiletical exegesis of the biblical text using literary and theological criticism; (b) deconstructed exegetical material and began to reconstruct it in a form easily used (i.e., concerns of the text); and (c) chose a few of these concerns for the sermon. We now continue a process of reconstruction and creativity that will culminate in the sermon itself.

Having planted our feet in the ancient soil of the text, and having also spoken with scholars, we can begin to consider what the text now can mean for us—the people of God—in our own particular situations. We apply it to our lives as a community, with norms and standards embedded in tradition. (If the text is received without authority, as if any individual can make of the application what personal experience dictates, then we are functionally atheist. God who resides in history and our community is lost.) We establish relevance, or rather God establishes the relevance of our lives through the One who is our purpose and truth. We call this stage of interpretation, "what experience says."

Liberation, black, feminist, womanist, and some western Pacific theologians took Rudolf Bultmann's cue seriously. They identified that the reader's own particular cultural experience, as well as the ancient writer's, was part of the interpretation process. Experiential factors uncovered material in texts that had not been seen before. For instance, Marxist criticism was the first to show that most of our traditional history and theology texts display the biases of the white, middle-class males who wrote them. Thus we might say that the notion of the biblical "text" expanded yet again to include even more material: beyond the biblical text itself, beyond its background (as discussed by the scholarly community), to the community background of the contemporary interpreter. Who we are as individuals and preachers affects what a text says through us.

This third stage in the hermeneutical process is a practical or praxis stage (for Aristotle, praxis = moral practice). The truth of the biblical interpretation that is being formed is tested in dialogue with the life of our community. This interpretation—rather than being determined by correspondence to philosophical or theoretical principles—is tested by practical experience (using principles such as logos, pathos, and ethos that are able to address a range of intellectual, emotional, and spiritual matters).

Experience has become central. Liberationists argue that no interpretation of a biblical text can escape being within a political context and worldview,[1] since politics and ideology are inescapable. José Miguez Bonino says, "Every interpretation of the texts which is offered to us (whether as exegesis or as systematic or as ethical interpretation) must be investigated in relation to the praxis out of which it comes."[2] Various liberation theologies are committed, as Elisabeth Schüssler Fiorenza notes, to those people who have been oppressed and ignored by history.[3] Now pastoral theologians like Don Browning, from a different perspective, also are claiming the essential role of experience in hermeneutics.[4]

Of course perceptive preachers have always known the importance of application: The truth of the text needs to be tested and applied in the lives of the congregation. This happens throughout the interpretation process, both in the reading of a text as we try to discern its meaning (as part of the hermeneutical circle), and continuing throughout the composing of the sermon.

A good preacher, as we have seen, is constantly pondering how this biblical understanding functions in the present world. For example, if using Isaiah's call, the preacher might be recollecting stories from today that speak of similar kinds of experience. For example, a preacher might think of this autobiographical story from Barbara Brown Taylor concerning the call to ministry that she experienced while listening to her childhood minister and friend:

One Sunday he asked me to sit up close to the pulpit. He wanted me to hear his sermon, he said, and as I listened to him talk about the beauty of God's creation and our duty to be awed by it, all of a sudden I heard him telling the congregation about a little girl who kept tadpoles in a birdbath so that she could watch over them as they turned into frogs, and how her care for those creatures was part of God's care for the whole world.

It was as if someone had turned on all the lights—not only to hear myself spoken of in the church, but to hear that my life was part of God's life, and that something as ordinary as a tadpole connected the two.[5]

Stories like this bring yet other stories to mind that will help identify the meaning we are developing for the present day.

Exegesis of Our Situation

It is not enough simply and freely to associate from textual images or ideas to situations in the present time. Some critical perspective is needed of our world, which is one reason why David Buttrick speaks of the "double hermeneutic" of the preacher: "We interpret revelation in light of being-saved, and we grasp being-saved in view of revelation."[6] In interpreting the biblical text, the text illuminates our world, and our world critiques the text, in a continuing hermeneutical spiral until the appropriate understanding is found. Even as exegesis of the biblical text is necessary, exegesis of our situation is also necessary, or we cannot adequately interpret the text. This exegesis of our world certainly means getting the facts right concerning any issue we might mention, which is one of the reasons why the preacher must read the newspapers, watch television, and stay informed. We must rely on trustworthy sources for our information, being especially wary not to accept the literature for instance of special interest groups necessarily as fact. If our facts are wrong, the congregation will not trust us.

Exegesis of our situation is more than correct facts, however. It refers to the evaluation of life around us from the perspective of a community that strives to be faithful to the Word, even as we constantly submit that community life to be under the Word. Don S. Browning calls this the descriptive task of theology—examining the theory-laden practice of communities to discern questions that we then address back to the biblical texts that shaped the community.[7] Said more simply, exegesis of our situation implies that the ground on which we stand to interpret the biblical texts, is often soft. We must be critical of our own attitudes, which have been influenced by the surrounding culture, even some that we might assume correspond to the gospel.

One important way of exercising this exegesis of our situation is through our understanding of social justice. Social analysis is part of the gospel, not a by-product of it. Jesus' own ministry was committed to the poor, the sick, the homeless, and the needy. He confronted the religious authorities. The only way we can ever ignore social justice is to retreat, says Art Van Seters, to a fractured view of the world: "Individuals have been treated [in sermons of the past] as if they could be separated from their corporate reality. With this separation the world becomes a mere backdrop to God's personal encounter with individuals as though the entire world is profane, no longer part of God's creation."[8]

> *Social analysis with a view to justice is not something we add to the gospel, it is part of the gospel.*

How might we bring a critical perspective of our situation to interpretation of the text? Three approaches in particular might help us here. One part of the clue, says Christine M. Smith, is to name radical evil for what it is, seen in a variety of prejudiced attitudes and actions (e.g., sexism, racism). She proposes a "homiletical methodology" to assist preachers. We are to speak with people who are suffering; and we are to experience the forms of oppression being addressed such that we "weep and passionately feel"; "confess the truth of the oppressions"; and "evoke resistance and action."[9] Notice also what she is not saying: She is not suggesting that we make the sermon into a lecture on abstract ideas (even though confession, for her, involves essential social analysis).

This threefold approach in preaching might begin with our own (or some congregational member's) "radicalizing moment" of experience that moved us to a new place of compassion. This is Smith's reflection on the prejudice against the aged shown to her own dying uncle:

> I will never forget one visit. Several family members were present. He began to talk about dying, and each time he tried to speak someone quickly silenced him with reassurances that he was fine and that he would get better. This happened more than once, and finally he gave up trying to communicate to us his feelings about wanting to die. To this day I have regretted what happened there.[10]

Such stories are an excellent way of awakening us as listeners to similar encounters we have had with our denial of death, or old age.

Another part of the clue, says William K. McElvaney, is to be open to where God is acting in the world. Our community as Christians is never the isolated community of our own family or circle of chosen friends, or even our own church. Rather it is the global community, no part of God's creation excluded. With this perspective our understanding of God, and our experience of God, is enlarged and deepened.[11] Increased challenges to our faith increase its depth and breadth. Thus we discover that while God cares about our own personal dreams for our futures, provided they are not born of greed or selfishness, "God has more in mind for us all than our privately imagined [blueprints], and that 'more' is basic to Christian preaching in whatever form it takes. Frequently God does . . . interact with us in ways we would not have imagined, chosen, or preferred. . . . God seeks to save us to become our deepest and truest selves for God and for others, to restore us to our intended purpose in community."[12] The experience of judgment as "a renewing and re-creating catharsis" and God's love as a "disturbing influence and power,"[13] says McElvaney, always leads from grace "to the inseparable claim on our lives."[14]

> Three Strategies for Social Analysis
>
> 1) Smith: weep, confess, resist
> 2) McElvaney: awareness of the gospel's global claim
> 3) Allen: 18 steps for research

There is yet a third proposal for responsible exegesis of our world through preaching. Ronald J. Allen has designed a process for recovery of topical preaching, a sermonic form that has received much criticism of late, yet which has been and will continue to be important for the church. His eighteen steps help prepare for preaching responsibly, imaginatively, and persuasively on topics of relevance to Christian life. Although he is discussing topical kinds of preaching, his approach is so balanced that it can serve as a model for responsible social analysis in any sermon:

(1) Determine that the topic is of sufficient size for the pulpit; (2) identify preassociations with the topic; (3) list everything you need to know about the topic; (4) search for biblical perspectives; (5) trace how the topic has been interpreted in the history of the church; (6) focus on two theologians on the topic; (7) bring out the denomination's position on the topic; (8) investigate other relevant dimensions of the topic; (9) inventory the congregation's experience with the topic; (10) imagine what it is like to be different persons in different situations relative to the topic; (11) evaluate the topic theologically; (12) state your own position on the topic; (13) articulate viewpoints other than your own; (14) consider the mindset and situation of the listeners in relation to the topic; (15) locate the listeners in relation to your position on the topic; (16) state what you want to say in the sermon; (17) decide what you hope will be the result of the listener's hearing of the sermon; and (18) design the sermon so that it will have a good chance of accomplishing its purpose.[15]

Though the steps are numerous, they flow readily, one from the other. If one is actually preaching on a topic, Allen's steps are likely to save time, not just in arriving at what to say, but also in finding a path around the swamp of congregational anger that some preachers enter by an unbalanced representation of controversial issues.

When preaching on controversial issues, three additional matters have general merit:

1) The preacher must give a balanced analysis of both (or more) sides of the issues, as fairly as possible.
2) The position to which the preacher calls the congregation must not be beyond their present ability to achieve.
3) The preacher's position needs to be identified as closely as possible to this reachable stance.

Preachers are wise to remember that reachable goals are often more prophetic for ministry than unreachable goals, which may cause the congregation to react against growth. As preachers, we generally are not to dictate what position a congregation must take, but rather are to invite them to responsible actions that honor their own ministries. A wise churchwoman once put the matter well: Try less to be a sage on a stage, than a guide at the side.

Critical exegesis of our situation is important throughout the hermeneutical process. It becomes essential when we begin testing "what experience says" in light of the biblical text, for our own attitudes, shaped by our own individual backgrounds and contexts, including the Bible, become part of what this text will say, in our expanding notion of the text.

Transposing Concerns of the Text

How does the preacher move from the biblical text to our situation? How can we know what connections are possible? The process is not simply random, the product of a brainwave in the shower. Principles can be learned for greater control and excellence; they are similar in nature to critical principles in the earlier two hermeneutical stages. The process that we follow in making bridges between the Bible and our time may be named rather than left to intuition. The preacher needs some tools to examine the field of meaning in the text and the field of meaning to which the text relates in congregational experience.[16]

We may use the following exercise to preview the strength of proposed ideas for a sermon. On one level it is a very difficult exercise, and many students rightly struggle with it. On another level, when we are able to do it, it seems deceptively simple, yet still it retains mystery and surprise.

Concerns of the text (= t) are simply paired with equivalent statements for our day, called concerns of the sermon (= s), since they deal with our time and culture, not the Bible. These pairs are natural links and provide the sermon with natural bridges of thought between the biblical text and today's experience. A concern of the text we defined earlier as any idea, expressed in a short sentence, with which the biblical text is concerned. It is true to the details of the text. We noted that it can arise from the text itself, from the commentaries, or from our scholarly background knowledge. A concern of the sermon, by contrast, is a transposed version of the concern of the text that makes a general statement about our time and culture we would affirm to be true. We affirm its truth by testing it, not as a true statement of the text (though intimately linked to the text), but theologically as a true statement of life either as we experience it in present or as our faith leads us to understand it. Moreover, we test it not as a complete, self-evident statement of the truth in itself, but rather according to what we sense it leading us to say, using our best theological skills and nuancing.

Earlier we saw the importance of using the phrase "concern of the text" as a way of identifying the wide range of potentially preachable ideas in a biblical text. We again saw the importance of our phrase as way of helping us to find the central idea of the sermon, designated as the major concern of the text. Now we see its importance in identifying how to cross the bridge between the biblical text and our time. The next step will be to select just a few of these bridges or paired statements to structure the sermon. They will be the bare bones of the sermon, for they will function as theme statements of individual paragraphs (the one deals with the text, the other deals with our time). Upon preaching, it will be essential to use their exact wording in the sermon in order to preserve the bridge for our hearers.

Rather than try to explain the intellectual process of transposition, accomplished elsewhere,[17] I provide numerous examples, for transposition is more readily observed than articulated. A helpful clue when transposing is to keep one key term constant. We will start with examples from our Isaiah text, and later move to more difficult examples from students. Judgment and grace are again identified according to how I imagine I would develop the idea, were I to choose this idea for development as a lengthy paragraph in my sermon. Here the neutral designation (n) is omitted because ambivalence is not a persuasive rhetorical strategy in the pulpit.

> In my own teaching no exercise or assignment has done more to help introductory students discover the connections they are proposing to make between the Bible and the present day, to correct and strengthen them, and also to show the range of rich possibilities of intersection between the biblical text and experience. We can isolate sources of problems, and also find stronger alternatives. Fundamental weaknesses of a proposed sermon can be spotted long before it is written, saving hours of potentially wasted work, on the part of both student and teacher. Students who do this exercise (and if necessary repeat it), can gain the experience equivalent to many sermons, in terms of identifying pitfalls and good connections to today. Equally important, the exercise done regularly strengthens our ability to do theology in the pulpit.

Exercise 8:1 Transpose your own list of concerns of the text.

Text—Isaiah 6:1-13: Isaiah's Call

  j = judgment   g = grace

Samples from the biblical text itself:

t: King Uzziah died. (j)
s: Many die today. (j) Or: Rulers die, or Earthly powers pass away. (j)

t: The country was in mourning. (j)
s: Many are in mourning. (j) Or: Our nations mourn. (j) Or: The
                                world lacks direction. (j)

t: Isaiah had a vision. (g) | Isaiah had a vision. (j)
s: Christ is our vision. (g) | We have no visions. (j) Or:
                                     | God seems absent to us. (j)

t: The Lord appeared to Isaiah. (g)
s: God appears to us. (g)

t: Six-winged seraphs praised the Lord. (g)
s: We praise God. (g) Or: God praises us. (g)

t: All earth is full of the Lord's glory. (g)
s: God's glory cannot be contained. (g)

t: Isaiah fears for his life. (j)
s: Many live in fear. (j) Or: Life can be lost. (j)

t: He is unclean. (j)
s: We are unclean. (j) Or: Our ways are unclean. (j)

t: He has seen God. (j)
s: God has seen us. (j)

t: The angel brings an altar coal. (g)
s: We have been made clean. (g)

t: The coal touches Isaiah's lips. (g)
s: Salvation does not stay remote from us. (g)

t: The coal does not burn his lips. (g)
s: Destruction of our sin does not injure us. (g)

t: His sin is blotted out. (g)
s: Our sin is blotted out. (g)

t: God needed a messenger. (j)   God needed a messenger. (g)
s: We need a messenger. (j)   God sent a messenger. (g)

t: God calls Isaiah forth. (g)
s: God calls us forth. (g) Or: God calls many forth. (g)

t: God gives Isaiah what he will need. (g)
s: God gives us what we need. (g)

t: Isaiah's word will dull the people's minds. (j)
s: Our minds are dull. (j) Or: We don't know salvation when we hear
                        it. (j)

t: God prevented some from understanding God's Word. (j)
s: We prevent others from understanding God's Word. (j)

t: They will not be healed. (j)
s: Many will not be healed. (j)

t: They will be made desolate. (j)
s: Much has been laid waste. (j) Or: We have made much desolate.
                                                              (j)

t: The Lord will send them away. (j)
s: God seems to have sent us away. (j)

t: Not one tenth will remain. (j)
s: Things will get worse. (j) Or: There is little hope. (j)

t: A remnant will survive. (g)
s: A remnant has survived. (g) Or: Hope is alive. (g)

t: The remnant will be a holy seed. (g)
s: The seed has sprouted. (g) Or: A new realm is breaking in. (g)

167

Samples from commentaries:

t: Judah is threatened with war from the north. (j)
s: War faces people on all sides. (j)

t: Isaiah sees heaven's holy courts. (g)
s: We glimpse God's heavenly realm. (g)

t: The holy realm is dangerous to the profane world. (j)
s: God's ways are not our ways. (j)

t: God creates a new identity for Isaiah. (g)
s: God gives us a new identity in Christ. (g)

t: God will not tolerate disobedience. (j)
s: God will not tolerate us. (j) Or: We tolerate disobedience.(j)

t: Isaiah pleads for God's people. (i.e., "How long?") (g)
s: Christ pleads our case. (g)

t: The desolation is like the destruction of the vineyard (Isaiah 5). (j)
s: God will not stand lack of fruit. (j)

t: The seed will sprout a light for all nations (Isa. 9:2). (g)
s: We are a light for all nations. (g) Or: Christ is a light for all people
(g)

t: God's purpose is larger than any one group of people. (j/g)
s: God's purpose cannot be stopped. (g)

t: God's purpose of salvation will not be thwarted. (g)
s: God is determined to accomplish our salvation. (g)

Samples from background knowledge:

t: Ability to understand God's Word is a gift of God. (j/g)
s: God illumines God's Word. (g)

t: This text influenced New Testament and Reformation attitudes
   about those who fail to understand. (j)
s: [not workable for the sermon in this form]

t: Isaiah as a whole stands as a text of strong judgment and also abundant promise. (j/g)

s: The God of judgment and hope Isaiah knew is our God. (j/g)

Student Examples of Concerns of the Sermon

Here are typical examples of concerns of the sermon from students working with various biblical texts. They are chosen to highlight typical pitfalls. I add my own comments to suggest stronger or potentially more interesting alternatives:

Matthew 5:13

t: Salt cannot restore its saltiness. (j)

s: Some people lack saltiness. (j) (Better: For many life seems to be without salt.)

t: Useless salt is not good for anything. (j)

s: Choose life or death. (j) (Stay closer to the above: Without God, we are not good for anything.)

t: You, the disciples, are the salt of the world. (g) (Better: The disciples are . . .)

s: The Christian community is valued as salt. (g) (For grace it is better to focus on an action of God: God in Christ gives us our saltiness.)

Matthew 21:23-32

t: Jesus questioned the religious authorities. (j)

s: We question the religious authorities. (j) (Or: We question God.)

t: The religious authorities argue amongst themselves about the right answer. (j)

s: Why would they do this? Do they know what they are afraid of? (j) (Avoid questions at this stage and make a direct statement that is true of the text: The religious authorities are confounded by Jesus. This is still a concern of the text, yet not of the sermon.)

t: The religious authorities failed to recognize God's action. (j)

s: We should consider our shortcomings. (j) (Better: We fail to recognize God. [We can still talk about our shortcomings in developing the sermon.])

169

t: Jesus' response was ambiguous. (j)

s: We rarely get clear answers from God. (j) (Another possibility: At times God seems devious.)

t: Tax collectors and prostitutes will enter God's Realm first. (g)

s: Red light hookers are eligible for salvation. (g) (This would be better at this stage if it were more general. In the sermon we can make it more specific, but now is a time to open possibilities. It would be stronger as a statement of grace if the action was shifted to God: God welcomes the sinners and despised.)

t: The religious authorities are not denied entry to God's Realm. (g) (This could be stated positively: Even the religious authorities will be given entry.)

s: God reaches to all with salvation. (g)

Matthew 21:33-46

t: The landowner rented the vineyard to tenants. (j)

s: We borrow and lend. (j) (Better: Our life at times seems on borrowed time.)

t: The landowner left the tenants to manage on their own. (j)

s: God gives us free will. (g) (Transpositions from judgment to grace, or from grace to judgment are more difficult for listeners to grasp, and are best used as emergency devices to help us find judgment or grace when it seems absent. Better: Sometimes God seems to have left us. "Seems" here reflects my own theological understanding, as is appropriate when dealing with a concern of the sermon. Our theology takes precedence since the biblical text is already secured in the sermon by the concerns of the text.)

t: The landowner sent servants for the rent. (j)

s: God sent the prophets to warn us. (j) (This idea could be developed with the concern of the text in the sermon itself. Concerns of the sermon are about us and our time. Better: God's messengers come to us.)

t: The tenants kill the son. (j)

s: We hurt Jesus by our hardness of heart. (j) (Better: We continue to crucify Christ today.)

t: The landowner sent many messengers. (g)
s: God sent Jesus to us. (g) (Better: God keeps reaching out to us.)

t: The landowner sent his son. (g)
s: God sent Jesus. (g) (Better if held to our time: God sends Jesus to us [i.e., even our worst actions will not have the final say].)

Item	Form in Sermon	Aids for Development	Test for Validity
concern of the text	paragraph on the Bible	the text, commentaries, background knowledge	the entire text
concern of the sermon	paragraph on our world and times	theology, social and cultural analysis	the theology of the church at large

Each of these sets affords a bridge that we can develop usually into two paragraphs (or one move) in the sermon. They link us with the text and move from Scripture to the present. Each concern of the sermon points us to a theological claim in our world that we develop in the sermon. It flows from Scripture and is expanded in relation to our world, experience, and theological insight.

This kind of analogical grid, far from being simplistic, is precisely what preachers must engage, knowingly or not, throughout the homiletical process. We cannot remain aloof from such judgments on the text, as though we were writing an academic essay on a Bible passage without concern for our own day. We must ask of every text, "What is the meaning of this for today?" recognizing that there are many possible meanings. In doing an exercise like this we make an otherwise unconscious process into a conscious one. We are thus able to discern the best potential ideas to develop. From these available options we will choose just a few for the sermon.

Implications of Concerns of the Sermon

In preparing to use transpositions of the sort just identified, students should ask two key questions of themselves: Can I see how a lengthy paragraph (two to three minutes or 200 to 375 words) developing a concern of the text using commentaries and scholarship would naturally lead to a second paragraph developing the transposed concern of the sermon? Second, Can I see how I might take a concern of the sermon and develop it into a lengthy paragraph about a contemporary culture or social setting using my best theological reflection?

Beyond these key methodological questions are two further implications for concerns of the sermon. The first is theological. Preachers need to be able to point to experiences of God if preaching is to be God's event and we are to proclaim God as loving and present, active and alive in the world. We cannot readily build up the community of faith with a theology of absence or despair and probably should not preach if this is all we have to offer. While not all students may share such an immanent and transcendent pulpit theology, and while faith is a gift, faith can also be taught. This, after all, is part of the purpose of preaching, to help people to see God in new ways. We remember that Jesus is called Emmanuel, or "God is with us" (Matt. 1:23); and his promise was, "I am with you always, to the end of the age" (Matt. 28:20).

Concerns of the sermon, such as we have developed on the previous pages, fall into six broad homiletical categories for theologically treating experience in the world:

1) God's judgment
2) the human condition
3) Christ's present suffering/crucifixion
4) God's forgiveness
5) God overturning the world
6) God using people

In other words, each concern of the sermon gives us at least one theological perspective from which to view or interpret the world.

This focus on God's action is very important. Most students (and some exhausted preachers) wonder how to find stories of today's experience for the sermon. Must we keep a file on one hundred different themes? No. Instead we can start to view events around us in terms of these categories. By using them, the vast range of experience becomes more manageable for preachers. For instance, any story about the human condition (e.g., human need and suffering) might be used to develop any concern of the sermon pointing to the human condition. Or any story about God using people can be used to develop a concern of the sermon pointing to Christ acting through people. Rather than have an unwieldy thematic approach to stories of experience, we have an approach geared to theological function. Thus we might try keeping only six main files for stories. We will work more on developing stories according to these six categories in chapter 12.

The second implication of our topic is for homiletical theory. Various writers have addressed the "double hermeneutic" for preachers.

Generally they speak to only one sermonic point of contact between the biblical text and our day, not the many that are potential. In other words, they speak of the one point of contact with the central idea of the sermon. There is some consistency in what is said.

Fred B. Craddock adapted Harry Emerson Fosdick's strong encouragement that the sermon have an *"object* to be achieved," not a *"subject* to be elucidated."[18] In other words, the sermon should have a need to be met or a problem to be solved. Craddock proposes something in addition to the common suggestion of identifying the central idea in one sentence. Preachers, he says, should also identify a related second statement that names a purpose of the sermon, that is, "What is the text doing?" He identifies this as a contemporary issue or need:

This question [i.e., What is the text doing?] is not only identifying the nature and function of the text but is also providing an early guideline for the sermon to come. After all, the preacher will want to be clear not only about what is being said in the sermon but also about what is being done in the sermon. And just as one's message is informed by *what the text is saying*, the sermon's function is informed by *what the text is doing*. If, for example, one were to state as what the text is saying, "Every Christian is a charismatic," and as what the text is doing, "Encouraging those believers who felt second-class," then *content and tone and purpose of the sermon* have come into focus.[19]

The usefulness of Craddock's purpose statement was spotted and adopted by others. Thomas G. Long thus speaks of a "focus statement" and a "function statement" that describe what the preacher "hopes the sermon will create or cause to happen for the hearers."[20] Henry H. Mitchell speaks of a similar pair: "One *controlling idea* and *behavioral purpose* is all any sermon can be expected to communicate with effectiveness, not great ideas from every [Bible] verse."[21]

Together homileticians are trying to identify recently neglected or previously unrecognized hermeneutical procedures that assist the preacher, and it is the procedures themselves that matter, not the terminology used to identify them. Most important is the instruction that the central idea emerging from the biblical text be directed in our time to meet a particular need in the lives of the hearers.

We have seen, however, that there are many potential points of contact between the biblical text and our time (not just one), as many as the number of concerns of the text and concerns of the sermon, though they are of varying potential for developing the fullness of the text. Without the

173

range of possibilities being exposed in a list it is hard to select a focus for the sermon in a systematic or purposeful way. By staying with our terms we can easily select a central idea for a sermon, complete with the double hermeneutic addressed by others.

Homiletical Method

1) Choose from the list of concerns of the text, an idea that normally focuses on an action of God (see chapter 7). Designate it as the major concern of the text (i.e., the central idea from the biblical text that will be our focus).

2) Pair it with what then becomes the major concern of the sermon, which continues to focus on God's action, but in our time and place. Either or both of these statements may be used and repeated in the sermon to express its central idea.

> The "major concern of the sermon" is the transposed version of the major concern of the text. It is the central idea of the sermon expressed in relation to our world.

3) Ask, "What question or need in the congregation does this statement answer?" Remember the distinctions made in chapter 1 between the expressed and actual needs of the congregation, and the preacher's need. Here we assume that the major concern of the sermon expresses the congregation's actual need, and it is up to us to identify their expressed need in their own words. Once identified, this statement or question becomes part of the sermon. In using it we make intentional the development of at least one possible relevance of the sermon.

4) Usually choose at least one additional pair of concerns (i.e., a concern of the text and a concern of the sermon) for the early part of the sermon. These will have some apparent link in the mind of the preacher with the pair designated as major, and will be developed in the sermon to serve the major pair that are the central idea. Thus if we are preaching hope, the minimal movement will be **text** (judgment), **situation** (judgment), **text** (grace), **situation** (grace).

For greatest clarity and simplicity, students initially might devote 200 to 375 words or one manuscript page or 2 to 3 minutes to each of these four. Eventually, longer sermons can be ventured.

5) Let these various "concerns" function as clear, obvious, and audible themes of their respective paragraphs, using repetition and

minor rephrasing as appropriate. Develop these ideas using complete sentences, rather than preaching just an image or picture contained within. Further, develop the idea from a particular theological perspective such that we have a sense of movement or progression of thought, instead of just talking around an idea. For example, a deepening sense of judgment or grace could provide this sense of movement.

6) So that the sermon flows smoothly and does not become mechanical, keep your concerns of the text fixed, once you start writing. As you develop a concern of the text, you may find that your thought leads to a slightly different concern of the sermon from the one originally planned. As long as this new one is an obvious link and easy bridge for your listeners from the text to our world, it will work. In other words, do not necessarily lock in your concerns of the sermon until the writing is underway.

We have been considering the third step in the hermeneutical process, what experience says. Thus on Wednesday, the preacher examines experience in relation to the biblical text. Next we turn to a final hermeneutical step that completes the interpretation process.

Exercise 8:2 From your list of paired concerns, pick one pair that designates your central idea. Identify what question or need of the congregation that major concern of the text answers. Now pick one or two other pairs that you might also want to include, and which can serve your central idea.

Review Questions for Chapter Eight

1) The third stage of hermeneutics (What experience says) arose
    primarily out of
    a) political awareness
    b) spiritual awareness
    c) biblical awareness
    d) existential awareness   [a]

2) "Double hermeneutic" means reading the biblical text
    a) first for personal and then for social implications
    b) two times to check for mistakes in our interpretation
    c) to be doubly critical of historical sources
    d) to be critical of our culture   [d]

3) Which is wrong: A "concern of the sermon" is a
   a) general statement
   b) statement about the biblical text
   c) bridge to our time
   d) thesis statement of a potential paragraph   [b]

4) The "major concern of the sermon"
   a) can be used to express a congregational need
   b) is the transposed version of the major concern of the text
   c) is the central idea of the sermon expressed in relation to our
      world
   d) all of the above   [d]

Questions for Discussion

1) The meaning of a biblical text in some measure is determined by
   the personal and cultural experience we bring to it. This being the
   case, how can we render an interpretation for everyone?
2) We use biblical scholarship and sensory details to develop paragraphs around a chosen concern of the text. When we shift to
   develop a concern of the sermon for our time, we stop worrying for
   the moment about the text. Instead, we use our best theology to
   reflect on the idea in today's context. In doing so, do you think we
   are in danger of distorting the biblical text?

THURSDAY/FRIDAY: WHAT THE PREACHER SAYS

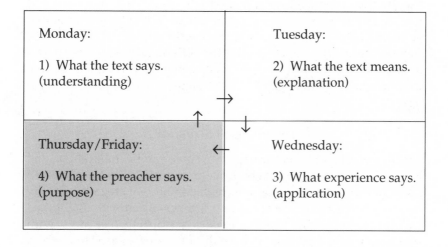

Monday:	Tuesday:
1) What the text says. (understanding)	2) What the text means. (explanation)
Thursday/Friday:	Wednesday:
4) What the preacher says. (purpose)	3) What experience says. (application)

As a concluding hermeneutical step, we consider composition. Sermon structure is considered in terms of body, introduction, and conclusion. The sermonic goal is considered from the perspective of lives lived out in faithful service. The idea of a "hermeneutical square" is completed (a) to redescribe the interpretation process through the preacher's week and (b) to help change attitudes that work against preaching by making homiletics invisible in the interpretation process.

We come now toward the end of the week and the fourth stage of the hermeneutical process: "What the preacher says." It could equally be "what the interpreter says," because it is the final stage in any interpretative process. This stage is a response to the initial text and is thus itself the making of a new text. In turn, in order to be understood, it will require its own interpretation in a continuing chain of communication. The focus here is on praxis, on creating a new text. It is on the purpose of the preacher (or other speaker) who shapes the future sermon (or other text) in such a way that it can be heard as intended.

Our topic of sermon composition is in fact the subject of the remaining chapters of this book; thus, we need not try to say everything at once. Instead, we may concentrate on two things: First, we will consider some basic, practical guidelines for the basic parts of the sermon. These may then be applied to any of the numerous forms we will discuss in detail in the next chapter.

Second, we will consider the goal we are intending to achieve through the sermon: an encounter with God such that lives are lived in faith and acted out in justice, mercy, and love. The interpretation we offer of the biblical text and our world will be affected by the rhetorical strategies we choose for the sermon. We therefore continue to anticipate the responses of our listeners, always attentive to a necessary, implied dialogue between the preacher and the congregation.

The Intended Structure

How we structure what we say in response to the biblical text and our world, obviously affects both the interpretation we render, and how it in turn is received and interpreted by the congregation. Whenever we communicate, we speak and listeners listen with established conventions in mind. Readers experience a detective story with expectations and demands that are different from when they read a history or romance. In a less dramatic fashion, listeners encounter parts of the sermon with differing expectations and demands. Here we briefly consider the structure of the sermon in three categories: the body, the introduction, and the conclusion.

The Body

Common to any sermon, whether it is a story or a sequence of "moves" or several "points," will be a central plot or idea that answers this question of listeners: What was the sermon about? Even as many interpretations of a biblical text are possible, it is fair to expect various interpretations of a sermon. As preachers, we simply should be clear about our own purpose in the sermon, our own meaning, and to communicate it as best we can.

The central idea of a sermon is appropriately understood as a developing idea or plot that gradually takes shape in the listener's consciousness. Everything in the sermon is in some way related to it, because it is at the heart of what we say (not least by emphasis and repetition). One of the most difficult tasks for many homiletical students is to keep the sermon focused upon or moving to develop one idea, not two or three, even though several minor ideas may be developed in stages toward it. In terms of our discussion here, that central idea is expressed as either the major concern of the text or its transposed version, the major concern of the sermon, or both.

At the same time, a sermon is a dialogue between the biblical text and our own situation. The biblical text is given central emphasis, although where we speak of it can vary. How many times we move into it and seek to apply it to our times can also vary.

> *Choose one idea, not two or three, even though several minor ideas may be developed in stages toward that idea.*

Sermon form can be pictured in a variety of ways: Eugene Lowry joins a descending curve and an ascending curve to form a pointed loop (or the Christian *icthus*, fish symbol, turned on its nose) as a way of describing his "homiletical plot." I use the circle and spiral (echoing the hermeneutical circle), with each loop constituting the development of a concern of the text along with its transposed concern of the sermon. Others use graphs, to highlight emotional climax for instance.

Perhaps a more universal picture that includes most conceivable approaches can be obtained by using a sine graph or curve, a symbol commonly used in science or math. Whether we are discussing the biblical text or our situation, the central idea or plot develops at the heart of what is said, explicitly or implicitly, throughout the sermon. The full development of a textual idea on a sine graph can be represented by a complete movement (developing a complete idea) in and out of the text, and back to the mean line. In the same manner, the full development of something in our situation is portrayed on the opposite side of the mean line. Partial developments are indicated by partial lines. Here are just a few basic possibilities:

1) Move once into the biblical text and apply it to our world. This is a standard exegesis-application format. On a smaller scale, it is a picture of one of David Buttrick's "moves" (composed of a theological idea from the text that is clearly stated at the beginning; the idea is

elaborated with an "analogy of experience" that anticipates congregational "blocks"; and the move is quickly concluded with a repetition
of the main idea).

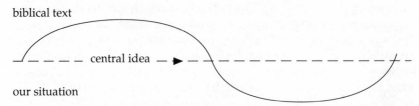

2) Move twice into the biblical text and our world. (If preaching
hope, any of the remaining forms can be used, although this is common: The first half is judgment, the second is grace.)

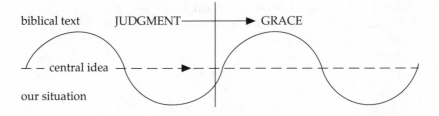

**3) Move partly into the biblical text at the beginning of the sermon
and complete the treatment of the text at the end.** (The number of
movements here may vary.)

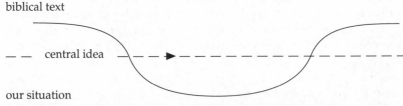

**4) Move from an experience to the biblical text and conclude with an
experience in light of the text.** (If our situation explores the inverse of
the Good News in the text, this structure can be used to preach hope.)

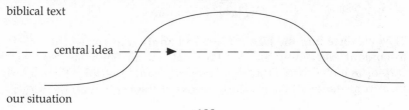

5) Move several times in complete movements. David Buttrick makes a literary analysis of the biblical text and isolates a number of key moments (which he phrases in conversational style) that lead to a transformation of consciousness. This is the sequence he develops for Matthew 2:1-12. It probably represents a twenty-five-minute sermon. The approach of this text is noted in brackets [ ] to demonstrate the same purpose using concerns of the text (= t) and concerns of the sermon (= s).

1. "Where is he?" asked the Wisemen. They belong in our world for they were looking for a savior. *[t: The Wisemen sought the child. s: We seek a savior.]*
2. "Where is he?" asked Herod, but he wanted to kill. Entrenched power will always be threatened by God. *[t: Herod wanted to kill Jesus. s: The world is threatened by God.]*
3. Well, guess who Herod turned to? To us religious people, that's who! *[t: Herod turned to religious people. s: Many would use religion to their own purpose.]*
4. Well, eventually Christ was crucified. *[t: Christ was crucified. s: Christ is crucified today.]*
5. But he rose again and still comes to us as threat and promise. *[t: Christ rose from the dead. s: The risen Christ comes to us in threat and promise.]*
6. So how do we respond? We worship and we offer ourselves. *[t: The Wisemen worship Christ. s: We worship Christ.]*[1]

biblical text

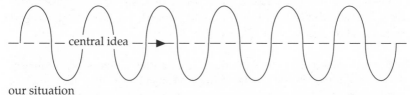

our situation

Students and accomplished preachers are encouraged not to switch too often between the biblical text and our situation, normally fewer times than in the illustration just given. Doing so can place too much emphasis on logos, demanding perhaps too much intellectual agility. Moreover, we expend energy and concentration to shift the scenery of our minds as listeners from biblical to our own times, even if we are treating the Bible mainly using the present tense in lively visual and oral ways. If the preacher uses too few moves with insufficient interest, the congregation will be bored. Too many quick moves on the other hand puts too great a demand on listeners, and the congregation will end up lost. Listening to such sermons is like trying to grab a housefly as it flies—you think you have it, but it is gone. Think of the preacher as a guide taking listeners through God's mansion of many rooms. Take us into a room, seat us, talk about the room, allow us time to note its features, and move us only when it will not seem as if we are being yanked.

The Introduction

The introduction is determined only after the central focus is decided, along with some plan for sequence of thoughts. Thomas G. Long offers excellent suggestions:

1) The introduction should promise something of what the sermon will be about. (i.e., Some need or question, like, Why do we pray?)
2) What is promised should be of value to the congregation.
3) The language and tone of the introduction should create a fair expectation of the language and tone of the sermon.
4) While the introduction should anticipate the whole sermon, it should also lead directly to the next step of the sermon.[2]

Clearly the introduction must get our attention, yet also not immediately plunge us into the heart of the issue. Listeners need time, as indicated in chapter 1, to establish a relationship with the preacher (ethos). David Buttrick (who provides our most detailed contemporary study of sermon introductions and conclusions)[3] is acknowledging this ethos dimension when he counters the old idea that the first sentence of a sermon should be a "grabber":

Evidence is to the contrary. People do not easily attend the first few sentences of a public address. Just as when we swing a camera on a scene, focus may be fuzzy before gradually clarifying, so the first two or three sentences in a sermon are seldom heard—they are fuzzy. Human syntax is individual, as distinctive as a fingerprint. Therefore, congregations must adjust to the syntactical patterns of a preacher.[4]

This does not mean that what we say is unimportant, but it means rather that we are modest in our expectation of what can be accomplished in the opening minutes of conversation.

Buttrick also cautions against the "step down introduction," one that keeps shifting the focus or subject (e.g., from the guest teacher, to the trip, to the first job). Pick one focus and point of view for an introduction and keep it.[5]

The simplest, though not necessarily the most imaginative introduction, may start directly with the biblical text, perhaps painting the situation of the biblical writer and remembering the lessons of oral thought and language from our earlier chapters (for instance about including the senses). To help remember these lessons, students should understand their assignment concerning the biblical text to be to create a movie in words. In other words, once a responsible, scholarly understanding of the text is assured, the preacher presents that understanding in highly visual and vital ways. Ask, "If I were to make a movie of this text, what decisions would I need to make" (e.g., Is it night? Is there a breeze? Who is present? What are people wearing? Is there something unusual? What sounds are there?) As in a movie, most of these items are background items, those that the camera merely notes in panning; central action and dialogue are what the camera seeks. A few of these incidental details need not distort the determined thrust of the biblical text. Rather, they are an important dimension of effective communication in a multimedia world.

The first encounter with the biblical text in the sermon should take on life. Create in words a movie of the biblical text. Do not retell the whole text at first encounter.

I encourage students not to tell the whole story or argument of the text at this time, particularly if they plan to return to the text later; they will then also need something to say.

Nonetheless, the first encounter with the biblical text in the sermon should lead us back into that text with sufficient detail and background that it starts to take on life. The Word of God should not be made to sound like boring, dusty history. We can make no immediate observations about the biblical text (e.g., "Who would have expected Rachael to do what she did?" or, "My own response to Rachael may be your own"), without its first being clearly focused in the listeners' minds. Too many preachers wrongly assume that the congregation is already fully immersed in the text and its times, simply because it was read aloud in worship as an earlier Scripture reading.

There are at least four easy alternatives, in addition to opening with the biblical text. One possibility is to repeat a conversation or event that was heard or seen, relevant to the central idea that we will develop. Another possibility is to use a central image from the biblical text or from our situation that will figure in the sermon. Third, we may use the introduction to speak of a doctrine or topic of relevance to congregational life. For instance, during Advent we might speak of the Incarnation; or during a congregational crisis we might speak of the doctrine of forgiveness.

Five Approaches to the Intro- duction

1) Discuss the biblical text.

2) Repeat a conversation or event rele- vant to the text.

3) Use an image that will figure in the sermon.

4) Speak of a doctrine or topic.

5) Tell a story that seems to contradict the major concern of the text.

Finally, we may tell a story from experience that seems to deny or contradict the central idea upon which we have decided to preach.[6] This can be an immediate way of developing relevance and of identi- fying the expressed and actual need of the congrega- tion. For instance, if the central idea is "God ministers to the needy," we might tell the story of someone in need who experienced God as absent. Or if preaching on "God answers prayer," we might speak of some- one who prayed that her husband would be healed, whose prayer did not seem to be answered. By the end of the sermon, we would return to this circum- stance in light of the gospel.

Although we do not plunge directly into the heart of the issue in the introduction, we do need to point in the direction we are taking, that is, to the central idea that we are developing, usually explicitly. Listeners need some signal as to what words will reveal the structure and flow of the sermon. These words also allow listeners to engage their own thought. Thus the preacher must help the listeners to hear what is being said; it is not enough simply to say it eventually. The old formula for essays (and sermons) is not far off the mark: "Say what you are going to say, say it, and say what you have said." This needs to be nuanced, how- ever: We merely point to where we are going rather than drive the congregation on a boring tour through the sermon's table of contents. We give them clues that will direct their access to our purpose in the sermon.

The Conclusion

Even as the introduction points to where we are going, the conclu- sion points to where we have been. Less is needed by way of conclu- sion than is often thought. We do not need to summarize the key points of what has been said; this may have been more important when sermons were normally an hour long, in which case a summary could serve to bring the hour into sharp focus. With the shorter norm of sermons today, such review may seem simply pedantic. If we think that the congregation will not grasp our meaning before the conclu- sion, it is time to rewrite the sermon, not write a summary. Said another way, if our meaning has not been heard before the conclusion, it is too late for it to be heard now.

David Buttrick makes a number of suggestions about conclusions; the wisest of these include:

1) Avoid ending the sermon with a question. A posed question (e.g., Will you or won't you bear witness to Jesus Christ?) "will neither be answered or remembered."
2) Avoid quotations in a conclusion that disrupt the point of view and interfere with the direct discourse appropriate to a closing.
3) Avoid personal testimony, for in the conclusion it "will leave a congregation with a consciousness of the preacher rather than the gospel."
4) Use direct, simple, concrete language.[7]

There is no general agreement, nor perhaps need there be, on the style or tone of the conclusion. David Buttrick is wary of the conclusion that seeks to be passionate through repetition of the same sentence structure for several consecutive sentences (e.g., We must go out into the world to . . . We must go out into the world to . . . We must go out into the world to. . . .) In this regard, Buttrick might agree with James S. Stewart, who advocated the decisive ending and "the quiet close": "You will never weaken the force of your final appeal by keeping it restrained."[8] On the other hand, we might agree with a part of the African American tradition, which is energized by passionate repetition, for it has "cultural roots which demand that a sermon end in a celebration,"[9] and this celebration leads us into the world with new hope and confidence.

Most of us do not know where to begin or to end. The problem is apparent when merely telling stories. This common error is most easily addressed if we eliminate the first and last few sentences of our story, for these are usually unnecessary commentary. It is not surprising that the same problem carries over to the sermon as a whole. Revise a sermon with a view to cutting out anything that is mere repetition or commentary. A number of additional principles may be kept in mind:

1) The conclusion should bring a sense of completeness to the sermon.
2) A return to the opening story, or a return to the ending of a powerful story begun in the first half of the sermon, almost always sig-

nals closure to the listeners. The sermon should not extend beyond this; thus, in itself the opening story can provide a fitting close if it is in fact the end. When used, the opening situation should now be briefly recast in terms of the message of the gospel. In other words, the gospel should be seen to make a difference.

3) The conclusion should be pointing to where we have been. It should therefore speak, directly or indirectly, about the major concern of the text (or its transposed version, the major concern of the sermon). Keep the conclusion crisp and clear.

4) The conclusion should also be pointing, directly or indirectly, to the world and our mission in it. The sermon is finished in the life of the congregation, not in the church on Sunday.

The Intended Goal

The preacher's purpose is what shapes the new text of the sermon, in response to the biblical text. While a specific sermon may be designed to meet specific goals, one goal remains constant in preaching: We want the congregation to be encountered by God such that their lives issue in faithful action. As Henry H. Mitchell has said: "The ultimate goal is not what the preacher will *say* about [God] but what [people] will *do*."[10] Lives lived in faith and service, after all, is one purpose of the whole Scripture. Thus of every sermon, listeners should be able to discern an answer to the question, What is required of us?

For our intention of the sermon to be met in this important regard, it should anticipate the kinds of situations to which the congregation is called. These situations need not be sprung upon the congregation at the end of the sermon, where their sudden appearance can impose an overwhelming sense of duty and burden. Again rhetoric can be our guide. What will move people to act? We can let the need for particular mission evolve naturally: Paint the picture of the need in the first portion of the sermon. In a latter section, envision or dream of that same situation, or one like it, transformed according to God's will. In other words, paint the picture of that need being met by God in a manner that is prompted by the biblical text. It is to God's efforts that we join our own work, by God's grace. The cause that we seek to assist is already begun. It is not merely up to us. We do not do our work alone.

Lives lived in faith and service is the intent of the whole Scripture.

Every situation that is named in the sermon becomes a mission situation for the church—an object of its prayer. We also anticipate situations needing ministry. I suggest five introductory principles for this:

186

1) Personalize: let the issue be connected to people, not left as an abstract principle.
2) Humanize: let us meet, through the sermon, people in situations of need so that we are identifying with their experience, not responding to abstract facts, figures, or opinion in the first instance.
3) Inform: relate only the most important information, making certain that all facts are correct and verified.
4) Identify: in addition to ensuring that listeners identify with the people we name, we must be certain they know that we also identify with them.
5) Visualize: allow us to imagine the particular situation (or one like it) transformed in the image of God's love.

I further suggest a few practical exercises to assist the mission focus of our sermons.

Exercises 9:1-4 Write your own example for each category below:

9:1 Develop situations and issues in ways that touch people where they are and mobilize them toward change, rather than leaving them frozen and immobilized by the immensity of the demand.

Example: To tell people that "everything we buy goes back into the ground" is to tell them the truth about the pollution of our environment, but if left there it can create a sense of despair. The problem is too big. What can we do that will make any difference? The clue here may be to involve the congregation. For instance, help us to see the positive consequences of even one small act of stewardship, repeated each day, starting with a few persons, working up to thousands, over several years. Help us to get a sense of the momentum of history and to remember also that human efforts on their own are never the whole story.

9:2 Enable mission by identifying God's action in relation to such situations. Listeners are not empowered simply by knowing of the existence of sin and evil. It is God who empowers the overthrow of these powers. If using an emotionally difficult story in the first section of the sermon, an equally powerful Good News story of God's action in the world is needed to balance the sermon.

Example: The first half of a student sermon contained an account of a woman in a Nazi prison camp. It was a powerful story, a horrible account of the reality of human sin. Specific details of violence were mercifully and necessarily omitted. By the end of the sermon, however, we had still not encountered God doing anything active, which might lead us to trust that God was more powerful, even than the worst of human deeds. Such a story cannot be used unless we have something of equal emotional and theological force to counter it.

9:3 If we lack a strong story of Good News to achieve the necessary counterbalance, as required, we may develop an idea with sufficient rhetorical passion and detail to provide the necessary balance.

Example: Someone might say in a sermon, "Christ's Reign is centered relationships, not worldly power." It is a good idea, rooted in the text John 12:9-21, but it needs development and focus to become an event we experience. Here is one attempt:

If Christ's love had nothing to do with us, it would be simply another abstract idea that we have to stretch our minds around, in a world of far too many abstractions, with far too much that is impersonal, and far too many broken relations. But this reign of Christ is personal, is intimate and caring. It is not something we need to read about in the morning paper or wait for the evening news to see. We may not have known Christ when we came here, but we may know Christ as we leave. Even in this brief time together, Christ has re-established a relationship with you. When you leave the doors of this church today, you cannot leave him behind, for he is going ahead of you, and with you. There are no doors you will enter this week that he will not already have entered. There is no trouble you can get into that will keep him away. Our ruler is a close relative of ours. We are part of his family. He is not a distant relative, like some cousin you see every few years, if it is convenient. Our Christ is the resurrected ruler who is ever present, in the power of the Holy Spirit, when the sun is setting, in the middle of the night, and in the blaze of the morning light, to help us see love through.

9:4 Create a sense of excitement about the wonderful things God will be doing this week, both with and without our help. Hear the closing moments of one of James S. Stewart's sermons, as follows.

Example: It is true that he is here in this church at this moment, and that if only we were not fast held behind the gates of sense and flesh we should actually see Him here, face to face, now. It is true that He can take our lives and interpenetrate them with his own, to enable us to say, "I live, yet not I, but Christ liveth in me." It is true that one day we are going to see Him face to face without any veil at all.

These things are true. And you believe them. But today I am begging you not only to believe them—but to imagine them, to visualize them, to see them, and to act on the basis of them. For it is as we let the shining, super-charged truth of them get hold of us, really take possession of us, that like Simeon we shall meet Christ reborn for us this Advent time.

And then? Why then, what does it matter whether life be long or short? If it is to be a long day's strenuous march, what joy, O Christ, to have Thy blessed companionship all the way! If it is to be a brief moment and a sudden call— "Lord, now lettest Thou Thy servant depart in peace, for mine eyes have seen thy salvation."[11]

These few suggestions with regard to sermon body, introduction, conclusion, and mission may be enough to get students started in the writing of their own sermons. Composing the sermon is also the focus of the remainder of this book. In the concluding chapter we will return in greater detail to mission goals of the sermon.

A Brief History of Stage Four

Here, at this fourth stage in the hermeneutical process, we preachers run into problems with other disciplines. From the beginning of our current study, one of the themes has been the importance of words. We devalue preaching by thinking of our task as simply "writing a sermon." This is a natural way of thinking because of the way in which our courses are usually arranged in seminary, divided into semiautonomous departments that can operate largely without direct concern for proclamation.

As a result we think of the interpretation process in compartmentalized ways: The first three hermeneutical stages (what the text says, what the text means, and what experience says) are often perceived as subjects generally covered by the biblical, historical, ethical, and theological departments. Moreover, if three stages are in fact recognized (since many follow Gadamer and Ricoeur in only recognizing the first two), we are given a message that this is the end of the hermeneutical process.

We do not often find writers in hermeneutics going beyond these three[12]—to consider how their own process of articulating a response affects the interpretation that is presented. This omission has caused serious problems for homiletics.

Invisible Homiletics

Our fourth stage of hermeneutics is of relevance to all disciplines, and is of particular relevance to preaching. Because this stage has

189

been generally overlooked, homiletics is rendered invisible in hermeneutical discussions. Why does that matter? We thereby conceive of preaching as an application of learnings already provided, a type of technique, such as "how to" do creative writing or music.[13] Preaching is appropriately conceived as creative, but this "how to" attitude discourages attention to proclamation and devalues the practice of the church. If something is thought to be "applied," so our thinking goes, it belongs in the Practical or Pastoral Theology Department. Simply the existence of practical theology institutionalizes the "how to" attitude, and encourages other departments not to consider aspects of preaching in case there is a violation of someone else's intellectual turf. Preaching however is our mutual interest.

Moreover, our courses in all disciplines, not just preaching, are concerned with "how to produce new texts," whether those new texts are essays (with requirements varying amongst disciplines), exegetical assignments, articles, journal entries, narratives, book reports, verbatim accounts, class presentations, sermons, or whatever.

The prevalent attitude that serves to diminish preaching and the Word of God conceives of the sermon as something that begins at the end of the hermeneutical process after the interpretation has been determined. However, we have seen that preaching is our focus from the beginning. The fact that we are going to preach instructs our study from the very start. We do not wait until our exegetical study of the text is complete and an interpretation of the text is rendered to contemplate sermonic possibility. If as preachers we were to organize our weeks in this compartmentalized manner (i.e., today I do Bible exegesis; tomorrow I do theology), and were to begin thinking about what we will actually preach only on Friday, our preaching might include many facts but it would probably lack unity and relevance.

Equally important, as we have also seen, is that our pulpit needs are focused needs. Homiletical interests are different from the interests of theology and Bible when preaching is ignored. For example, as preachers we concentrate on central doctrines, we formulate what we say for oral delivery, we treat the exegetical process in relation to faith, not only as history in the first instance, and we use it to a specific purpose—to identify potential preaching needs. The more we bring our preaching needs to our study of theology and Bible, the more directly those disciplines will contribute to proclamation. We can no longer merely assume that courses in other disciplines will necessarily result in better preaching or greater ability to meet the needs of congregations.

The current invisibility of our fourth stage in hermeneutics results in another problem. Preaching is seen as different in nature from other theological pursuits—as though it is a form of technology. However, interpretation of the Bible and our world is its task, and every discipline must produce new texts (spoken or written). Texts are responses to something that is said. Texts are communication itself. Thus practitioners in every discipline need to be attentive to the process of their formation. Texts never happen out of nowhere. They are purposely composed to conform with established genres and recognized rhetorical standards.

Visible Homiletics

Hermeneutics is concerned with how understanding takes place. Without the words that make our response to a text, no interpretation of that text has happened. The response is the interpretation; thus, how this response is made is an essential part of the hermeneutical process, not something added to it at the end. We all depend on new texts and promote their established conventions, even in parenting; for example, when teaching children the right kinds of things to say. Mostly we promote these conventions without being conscious of it, or without recognizing their importance. "How" and "what," form and content, theory and method, purpose and function repeatedly intersect in a tight weave. In the case of preaching, we choose to be exceptionally conscious of what and how we are (and are not) communicating. Much depends on this consciousness.

Our understanding of hermeneutics is being pushed to expand, not least by postmodern literary criticism. We are now attentive to the manner in which technology for communication affects the apprehension of its message. Boundaries that were formerly fixed have started to crumble: between a literary text and its interpreting commentary, between the writer and the critic, and between the literary text and its receiving community. Roland Barthes, the famous French literary critic, for example, helped to extend hermeneutics by inverting the usual meaning of "text" and "work" (i.e., that which results from a text). In his inversion:

The work is concrete, occupying a portion of book-space (in a library, for example); the Text, on the other hand, is a methodological field. . . . The work can be seen in bookstores, in card catalogues, and on course lists, while the text reveals itself, articulates itself according to or against certain rules [e.g. grammar and syntax]. While the work is held in the hand, the text is held in language: it exists only as discourse. The Text is not the decomposition of the work; rather it is the work that is the Text's imaginary tail. In other words, the Text is experienced only in an activity, a production. It follows that the Text cannot stop, at the end of a library shelf . . . [14]

In other words, in postmodern criticism, the ground shifts from in and behind the literary text to in front of the text, in the reader's encounter of it, such that Barthes claims this activity to be the real text.

Stanley Hauerwas, by a similar venture, claims that there is no "real meaning" of biblical texts that may be determined abstractly by an individual scholar or preacher. Only recipients acculturated within a community of faith supply the meaning: "The practice of preaching is just that—disciplined practice. I make no claims to be interpreting the Scripture in order to get at the 'real meaning.' The 'meaning' is that use to which I put these texts for the upbuilding of the Church."[15] Barthes, Hauerwas, and others would find suspect the modern attempt to keep preaching invisible, excluding it from hermeneutics, though they might vary in their estimation of preaching's relevance.

We conceive of preaching as God's event, not as a process that happens at the end of the hermeneutical process, but as something that is an integral part of it, and that gives direction to each stage. The sermon is composed only in continuing dialogue with all of the preceding stages of interpretation. The rules for sermon-making that sometimes give rise to "how to" assessment and dismissal, are in fact no different in kind from the theory of translation and interpretation used in biblical study (for instance in stages one and two).[16] Such rules are merely their counterpoint in praxis.

For example, an explanation of the biblical text sought to discover, or critique, the unity of a work that already exists (how its parts relate to its whole, and its whole to its parts). Our final stage of authorial purpose or intent in composing a sermon, by contrast creates a text such that its parts and whole work to unified purpose and effect. Only with the union of all four stages do we have the true fusion of horizons (biblical and contemporary) which Hans-Georg Gadamer names as the purpose of hermeneutics. In other words, we claim here a simple truth: The completion of interpretation is the creation of a new text, be it sermon, essay, or article, and this alters our understanding of hermeneutics.

This hermeneutical square requires a positive revaluing of the task of preaching, necessary if it is to be reconceived and communicated as an event of God. How we think of something affects practice. The words we use to describe it affect how we do it. If we are to give our

best efforts to preaching, we need to understand it correctly in relation to other disciplines and honor it accordingly.

To develop in detail how we give expression to our intent as
preachers, the fourth stage of our hermeneutical process, we turn in
the next section to study the tradition of poetics and preaching. In
particular we will explore the well-traveled paths of propositional
and narrative preaching. In doing this we will further uncover helpful
tasks for the last half of the preacher's week.

Review Questions for Chapter Nine

1) Which of the following was represented as an expansion of the
   text?
   a) translation as substitution, grammar, and syntax
   b) consultation of the commentaries
   c) consultation of experience
   d) intent of the preacher
   e) all of the above   [e]

2) It was suggested that one of the most difficult tasks in sermon
   composition for many students is to
   a) keep the sermon moving between the biblical text and our
      situation
   b) focus thought on or toward just one idea
   c) feel good about themselves
   d) feel good about their congregations   [b]

3) Which of the following is identified as true of the practice of
   frequent switching between the biblical text and our situation?
   a) establishes a pleasing rhythm
   b) demonstrates the preacher's keen mind
   c) helps the congregation to lose their way
   d) shows concern to connect with the Bible   [c]

4) Which was not one of the five suggestions for the introduction?
   a) discuss the biblical text
   b) develop a central image
   c) tell a story that contradicts the gospel
   d) go to the heart of the matter
   e) repeat a relevant conversation or event
   f) speak of a doctrine or topic   [d]

5) Which is right? The conclusion should
   a) avoid quotations
   b) avoid personal testimony
   c) point to the world
   d) point to where the sermon has been
   e) all of the above   [e]

6) Homiletics is mistakenly invisible because
   a) sermons are spoken not seen
   b) it is interpreted as "how to"
   c) preaching is similar to other disciplines
   d) none of the above   [b]

Questions for Discussion

1) Try to explain how you understand the "meaning" of Scripture, with particular reference to God, the biblical text, and the community living its life in faith.
2) In your opinion, can a preacher be effective if God seems hidden and remote?

Sermon Exercises for Section III: Hermeneutics

Exercise 9:5 Students have already completed most of the following exercise, with the exception of ordering the paired concerns for Wednesday. Do that now, paying attention to focusing the entire sermon on just the central idea. Each time we preach we might try to complete the following worksheet. Students may now wish to try a first quick draft of a sermon, saving a more substantial draft until after the next chapters.

A Preacher's Practice Worksheet

Romans 8:1-11 (See pages 255-59 for a full sermon on this text.)

1) *Monday: What the text says*—Here give answers to the literary and theological questions of the biblical text, based on your own reading, without commentaries (only a sampling of these is included here):

• The form is a letter of Paul sent to Christians in Rome, whom he mostly does not yet know.
• The situation is a debate between Jewish and Gentile Christians about the law.

194

- The message is radical, that is, no condemnation for Christians; Christians are free of the power of sin and death; Jesus' death condemns sin to death; Jesus' death makes followers alive to the Spirit; people of the Spirit keep their minds on things of the Spirit; thinking of the flesh leads to death; thinking of the Spirit leads to peace; God's law opposes the flesh.
- My initial naive response: I like the positive overall tone, but I get stuck on keeping our minds on things of the Spirit. How is this not acceptance of injustice and suffering in this world, in favor of another world to come?

2) *Tuesday: What the text means*—Various concerns of the text confirmed by study of the commentaries are listed, and a major concern of the text is identified (again, only samples are given here):

- Christians are free of the power of sin and death. (g)
- Rome's Gentile Christians are unwelcoming of their Jewish Christian returnees from exile. (j)
- Paul's upcoming Jerusalem hearing depends upon Gentile-Jewish harmony in his ministry. (j)
- The power of the law to condemn is broken by the Spirit's purpose of life. (g)
- Jesus' death makes us alive to the Spirit. (g)
- Spiritual things lead to peace. (g)

Possible major concern of the text: (g) God is the source of all hope. Or, more active: God gives hope. (I am trying to identify an idea that gives me a sense of the whole.)

3) *Wednesday: What experience says*—Notes in the form of concerns of the text and concerns of the sermon (Buttrick's "moves"; our possible paragraphs) are selected and arranged in an appropriate sequence. If hope is the focus, the movement is from judgment to grace. In these transpositions, remember that the concerns of the sermon are true for our day (not necessarily true to the text, although prompted by the text).

t: Paul's upcoming Jerusalem hearing depends upon Gentile-Jewish harmony in his ministry. (j)
s: The survival of humanity is threatened by our divisions. (j)

t: Things of the flesh keep the mind on the flesh.
s: Many of those who suffer have not energy for the Spirit.

Major t: God gives hope. (g)
Major s: God gives us hope. (g)

t: Christians are free of the power of sin and death. (g)
s: Christ frees us from death's power. (g)

4) *Thursday/Friday: What the preacher says*—The full sermon is written, perhaps the first half on Thursday morning and the second half on Friday morning.

SECTION
IV

The Tradition of Poetics

Perhaps no word is so readily associated with rhetoric as poetics, largely because of Aristotle's writings on each. Given their comparative lengths (his *Rhetoric*, including *Topics*, is three hundred pages in his *Collected Works*—his *Poetics* is only twenty-five), their equal status in our minds is surprising. Of course some matters relating to classical poetics were discussed as rhetoric, for instance metaphor. Also, the fields naturally overlap, for both are concerned with words and communication. Moreover, in the ancient world, rhetoric was dominant. Although it evolved to provide the basis of education, forms of entertainment (e.g., debate), and social grace, rhetoric was solidly rooted in the legal, economic, and political systems of the day.

In our world the situation is largely reversed: Poetics, relating to the arts and literary criticism, has dominated rhetoric, and in fact helped to revive it. Some preachers narrowly associate poetics with the insertion of a poem to the end of a sermon, as once was popular, or with matters of rhythm and rhyme related to poetry. However, even for Aristotle poetics was far-reaching. It included a number of topics: language, form, rhythm, rhyme, meter, diction, character, unity, imitation, fiction, tragedy, comedy, epic, plot, and the like. Today it is larger still. It includes unity, content, and function; narrative (Aristotle's focus on plot); genre (beyond Aristotle's tragedy and comedy); effect (beyond *catharsis*, which for Aristotle was the purging of undesirable emotions); imagination; imitation of reality (Aristotle's *mimesis*); and a host of modern ideas having to do with various kinds of literary criticism (e.g., feminist, psychoanalytic, sociological, postmodern).

In this section we continue to explore the fourth stage of the hermeneutical task, for here we compose the sermon. In successive chapters we will examine: the structure of the sermon and issues concerning narrative and propositional sermons; devices for strengthening linear thought and polar thought in preaching; and ways of telling stories to strengthen God's purposes of mission in the sermon.

ARRANGING THE SERMON: UNITY AND FORM

A new appreciation of organic unity contributes to the current homiletical revolution. Form and structure of sermons is explored through discussion of propositional and narrative preaching. It is suggested that these terms have been stretched beyond their limits and, as a result, that they encourage preachers to make false homiletical choices. A synthesis of the best of both forms is advised, as well as more attention to subforms.

As we begin to consider homiletical poetics, we will confine ourselves primarily to issues of unity, form, function, and content as these have been traditionally discussed. We begin by considering a change in attitude toward unity in preaching that in some ways began the current homiletical revolution. It led to two parallel streams in current homiletics. Propositional preaching emphasizes propositions and principles of logical thought. Narrative preaching emphasizes story and principles of art. Whatever the form, our controlling purpose throughout is reflected in James S. Stewart's theological test of a sermon for a congregation: "Did they, or did they not, meet God today?"[1]

Unity

H. Grady Davis was a key founder of homiletics as practiced today. In 1958 he was one of the first voices to signal a shift to a new understanding of unity in the sermon. Two decades of teaching homiletics had led him to conclude that the solutions for good preaching "lie neither in the traditional study of homiletical forms, nor in a preoccupation with the vital content of preaching apart from the form it takes, but in a sharper awareness that content and form are two inseparable elements of the same thing."[2] One of the first steps in this move to unite form and content was to argue for organic unity in preaching theory. (He was not its first practitioner, for many predecessors throughout the ages used organic form. In fact, Romantic literary theorists had been urging union of form and content in art in the early 1800s.) A decade later David James Randolph was making a similar point about the need to unite message and form: "The sermon seeks forms of construction and communication which are consistent with the message it intends to convey, not necessarily those which are most traditional."[3] We in our own time have been locked in a debate between propositional and narrative form; while we have discovered the importance of organic unity, we may still need to be reminded of Davis's point that form in itself is not the issue.

When we say that the unity of the sermon is organic, we mean more than that it has movement, serves one central idea or plot, and must hold together as a unified whole. Organic unity implies that a sermon, like an organism, has a life of its own. It lives by principles that have to do with how parts relate to one another and contribute toward the whole, and how the whole influences each of the parts. There is often an organic quality to thought itself, particularly in conversation where the subjects flow easily from one to the other without formal announcement or closure.

Moreover, the growing recovery and influence of rhetoric is helping us to understand that even unity of form and content is insufficient. They must be united with function. We speak for a reason. We speak in a specific setting to a specific purpose, often of persuasion or identification. Thus we not only consider the unity of our composition as a whole, but also the unity of our composition as a rhetorical event that hospitably anticipates listeners and their needs.

Static unity, by contrast, is unity imposed on material by a predetermined structure or genre. The unity thus generated conforms to standards that do not primarily originate within the particular work itself. It is important not to equate static unity with bad art. For example, Leonardo da Vinci's painting *The Last Supper* leaves the near side of the table unoccupied, not because people actually ate that way, but because he wanted to capture faces, and he was painting in a classical style, which did not pretend to imitate what was natural or authentic. Nonetheless within that style there is much that is exceedingly natural. Similarly, when the great preacher and poet of the early 1600s, George Herbert, wrote the poem "Redemption," he chose to write it as a sonnet in trochaic pentameter (/ˇ ˇ/ˇ ˇ) with a definite rhyme scheme (abba, cdcd, effe, gg). This largely predetermined structure (the sort we find in most hymns) meant that words were often chosen to fit the verse and rhyme scheme, rather than flowing in a more natural, less structured way, *guided by developing patterns of thought and imagery.*

A preacher who sets out to write a sermon with three points and subpoints, without considering the biblical text, is choosing static unity. However, sermons often employ static unity not by virtue of their having points but by having points that are not inherent to the biblical text, or that do not grow one from the other. Here is static unity of a clumsy sort in a three-point sermon: God is good; God is glad; God is gracious. The unity here is from parallelism, alliteration, and God as the consistent subject. The same points could conceivably be found in a variety of biblical texts (even though they might not derive from the most important concerns of the text). The points could be shuffled in a different order, largely without affecting the meaning of the whole.

Organic unity implies that a sermon, like an organism, has a life of its own. Static unity, by contrast, is unity imposed on material by a predetermined structure or genre. Sermons often employ static unity not by the fact of their having points, but by having points that are not inherent to the biblical text, or that do not grow one from the other.

Similarly, a preacher may be using static unity of the worst sort in developing for instance a concern of the text: the idea may be treated as a general topic that is loosely discussed, one in a continuing series, yet without much direction or purpose, other than to cover the subject. For organic unity, this development needs direction, theological purpose, and some sense of movement, for instance a deepening sense of judgment or grace. The overall thought needs to be seen to arise from this one idea and lead back toward it, once completed. The development of the concern of the text thereby ceases to function as a static collection of thoughts or images.

Static unity of the worst sort can also be present in the delivery of a speech. If what is said connects to nothing obvious in the listeners' lives and is not altered by the nature of the audience, the event has static unity. The speaker's agenda is the imposed structure of the occasion. Obviously this can be accentuated by a monotone voice, lack of eye contact through reading, or the fact that the delivery in other ways ignores the listeners.

Static unity of the best sort is seen when structure serves the purpose, the purpose being more than just identifying three points. For instance, if the purpose of a sermon is to explore a certain issue, it might be good to follow some form of thesis, antithesis, synthesis, dealing with essential, interrelated matters.

Organic unity came to prominence in the Western world through the Romantic revolution in the arts roughly between 1790 and 1840.[4] The Romantics were reacting to classical art, urbanization, and the industrial revolution. Their art valued the wildness of nature, people and nature living in harmony, metaphor, human emotion, spirituality, imagination, and the inner workings of the mind. In important ways the Romantics broke ground, for instance, for fields as diverse as today's contemporary art, education theory, hermeneutical theory, and psychoanalysis.

Concerning issues like unity, form, imagination, and metaphor, theology apparently never had a Romantic revolution. It may be this that is happening now.

Theology was directly affected by the Romantic movement, particularly through Schleiermacher (1768–1834), whose emphasis on experience may be said to have started the recent revolution we have seen in theology. His "On Religion: Addresses in Response to Its Cultural Despisers" reduced doctrine to a secondary role in favor of faith, intuition, and absolute dependence upon God. He said that "all doctrines and dogmas that many take to be the essence of religion, . . . simply result from that contemplation of feeling";[5] they refer less to attributes of God than to our feeling of absolute dependence upon God.

Concerning issues like unity, form, imagination, and metaphor, however, a Romantic revolution only recently appears to be underway in theology, under different labels.[6] A few individuals in theology clearly appropriated and advanced the learnings of the Romantics, to be sure. Horace Bushnell in the 1840s developed an organic theory of education, a theology of language centering on imagination, and defended multiple meanings in a biblical text as both natural and organic, "even as a stalk of corn pushes out leaf from within leaf by a growth that is its unsheathing."[7] Paul Tillich and others were key voices in correlating biblical truth and theological language to situations of changing culture, and art to theological purpose.[8] Until recent decades, and in contrast to many disciplines in the arts, such influential voices have been few.

Davis wrote the following words, which are the best description we have of organic unity in preaching. He claimed that this is not a poem but an alternative to a traditional sermon outline. The first line is his "idea that grows" (anticipating in some ways both Craddock's inductive approach and Buttrick's idea of the listener's developing consciousness). His words echo both Horace Bushnell, and the 1926 poem by Archibald Macleish, "Ars Poetica" (the epigraph of this book).[9] Note also his reworking of Augustine's injunction that preaching should teach, delight, and persuade (*On Christian Doctrine*, IV, 9ff.):

Design for a Sermon

A sermon should be like a tree.

It should be a living organism:
 With one sturdy thought like a single stem
 With natural limbs reaching up into the light.

It should have deep roots:
 As much unseen as above the surface
 Roots spreading as widely as its branches spread
 Roots deep underground
  In the soil of life's struggle
  In the subsoil of the eternal Word.

It should show nothing but its own unfolding parts:
 Branches that thrust out by the force of its inner life
 Sentences like leaves native to this very spray
  True to the species
  Not taken from alien growths
 Illustrations like blossoms opening from
  inside these very twigs
 Not brightly colored kites
  Pulled from the wind of somebody else's thought
  Entangled in these branches.

It should bear flowers and fruit at the
 same time like the orange:
 Having something for food
 For immediate nourishment
 Having something for delight
 For present beauty and fragrance
 For the joy of hope
 For the harvest of a distant day.

To be all this it must grow in a warm climate:
 In loam enriched by death
 In love like the all-seeing and all-cherishing sun
 In trust like the sleep-sheltering night
 In pity like the rain.

     —H. Grady Davis[10]

Davis's pioneering work with organic unity (which he found operating in many great sermons of the past) also pioneered discussion of both deductive and inductive preaching, topics that would later become of great importance to homiletics and to which we will return. His influential book arguably was the beginning of the current revolution in homiletics. Recently, Henry H. Mitchell has helped move organic unity in the direction of shaping consciousness, purposely echoing David Buttrick: "Am I struggling to get a point across or am I working at a flow in consciousness which will be used to beget trust and change behavior? Another way to put it is, Do I see and feel what I'm talking about, or am I myself obsessed with clever, scholarly data and abstract ideas?"[11]

It would be fair for us to ask why we should be concerned about unity, beyond making sure that what we say "holds together." The preacher's art, we could argue, is not the proper focus for the preacher or the congregation. God can use whatever faithful offering we make, unified or not. What matters is the unity with which people perceive all creation, under God.

While true, the other side of this particular argument has had less exposure. Organic unity in preaching has implications in at least four areas in addition to form:

1) Communication—In a television world of largely organic communication, a preacher's lack of art through mechanical or static use of rhyming points can itself become a focus of attention, distracting attention from the Word.
2) Pastoral relationships—Organic unity implies treating people as God's loved ones, valuing what they have to offer as listeners with ministries, and recognizing that they respond with more than just their emotions, or just their heads, to what is said (in ways we have identified with logos, pathos, and ethos).
3) Theological worldview—Theology at times has imposed a static structure upon reality, such that experience is deemed irrelevant (in the manner, for instance, of some of the worst neoorthodox theology). Alternatively, experience becomes our primary determinant (for example, in the manner of some of the worst liberal theology). If we perpetuate this in preaching we encourage lack of unity in life and faith.
4) Mission—If we think organically, our theology will be holistic, modeling the connectedness of all things and all acts. This assumption is common in postmodern thought and has particular implica-

tion for preaching. We may be boldly positive toward our congregations as we preach, assuming: that in our baptism we have already chosen Christ; that as a congregation we long to be doing Christ's work; that faith is expressed in lived life; that our joy is incomplete while others suffer; and that in encountering us, God empowers us for mission.

Of course when unity was understood statically, as something to be imposed on material rather than arising from it, inclusion of these matters in discussing unity would have seemed strange. Static unity tends more easily to be confined to form, while organic unity of necessity is also concerned with matters of content and systems of interconnection.

Up to this point we have maintained the union of form, content, and function. We do not abandon that idea now as we turn to consider more closely matters of sermon form.

Propositional and Narrative Poles

The current revolution in homiletics has the issue of form as its catalyst and center—in particular the differences between propositional and narrative preaching. In fact, these two have been so polarized, and the issues behind them so distorted that we may be in need of additional categories (and hence new practice).

The "propositional" or "propositional-discursive" form is sufficiently elastic to include most traditional sermon types. Propositional refers to logical proposals, statements, or claims. Discursive comes from the Latin word meaning "to run about," implying an argument that moves from point to point, gradually building a strong, reasoned position.

Commonly referred to as the three-point or point-form sermon, it in fact has many varieties (even as it can have many or few points). Common to all, in theory at least, has been the encouragement of one central proposition or idea. Other ideas become lesser propositions, often with their own subpoints.

This has been the bread-and-butter sermon of the church for the last eight hundred years, for it has great flexibility, versatility, and possible enduring potential. It came to prominence around 1200 with the recovery of Aristotle and thus of empirical evidence based in reason.[12] Already in 1300, Robert of Basevorn was commenting, "Only three statements, or the equivalent of three, are used in the theme—

either from respect to the Trinity, or because a threefold cord is not easily broken, or because this method is mostly followed by Bernard [of Clairvaux], or, as I think more likely, because it is more convenient for the set time of the sermon."[13]

Three historical subforms employing static unity influenced the development of propositional preaching:

1) The propositional sermon commonly exhibits an exegesis-application approach. This form dates back to the synagogue, if not to the time of building the Second Temple (see Neh. 8:1-8), where the norm was to read Scripture and comment upon it. Under Charlemagne, priests were to read the Latin New Testament and then to follow with a translation, an explanation of the text, and an application of it to the people's lives. The Puritan plain-style sermon (exposition, doctrine, application) was yet another modification, in which brief exegesis led to a specific doctrine that then became the subject of the sermon applied to the life of the people.
2) Another practice that had impact was the medieval disputation, followed by nearly all of the great teachers of the period. Teachers like Thomas Aquinas would begin with a question, move to arguments against the position, and then move to arguments for it. This approach is more commonly known from Hegel's thesis, antithesis, synthesis. Its three-part movement was easily adapted to the point-form of preaching.
3) A third form from classical times has been the syllogism, the basic unit of ancient logic. It also has a natural three-point movement: if A, and B, then C.

We can already see that point-form can encourage an idea-centered approach. Propositional preaching can be excellent for the communication of information. Does this mean that propositional preaching must be identified with preaching as information? Probably not, although this is one area (to which we will also return) in which current homiletics may be at fault.

For precisely this identification with preaching as information, propositional preaching has drawn fire in recent decades. It seemingly represents, correctly or incorrectly, an authoritarian style of ministry, in which the preacher stands over the congregation rather than with them under the Word, using a lecturing style of proclamation.

Of course there were other reasons for change. For example, propositional preaching seemingly arose: when the preacher was automatically granted considerable authority; when little distinction was made between the preacher's opinion and actual fact; when fewer things in society were open to interpretation; when church attendance was a social duty and congregations were a captive audience; and when, because of lack of formal education, congregations sought information and learning more than, for instance, integration and shared perspective.

Many preachers used propositional form as a static three-point structure for every sermon. The problem with points is not points: They can be helpful on occasion for listeners to hear what is being said; for instance, if there are three practical things to try in our exercise of Christian life this week. They can easily be misused or overused however, when the preacher's agenda becomes imposed on the text or on the listeners. Points are chosen primarily to help the preacher not the listener. The thought line of the preacher becomes our rule rather than our guide. In the most extreme instances, the overall purpose becomes the preacher's information, rather than the listener's process of reflection and identification with the material in arriving at his or her own understanding.[14] The difficulty is heightened by a general lack of tolerance for authority that is prevalent today: Listeners are often unwilling to be submissive to the agenda of a preacher who wishes to be controlling, particularly if the preacher's agenda does not take account of the congregation's need. The problem with points arises when the listeners, in hearing the points, become bored and ask, What is the point? In actual practice, many homiletical points did not merit the attention that they were given.

> *The problem with points is not points. The problem with points arises when the listeners, in hearing the points, become bored and ask, What is the point?*

Moreover, those at the forefront of change perceived a revaluing of experience for education. In 1970, Charles L. Rice argued for the use of imagination along with reason in preaching, and suggested several story-based forms modeled from literature: He was against "the marshaling of arguments and neat regimentation of propositions. Life does not present itself in that form—life does not feel that way."[15] Stephen Crites, in a landmark essay in 1971, argued that narrative or story, far from being an abstraction from reality, is in fact the way in which we experience it.[16]

Also in 1971, Fred B. Craddock published *As One Without Authority*, in which he developed ideas of H. Grady Davis in advocating a new model of inductive preaching based on the preacher's own experience of the biblical text.[17] There was new interest from European Americans in the rhetorically sensitive, story-based, oral traditions of many African American churches. The possibility of objective knowledge was increasingly in question from a variety of sources, even as authority in general came increasingly under suspicion in a post-Watergate, post–Vietnam War era. The Bible was recognized as largely story, as were the parables central to Jesus' own preaching. Perhaps more compelling than any of these changes, however, was the effect of television: Its medium was mainly narrative, and it was shaping the way listeners in the congregation actually thought.

Narrative in one form or another had always been present in preaching. It had largely lost its strength in some traditions, having been reduced to canned stories or merchandised illustrations that only served to make plain a point that had already been established. The power of narrative to make its own points in its own ways had never been lost for instance in many African American and some regional churches that were in touch with their oral roots. When preaching seemed in decay, oral storytelling and literature (including biblical) were examined more closely. What we call narrative preaching thus arose to meet the changing needs of re-forming congregations, many of whom were in search of narratives that would bind them together.

A narrative sermon is a sermon that makes primary use of story to develop an idea, attitude, or experience for the congregation. It proceeds not by argument and propositions but by plot, character, and emotion (another version of logos, ethos, and pathos). Its truth is recognized not through logical reasoning and objective proof. Rather, the sermon is tested by its correspondence to Scripture and life experience: "Does this reflect life as I know it in faith?" Its source of unity is poetics (principles of art and literature), for example: plot; controlling images; a particular event, location, or time; identification; a sense of completed action, growth, or emotional resolution. Narration implies a flexible organic structure and varied forms: Structure is experienced to emerge out of events of the story rather than to be imposed on them. Narration implies style as well as form: Something is told, or related, in the conversational manner of life experience. The model for language shifts from the essay to the novel and short story.

The chart on pages 210-13 lists common varieties of propositional and narrative sermons.

208

Problems in the Homiletical Camp

How we think about sermon form affects how we practice our craft. For all of the gains of recent decades, there are also troubling signs that we have built our homiletical house above an underground stream. The terms *propositional* and *narrative,* helpful though they have been in helping us move in new directions, are inadequate in themselves to serve as our only foundations. With so much weight on them already, they are starting to show the strain. Many preachers are practicing a middle way, at neither end of the propositional or narrative extremes.

Consider, for instance, the common identification of propositional preaching with abstract thought and preaching as information. We have seen that this form is indeed well suited for communicating information, abstract or concrete. But as preachers newly awakened to the persuasive power of logos, ethos, and pathos, we may also begin conceiving of points in relational (ethos) and emotive (pathos) ways. Moreover, we may see that the issue with propositional preaching at times has been with static structure. Propositional preaching can employ organic form, however.

Consider also the common identification of some propositional preaching in history with poor biblical exegesis. Verses were often quoted out of context. Even when historical-critical approaches began to flourish in schools, preachers were unsure of how to use such methodology in the pulpit. Without defending these preachers—for problems persist with our use of historical criticism as well—we can say that Christian faith was their priority: Rather than a specific verse or verses, their text was the entire canon. So there is nothing inherent to the form of the propositional sermon that prevents proper treatment of Scripture, or that merits its rejection on biblical grounds.

The adjective *narrative* is also being stretched. Imagination or creativity has been identified with narrative, when in fact creativity can be found in any genre,[18] and poor narration can be as devoid of imagination as any computerized telephone answering message. It could be argued that though in narrative preaching we have a newly recovered form, genre, function, and style, we have not yet found sufficient ways to identify quality, whatever the form.

We could go a step farther. Narration is associated with sermons that treat listeners as partners in learning and as participants in what is said (i.e., in the man-

Although in narration we have a newly recovered form, genre, function, or style of preaching, we have not yet found sufficient ways to identify quality, whatever the form.

209

PROPOSITIONAL PREACHING

TYPES OF PROPOSITIONAL SERMON

Exegetical Sermons: A biblical text is treated line by line, or verse by verse, to explain its meaning and relevance for today. Examples of this form extend from at least Cyprian *(On the Lord's Prayer)* to Karl Barth.

Expository Sermons: Preachers frequently begin with an introduction, exposit the biblical text (i.e., explain and interpret a theme) in one lengthy exegetical section, move to some form of bridge to our own time and situation, apply the text to our own lives, and end with a conclusion, possibly including an exhortation to action.

Topical or Thematic Sermons: A theme is developed from contemporary life or from pastoral experience. Harry Emerson Fosdick (1878–1969) and others used this form, often without reference to a specific biblical text, and perhaps unfairly earned for it the label "unbiblical." Preachers could progress up a ladder of points of increasing importance; or could examine a single idea from many angles, as though it were a faceted jewel; or could begin with an emotionally powerful story that would culminate in some spiritual insight, with appropriate lessons for the congregation. Ron Allen has recently revived this form (see pp. 163-64, 216-17).

Doctrinal Sermons: Similar to the topical sermon, the theme is a particular Christian doctrine, and often free use is made of theologians and Scripture.

Puritan Plain Style Sermon: This label originally identified a sermon that used plain imagery, minimal structural divisions, and that was delivered in the plain style of rhetoric classically reserved for teaching (in contrast to the middle and grand styles for pleasure and persuasion, respectively). Although now perhaps disappearing, it evolved with Wesley and others to follow the pattern: exegesis of a biblical verse in the introduction; identification and development of a particular doctrine, which forms most of the body of the sermon (with reference to any Scripture); and eventual application and conclusion.

TYPICAL USE OF POINTS

Two or more points are taken:

—from one verse of Scripture: For example, John 1:1 "In the beginning was the Word, and the Word was with God, and the Word was God." Here the verse is a three-part verse. Preachers have sought to process verses through the lens of pastoral and prophetic need; hence the possibility: (1) God made all in the beginning, (2) the Christ we know was with God, (3) we may trust Christ eternally. This triad is modeled on syllogism. The third point would be strengthened if we imposed our judgment-grace paradigm to focus on God's action, instead of ours; thus, "Christ embraces us eternally."

—from one long passage of Scripture: For example, Psalm 23 might be preached thus: (1) Our paths are dangerous, (2) The Lord is our Shepherd, (3) There is nothing to fear.

—from several verses or passages, that is, using a Bible concordance to find a variety of texts to make related points: For example, (1) Bear your burdens—Galatians 6:2, (2) Bear each other's burdens—Galatians 6:5, (3) Cast your burdens upon the Lord—Psalm 55:22.[19]

—from traditional doctrinal understanding, largely outside the biblical text: For example, using I Thessalonians 1:5 ("Our message of the gospel came to you not in word only, but also in power and in the Holy Spirit and with full conviction"), we might discuss the doctrine of the Word. Here the divisions might come from our own understanding of the Word that would then be related to this text. Thus, (1) God dares to become known through word, (2) Human words differ from God's word, (3) God's word is action and power, (4) God's final, eternal word is Christ.

TYPES OF NARRATIVE SERMON

One-story formats (pure narration):
1) the biblical text retold in its time[20]
2) the biblical text retold in our time
3) a story of our time is told that intersects with the biblical text in such an obvious manner that only minimal linking commentary may be required, somewhere in the sermon. These modes were anticipated by H. Grady Davis.[21]

Multistory formats (pure narration):
Here are the simplest:

1) "One-two": one story of brokenness is countered by a second story of hope, the biblical text intersecting in obvious yet minimalist fashion.
2) "One-two-one": a story, broken midway by the story of the biblical text, returned to in the final third—a format first advocated by Charles L. Rice.[22]
3) "One-two-three": The first story leads to the second story, usually the biblical text, and is followed by a third story which counters the first. Again, Rice's work is an early source.

Hybrid formats (mixed narration):
Preachers employ narrative principles and varying amounts of narrative. The varieties are too numerous to categorize helpfully, for the sermons include anything combining narrative with non-narrative material.[23] Eugene Lowry's "homiletical plot" may be considered in this category:

1) Upset the equilibrium by posing a problem in the "felt needs" of the hearers,
2) analyze the discrepancy,
3) disclose the key to resolution from the gospel,
4) experience the gospel in the lives of the hearers, and
5) anticipate the consequences.[24]

SAMPLE USES OF STORIES

Retelling the biblical story in its own time (a one-story format):
Ella P. Mitchell preached on Esther, amplifying a sense of God's call that is hidden behind the original story more than it is central to it. Her sermon used the following moves:

1) Esther's background,
2) Esther's dilemma,
3) Esther's action,
4) Celebration of God's work through Esther.[25]

Telling a contemporary story (one-story format):
Thomas H. Troeger preached a wedding sermon on the wedding vows. He told the story of a couple who, each year, on their wedding anniversary, donned their wedding clothes and had their picture taken in their front room. He pictured them on their fifth anniversary and the meaning of "poorer"; on their fifteenth and the meaning of "worse"; and on their forty-seventh, discovering the rich delight in having kept promises and in meditating on "in sickness . . . until death."[26]

Using a multistory format:
Fred Craddock preached a sermon on Galatians 1:11-24 in which he asked the congregation to envision a face when he said the word "bitter." He told five stories (each introduced with, "Do you see a face? I see the face . . . "), before turning to Paul in the same vein and identifying the bitterness with which Paul himself is struggling.[27]

ner of storytelling), even though one of the early proponents of this strategy was not also a voice for narrative preaching.[28] Narration is further identified with the descriptive and evocative; with involving hearers, calling forth their own experiences, and inviting them to draw some of their own conclusions; and with inductive as opposed to deductive.

When Fred Craddock advocated inductive preaching (a term he later dropped), he was referring to sermons that gradually narrow to a point or conclusion, modeling the preacher's own inductive and experiential journey through the week. A deductive sermon, by contrast, became identified with a traditional propositional sermon that starts with its conclusion stated as a proposition, and then widens to consider evidence to prove it. The conclusion is never in doubt from the beginning; rather, in doubt is the manner of proof.

Here is the problem: Inductive and deductive categories may work to describe styles of preaching, but they do not work when each is attached to a particular form of sermon. Both are categories of formal logic. Inductive thought is as easily employed in propositional preaching as in narration. If we were to be strict, since theology is not, for long, based in empirical evidence, we could say that all theology is inductive. We do not need to become abstract or technical, however, for the problem is easily seen: If an inductive sermon identifies its conclusion at the beginning (in the manner of deduction), it presumably ceases to be inductive, even though its thought proceeds in an inductive manner.

Let us be clear: By attaching too much weight to terms dealing primarily with form, preachers recently have been encouraged to make a simplistic choice between one or the other, when the grounds for this choice are false. As students, we do not need to make this choice. Preaching can be authoritarian in any form. The one would make us a slave to the preacher's reasoning; the other would make us a slave to his or her imaging. Weak content is a liability for any form. Moreover, both forms, in either extreme, can be flawed.

Preaching can be authoritarian in any form: A paternalistic preacher using a propositional format is little different from the preacher who uses narrative to wander through hill and dale without purpose.

For example, the single-story sermon (using a story from the Bible or from today) can be as flawed—for different reasons—as the propositional sermon that sacrifices the Bible and determines points solely by words that rhyme (e.g., "God works by finding, minding, and binding"). When a single story is used, unless the preacher is very skilled indeed (as some are),[29] the congregation can be left struggling to make some direct, substantial connections with God in their lives. These connections should become conscious in our minds, not left in the subconscious.

The point of the sermon is not a surprise at the end, discovering what it was about. Ideally listeners should be clear about the import of the sermon at least by midway, if not from the start, such that they are already applying it to their lives by the end. A simple story may help the congregation to recognize their common humanity and Christ in their midst. Still, identification with a character in the gospel story is often not sufficient to make explicit, or conscious, the gospel. Recognizing a familiar situation as described in a story does not necessarily mean we will in fact make the connections the preacher makes or desires us to make with our own lives. Even appreciation of this type of sermon by a congregation on the church steps after a service may not mean that they met God.

In many cases, as listeners, our interpretation of the narrative sermon gets stuck at stage two of the hermeneutical square with our asking, What does this mean? (The same thing is true of propositional sermons that exclude experience.) When this happens, as preachers, we fall short of one purpose of proclamation, which is to facilitate a relationship with Jesus Christ. Thus such narrative sermons may convince more by their ethos and pathos, and not enough by their logos.[30]

Neither form then, considered merely as form, itself offers the improvement in preaching that we seek. Moreover, as soon as we start to think of hybrid forms, combining propositions and narratives, we have little justification for calling them one or the other. This is one reason why categories of overall form are of limited value (which may also be why David Buttrick prefers speaking of narrative and propositional sermons as "preaching in the mode of immediacy" and "preaching in the reflective mode," that is, reflecting on experience).[31] We are, after all, free to use whatever form facilitates our purpose in proclamation, and might be better off to pay more attention to matters of form, content, and function that can improve quality. Higher quality is achievable through an integration of the best of both forms.

Synthesis

Much exciting work on sermon form in recent years provides the kind of integration and flexibility of overall form being advocated here for preaching as God's event. Some of the pioneering work done in narrative by teachers such as Henry H. Mitchell, Edmund A. Steimle,[32] Charles L. Rice, and Fred B. Craddock in fact paved the way for and anticipated some of the synthesis that is now happening in pulpits.

Currently, much synthesizing work is underway in relation to form, content, and function. In particular, two of Eugene L. Lowry's works, *The Homiletical Plot* and *How to Preach a Parable: Designs for Narrative Sermons*,[33] while specifically arguing for narrative, in fact articulate how sermons that were not necessarily narratives can nonetheless employ organic principles from narrative. Both Christine M. Smith and Carol M. Norén have shown how feminist concerns move sermonic form away from models that stress authority and toward models reflecting relationships.[34]

The work of at least three other writers stands out. Thomas G. Long's approach to the sermon through the literary forms of the Bible is richly suggestive of varieties in homiletical form. He uses a number of questions to discern from a biblical text the form that a sermon might take:

1) What is the genre of the text? (psalms, proverb, miracle stories, parables, prophetic oracles, short stories); 2) What is the rhetorical function of this genre? (A joke is . . . to make us laugh. A ghost story is . . . to frighten us. . . . A parable does something to a reader that a psalm does not do, and vice versa); 3) What literary devices does this genre employ to achieve its rhetorical effect? (*How* does the text do what it does?); 4) How in particular does the text under consideration, in its own literary setting, embody the characteristics and dynamics described in the previous questions?; 5) How may the sermon, in a new setting, say and do what the text says and does in its setting?[35]

One of the strengths of this approach is that the intended result or effect of the biblical text is considered as part of the text's meaning, and thus becomes a source for our own direction in creating a similar event through preaching.

Another formal approach worth detailing here is Ronald J. Allen's proposal for the recovery of topical preaching, in *Preaching the Topical Sermon*. This topical form, as noted, has served the church well through history, yet has come under considerable criticism in recent years, not least for its failure to treat the biblical text in responsible ways. Allen corrects this, and suggests a variety of intriguing possibilities in form for preachers to try:

1) deductive form of description, evaluation and application—(a) introduction: 5-15% of the length, (b) statement of the main point:

5%, (c) description of the topic: 15-25%, (d) theological evaluation of the topic: 15-25%, (e) application: 15-25%, (f) conclusion: 5-15%

2) Methodist quadrilateral—(a) Introduction, (b) the Bible: 15-20%, (c) the tradition: 15-20%, (d) experience: 15-20%, (e) reason (i.e. learnings): 15-20%, (f) synthesis: 20-25%, (g) conclusion: 5-10%

3) practical moral reasoning—(a) experiences of the topic in the congregation: 10%, (b) listening to (i.e. learnings from) the experiences: 20%, (c) critical analysis: 30-50%, (d) decision and strategy: 20-30%

4) general inductive—(a) preacher's story of becoming aware of the issue, (b) connection to the congregation, (c) explore the issues together, (d) resolution

5) structure as praxis (borrowed from David Buttrick)—four to six moves of four minutes each, each composed of a three sentence focus, the move itself, and a three sentence closure: e.g. (a) introductory framework, (b) critical examination and analysis, (c) reevaluation or interpretation in light of Christian vision, (d) new understanding and revisioning of the future

6) focus on mind, heart, and will [or logos, pathos, and ethos]—(a) introduction, (b) statement of the claim of the sermon, (c) focus on the mind (i.e. what must we know?), (d) focus on emotion, (e) focus on the will, (f) conclusion.[36]

Note that none of these forms precludes the possibility of choice about theological emphasis; for instance, whether or not to preach hope.

Finally, we may return to David Buttrick's work, not only to what he called the "macro-matters" of overall sermon form but also to the "micro-matters" of individual parts of the sermon, in particular his "moves." We saw earlier that he uses the term "moves" in a manner to emphasize "a movement in language," as opposed to static "points."[37] He suggests, as we have just glimpsed in Allen's fifth form, that the sermon is composed of a variety of these moves. They consist of (1) a theological idea from the biblical text (i.e. our "concerns of the text"), and (2) analogies of experience (i.e. our "concerns of the sermon"), developed in anticipation of congregational blocks (our expressed and actual needs of the congregation).[38] Thus one move in a sermon on Jesus' healing of the lepers is based on this idea: Jesus commands the lepers to show themselves to the priests. Buttrick develops it as follows:

a. Theology: We should be shocked by the abrupt command. Jesus had flunked Pastoral Care 101: Surely, he should have said something like, "It must be difficult being a leper . . ." Instead, we get a hard-line command, "Go!" Luke is presenting an imperious Lord Jesus Christ who, as God-with-us, has authority.

b. Analogies of Experience: Analogies of experience are difficult to get at in an age as secular as ours. Again and again, however, our cries for pity do seem to be answered by commands of God. The saints tell us that when they have hustled up to God, filled with personal pathos, God has often answered with "Go!" "Love!" "Serve!"

c. Congregational Blocks: Popular piety has painted a picture of caring Jesus, who, when we pray in desperate need, responds with warm support. Jesus' abrupt command may be unexpected and quite inexplicable.[39]

From this passage, one can already sense subsequent movements of thought about to take shape.

This kind of attention to smaller units of form within the sermon is of growing importance in homiletics. If we are to improve the quality of our preaching, not just change its shape and motion, we need to find additional ways to identify some currently hidden forms in sermon process. We need ways of improving the quality of whatever forms we use. In our discussions we need to place less emphasis on choices between either propositional or narrative form. Buttrick wants us to think of form in terms of shaping the consciousness of our hearers, and how the hearing needs of the listeners can be met. In our next chapters, we will be thinking in different, though related terms, using the categories of "how language works" and "how language shapes thought" rather than the slippery phenomenological notion of "consciousness."

Review Questions for Chapter Ten

1) Static unity
   a) implies that a sermon has a life of its own
   b) is like static electricity, creating "sparks" of interest
   c) arises from imposing a predetermined structure
   d) arises out of the purpose and material being discussed   [c]

2) Which was not suggested to be true of propositional sermons: They
   a) have been the bread-and-butter sermons of the church
   b) "run about" from point to point
   c) came to prominence in the Reformation
   d) may tend to be the preacher's agenda   [c]

3) Which was not one of the reasons given for the rise of narrative:
   a) congregations are tolerant of authority
   b) congregations have many opportunities for education
   c) congregational experience is appreciated
   d) Jesus' preaching   [a]

4) The following describes which sermon type: introduction to
   exegesis to application to conclusion?
   a) topical
   b) exegetical
   c) hybrid narrative
   d) expository   [d]

Questions for Discussion

1) If mission were understood statically rather than organically or
   holistically, what might it look like in a sermon?
2) What is the best sermon you remember? What made it excellent?
   Was it propositional? narrative? a mixture?

LINEAR THOUGHT AND HOMILETICAL MOVEMENT

Modern poetics is used to distinguish two axes of thought that are found in language. Preachers tend to be dominant in one or the other. Through attention to linear thought (i.e., definition or description, sequence, and metonymy), preachers dominant in polar thought are shown practical ways to strengthen their preaching. All linear modes may be considered metonymic.

We all think that what we are saying is perfectly clear, simply because what we are saying is usually clear in our own minds. However, people think in different ways. If we look to language, we discover that in addition to unity (static or organic), two broad principles assist clear communication. These are linear thought (or progression and movement) and polar thought (or digression).

Linear thought has a sense of movement or progression along a line. It is deductive, convergent, or focused on propositions. Some people speak of it as influenced by the left hemisphere of the brain, which is logical, informational, and sequential. Propositional preaching is associated with it, yet linear thought is needed in any preaching. One mark of poor narrative can be the absence of linear thought: Listeners may ask, "Where is this going? What is the point?"

Polar thought, by contrast, allows for digression from a linear line of thought to related topics. Modest forms of digression are in fact essential to all preaching as a means of establishing relevance in the lives of the congregation. Without it, listeners may ask, "How does this connect to my life?" or "How does this connect with the Bible?"

Each of us tends to have a dominant and subordinate mode of thought. Students will be encouraged to concentrate on one or the other, whichever is weaker, that it might be strengthened.

How do we know our own dominant mode? An over-simplistic guide, perhaps, is this: The preacher who likes to develop a clear line of rational argument, and feels insecure about using imagery and metaphor, is likely a dominant linear thinker. On the other hand, the preacher who prefers imagery and metaphor to formal doctrine is likely a dominant polar thinker. Both modes of thought are conceptual, and both are essential for preaching. Each can be learned.

We need to be attentive first to the structure of language. Many structures in language contribute to meaning. For instance, linguistics looks at grammar and the relationships between the language as a whole *(langue)* and a specific utterance *(parole)*. Semiotics focuses on the rules of signs and symbols. Anthropology looks at social matters (e.g., kinship, mythology) that affect language. For preaching it is important to identify structures that directly assist theological expression.

We begin by understanding that linear and polar are the two axes of our thought (see p. 317n. 5). What differentiates them? For each I isolate three dominant paradigms from poetics. Linear thought (definition, sequence, and metonymy) progresses along lines. It connects points along those lines, and makes claims concerning the nature of their relationships (i.e., "this is part of this"; "this leads to this"; and "this links with this"). Polar thought (comparison, contradiction, and metaphor) digresses from linear lines of thought. Two ideas are connected as poles on the basis of some shared identity, yet often not in strictly logical ways. The degree of perceived identity varies from assertion to assertion (i.e., "part yes and part no"; "yes is no"; and "both yes and no").

The following chart sketches these six theological paradigms. Each will be explored in detail in this or the next chapter. Exercises are designed particularly for students who have written a draft of a sermon and are in the process of revision (perhaps who have even already read chapter 13). Some readers might wish to turn directly to the pages dealing with their area of weakness, while others may benefit from working through all six paradigms.

Micro-forms for Preaching

Three Modes of Linear Thought (Progression)

Three Modes of Polar Thought (Digression)

1) Definition or description of an idea • by family • by part • i.e., " this is part of this "	1) Comparison of two or more ideas • by similarity (simile, analogy) • by difference (negation) • i.e., " part yes and no "
2) Sequence of ideas • time (chronology; cause/effect) • space (form, lesser/greater) • emotion (order of feelings) • logic: syllogism (if a and b, then c) • i.e., "this leads to this"	2) Contradiction • real • apparent (paradox) • opposition or antithesis • i.e., "yes is no"
3) Paradigm of Metonymy • a thought group becomes symbolized by one idea, image, or part and is then linked to something that comes before or after • as in the figure of speech known as metonymy (and including synecdoche), one part or association leads to the whole, e.g., "wheels" for car • i.e., "this links with this"	3) Paradigm of Metaphor • a thought is identified with an experience, or an experience with a thought, in a lateral departure from the chain of thought • as in the figure of speech known as metaphor (and including simile) one thing is identified with another, e.g., "love is a rose" • i.e., "both yes and no"

Linear Thought for Preaching

Whatever overall sermonic form we use, the sermon must have movement, our thought must go somewhere. It is not enough to have a central idea. It must develop. It must grow. Something must happen. Movement (or what is called plot in narrative) is one of the expectations that listeners bring. Linear thinkers are excellent at arranging thoughts in sequence, like points on a line, all progressing to a purpose. Whether we call this sequence an argument, theme, or plot, it communicates information and gives shape to the authors' intent. Linear thinkers have a gift in knowing how to order their material for the most logical, easily followed presentation.

Exercises for Strengthening Linear Thought

Here are some basic exercises, with examples from sermons, designed for those of us who need to strengthen linear thought.

1) Definition—define key terms or doctrines. One of the best ways to be clear is to define what we mean. Long ago, Aristotle identified what continues to be our method for defining (*Topics*, IV): Begin with identification of the general family to which something belongs, using an equivalent or coordinate term or phrase. To define is to say, "This is part of that." Thus we might say that "preaching is a form of public speaking." Next move to discuss its parts: ". . . that interprets the meaning of the Bible for today and usually takes place in the setting of worship. It is an offering of the incarnate Christ to the world, and offering of both the preacher and the people in service to God." Effective use of definition, often allowing definition to provide structure and order for ensuing thought, can instill trust and confidence in the speaker (ethos).

Definition can be used to structure a paragraph. In some circumstances, if the subject is of sufficient importance, it can be used to structure an entire sermon in which each part of the definition is dealt with in turn.

Description is closely related to definition and perhaps has been more common, yet need not continue to be, in narrative genres than in propositional. In description, the parts are visually shown as part of the family, or the family and its parts are discovered through the action. The best description does not report the facts but creates the event.

James S. Stewart, the great Scottish preacher, began a sermon on John 3:8 in the following manner. Note how he does not lose the visual and other senses during the defining, and thus holds our interest. In other words, his definition incorporates description, an appropriate synthesis for sermons:

To anyone brought up in the Jewish tradition, it was natural, almost inevitable, to compare the Spirit of God with the wind. For in the Hebrew tongue the same term was used for both. The word *ruach* stood in fact for three things. It meant breath, that most palpable part of existence, the breath of life. It meant also the desert wind, tearing violently across the land with primal energy and elemental force. And it meant the Spirit of God, the super-natural power that sweeps across the ages, and bursts into history, and takes possession of the lives of men.

Now here was Jesus with Nicodemus on the Mount of Olives . . ."[1]

Exercise 11:1 Examine the focus (central statement or major concern of the text) for your sermon. It might be an action of God. Identify a key doctrine in that statement. Look to a dictionary or a theological commentary to determine how you might helpfully define, interpret, or clarify it in your sermon, keeping in mind that we define something by its family and its parts. Now rework the definition to make it descriptive in the manner of Stewart. For example:

Central idea: God blesses us in our need. (from the Beatitudes of Matthew 5)

Doctrine: Blessing

Definition: A blessing is a gift from God, something through which God acts to bring about God's purpose. It may also be the invoking of God's favor on a person, object, or a situation through the power of the Holy Spirit invested in us.

Reworked version also using description: Who could have predicted that God would have acted when that woman needed help? Perhaps no one, but she might have trusted. For God always hears our prayers. No, things did not happen just the way she hoped. But in the way it did happen, she encountered God, or rather, God encountered her. She has one very simple, time-honored word for what happened to her. That word is "blessing." It is what has happened to us as well.

2) Sequence—determine the logical order in which ideas need to be linked. If your sermon manuscript seems to lack sufficient clarity and purpose, go over it to trace the logic of your thought. For example, even a sequence built on the words "afternoon," "lunch," and "supper" is irregular: The norm lunch, afternoon, and supper. Nonlinear thinkers often think that the steps of their thought are unimportant, but linear listeners need to hear clear steps of progression to understand, test, or accept what is being

> Nonlinear thinkers often think that the steps of their thought are unimportant, but linear thinkers need to hear clear steps of progression to understand, test, or accept what is being said.

224

said. Sometimes it is even advisable to insert numbered points at this stage of revision to sharpen your own thought to help listeners. To offer a logical sequence, you imply that "this leads to this."

One basic logical movement in a sermon is from the biblical text to our time. An expository sermon moves once from exegesis to application: This may be its dominant linear movement. (In other forms, those with more frequent exchange between the biblical text and our situation, we will be arguing that these movements are predominantly polar, rather than linear, seeking to establish parallels or analogies in our time that break the linear flow. Sometimes when distinguishing linear from polar, it is a matter of determining which mode is dominant, for, depending on perspective, both may be present.)

The Scriptures of course are not arbitrary to preaching: They are the foundation of what we preach. Listeners listen, in the first instance, not because they want to know our opinion, as preachers, but because they want to know God, and what God is saying to our community. The church has always regarded the Scriptures as God's voice. Thus we do not seek to muffle God, and we conform what we say to what we have already heard there. In topical preaching, what we say should be seen to emerge from the biblical text or texts.

This means sustained focus on the biblical text in the sermon, in paragraphs of thought that are sufficiently long for the thought of listeners to become focused on the text. (For introductory students we suggested a focus of 200 to 375 words, or two to three minutes at 100 to 125 words a minute.) Help listeners to "see" it by creating it as though making a movie. Preachers soon find themselves in trouble if they are heard to be preaching their own opinion, ideology, or political persuasion. This requires theological discipline, biblical responsibility, and willingness to submit to the Word. Check to be sure that you have given sustained attention to the biblical text (including what commentaries have said about it) at least once, but normally at least twice in the sermon, if preaching hope. Once again, introductory students, or preachers confined to sermons of twelve minutes or less, are wise to limit their efforts to two ventures into the biblical text.

Progression in a sermon may be fostered by: theological movement; stages of a definition; chronological order; rhetorical impact; cause and effect; spatial order; emotional sequence; accumulation or elimination; or syllogism.

Here are some of the ways in which progression can be fostered: *theology* (e.g., judgment to grace); *definition* (exploring in turn the various elements of a definition);

chronology (e.g., this, then this, then this, and this); *rhetoric* (the old rule for three ideas of unequal strength is to start with the second strongest, then go to the weakest, and conclude with the strongest); *cause or effect* (e.g., if . . . then; or, because of this . . . this; or, sin leads to death and the cross leads to salvation);[2] *space* (e.g., starting with the foundation; or moving from lesser to greater; or greater to lesser); *emotion* (e.g., leading to a climax;[3] or Elisabeth Kübler-Ross's stages of grief); *accumulation or elimination* (e.g., this, and this, and this, and this; or, not this, or this, or this, but this); or *syllogism*, from formal logic (i.e., if a, and b, then c).

Frequently in theology a modified form of syllogism (i.e., the enthymeme) is used, in which one premise is left out but implied: If a [and b] then c. For example: Christ died for sinners; [you have sinned;] Christ died for you. In preaching, however, this omission of a premise can reduce clarity. Note how small each step of thought must be in order for a developing idea or plot to be easily followed.

Some traditional propositional sermons use an obvious syllogistic structure. If we were preaching on John 3:16, we could try this:

major premise: God loves all people
minor premise: We are people
therefore: God loves us

Emotional sequences are possible, although we ought to be careful not to psychologize or moralize where it is not warranted. One preacher developed the following emotional sequence in Luke 10:38 concerning Martha: (1) Distracted by many concerns, (2) Doubting the Lord's concern, and (3) Demanding other's concern.[4] If there is a potential problem here, it occurs in turning the text into a moral lesson that scolds Martha. (That this preacher was a man scolding a woman in paternal fashion adds to the problem in our day.) An alternative sequence that honors Martha might be: (1) Martha is anxious to serve Jesus, (2) She becomes distracted in her anxiety, (3) Jesus gives her peace.

Exercise 11:2 Review what you have written of your sermon. Check the sequence of ideas. It was common in the past to have students prepare a sermon outline, prior to writing, consisting of points and subpoints. This process may be helpful for some people, but they are apt to be linear thinkers. Here we are trying to assist primarily polar or imagistic thinkers, and for them (as well as for some linear thinkers) the results of outlines are often mechanical and boring. Instead, on a separate piece of paper, try to construct the sequence of your thought from what you have already said in your first draft. If the order is not yet clear, make it clear using points if possible. Remember that your thought should move forward, in steps that follow one after the other, neither too large nor too small. Ask, What is the link here with what went before, or what follows? Ask, If I cut out this sentence or paragraph, is my message clear? Listeners need time with each movement of thought to catch up to the preacher. Stay with the thought awhile. Say it in other words (much in the manner of transposing concerns of the text). Most polar thinkers need to be more explicit about steps of thought than they think is necessary.

3) Metonymy—the basic linear paradigm. The subject of metonymy (rhymes with *economy*) addresses the problem of sermons that seem the product of mere free association. One thing moves to the next without any apparent order or progression. Perhaps the sermon moves from Jesus feeding the five thousand, to the church picnic last July, to when the preacher last went home, to the building that is being built downtown, to Jesus walking on water, concluding with mention of the rain last week. The preacher can be taught how to take these apparently random episodes and shape them to one purpose expressed in the central idea of the sermon. Moreover, the preacher can be shown how to link sentences and paragraphs, to identify where logical steps are missing, or to discover the order that is already inherent in the material, although the mind may not consciously have identified it.

Thus, such a random sermon might be revised to move as follows: Jesus taught, and when he finished, the five thousand people were hungry. In feeding them he made community, of the sort we experienced for instance last summer at the church picnic. My journey home reminds us of how many people are homeless and without community. What if we could help house the homeless in a building like that being built downtown? All things are possible with Christ. Did he not feed 5,000, walk on water, rise from the dead? Does God not rule over all, even watering our crops with the rains this past week? God will continue to feed us and nurture us, and meet our needs as we reach out to others with God's love.

Metonymy allows these ideas to be linked into a unified, developing chain of thought. The most important idea about metonymy is the way in which it forms a chain of thought that moves somewhere with an evident objective. Let us now turn to examine our subject more closely.

> *Metonymy makes chains of thought. It connects ideas and images, or steps of an argument or narrative, to form one dominant movement of developing thought.*

Metonymy is little recognized yet is perhaps the most basic and common form of linear thought. When we come into a movie midway, we can figure out much of the earlier action on the basis of metonymic traces or clues that are embedded in the unfolding events. Metonymy allows us to recover material as well as to predict new material. The device is more than arranging thought on a continuous line. It is creative. *Metonymy* literally means "to change a name," in other words, to substitute the name of one part for the whole, or the name of something adjacent in time or space (i.e., contiguous) for the whole. Here is an example of metonymy as a figure of speech: The White House signed a paper. We mean, of course, that the President signed it. President and White House are so connected with each other in time and space, that the substitution of one name for the other (on the basis of what is called *contiguity*) makes sense.

Metonymy is not merely a figure of speech, however. If it were we might ignore it as ornamental. It is, along with metaphor, one of two basic paradigms in thought first identified by Roman Jacobson in his now classic study used in a wide variety of disciplines, *Fundamentals of Language* (1956).[5] David Lodge provided the most detailed study of Jacobson and concentrated on the macroforms or typologies of modern literature.[6] Neither Jacobson nor Lodge explored in detail the specific expressions of metonymy in language, as we venture here, as microforms for preaching.

Metonymy as a paradigm of thought seeks movement, sequence, progression, or direction by linking a series of ideas, on the basis of some developing order, or of a part connecting with the whole, or on the basis of one thing's being adjacent another in time or space.

There is a way in which all linear thought, including definition-description and sequence, may be conceived as relating to metonymy. Metonymy as a paradigm of thought seeks movement, sequence, progression, or direction by linking a series of ideas in a developing chain of thought, on the basis of some order, or of a part connecting with the whole, or on the basis of one thing's being adjacent another in time or space. Metonymy generates movement along a series of points in lines, for progression, development, and direction. It develops a central line of thought, linking individual steps in one long developing chain.

It also makes many smaller chains within the sermon that help sentences and paragraphs stick together. These do not necessarily follow logic. An idea or image here may be picked up there, in the next sentence or many paragraphs later. The resonance or repetition signals the mind to recall the last instance of its

228

use, and to anticipate a future use. Such chains help to hold the whole together.

Whenever we write or preach a sermon and it does not seem to hold together, or does not flow, metonymy is always lacking. Sentences do not link with other sentences, paragraphs do not connect with other paragraphs, and every idea seems scattered. Metonymy is also lacking when theological language does not sufficiently link with the larger Christian story. However, metonymy in sermons—and hence unity—is primarily a chain of thought, like the steps in an argument, or the movement of a plot, or some other sequence that shows both movement and development.

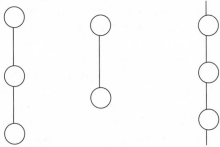

Practical Uses of Metonymy

Let us now turn in a more practical direction to see several metonymic structures at work. Here are some of the most important forms of metonymy to use in sermons:

1) *Metonymy between sentences*—Try consciously to develop links: Check to make sure that each new sentence picks up some thought from one or more foregoing sentences. If you are not clear why you are saying something, your listeners also will be unclear.

Whenever a thought group becomes symbolized by one word, phrase, or image (i.e., the whole being recalled by the part, or by something associated with it in time or space), and is then linked to the next thought group, we have metonymy.[7] Alternatively, when one word foreshadows a later line of thought, that too is metonymy: that is, a part (or something associated with it) anticipates the whole. In other words, metonymy functions by recalling or foreshadowing, and is always reaching beyond itself for further links elsewhere in what is being said.

Of course any sequence of sentences should be able to serve as an example here, but this one from a sermon by Lucy Rose displays clearly some links between words such as communion, bread, wine, Lord's Supper. Notice the smooth flow in her speaking:

The *communion table* was empty today. Last week there had been a *pitcher of wine, two chalices, two plates, and a loaf of bread*. The *bread* was always tasty with chewy seeds her mama never used in cooking. She didn't like the taste of *wine* much, but she never drank much, just enough to wet the tip of her tongue. What did it all mean, the *communion, the Lord's Supper?* It was something they did once a month. She knew all the proper theological words to describe *what they were doing.* But what did *it* mean to her, to Louisa, on this day, June 14, 1987?[8]

Exercise 11:3 Review a paragraph of the sermon you are composing. Circle words that link sentences. If you are unable to find them, rewrite to make sure that you incorporate them.

2) Metonymy between paragraphs—Ensure sufficient links. The sermon may be conceived as having a variety of minor chains, as in the excerpt just quoted. Additional unity is provided, however, by carrying forward one developing line of thought, for instance a major concern of the text or its major concern of the sermon. It will be present through various discussions of the Bible and our times, which weave the sermon. Check to see if the predominant chain carries through to the end.

Robert F. Smith based a Palm/Passion Sunday sermon on Isaiah 50:7ff.: "I have set my face like flint, / and I know that I shall not be put to shame; / he who vindicates me is near." The image of "face like flint" was used from beginning to end, in various ways, to give both progress and unity to the sermon. He began by talking about "faces like flint": of his Scottish ancestors, of people he saw in visiting Scotland, of refugees in Bangkok airport, of his mother five days before her death, of Jesus entering Jerusalem (Matt. 26:14ff.), of Jesus setting his face resolutely to Jerusalem (Luke 9:51), of the prophet Isaiah, of any of us who enter tough situations. He moved in a progression here from ethos to pathos to logos and back to pathos. Then, in an apparent break, he returned to Isaiah ("The Lord God helps me; / therefore I have not been disgraced") and told two stories. The first was of the eight martyrs—six Jesuit priests, the housekeeper, and her daughter killed in El Salvador in 1989; and this next one. Notice how the final sentence functions to bring together the entire sermon:

A year later I was part of the ecumenical group who gathered in the Romero chapel to commemorate the death of the martyrs. The evening was long, the air close, and those of us who had traveled long miles to be present were beginning to flag when Jon Sobrino, the seventh Jesuit who, but for the fact he was out of the country that fateful night, would have also been assassinated, came to the microphone. He held in his hands a tray on which rested eight clay flower pots filled with earth. His hands shook as he solemnly planted a single frijole, the bean which is the staple food of the Salvadoran peasant, in each of the pots. He placed the tray before the tomb of the martyrs and turned and said softly the only words he could have said, "Unless a grain of wheat falls into the ground and dies it remains alone, but if it dies it bears much fruit."

Would you be surprised if I told you that his face was set like flint?[9]

Exercise 11:4 Examine five paragraphs of your sermon in progress. Identify in one short, crisp sentence the main thought of each paragraph. Out of five, how many have the subject of the paragraph clearly stated in the first sentence? in the last? in both? How many of the paragraphs develop only one thought? Circle the word in the last sentence of each paragraph that links to a word in the first sentence of the next. Again, in one short sentence, what is the doctrine or image that links several paragraphs, as in the Smith passage?

3) Metonymy as history and tradition—Metonymy not only provides a sense of progression and movement through the sermon, it is also needed to provide a sense of progression and movement through history. In other words, an important dimension of metonymy in the sermon is to establish a sense of history, tradition, continuing revelation, and hope for the future. Thus a specific event in history is chosen to represent an entire century; a specific quotation is meant to represent an entire community of thought (e.g., a quotation from St. Bridget of Sweden might be used to represent the entire Middle Ages); various events and people are linked through time in a chain of tradition (e.g., women preachers). Strategic use of metonymy in this manner helps remind us that we preach on behalf of the entire church, not as individuals preaching our own individual theologies.

4) Metonymy in theological expression—Though a new idea to most of us, metonymy is in fact an essential chain for theology. We can use it to strengthen our theological expression in several ways:

a) Metonymy connects one sign of God to the larger truth of God: Individual experiences of God, when linked to a larger developing picture of God, can function as metonymy. This happens with synecdoche, which scholars following Jacobson commonly identify as a subform of metonymy. In this, the name of God is substituted for the actions with which God is associated. Thomas G. Long speaks of the "synecdoche-style illustration": "We can point to places in human life where grace or hope or sin or love has been experienced and allow those experiences to stand as signs of the larger truth toward which they point."[10] For example, in a sermon on bearing one's cross, he suggests telling a story of a family that did not have difficulty adopting children, because they were willing to adopt whoever needed adoption, usually those children that for medical or physical reasons were difficult to place. The story, Long says, "does not say everything that can and should be said about cross-bearing. . . . But if cross-bearing is indeed choosing to embrace suffering in selfless service of others, this episode gives us one incident in human experience of the thing itself."[11]

Our analysis of this and similar stories as metonyms need not preclude these stories from also functioning in another way, for instance as metaphors of God's love. Even as a popular line drawing can be seen as either a duck or a rabbit, yet not both in the same instant, the mind allows only metonymy or metaphor to be seen at one time.

b) Metonymy connects one idea or image to the larger Christian story: Words such as "Christmas," "birth of Christ," "Bethlehem," "star," "stable " are used as metonyms when we substitute them for the larger story of Jesus' birth or for the doctrine of the Incarnation of God in Christ. Similarly, we use metonymy when we say, "By the cross we are saved," by which we really mean by Christ's death and resurrection. Conversely, we speak of the empty tomb as a way of recalling the entire Christ event, including both Good Friday and Easter. We speak of the "throne" of heaven when we mean God's authority over all. We allow a few biblical texts read in worship on Sunday to represent and speak to the entire biblical story. We teach that one sermon is only a part of the church's entire proclamation, and functions to represent the whole within which it is properly understood. Similarly, we affirm that when two or more persons are gathered in Christ's name, the church is at prayer.

c) Metonymy allows us to speak in important ways that are different from logic and transcend space and time: Neither space nor time is absolute. Within language, metonymy normally allows us to transcend the limitations of geography or chronology. Such ways of speaking are more common than we may have thought. Metonymy allows us to say that though there are many Tables around the world, and many loaves of bread, and many flasks of wine, there is only one Table, one loaf, and one cup, and that is the one body and blood of Jesus Christ which is given in this moment. Similarly, using metonymy we say that Christ may be found in many places at any moment, though there is only one resurrected Christ. In compassion we speak of anyone's suffering anywhere as being our pain (and Christ's). We affirm that wherever the church is ministering, we are present.

> **Common Metonymy Locations**
>
> 1) between sentences
> 2) between paragraphs
> 3) as history and tradition
> 4) in theological expression
>   a) connecting a sign of God with a larger truth
>   b) connecting one idea or image with the Christian story
>   c) breaking with logic and transcending time and space

On a temporal axis, metonymy sometimes dissolves time. For example, preachers who observe Advent speak of Christ's coming (in the historical Incarnation, into our lives in the present, and at the end of time), yet in contradictory fashion we also appropriately continue to affirm that Christ has already come. Moreover, we continue to affirm during Advent, that the One who is coming in a child is the One who was crucified on the cross for our sins.

Other examples of metonymy dissolving time in theological language can be given. Many people are being crucified today, suffering torture or injustice in various forms. In our theology, however, we identify these individual acts of suffering and oppression with the one historical crucifixion of Jesus Christ that happened long ago. We speak of Christ being crucified today. Though we were not present at that historical crucifixion, we nonetheless say that we were there—"Were You There When They Crucified My Lord?"—even as we affirm that we continue to participate in the crucifixion of Christ. Though death lies ahead of us, the New Testament says that the important death about which we are to be concerned has already happened through our baptism; thus in Christ we have already died and participate by faith in the resurrection that occurs even now and at the end of time. Important theological truths depend on metonymy.

Metonymy also sometimes generates time. Eschatology (the doctrine of the last things) is the result of revelation and is communicated often in language by metonymy. Our present understanding of God as a loving God who both judges and saves, reaches into the future. Thus failure to speak of heaven speaks volumes about our under-

233

standing of God's power. We may speak of heaven, not with language that conforms to science, but with language that conforms to our faith. The God whom we know now is the same loving God of the cross, who awaits in the future, pleased to use our words even now to help people live lives of expectation.

Exercise 11:5 Identify one additional example of metonymy for each of the theological categories just presented, perhaps by reading the texts of hymns. For example:

a) One sign of God represents the entire truth of God:

—in "Now Thank We All Our God," find the line "who from our mother's arms hath blessed us on our way." The one image stands in place of our lifelong journey with God. (This is another instance in which the image can also function as a metaphor of God's love.)

—in "Be Thou My Vision," each verse focuses on one attribute of God, which stands for God's nature. Thus verse two begins, "Be Thou my Wisdom," and verse three, "Be Thou my Battle-shield," contributing and leading to the fullest expression of praise in verses four and five: "High King of Heaven."

b) One idea links to the larger Christian story:

—in "Come Down, O Love Divine," the image of the descending Spirit links to the descent of the Spirit on Jesus at his baptism and on the disciples at Pentecost, although neither is mentioned explicitly.

c) Space and time are transcended:

—in "Thine Is the Glory," we sing, "Lo, Jesus meets us, risen from the tomb," as though we are now at the first Easter, or in that faraway garden across the seas.

Common Errors When Using Metonymy

Four common errors are made by preachers who are strong in linear thought.

1) First, they often preach without using words to re-create experience cinematically. Generally, they may communicate many ideas abstracted

234

from experience, but portray no people in the midst of the experience itself. Or, if there are people, they are abstract and seem unreal. For example, in a sermon we may hear about a mother yet never hear her voice or words, or about a father whose face and hands are never seen, or about a child who is never named or seen or heard. Portraying people in relationship should be the constant goal of preachers when dealing with experience, yet the people may end up as stick people, or cardboard characters who lack ambiguity and emotion, who are extracted from life but abstracted into principle. As preachers we seek to counter the dehumanizing influence of the world and media, not contribute further to it. Thus we rehumanize issues and relationships by bringing them properly into focus before God's Word.

One reason for cardboard characters is that some linear thinkers may think that details do not matter, since they do not get to the heart of the matter. While there is always a real danger that details can be excessive and distracting, preachers should cultivate appreciation of the manner in which a few appropriate details (like designer labels or the names of foods if a meal is central) allow listeners the opportunity actually to experience what is being discussed. Preachers might learn to imitate the concise descriptions of people often found for instance in short stories. The best descriptions are never for their own sake, for instance for the sole purpose of saying what someone is wearing, but are rather a means of purposely disclosing the character of the person and a developing action. The clothes are being discussed (sometimes to symbolize social status), but the real subject may be the character's emotional state.

2) Linear preachers often give excessive factual material and use abstract theological language. These preachers know the importance of facts and of proper framing of theological issues. Often, however, they confuse their own perception that the congregation needs particular theological information, with the actual need of the congregation. The actual need of a congregation is rarely for information, in itself. For instance, the preacher might decide that the congregation should know the doctrine of the Trinity, for it is there that they may learn about relationship and the need to be loving. In fact, the actual need within listeners is more commonly an understanding of those theological factors that prevent our love from being enacted, such as fear, and then for God's countering word to that fear.

3) Linear thinkers tend to stay with the familiar explanations of difficult subjects, rather than to risk trying a new approach. As theolo-

THE PRACTICE OF PREACHING

gians we need to be at least suspicious of understandings that everyone accepts and takes for granted. In this manner, fresh and deepening understandings might be opened, and preaching will not settle
into the staid and boring tracks of other years. Perhaps the best way
of learning to venture anew is to trust the value for both preacher and
listener in bringing fresh experience alongside comfortable formula-
tion, to see what new doors of learning can be opened.

4) Linear preachers may put in too many logical steps, providing
explanations of things at too slow a pace or where they are not needed. To correct this, look for steps that can be omitted without destroying the sense of flow.

We have been talking about errors often made by linear preachers.
A further word of caution concerning metonymy is needed for polar
thinkers. We have seen how easy it is for metonymy to make links
between sentences and paragraphs. One preceding idea or image is
carried forward. Used poorly, metonymy is simply a way of making
it seem like there is progression when in fact there is no substantial
development of thought. Thus we might end up with a series of
images (for instance about someone's life) that in fact lead nowhere
and connect to no progression of understanding.

A chain of similar images or stories that are linked through free
association is not generally what we are after. The preacher's mind
(or that of anyone else) in itself is not our proper focus. We want progression, purposeful development of thought, expansion of an idea,
complication and resolution of events, whether this is in terms of
propositional movement or plot. Various chains, important though
they are for unity, need to link to a larger chain or developing consciousness of the hearer. This central idea as it develops must be clear.
As listeners we simply need concrete, specific evidence that what is
being said is indeed going somewhere, that the preacher knows
where it is going, and that we are made part of the journey, rather
than left as anxious watchers of a merry-go-round circling in the
preacher's mind.

Metonymy seeks links with material around it. Metaphor, we will
see in the next chapter, establishes self-sufficient polar units, the interaction occurring between the poles. Metaphor breaks progression, or
seems to break it, as it looks for similarity and dissimilarity. We have
seen that sometimes a story that functions as metonymy can also function, for instance, as a metaphor of God's love. In these instances it is

important not to get stuck by trying to decide whether a set of propositions, or a narrative, is metonymy or metaphor, when it may be both.

Review Questions for Chapter Eleven

1) What is generally not true of dominant linear thinkers?
   a) they are confident in using stories and images
   b) they are good with propositional and doctrinal expression
   c) they prefer logic to imagination
   d) all of the above   [a]

2) Your sermon does not display clear movement of thought. It
   was suggested that you
   a) throw it away
   b) start again, this time using a sermon outline
   c) find the order behind your thoughts and put in points
   d) all of the above   [c]

3) Pick the answer that does not fit for metonymy:
   a) is a figure of speech
   b) links a part with the whole
   c) is a paradigm of thought
   d) seeks similarities   [d]

4) What is true for metonymy in theological expression:
   a) it allows us to speak as though we are somewhere we are not
   b) it connects to the larger Christian story
   c) we are present with the historical Jesus in his earthly ministry
   d) it enables speech about heaven
   e) all of the above   [e]

Questions for Discussion

1) What actions of God could we not discuss if we did not have
   metonymy in language?
2) What did you learn in this chapter about your own ways of
   thought? Identify and discuss the modes of metonymy you use
   most readily, and those you need to develop.

POLAR THOUGHT AND HOMILETICAL RELEVANCE

The ability to depart from a line of thought can be indicative of developed relevance. Three modes of polar thought are explored in turn: comparison, contradiction, and the paradigm of metaphor. Preachers dominant in linear thought are shown practical ways to strengthen their preaching. Some dangers of metaphor are discussed. Implications of linear and polar thought for homiletics are explored following a sample sermon.

Polar Thought for Preaching

In addition to progression and linear movement, the sermon must also have polar thought or digression to establish relevance. If we can imagine an entire sermon devoted only to what Paul said on fleshly sin in Romans 7, we can begin to see the need for polar thought. We expect the preacher to make connections with our lives. We want variation in pace. Digression is the ability to involve listeners, to depart from a certain chain of thought and to incorporate a variety of thoughts, feelings, and experiences. Thus if the central line of thought or metonym is moving down the page in a linear chain, the digression may be pictured moving more or less at a right angle to it.

Our thirteen-year-old son, Adam, decided to purchase one of the memory systems that is advertised on television. He is learning that the mind thinks in pictures, not words, and that people have the ability for "photographic" memory. One of his exercises is to memorize a list of numbered pictures. Each picture is associated with an object that naturally connects with it: thus one is a tree trunk (it looks like a "1"); two is an on-off light switch; three is a three-legged stool, and the list continues to twenty. We are now in the midst of constructing lists of twenty objects, that once told, he can rhyme back to us. Every object we name (pillow, typewriter, book) he numbers and pictures doing something ridiculous in relation to the previous list. Thus the pillow might be falling from the tree, the typewriter is balancing on the switch, the book is being read by the stool.[1]

Do you perceive what has happened? The conversation takes a ninety-degree turn with the discussion about Adam. (It takes another shift now, back in the original direction.) The previous line of thought is broken and as readers we begin searching for some connection with what was said before. As a story with a plot it has its own secondary metonymy that carried us along, but we keep searching for the dominant polar connection, the purpose of the digression, which is not given.[2] We ask, "Why is this story being told now?"

Here is the link: For memory in that program, two things were needed. One was sequence or movement, provided primarily by the numbers one to twenty, and secondarily by the actions (falling, balancing, reading). The second was polarity: pillow vs. tree, typewriter vs. bike, book vs. stool. Each step involved linear progression as well as polar digression. The same movement is helpful for our sermons: Each important linear step of thought may have its own polar movement to help listeners understand and remember. Memory needs both.

Polar thinkers are gifted in moving from a line of thought to establishing relevance in experience. They know how to interrupt a line of thought, to make connections, and to present their material in interesting ways that we often associate with imagination. As we saw in the last chapter, metonymy is also highly creative in its own way.

At the beginning of the foregoing chapter (11), there is a chart identifying three modes of polar thought: comparison, contradiction, and the paradigm of metaphor. We will discuss each here, primarily for the benefit of dominant linear thinkers who wish to strengthen polar thought.

One of the simplest ways of keeping polar and linear thought distinct in our minds is to remember

Polar thought allows for digression, the ability to involve listeners and to establish relevance. It permits us to depart from a certain developing chain of thought to incorporate a variety of thoughts or experiences and thereby to establish relevance.

that metonymy makes chains and reaches beyond itself; polar thought functions between two poles, reaching within as it were. Polar thought functions in semi-autonomous units. It depends on metonymy to be linked to the chain of thought.

Exercises for Strengthening Polar Thought

We turn now to explore each of our three modes of polar thought (see the chart on p. 222). At the end of this chapter a sermon is provided in which aspects of linear and polar thought are highlighted.

1) Comparison—Look for ways to compare what you are saying with something similar or different, to bring a sense of freshness to our thought. This may be done in small, incidental ways. For instance, Samuel D. Proctor was preaching about the problem of knowing the parable of the good Samaritan so well. He makes lively even this simple idea by brief digression: "This is a familiar story, but it's like some hymns we sing: the words are so well known that we don't really hear them. It's sort of like a siren wailing on a downtown street at night or a barking dog—both are heard but unheeded."[3]

Comparison, in looking for similarities and differences, says, in effect, "Part yes and part no."

Of course comparison may be used effectively in larger ways. Comparison may be made, for example, by contrasting what the world says (e.g., about worship, thanksgiving, or love) and what the church says. Other approaches are with simile (comparing two similar things, e.g., "We are like Martha") and analogy (comparing two different things, e.g., "Faith is like a tree").[4] Generally avoid allegory, at least in biblical interpretation, for it usually distorts the text, especially if every detail of a biblical story is bent to correspond to our own superimposed code (e.g., the tree = sin; Zacchaeus in the tree = the human dilemma; and Jesus walking down the road = the Second Coming).

In this Christmas Eve sermon, Luther used several comparisons: between Christ in a stable and rogues in seats of honor; between God's disregard for the powers of the world and the world's disregard for God; and between what the rich people who had everything in Bethlehem have now and what Mary and Joseph, who had nothing, now have:

Then when they came to Bethlehem, they were the most insignificant, the most despised people, as the evangelist indicates. They were obliged to make room for everyone, until they were shown into a stable and had to be satisfied to share with the animals a common hostel, a common table, a common room and bed! At the same time many a rogue occupied a seat of honor in the inn and was treated as a gentleman. Nobody notices or understands what God performs in the stable. . . . Thus God indicates that he pays no attention at all to what the world is or has or can do, and on the other hand the world proves that it knows nothing at all of, and pays no attention to, what God is or has or can do, and on the other hand the world proves that it knows nothing at all of, and pays no attention to, what God is or has or does. . . . What did Bethlehem really have, when it had not Christ? What do those have now, who at that time were well off? And what do Mary and Joseph lack now, even though at that time they had no place to sleep comfortably during the night?" [5]

Exercise 12:1 Pick one idea in your sermon draft that seems difficult or in need of a little life or spark. Identify a few things in our own experience that it is like. Alternatively, see if there is a series of things you might picture that are dissimilar; for example, "We do not think that this is what is meant . . . or this . . . or this. . . . Rather . . ."

2) Contradiction—Seek real or apparent contradictions to develop in preaching. Normally we avoid contradictions, knowing they hinder persuasion. We may be unaware of how useful contradiction is in both poetic and theological expression. We may have been taught that contradictory images or statements have no place in logical thought; in fact, Anselm of Canterbury used his law of noncontradiction to prove the existence of God.[6] We often prefer to avoid use of the term *contradiction* and speak instead of *paradox*, or apparent rather than real contradiction.

Samuel Taylor Coleridge once said that "except in geometry, all symbols of necessity involve an apparent contradiction."[7] Together with Kant, Hegel, and Kierkegaard, he awakened us to contradiction as one of the most important principles of theological method. Ebeling called contradictions "dead ends [that are] the expression of ultimate mystery."[8] Henri de Lubac said of paradoxes that they "do not sin against logic, whose laws remain inviolable: but they escape its domain."[9] D. M. Baillie stressed the importance of contradiction in theology and went on to say: "When we 'objectify' [the divine reality] all our judgments are in some measure falsified, and the higher truth which reconciles them cannot be fully expressed in words, though it is experienced and lived in the 'I-and-Thou' relationship of faith towards God."[10] Contradiction says, "Yes is no."

Some teachers would say that many of the central tenets of our faith use paradox, that is, that they seem not to make logical sense but are nonetheless true. In fact, paradox is simply a subform of contradiction: To those outside the faith, and even to believers at times, contradiction is both the thought form and the issue. Said another way, paradox is a contradiction that the listener has resolved through faith or by some other means, such as experience.

Here are some of the central tenets of our faith that use contradiction:

> Creation is out of nothing.
> God is Three in One.
> God became human.
> God is with us.
> Jesus was born of a virgin.
> Christ is fully human and fully divine.
> Christ died that we might have life.
> Christ is no king and king.
> Christ has come and is coming.
> We must die to have life.
> We must lose self to find self.
> We must be born again.
> In wealth we are poor.
> By giving we receive.
> In loving we participate in eternity.
> Love is stronger than violence.
> Blessed are those who mourn.
> The only certain knowledge is the knowledge of faith.
> For the unreconcilable there is reconciliation.
> We who are many are one in Christ.
> The first will be last and the last will be first.
> The obedience God demands is the obedience God supplies.

Preaching that puts wallpaper over the contradictions in our theological halls honors neither reason nor faith. Rather, we should highlight unavoidable contradictions in faith language such that what is at issue in faith becomes clear. Like Jesus' parables, we must participate in some contradictions to make sense of them. Though lying at the edge of reason, some contradictions are also doors to faith. They open near the center of truth, that Jesus died yet is alive. They allow us to see how we are condemned by the fact that Jesus died for our sins, yet also to see how the same statement, Jesus died for our sins, stands as our hope.

Theologian and preacher Horace Bushnell once argued that "we never come so near to a truly well-rounded view of any truth, as when it is offered para-doxically; that is under contradictions."[11] His sermon "Free to Amusements and too Free to Want Them" displays stunning theological use of contradiction at a number of levels. It is based on I Corinthians 10:27. If

> *As with Jesus' parables, we must partici-pate in some contradictions to make sense of them.*

you go to an unbeliever's house who does not observe our rules of eating, he cautions, go freely, unhampered by any foolish scruples that will become an annoyance to the host or other guests. In that we are free, we do not need to exercise "the other kind of freedom, or care anything for it." He then returns to criticize those who would sin by their avoidance of sin:

Do not reduce religion to the grade of a police arrangement, and make it a law of restriction upon the world's innocent pleasures. It can not afford to hold a position so odious, and withal so nearly false; for there is no sound principle of ethics that makes it a wrong, or a sin, to indulge in plays and games of amusement, save when they are carried beyond amusement, and made instruments of vice, or vicious indulgence; when of course they may be wrong, even as feeding itself may be. Why strain a principle of restriction till it breaks, and lets out the waters of sin to sweep it clean away, and all sound virtue with it? . . . Every thing in short requires self-regulative prudence. Innocent in itself, it can be, and very often is, a gate that opens excess.[12]

Exercise 12:2 To bring the issue of faith more front and center in our preaching, we might ask of our sermon, "Is there some theological contradiction inherent in this doctrine or biblical text that I may enhance?" Rewrite the paragraph of your sermon draft that contains this doctrine to enhance the contradiction you find.

3) Metaphor—the basic polar paradigm. The most basic form of polar thought is found in the figure of speech known as metaphor. The Greek root of the word *metaphor* means "to cross over," or "to carry over," from one thing to another, assuming some point of comparison between them. Strictly speaking, a metaphor is a figure of speech that compares two things and does not use *like* or *as.* Aristotle said, "The greatest thing by far is to be a master of metaphor."[13] He spoke of metaphor's importance: "Now strange words simply puzzle us; ordi-nary words convey only what we know already; it is from metaphor that we can best get hold of something fresh. When the poet calls old age 'a withered stalk,' he conveys a new idea, a new fact."[14] The simi-larity of two ideas (old age and dying plant) is asserted. Metaphor says, "Both yes and no." For any metaphor to work, that is, for it in fact to be a metaphor, our yes (i.e., "They are similar") must be accompanied by our no (i.e., "They are different").

Metaphor is not merely a figure of speech. It is also the second of two basic paradigms in thought identified by Roman Jacobson. In studying language loss among aphasiacs, he discovered that some of his patients had lost the ability to combine thought in sequential ways, ways that he connected with metonymy. Other patients had lost the ability to recognize similarities or to connect thought in associative ways, which he connected with metaphor. He helped establish these as the two axes of thought.[15]

Metaphor, as a paradigm of thought, takes one word, phrase, image, or story and sets it alongside another, thereby establishing a meaningful link or comparison that (a) may not be strictly logical and (b) is made on the basis of perceived similarity and dissimilarity. An idea or attribute that is properly associated with one object or person is "carried over" to another.

Metaphor incorporates both comparison and contradiction: One thing is said to be another, which is in a strict sense logically impossible. Consider, for instance, the metaphor in Luther's great hymn, "A Mighty Fortress Is Our God." We cannot say in logic that God is a castle or fortress. Nonetheless a legitimate comparison is made.

To take another example, love is a red rose. Love is not a rose. Love is an emotion. Nonetheless, the beauty, fragility, and color of the rose are "carried over" to the idea of love. The metaphor starts to make sense.

Jesus spoke in metaphor in saying: "This is my body," or, "I am the good shepherd," or "I am the true vine." Similarly, Jesus' parables have the structure of metaphor: He brought a basic idea (the Realm of God) alongside a simple story, to make a profound theological statement.

A subform of metaphor that need not concern us at length is simile, which compares using like or as: "Love is like a red rose." The addition of the word "like" or "as" removes the apparent illogic, and, in reducing metaphor to simile, shifts us back to the first of our polar categories, comparison itself.

Metaphor as a paradigm of thought incorporates comparison and contradiction. One word, phrase, image, or story is set alongside another to establish a meaningful link or comparison that (a) need not be strictly logical and (b) is formed on the basis of some perceived similarity or contradiction. An idea that is properly associated with one object or person is "carried over" to another.

It can be argued that metaphor as a paradigm of thought is identical to the structure of imagination as it was conceived by the English Romantics (c. 1790–1840). Imagine a hand-cranked generator from an old telephone. The two wires leading from it carry an electric current, as long as the generator is being turned. When the wires are touching, no spark is visible. Much of our normal conversation is like that: Meaning flows but without the flash of imagination. When the wires are a few inches apart from each other, however, a steady spark will jump across the gap between them. Imagination is like that: Two ideas are brought into relationship, one with the other, and a spark leaps between them, a fresh insight, visible energy. This sparking can occur at various levels in the homiletical process: with individual words (i.e. metaphors), between the biblical text and our situation, between judgment and grace, between story and doctrine, and between pastor and prophet, to name a few of the more important areas for polar thought.[16]

Metaphor functions as a unit and is dependent upon metonymy to link it into the chain of thought, to make it part of the whole.

Practical Uses of Metaphor

There are several key ways of conceiving of metaphor and experimenting with it for preaching.

1) Metaphor as points of contact between the biblical text and our world. We are using metaphor from the beginning of our sermon when we conceive of comparisons between the biblical text and our time. Whether we follow Buttrick's "moves" in a sermon, or Long's "focus" and "function," or my "concern of the text" and "concern of the sermon," "major concern of the text" and "major concern of the sermon," the overarching paradigm we are following is metaphor. A theological idea from the biblical text is first developed in relation to that text, and is then transposed to our situation as an "analogy of experience." This movement to our time breaks the metonymic progression of the text as we step aside from it to explore relevance.[17]

The primary energy now shifts from unidirectional development of the text, to polar energy that flows back and forth between the text and our situation as we explore similarities. Together as a polar unit, the poles say, "This is that: this situation in the Bible is that situation in our life" (or vice versa). In the sermon they become a full paragraph or two (or in Buttrick's terms, several minutes of developing consciousness).

2) Metaphor as a dominant image of the central idea. A dominant image in a sermon is frequently the dominant image from the biblical text. This image becomes identified with the central idea of the sermon. For instance a sermon might have primary focus on the image of a burning bush, or of a still, small voice, or of water being turned into wine. While some readers might already interpret the image as a metaphor of God in the biblical text, it becomes a metaphor of God in the sermon when it is developed in relation to God, in other words, when its biblical significance is represented by the preacher.

It is equally possible to draw a dominant image from contemporary experience, for instance a civic election, or a flood, or homecoming, or harvest. The biblical text might suggest the image in our world: for instance, a student preaching on Jesus' cleansing of the temple chose to speak about God in the whirlwind. Another student using that text might find in Jesus' no-nonsense attitude the image of a bicycle courier who does not stop for traffic lights, cars, or pedestrians. Images thus become theological metaphors.

A dominant image or metaphor is dominant simply because it is given central focus. It becomes more than this, or what we might call a unifying or controlling image or metaphor when it is repeated, appearing in a variety of contexts within the sermon, rather than being developed in just one place. When images and metaphors are treated in this repeated fashion, such that they form a chain of references linking the same image throughout the sermon, they are functioning metonymically (e.g., see Robert F. Smith's use of the image "faces like flint" in the metonymy discussion).

The most daring or risky kind of dominant, unifying, or controlling image or metaphor can be one for which there is no biblical link (see the sermon at the conclusion of this chapter). Let us take the common image of a bus. If preaching on the great commandment, one could weave in a story about a woman who wanted to find out what Jesus meant by it. The story is an allegory, but used in this way it does not distort the biblical text, as allegory in a sermon so frequently does:

She went to the curb and boarded the bus that read across the front at the top, as its destination, "Love God and Your Neighbor as Yourself." At the end of its run she got off, only to discover that she was in the heart of suburban Impossible. She went to the minister of Impossible Community Church, only to be told that it was up to her to love God and her neighbor. She had to rely on her own resources. She left that church thinking it was impossible. She caught the same bus back, surprisingly with the same text cited as its destination. It was on the way back that it occurred to her that the impossible is possible only with God. Only by God's action was it possible for her to fulfill the great commandment. All things are possible with God.

Exercise 12:3 Should you wish to explore this use of image, decide to do so only after your exegesis is completed, when the biblical text is not likely to be distorted. Identify your central idea or action statement. Now simply search in your mind for some location or event in which those words might be heard, or seen. They might be scratched into the metal of a telephone booth, stamped onto a letter, sung in a Country and Western song, read from a newspaper by grocery shoppers in a queue, carved into a hospital window sill, written on a bumper sticker, flown on a banner at a football game, or stuffed into a garbage can. Now, imagine that you are there. Use exercises like those of the literary and theology students in chapter 3, only now use them to explore the imaginary scene, and to determine how the words got there, who wrote them, how God was seen, and so on, always in a way that will lead us to the biblical text and God in our own lives. In other words, use the same literary and theological exercises we used to deconstruct the biblical text, now to construct the new text of the sermon itself.

3) Stories as extended metaphors. As preachers we need particular help in finding stories of God in our world. On one hand it seems so obvi-

247

ous that the preacher's task is to name God in our world. Yet on the other hand, so many preachers have tremendous difficulty when it comes to this. "How can we be sure what is God?" some ask. "What does God look like?" others may cry. Yet Jesus used his parables in this manner.

Obviously there is boldness in claiming God's presence or action in certain events. We cannot have absolute certainty in naming God in the present moment, yet we proceed in faith.

One of the most important things we can do to name God in the present is to look for signs of the inbreaking Realm of God. Thus we may say that we see God acting wherever there are acts of authentic love, peace, mercy, justice, reconciliation, righteousness, comfort in the midst of suffering, compassion, healing, order out of chaos (and sometimes the reverse), hope out of despair, and the like. While we do not overlook or underestimate our capacity for deception, or the possibility that God's inbreaking in this moment could yet be temporarily thwarted by the power of evil in the next, we nonetheless in this moment proclaim God's activities in our midst.

Thus entire stories from experience can function as extended theological metaphors when held adjacent to that dimension of God's inbreaking realm to which they point in the biblical text. The story and the idea become the poles between which metaphoric meaning is generated.

A common mistake of preachers who have discovered ways of naming God in experience, is to think that these stories can stand on their own, almost as self-evident "proofs" of God or God's nature. (Medieval preachers did the same thing with arguments of the church fathers: Simply to cite the argument was to "prove" the theological case.) However, every story and experience has many possible interpretations. Stories cannot escape ambiguity. Some of our stories, if separated from the Bible, can imply things that are not true of God. To ensure that stories of God are heard correctly, and have the appropriate kind of theological nuancing, we use them in polar fashion alongside the biblical text to demonstrate what we have learned about God from it.

> *Four Homiletical Uses of Metaphor*
>
> 1) *Points of contact between the biblical text and our world (i.e., concerns of the text and concerns of the sermon)*
> 2) *Dominant images of the central idea*
> 3) *Stories as extended metaphors*
> 4) *Theological categories of experience*

4) *Metaphors and theological categories of experience.* Consider another important

approach to metaphor for the sermon: I recommend that as preachers we view the world around us in terms of six theological categories of experience. (These are the six categories for "concerns of the sermon" identified in chapter 8.) If we train ourselves to view the world theologically through these categories, we will know what stories connect most readily with our concerns of the sermon. In other words, each experience that we may relate, and each concern of the sermon we may use points us to at least one of these theological perspectives. We need simply to match categories and interpret what we say in their light.

a) Metaphors of God's judgment. Theologically and pastorally, this is the most difficult kind of metaphor to establish, if only because so much harm has been done by Christians ascribing God's punishment to some suffering or tragedy in people's lives. For instance, Billy Graham recently recanted what he said to a reporter from the *Cleveland Plain-Dealer* that AIDS was a judgment of God, acknowledging that such a statement was both wrong and cruel. What can prevent us from this kind of mistake is the incarnation, cross and resurrection, which loudly proclaim that God is a God of unrelenting love. God may help us in ways we find difficult, but God is not the author of suffering and misery; and it is God who brings good out of all evil.

Jesus denied validity in this approach of attributing God's punishment to current human suffering. For instance, Jesus refused to grant that the eighteen Galileans, killed by the fall of the tower in Siloam, were being punished for their sins. His homiletical approach can be ours. He used their story as a metaphor of the judgment that rests upon us all: "Do you think that they were worse offenders than all the others living in Jerusalem? No, I tell you; but unless you repent, you will all perish just as they did" (Luke 13:4-5).

An elderly woman was recently found in her home where she had been dead for more than a year, her neighbors unaware, though they kept cutting her lawn! Such a story can stand as God's judgment against us for how we live.

As I write, tragic fires sweep through California, fed by the annual Santa Ana winds. Their description in the *New York Times* (Oct. 28, 1993) is poignant:

The winds rush [from Utah] toward the sea, growing hotter and drier as they are compressed at lower altitude. As they are funnelled through mountain canyons, they gain speed. For restless days and nights they blow, hot and unsettling. Humidity drops to nearly nothing. After a couple of days the wood of houses dries so much it begins to creak. Soon cabinets, doors and drawers that used to fit warp and stick ... even plants with high water contents, like cactus, can burn like tinder. A few hours of Santa Anas puts people on edge. They feel as if they cannot drink enough liquid. When the winds last for a week or more, as they often do, moods become worse. "It is the season of suicide and divorce and prickly dread, whenever the wind blows," Joan Didion wrote.

Once the fires are out and danger past (thereby not making light of anyone's suffering), might not this passage be used in an Advent sermon to speak about the nearness of God's judgment on us all (not specifically on those threatened in California)?

Exercise 12:4 Read Matthew 18–25 and identify various images of God's judgment that Jesus used from his culture. Now identify several scenes from your own world and how you might use them to similar effect.

b) Metaphors of the human condition. These are the tragic stories we see every day on the news: the story of a young boy afraid to walk to or from school for fear of violence; the story of a woman, formerly a music teacher in Sarajevo and now a sniper in the army; the story of someone who is unemployed; the story of a wealthy executive whose addiction is destroying everything. We may hold up one of these stories as saying something about our human condition and the choices we make.

Never relate details of violence, or spend more than even a sentence or two on a story that evokes vivid images of violence: the images are too common, too powerful, and besides being too hard to counter in another part of the sermon, they can easily become a form of negative manipulation that can undermine the pastoral relationship.

Rather than identifying a separate category of theological metaphor for nature, it is arguably best to treat experiences of nature as metaphors of the human condition (or possibly in one of the other categories). There are three reasons for this: (1) The sermon should remain theologically, not ecologically focused; thus, treat human abuse of creation in the first instance as a metaphor of the human condition (e.g. as sin). (2) Listeners are primarily interested in stories of people in relationship, not facts about nature, isolated from people who are affected by natural events. (3) Stories of God perceived in nature are best used only with great caution, and not as evidence of the existence of God. Discoveries of God in nature are so greatly determined by the situation of the viewer, that they are not often persuasive to the situation of listeners.

For example, bright sunlight might be as depressing to one person in mourning as it is uplifting to a patient just out of the hospital. Sunlight does not make God closer, nor does its absence make God further away.

Some restrictions apply: We tell stories of the human condition as a way of pointing to what is wrong with ourselves and human society, not what is wrong with the people in the stories. (The finger of judgment in the sermon almost always points first at ourselves, not at others, for we are the ones the Word initially convicts.) We tell the details of these stories, but we never relate details of violence, or spend more than even a sentence or so on a story that evokes vivid images of violence, for to do so is similar to using the techniques of horror films to evoke a voyeuristic emotion. Name and denounce evil, do not paint it in detail, for it is not evil that we preach, but God's condemnation of it and victory over it in Jesus Christ.

Exercise 12:5 Watch the evening news of one of the leading television networks and pick one story to write as a metaphor of our human experience. Write the story to conform as nearly as possible with what you would actually use in a sermon.

c) Metaphors of Christ's present suffering and crucifixion. In every corner of the world we hear stories of innocent people being forced to suffer at the hands of others, or because of greed, malice, envy, sickness, and so on. The stories may describe the homeless, or those without needed medical assistance, or those in prison, or the person who is betrayed. We hold the cross up to these situations and claim them to be both Christ's concern and places in which Christ may be found suffering.

d) Metaphors of God's forgiveness. Many preachers tell stories of people whose lives were turned around, often in dramatic ways, through discovery of a new beginning in Jesus Christ (e.g., the alcoholic or drug addict who goes into recovery, the workaholic professional who starts to care about people).

e) Metaphors of God overturning the world. Here we do not resort to simplistic stories of the happy-ever-after variety, for they do not speak the truth about life, and do not serve the gospel well. Even stories in which everything turns out all right in response to prayer must be used with caution. These incidents may be mentioned, but they tend to imply that God is punishing those listeners whose situations did not turn out well. Rather we use stories where, in the moment, irrespective of other realities, God is glimpsed at work. The ambiguities of life are not erased. Here is an example:

A father was despairing of reaching his teenage son who for some months had been withdrawn to all but his small circle of friends. Questions were met with one-word responses. Invitations to do things together were refused. Attempts to communicate were foiled. "Sorry, Dad, I have an incoming call." Or, "Sorry, I am just going out." Anger did not work. And it seemed that neither did love. Or prayer. Trust that had built over the years now fell like clumps from the bank into a swirling stream: Too much secrecy about nights out. Slipping grades.

One night the father tried again, as he had many nights. He spoke about his own experiences at the same age. He told his son that if he worked hard he could do almost anything he chose. Most important, he told him, "I love you."

Later that night his son came to him. What he said was not much, but it was something that he had not said in two years. He said, "Dad, do you want to play a game?" It was not much, but it was more than enough, and more than his father had even dared to hope for. In those words, just for a moment, the father thought he heard God saying, "I'm still here. Do not despair."

Exercise 12:6 Tell a similar kind of story in which the ending could be seen as ambiguous, yet is interpreted in light of God's grace.

Six Theological Metaphors of Experience

1) God's judgment on us
2) the human condition
3) Christ's suffering and crucifixion in the world
4) God's forgiveness
5) God overturning the world
6) God using people

f) Metaphors of God using people. God may act independent of people, or through people. In sermons we commonly try to tell stories of people doing loving acts. One of the common errors we make is in letting the people shine on their own merits, instead of pointing to God who enables them to love.

Note the skillful manner in which Gardner C. Taylor uses this next story, a sermonic digression, to point to God. A man approached him at the close of a service. They had not seen each other since youth, and the man had become a doctor. The man tells him how he would never have become a doctor had someone not helped him out. Also notice how relevance is established by the end:

And he told me about a man, dearly loved of me, who let him have sixty-five dollars, so that he could get back to his job, so he could go to school. He said to me, "That man did not know that right then I was at the end of my courage, and if he had not given me that sixty-five dollars, I would have given up."

Now that man *did not know*—but as surely as I stand here, my faith says to me that there was somebody who *did* know, somebody who *knows* when we reach the end of our patience, somebody who *knows* when our strength has all but failed, who *knows* when we have borne the last sorrow. He is the One who cares.[18]

A Word of Caution Concerning Metaphor

Three common errors are made by preachers who are strong in polar thought:

1) Preachers dominant in polar thought sometimes make the mistake of preaching biblical images, neglecting to identify a specific connection with God, thereby failing to develop theological metaphors. Whether the image is that of "being swallowed by the whale" or of "the blind man seeing," the image is treated as though it unambiguously carries the intellectual and theological freight of the biblical passage from which it comes. Not every image in a biblical text communicates God. Again, to develop an image in a fine poetic manner, that is, to show that image in a variety of unusual settings, does not ensure that the Good News we are seeking to proclaim has in fact been presented or understood. It may be functioning as a metaphor of the biblical text, but may not yet be functioning theologically, for instance as a metaphor of God in the sermon. It is often the central idea of the sermon, with direct focus on God, as much as any image itself, that needs emphasis. Thus when the image is recalled, it is restored to the theological and metaphorical significance we discovered it to have in the biblical text.

> **Working Definitions**
>
> *image: a word picture*
> *metaphor: an idea (e.g. love) is connected with a picture (e.g. rose) in a relationship of assumed similarity (e.g. love is a rose)*
> *theological metaphor: an image is connected to an idea about God.*
> *story: a plot involving characters and emotions*
> *parable: an extended metaphor in which a religious idea (e.g. the Realm of God) is connected with a story about ordinary life*

For example, to preach the image of the burning bush is not enough, no matter how many locations in which we might imaginatively portray the bush burning in life today. The image in the Bible is connected with God; it is a vehicle of God's message. Literary critic I. A. Richards once defined metaphor as consisting of two parts, the vehicle (i.e., that which carried the message) and the tenor (the message itself).[19]

253

The norm here is simply this: Repeat explicitly the major concern of the text, and ensure that the dominant image is fully associated with this central message in the minds of the listeners. Thus the dominant image becomes a metaphor of God.[20]

2) Preachers to whom images very readily come will often load their sermons with images. In the worst cases, competing images shift the focus to a new scene or example every sentence or two. Rather than the images serving the central idea of the sermon, the central idea is subverted into serving the images for they take over. A sermon that functions in this way is as demanding as a highly abstract treatise. As a sermon, it may have little reward and may frustrate or anger its hearers.

Sometimes the biblical text itself may seem to prompt us in this direction of multiple images. For instance, the transfiguration account in Mark 9 suggests a blazing array of potentially confounding images for one sermon: mountaintop experience; valleys [of life]; enveloping clouds; transfiguration; dazzling white clothes; garment of light; voice from heaven; and, by the frequent relationship of this text with approaching Lent, the wilderness.

To counter excessive imagery: (a) Focus more on developing linear thought, (b) focus in one place or on one idea for a sufficient length of time (perhaps one manuscript page) so that hearers may appropriate what you are saying with ease and clarity, before moving to the next focus, and (c) most important, choose just one image to develop in a paragraph or even throughout the sermon. This may come from the biblical text, or from some story of experience to which we relate the text.

3) Frequently preachers who are imagistic in their thinking bring new images to established ones. For all the benefits of this talent in preaching, dangers are present as well. An attempt to say something fresh can end up as muddied thought. Thus baptism, for instance, which Christians already connect with being washed of our sins, might be imagined as "birthing" (which also involves water), perhaps on the basis of being born again (John 3:3). Alternatively, the meal in which we share the body and blood of Christ, might be pictured as a picnic. Or again, the cross, which can be variously a metaphor or symbol of crucifixion, atonement, sin, suffering, injustice, and so on, might instead be described as having the shape of a pickax used in a murder. Or, once more, the Reign of God, which can be a metaphor for God's just and merciful authority over all, might be addressed by using a pun on rain, thus the rain of God that falls on all. In this manner, cluttered images and mixed metaphors are produced (sometimes consciously) in which meanings clash and communication falters.

A simple rule helps to avoid this. When dealing with any of the central symbols and doctrines of our faith, stay with the original biblical images and common theological understandings. Nurture the community of faith by expounding a good traditional meaning. Then introduce someone's actual experience to help provide the desired freshness or newness of understanding.

A Sermon Demonstrating Linear and Polar Thought

The following sermon attempts to demonstrate our learnings. It was preached at Timothy Eaton Memorial Church in Toronto on Sunday, July 11, 1993, using Romans 8:1-11. Since the text itself does not supply much narrative or imagery, I supply it, remembering the need for preachers to make a movie with words.

The Coin of Hope

What a delight it is for me to be worshiping with this wonderful congregation once again, on another great Sunday to celebrate the resurrection of Christ. God has issued no apologies for the hot weather, so to any guests with us, or listening on radio, at home or in hospital, let me simply extend what you have already felt, God's warm welcome to this service of worship, and into God's presence.

I opened my Bible this week to the book of Romans, chapter 8, our lesson for today, and a coin fell out. I do not know how long it had been there. It just fell out onto the floor, and lazily rolled a curling path across the kitchen to where it finally wobbled to rest near the dog's dish. It was about the size of a silver dollar and was the color of a faded old penny. Even before I ran my thumb over it, I knew it was well worn. The letters, both to my eye and thumb, were smooth, and I could hardly read them. I thought at first it said, In God We Trust. But that is not what it said. On closer examination it said, God Gives Hope. God Gives Hope. *[This is the central action statement or major concern of the text around which I will develop this sermon. I have chosen a coin as a common visual image from daily life with which I might speak of this idea in a way that interests me, in the first instance.]* The words circled the perimeter of the coin, and in the center there appeared to be the face of someone I assumed was Jesus Christ. It was a Hope coin, and I could only imagine the sweaty palms or the white knuckled fingers that had clutched it in previous years. You probably have some at

255

home, hidden in a coin jar, or in the bottom of a drawer, or in the pages of your own Bible. Your coins are probably old and well worn, almost done in, like mine.

I could see from the imprint on the page of the Bible that it had been pressed into these verses written by Paul [the coin image is functioning metonymically to link with the previous paragraph and to take us into the biblical text to develop the central action]: "For those who live according to the flesh set their minds on things of the flesh, but those who live according to the Spirit set their minds on the things of the Spirit. To set the mind on the flesh is death, but to set the mind on the Spirit is life and peace." It seemed appropriate that this Hope coin lay wedged in these verses. Paul says, if we want to live life in a hopeful and positive way, then we have to look to spiritual matters, not the things of this world. [This idea will be restated now with small, linear steps forward in each sentence, primarily using "if . . . then," to begin developing a sense of judgment.] If we want to be able to get up in the morning, and throw open the drapes saying, "Isn't it great to be alive!" then we must have gone to sleep trusting, at least in some small way, in God to watch over us and our loved ones. If we want to believe, as the coin says, that God gives hope, then we may have to read our Bibles to know that God is hope, that when we've got hope it comes from God, and that there is no hope without God.

I met a woman who had a coin like mine. [The coin continues to function as a linking metonym as we move in polar fashion into the experience of parenting.] She carried it around in her purse. She has arrived at that place that all parents hope they will avoid and perhaps few do. It's the place where you stand, as you watch your children run off to the park, like they did those hundreds of times with footballs in fall, skates in winter, baseball mitts in spring, and swimming trunks in summer. Only now it's not daytime, and they are not little any more, and they don't come back with clutches of wilted dandelions in their sweaty little fists: They are twelve and thirteen. And they aren't staying in sight. In fact, they may not even be telling you where they are going. But you know, or think you do. If it is not this park, its another, or some deserted schoolyard. And you imagine that if they aren't smoking cigarettes, maybe they are smoking something else, or drinking. It is innocence we are waving good-bye to. We knew we would have to sometime, only not so soon, just in their early teens. We don't know what will return in its place. It is so hard to trust. And the worry will not subside. This woman said, "I want to blame the school system, if only it was more strict; or the church, for turning them off; or society, for having no respect for authority; but really, I fear, somehow it is my own fault. Somewhere I have failed." *[Parenting has become a new chain of thought uniting this paragraph.]* Strange how we can have a coin as big as a Hope coin, in a purse or pocket, and forget that we even have it. *[This sentence pulls us back to the central line of thought.]*

Of course we know what that is like. *[More comparative moves or digression, in an attempt to try to include everyone.]* Many of us have forgotten that we have Hope coins, if we ever noticed. We could just say a few words—words like drugs, population explosion, ozone layer, destruction of the rain forests, recession, unemployment—and see how quickly despair starts flooding with waters deeper than the swollen Mississippi. *[Tragic flooding was occurring at this time.]*

Another man had a coin of hope. *[The central chain of thought is continued in earnest.]* His name was Paul. He couldn't wait until he would be in Rome in person to spend his coin. So he sent it on ahead of him, together with his letter, to people he didn't even know. They had conflicts in their church. Some were just returning from being exiled for their faith, and were now being treated as immigrants, foreigners. You need this coin now, he wrote. I want you to spend it as soon as you get it.

Sometimes it is better to wait until you see someone face-to-face, rather than send a letter, and risk being misunderstood. In the little house church by the vineyard in Rome, some would have misunderstood Paul. His letter was being read aloud, "To set the mind on the flesh is death, but to set the mind on the Spirit is life and peace." The coin dropped out onto the dirt floor, unnoticed by some. "Oh sure, honey," one man in the doorway clucked to his wife, "When the world of the flesh is running amok, look to spiritual things. Keep your eye on heaven. It's more like, stick your head in the sand." *[One possible dimension of the biblical text is developed to stand in contradiction to Paul's intent.]* Is that why Paul sent his hope coin in the mail? Forget the world! Think of heaven! In some circumstances, that can be like taking drugs—a form of escape from reality.

Let us be clear about this. As the couple in the doorway eventually understood, Christ is not an escape from reality, but an escape to reality *[two poles are set against each other]*. For this Christ that you have met in your life, is the same Jesus that was put to death, and yet lives, his life being stronger than the grave. *[A series of similar metonyms reaching to the past is now developed.]* If you want hope, side with a God who is love. No power is stronger. This is the God who created everything out of nothing, and brought order out of chaos. This is the God who set in motion a million tiny balances that, a few degrees centigrade one direction or another, a little less tilt of the earth's axis, would have meant no life on earth. Is this not also a God who may be trusted to bring order out of the chaos of your life? *[Metonyms of the past now switch to metonyms reaching to the future.]* It is the God who created all things, who will bring order out of the chaos of our times. It is the God who brings order out of the chaos of our times, who is raising our children to be fine leaders, more responsible than we have been in caring for the earth. It is the God who is caring for our children, and our children's children, and our great grandchildren, who brought forth Christ from the dead, that we might have faith, and live lives of hope, not despair.

So hope. Lift your eyes, not to heaven and away from the suffering of this world. Rather, look to the brokenness of this world, even to your own, and see Christ laboring in the midst of it, with your children and mine. *[Again, this is a lateral, polar movement into our experience.]* Think, for instance of the eight-year-old girl, Jocelyn McDonald, recently given the Governor General's Star of Courage Award in Ottawa. She is the youngest person ever to have received this second highest possible Canadian honor. When a man took her five-year-old friend, she followed. She threw a stone that made him let go, only for a moment. When they entered the man's house she waited a minute and then against better wisdom snuck in, found her friend in an upstairs room, and snuck her out before any harm could come to them. It was God acting in that girl.

Go into the brokenness, doing your part, and experience the power of the Holy Spirit giving you hope and strength and courage to carry on. *[We continue to look to experience, to include everyone, and to establish mission.]* Keep your eyes on the things of the Spirit, on peace, mercy, justice, righteousness, both here and in heaven; and your heart tuned to the compelling desire of the Spirit, to bring goodness in the midst of this world of flesh, and in the world to come. And when at last the Father calls us home with a mothering love, we may close our eyes in peace, knowing that all is in good hands.

I have my Hope coin right here. *[A return to the central metonym, which has also become a metaphor of the text for our lives.]* I'll just hold it up so you can see it in the sunlight. Of course, even if you are in the front pews, you need to be looking with the eyes of faith in order to see it. I have one in my hand even as you have one in yours. No matter how old and worn, as soon as we spend it, it becomes shiny and new. The words, God Gives Hope, stand out in bas-relief, and the face of Christ is there before us. Check it out. Look in the offering plate as it goes by this morning, or try it during the week, as you share your coins with everyone you meet.

Implications of Linear and Polar Thought for Sermon Form

We have considered three kinds of progression or linear thought (definition, sequence, and metonymy) and three corresponding kinds of digression or polar thought (comparison, contradiction, and metaphor). What is the importance of such attention to poetics? Although homiletical discussion of recent decades tends to focus for instance on inductive-narrative and deductive-propositional categories, we saw that these distinctions are no longer adequate to the homiletical task, at least in the manner they have popularly been stretched through overuse. The terms are good, we need simply to be more guarded in our use of them. Instead of being restricted primarily to two categories for discussing many homiletical issues, we now have a variety of subforms that are reliably based in the structure of language itself. Each allows us opportunity for improvement.

Moreover, preachers can identify structures that can be strengthened in preaching, structures that support theological discourse. Thus if linear preachers can learn to incorporate controlled digression in their preaching, their sermons will have more relevance and interest. And if polar preachers can learn to incorporate stepped movement and progression of various sorts in their preaching, they will be more easily followed.

Preachers can monitor their own writing, seeking to alternate between linear and polar thought. More than one or two paragraphs of intense linear progression, developing the central idea of the sermon, is too much. Some digression is needed. By the same token, more than one or two paragraphs in apparent digression might be too much. Listeners should be reminded where the sermon is going. The progression of linear thought and the digression of polar thought are part of the warp and woof of the woven Word, and need to be interspersed.

In spite of the revolution in homiletics, and for all the impact of narrative in the pulpit, we hear no groundswell of voices saying that we have yet entered a new era in which the quality of preaching has radically improved. Style has changed. In fact, one experienced homiletician has claimed that with the widespread adoption of the lectionary, sermons have become more biblical, but they are also "somewhat more boring."[21] Important work has been done. Theory and praxis are rapidly evolving. However, we are still in the midst of a long process of change that, with the Holy Spirit, may yet lead to a rebirth of preaching. To date, all that we can say for certain is that there are more varieties of sermon available, many more resources for preachers, much creative scholarly and practical exploration, and much promise afoot.

Another important aspect of our study is the similarities between narrative and propositional genres: Each needs both linear and polar thought, though each may have its own expression of these. For instance, propositional genres are likely to have logic as a dominant sequence, narratives are likely to have plot (i.e., other forms of sequence like chronology, emotion, etc.). Yet both need metonymy. Propositional genres are more likely to define an object, narratives are more likely to describe it. Yet both need metaphor. Both genres need each other, and both need creativity, which is one of the reasons it is mistaken to identify imagination in a simplistic way with a genre such as narrative. In addition, metonymy has its own way of being creative, for instance in dissolving time and space, and it is present in both genres.

Metonymy and metaphor are subjects that deserve more attention than can be given here, not least to understand creativity. A second area of future importance will be the subject of performative language; that is, language that does what it says. How do linear and polar thought accomplish what they speak? What is the connection between theological language as event and preaching as God's event?

One essential aspect of preaching remains for us to consider here: the mission of Christ. No sermon is truly complete until it is incarnate in lives of faith and service. Every sermon should contain some pointer or invitation to action for Christ's followers. In our final chapter, then, we look to poetics for contributions to our mission purpose.

Practical Questions for Use of Metonymy and Metaphor

Practical Questions to Assist Preachers in Using Metonymy:
- Have I clearly stated an action of God in my sermon?
- If I were to state the central idea of the paragraph I am working on, what would it be? Have I stated it clearly in the paragraph?
- When I start a new paragraph, do I make clear the link to the central idea of my foregoing paragraph? Do I also make clear the subject or central idea of this one?

- Have I had one dominant chain of thought throughout, which will be evident to my listeners?
- Is there sufficient sense of something happening, or of thought progressing or developing?
- Did I allow metonymy to dissolve time and space, speaking of Jesus now, in various places, or us in Jesus' time?
- How does this sermon link to the resurrection?
- Given all that I have said in the sermon, what do we do, to where are we led, what is the mission to which Christ is now inviting us?
- In rehearsing my completed sermon, can I remember the linear progression of it, step by step? If not, have I made it clear enough (both for myself in the delivery and for my listeners in the hearing)?

Exercise 12:7 for Polar Thinkers: As a creative exercise, write a paragraph (one that you would not use in a sermon) on any topic. Demonstrate in that paragraph each type of linear thought that was discussed in chapter 11 (i.e., definition, description, various kinds of sequence, various uses of metonymy).

Practical Questions to Assist Preachers in Using Metaphor:
- Have I tried to employ polar thought, looking for helpful places to draw comparisons? Are there any worthwhile surprises in the direction of my thought?
- Is there some contradiction to be identified that is worth exploring?
- Have I used digression to create interest, evoke feelings, and involve listeners?
- Have I enabled the biblical text to stand as a metaphor of life today?
- Have I made clear the relevance of my topic in the lives of the people?
- Have I linked digressions into the chain of thought with metonymy?
- Is there some dominant image I can use to support my central idea?
- Have I used it repeatedly?
- In rehearsing my completed sermon, do I have a balance of experience (e.g., men and women, young and old, near and far, rich and poor, various cultures and countries)?

Exercise 12:8 for Linear Thinkers: As a creative exercise, in two separate steps, write the following: (1) a brief one-paragraph story about any object of interest, omitting any comparisons whatsoever. (2) Now rewrite that paragraph such that the object is now used as a comparison to describe one of your parents. The object is still your focus, but the parent is your subject.[22]

Review Questions for Chapter Twelve

1) What is not said to be generally true of polar thinkers?
   a) they think through steps in order
   b) they find relevance
   c) are imaginative
   d) none of the above   [a]

2) From the foregoing two chapters, which is correct?
   a) paradox is a subform of contradiction
   b) synecdoche is a subform of metonymy
   c) simile is a subform of metaphor
   d) all of the above   [d]

3) Metaphor is
   a) a paradigm of thought
   b) the ability to see similarities
   c) the structure of imagination
   d) a figure of speech
   e) all of the above   [e]

4) Which of the following was not suggested as a homiletical
   category for experience?
   a) God's judgment
   b) the condition of nature
   c) the human condition
   d) God acting through people   [b]

5) One of the following is a danger for predominantly polar
   preachers:
   a) preaching images not ideas
   b) not knowing what images to use
   c) staying with traditional helpful metaphors
   d) all of the above   [a]

Questions for Discussion

1) Is it possible to do theology and omit metaphor?
2) What practical steps might you devise for your own ministry to
   ensure that you keep working to develop the weaker aspect of your
   own thought and expression?

CHAPTER THIRTEEN

MISSION, TRUTH, AND STORIES

Mission begins in the sermon itself. Use of story in service of mission means that preachers must at times decide between loyalty to fact and loyalty to faith. Imitation of reality or verisimilitude has practical implications for a preacher's voice and delivery, use of character and plot, and use of contemporary stories from personal life, the arts, or news. The event of Christ in the sermon has implications for the world.

Preaching is distinguished from other speaking events by functioning as an event of divine encounter. The sermon initiates a response in the hearers that becomes Christ's mission in the world. Our thrust here is bold: It is to claim that preaching is more than an individual and congregational event, and more even than a regional or national event. It is a global event, the proportions of which are to be found in God's saving purpose for humanity.

The sermon begins doing Christ's work through being the word Christ chooses to make his own, but also through becoming what Christ speaks, Christ's presence in our midst by the power of the Holy Spirit. The sermon is the Word, the meeting, the message, the relationship, the action—the event of salvation that becomes completed and enacted visibly in the sacrament of Eucharist.

Thus we may say that God's inbreaking truth, of which our words are effective bearers, comes more as transformation than information, more as action than abstraction, more as gift than burden. Even our language is transformed by the import of its message. We do not hedge our words with hesitancy and tentativeness, by saying "I believe" or "I think," for the focus is not the preacher, and the force of the Word is proclamation. We are also unable to speak about a personal God in impersonal ways, about the love of God in unfeeling ways, about the actions of God as though they themselves are passive, or about the privilege of mission as though it were mere duty.

Moreover, God's Word goes forth in power. As preachers, we utter dreams for humanity to which we and our congregation have been led by faith. God's will is not left to the "musts" and "shoulds" that are required of us. No matter how familiar the scenes we paint, we picture new possibilities with God in ways that God actually enables. These possibilities are already in the process of being realized, overcoming the realities of sin, evil, and indifference to which we may have grown accustomed. Thus the peace which we proclaim participates in the peace which its proclamation initiates. The love and justice we speak become part of Christ's expression of that love, and doing of that justice, in the world. It is not mere information about grace we are communicating; it is the experience of grace that we are sharing in the person of Christ through the Holy Spirit.

The question, of course, is, How do we do this in authentic ways? How do we help restore metonymy to Christian faith, to the degree that past, present, and future in our minds become what they are in fact, an unbroken story of God's love? Further, how do we help restore metaphor to Christian faith, such that the suffering of our neighbor becomes a metaphor for our own and Christ's suffering, and yet by the grace of God somehow also an invitation to promise? To begin answering these important questions we turn to raise one final issue concerning poetics: the question of fact, fiction, and truth.

Fact, Fiction, and Truth

Often to tell a story in a lifelike way, as preachers we must include details that are beyond our direct knowledge (e.g. weather, time of day) because they were not part of what we heard or remember. If we are going to re-create biblical stories or current events, and not just report them, in a small way we again become movie directors making essential decisions about background details not in the script.

Or we might decide, for legitimate pastoral reasons, to alter the details (names, location, gender, age, etc.) of a story that was important to use in a sermon. Here is one of the great dilemmas for any preacher: How can I, as a proclaimer of truth, say something that I know to be less than wholly true? If I say something that we do not know to be fact, have I crossed into untruth? What is the role of creativity in the sermon?

The preacher must never lie; or claim that something is factual that is fictional; or say that something was a personal experience that was not; or disclose something that was told in confidence. Most of us would agree to the corollary, that what we say must be true, yet it is here that the problems arise.

Stories for the sermon are not meant to be verified primarily by logical tests, for instance by strict assessment of fact. They are accounts of experience, and experience is always limited by the viewer, who is selective in describing experience. The primary test of stories is known in poetics as verisimilitude. Verisimilitude is the lifelike imitation of reality such that what is told resonates with the listeners' experience as being true. In other words, does it seem like this happened or could happen? Thus a story about a woman who spoke French to the sparrows in her feeder, might have verisimilitude; but a story of a woman whose sparrows spoke French to her would not. Verisimilitude is about more than being believable and convincing, however. It is about making truth claims through our own imitations of reality. This is the same test that we apply for instance to popular movies. At some level they must convince us of their truth, of their correspondence to some aspect of reality as we know it. Can something be true if it is not fact but fiction? How we view art and works of imagination will help determine how we answer this question. Humorist Garrison Keillor likes to tell the audience that he has made his living telling lies, but anyone who listens carefully to his monologues knows he is more frequently telling the truth.

Verisimilitude is the lifelike imitation of reality such that what is told resonates with the listeners' experience as being true.

We may look to what may seem like an unlikely place for imagination—the Bible. We may recognize that Jesus' parables are a creative treatment of the world around him. As Fred Craddock notes, "Someone might have asked Jesus after his telling a parable, 'Did that really happen?' but probably not, since such stories were familiar in that culture."[1]

The issue of facticity is turned up a notch, however, when we consider the dilemmas faced by the Gospel writers. Parallels indicate that they clearly had the earliest Gospel in front of them as they wrote (most scholars concur that this was Mark), yet they altered details to suit their own theological accounts. They changed locations, the chronology of Jesus' life, and extended or otherwise altered the words of Jesus himself. To us this tampering with an earlier source might be a form of lying or distortion of the truth. To them it was not. Rather, they were operating by a notion of spiritual truth rooted in fact, witnessing to their faith, not in modern historical truth that gives sole priority to documented detail.

To seek a simple answer for our question concerning truth and fiction may not be possible. Theologian Julian N. Hartt argues with an appropriate subtlety and nuancing: "A story may be truthful, that is authentic, whether or not it is factually accurate. Which is to say it may square with our perceptions and value structures even though it may be faulted by our memories or by some public instrument for ascertaining the facts."[2] Our problem may be improperly framed as a bald choice between truth or untruth. Elizabeth Achtemeier is close to the heart of the matter in observing in *Preaching as Theology and Art* that "art allows the one seeing or hearing it to enter into a new experience . . . to participate in reality a new way."[3]

"Fiction is not different from truth; fiction is only different from fact."
—Don Chatfield[4]

We can take a different approach to our problem, however, by exploring whether, in using fictional elements, we are closer to the truth than if we omit them. For instance, if we add fictional details to a portrait of someone who is unemployed (or if we even create a fictional unemployed person), have we departed from the truth or come closer to it, particularly if the details are drawn from a number of true accounts of unemployed people? By the same token, if we stick to actual fact, can we ever speak of an unemployed person without violating privilege or honor? Without violating confidentiality, could we ever paint anyone's struggle in any situation in sufficient detail to move others to action on that person's behalf? Instead of allowing the congregation to meet these people through our words, and to experience the world through their eyes, we can be reduced to reporting just the facts. It is similar to what Craddock referred to as boiling the water and "preaching the stain in the bottom."[5] In the end, turning experience into mere statements of fact can often distort experience more than the addition of fictional detail to support verisimilitude.

Our choice may also not properly be conceived as a simple choice between good and bad communication. Rather, it may be between honest proclamation of our faith, on the one hand, and absolute loyalty to historically verified detail, on the other: "Am I proclaiming faith that is rooted in history, in the first instance, or am I proclaiming history that is a foundation for my faith?" I believe that in dealing with contemporary experience in preaching, we are more concerned with the former, with proclaiming faith. Thus the issue may be whether what is presented is recognizable in human behavior, and whether we have misrepresented something as fact when it was not. In other words, did we imply, "for instance," or "this is a fact and I was there"? As preachers, making movies with words, we are not limited to making documentaries. In many cases verisimilitude is the source of our truth claim rather than confirmed fact.[6]

No safe way out of this problem is available for any of us: Each of us must make our own decision. Every time we speak, truth is an issue, not because our intent to tell it is in question, but rather that our ability to tell it is faulty. In addition to the reality of sin, we are dealing, once again, with the issue of objectivity and human limitation. Our perception is only partial and usually flawed. Nonetheless, we are called boldly to witness to the truth as we know it. At whatever resolution we arrive for ourselves, there can be no tolerance for lying, and personal integrity must be both maintained and apparent.[7]

Consider one further dimension of verisimilitude. In preaching we are concerned with presenting at least two kinds of reality. We certainly present life as most people know and experience it. We also present life as we know it to be true when seen from the perspective of faith. We affirm as Christians that life understood in relationship to God is reality, not the world as it may appear, separate from God. It is this verisimilitude we are also after. A primary purpose of preaching is to move us all from the one perspective to this other one, for it is God understood in relationship to the world who is deserving of our trust.

Practical Exercises for Verisimilitude

Here are some practical ways in which we may put verisimilitude to work in our preaching. We will look at three diverse dimensions of imitation of reality in sermons: delivery, character and plot, and stories of contemporary life and culture.

Delivery

The pulpit requires a heightened sense of the natural self. Small gestures, like the turn of a hand, or frequent gestures that would be quite appropriate in conversation around a coffee table, become ineffectual and distracting in the pulpit. Our pulpit voice should not be a normal speaking voice (even if we are in a church with a microphone), yet it must not be perceived to be a false "pulpit voice" or "preacher's voice" that projects piety or pretense. Our voice must be large enough to reach the far corners, and our gestures must be deliberate and big enough to make a statement, yet seem perfectly natural themselves.

In many seminaries voice training is all but neglected, when at one time, most seminaries had full-time instructors of public speaking (in addition to homiletics instructors). Voice is one of the first things people notice, and it can mean the difference between people listening or not. Even our reading of Scripture should capture attention. As James Forbes frankly says, "A preacher who doesn't respect the word enough to strive for excellence in leading the congregation to hear it doesn't deserve the opportunity to present his or her manuscript as if such words are somehow more important than the Bible."[8]

Voice involves posture, gesture, pauses, emphasis, pace, volume, tone, breathing, and a host of other essential elements. Those who teach what today is called speech communication no longer pursue one universal standard of good speech. Their own discipline has undergone an organic revolution, and speakers are now advised to draw on their own experience, to find their own "inner voice" and a natural style that "embodies" the truth. Richard Ward notes, "The authentic sound that a preacher makes comes from the interrupted cries within the unexplored recesses of the preacher's own experience."[9]

> *Speakers are now advised to draw on their own experience, to find their own "inner voice" and a natural style that "embodies" the truth.*

Nonetheless, timeless practices still need to be learned, like breathing from the lower abdomen (a heavy book, placed on the stomach while you are lying down, should move up with each breath in), learning to use the lower registers of voices, and proper projection. Perhaps the best guide available, complete with practical exercises, is by Patsy Rodenburg, *The Right to Speak: Working with the Voice* (London: Methuen, 1992). Make use of any occasion to read aloud, particularly to children or with a partner. Tape-record your own sermons and play them back, listening to your use of voice. Even in a small town preachers can often find a musician who can give helpful coaching. Developing the voice, like becoming an excellent preacher overall, takes many years of work. Generally the two can be developed at the same time, as part of one process.

In addition to voice, we seek passion. Passion is the natural outgrowth of deep faith and an integrated self, but there are some other things that also can help. If a topic is sufficiently large and important, passion will come from listening to the pain or joy that is touched by awakened memories. John Mason Stapleton identifies passion as a theological issue: "Passion is evoked as the gospel is yet *re*apprehended, *re*experienced, and *re*understood—in a word, *rediscovered*."[10] Again, Robin R. Meyers says that identification with the experiences that are portrayed is the clue: "We do not necessarily need a rhetorical strategy to arouse emotion in others so much as we need a rhetorical strategy to exhibit the authentic emotions in ourselves."[11]

Of course, sentence structure, rhythm, emphasis, and pace also can be used to communicate feeling. Read the sermons of great preachers through all ages and learn to spot passages that were delivered with passion. (Augustine followed Cicero in identifying three styles of speaking in a sermon: subdued, for teaching; temperate, for pleasure; and grand, for emotional persuasion.)[12] Read sermons of our own times for parallelism, repetition, and short clauses and sentences of the sort that signal passion, as in this excerpt from Jini Robinson:

The fact is that the overwhelming love of God causes us to love ourselves and our neighbors as ourselves. The fact is that love brings us togetherness. The fact is that Jesus saves, strengthens, and preserves. He lifts up the broken-hearted; he restores the lost. Jesus befriends the lonely. He comforts the despairing. The fact is that I wouldn't want to live without Jesus. I don't know how I could make it from day to day without him. I believe my story would have a tragic ending without the love of the Savior. The fact is that Jesus is all the world to me, my life, my joy, my all. No feeling can overcome the fact of Jesus' presence. This is my story! Church, is this your story? Jesus is my reality! He is my strength from day to day. He is the fact, hallelujah! Praise the Lord![13]

Exercise 13:1 Try imitating this passage, using words that are natural for you, perhaps as a conclusion to your own sermon.

Often this kind of energetic oral prose can also be used to communicate important but mundane material in an interesting manner. When we do this, the general theme and rhythm of speech helps to carry listeners. Whether they comprehend each phrase (though each must be comprehensible), or follow each shift of thought in such portions of a sermon, matters less than that they gain the thrust, tone, and beat of the preacher's comments (see Charles G. Adams, p. 56). The appeal includes logos, but it draws strongly on pathos and ethos.[14]

Character and Plot

We are primarily concerned in preaching with situations that imitate experience. These can be told in such a way that they carry theological implications for how we are to live, behave, and believe. In fact we cannot conceive of homiletical theology without this connection to daily life. The number of basic "plots" in experience that touch us deeply and awaken our humanity are probably few in number. Most tragic stories have a plot that is some version of either abandonment, betrayal, oppression, defeat, loss, injury, or illness. Most joyful stories, by contrast, have a plot that is either courage, reconciliation, justice, accomplishment, discovery, healing, or recovery.

Plot and character in stories are related. We tend to think of plot as a series of events that will happen to characters. However, creative writers know that most plots, "can, do, and should evolve according to the qualities of their chief characters, the battles they face with reality, their responses."[15] In fact, contrary to Aristotle, who had a static notion of character,[16] we may claim that plot is appropriately the result of character, not the other way around.

> **Basic Plots in Experience**
>
> *Tragic: abandonment, betrayal, oppression, defeat, loss, injury, or illness*
>
> *Joy: courage, reconciliation, justice, accomplishment, discovery, healing, or recovery*

Plot is the necessary outcome of some conflict within a character. It is this inner conflict that gives the verisimilitude we are after. Resist portraying any character in a sermon as a romantic ideal. The story of an ideal mother who never spoke an angry word in her life is generally less authentic than the story of a mother in whom a sense of duty and a longing for fulfillment are in conflict.

Foster-Harris, a gifted teacher of creative writing during the 1940s, taught the value of contradiction in character portrayal:

Do not hesitate for an instant to give your hero or heroine . . . impulses to evil. . . . For these dark powers, fused with their opposites—the will to good, the moral impulses, the powers of the spirit [are what] make your central character. The real purpose of the story is to test the fused contradictions which we cannot see but know to exist.[17]

The conflict, he said, must be within one character, and the plot then becomes the conflict and its resolution. Thus the story of Abraham and Isaac, when told from Abraham's perspective, is the conflict of piety and parental love.[18]

Conflicting values or emotions generate the action, yet they are never literally named in the story itself. Rather, we view the relationships in which these emotions arise. We may also remember that motives in themselves need not be our particular focus. Listeners can discover a character's values, emotions, and motives the way they often do in real life, through the action, or through conversation.[19] Trust stories to say what they mean, and listeners to get the point of stories on their own. Stories make points in their own ways. Simply supply sufficient interpretative material to link the story metonymically to your overall progression of sermonic thought. Usually only one sentence is needed for this link.

Foster-Harris made the following recommendations for telling a story: (a) Set the situation and characters in place with no flashbacks until the action is well underway, making sure that you start with action having already happened. (Too many preachers using narrative get bogged down in description that involves no action. Start with action already begun for that will carry us through, and use description only to serve the action.) (b) Develop some complication at the beginning arising from the internal conflict and the character's decisions and actions. Do not discuss the emotions; simply show the signs of the emotions in a character's actions or appearance. (c) Move to a crisis in which the character makes a decision the way he or she always has, that is, for the good or for the bad. (d) Conclude with a climax or an answer or reward.[20]

Exercise 13:2 Tell the story of a powerful emotional scene, but do so without: discussing emotion, using interior monologue (i.e., telling us what the character is thinking), or using commentary (i.e., standing apart from the action as an intellectual observer).

Stories of Contemporary Life and Culture: from Personal Life, the Arts, the News

Most stories we see around us can be categorized theologically, as well as by plot. For instance, we said that we can use stories in the world around us as theological metaphors of:

- God's judgment
- the human condition
- Christ's present suffering and crucifixion
- God's forgiveness
- God's overturning the world
- God using people

The advantage of using these categories has already been discussed. Informed preachers generally have no shortage of potential

271

stories for homiletical use, although they may not recognize this. Rather what most of us suffer from is an inability to isolate stories, or to know how to use them to theological advantage. If we know the potential theological purpose any story may serve, we are more easily able to recognize stories around us. Moreover, we may learn to tell the same story in different ways to meet a variety of these theological purposes, and thereby be able to adapt stories to sermonic use.

As mentioned earlier, none of these kinds of stories is of the "happily-ever-after" variety. For instance, we might tell a story of several youths who are out on a boat late at night when a storm comes up. Their families are worried and send for help. The youths see lights on the shore and make it to safety.

Whatever power this story might have if properly told (which it is not here) is lost if the purpose of telling it is to say simply that God is good. (Listeners then ask, "Why wasn't God good when my friend drowned?") However, a story such as this might be told if we also include the worst case scenario. Thus we could conclude: "What if safety had not been found? Even then, we know in faith that there is One who stands on a distant shore who guarantees safe harbor, and from whose love no one can be lost. . . ."

Three common sources for stories about contemporary experience are available to the sermon, and these are stories from personal life, the arts, and the news.

1) Personal life. From people come personal stories, about ourselves or about others. They allow us a glimpse beneath the surface of appearance. More than one story about ourselves in a sermon is often unwise, for the focus can be too much on ourselves and away from the lives of our people before God. If necessary, drop "I" references, or tell the story from the perspective of another person who was present. Moreover, after telling an "I" story, it is a good rule to spend a sentence or two shifting the attention back to the congregation (e.g., "But we have all had similar experiences . . ."). Richard L. Thulin has provided excellent suggestions for appropriate use of autobiography in *The "I" of the Sermon* (Fortress Press, 1989).

The usual reason we tell stories about ourselves is to deepen our relationship with the congregation. It is to discuss some common human weakness (not a vice, and similarly not a strength or virtue). Avoid private stories of the sort one tells only a confessor or intimate friend, as well as stories that might damage the office of preacher with which we are entrusted.

Susan May told the following story in a sermon on God's love. In terms of our discussion here, her daughter's action stands as a metaphor of Christ:

I had been having one of those mornings when everything was going wrong. The alarm clock had been late. My skirt wasn't ironed. The kids argued about what kind of cereal to eat. I remembered that I had to stop and get gas on the way to school. The pressure began to build, and my impatience grew.

I don't remember now whether it was that one more trip to the bathroom, or the spilled cup of juice, or the lunch box that broke open at the last minute. Something pushed me past the breaking point, and I began to yell. I yelled and screamed. Me, a college-educated, sophisticated, civilized, mature, training-for-effective-parenting me.

I was horrified and embarrassed, completely aware that I was making a fool of myself. But I couldn't stop. Until my daughter came across the room, put her hand on my arm, and said, "Mom, maybe you forgot that we love you."[21]

Homiletical Analysis

Conflict: need for control + parental love
Plot: loss (of control)
Metaphor: Christ acting through the daughter.
Possible central idea of the sermon: God loves you.

In neither this case, nor the next, is there any question of the preacher's current well-being. When there is such a question, it inappropriately draws attention away from the Word, so that the preacher, not the congregation, becomes the object of pastoral focus. The pulpit is simply not the proper setting for this kind of self-focus.

Peter Vaught is preaching on the red dragon of Revelation 12:1-6, which represents the force of evil. He tells powerful and sad stories of the dragon in his childhood. They are important stories to hear, for, as he says, the vast majority of families are dysfunctional. People in the pews are dealing with similar stories of alcoholism, physical or sexual abuse, and neglect. He is explicit in using his story for mission purpose. One brief excerpt must suffice:

I hope you came from a family where Mom and Dad did look out for you. I hope you came from a family where you were cared for and loved and protected. If you did, you were lucky.

Most of the people I will come in contact with in my life were not so lucky. One of the most ugly faces of this mess is that most of the people I meet—people who have been raised in homes that did not work the way they were supposed to—have the biggest chance of doing the very same thing all over again to the people they love. Friends, the red dragon is a frightening face of evil.

Both of my parents are dead now. I received an inheritance from them. I have inherited feelings of being responsible for everything that happens. I have inherited not trusting my feelings. I have inherited not trusting others. This is the legacy my parents have given me. My mom and dad were not evil. They were weak like the rest of us. They were misinformed about many things. Like the rest of us. The dragon was there knocking at the door. . . ."[22]

Vaught continues his sermon with a discussion of God's saving the woman giving birth from the red dragon in Revelation, and ends with his own vision, a dream in which his dad calls him to the center of a family gathering to tell him of his love. His last line: "With this dream of reconciliation and peace, God brought this child out of the reach of the red dragon."[23]

Homiletical Analysis

Conflict: understanding of parents + anger at parents
Plot: betrayal
Metaphor: the human condition; or, God's overturning suffering
Central idea of the sermon: God disposes of the dragon.

Vaught demonstrates what can be a very important homiletical rule for all of us: He shows compassion for even the worst person he mentions. Whether this person (or group) is in a story that we tell or in the biblical text, always empathize with the worst person. This means "try to understand" not "condone the actions." Someone in the congregation will always identify with that person, and that person needs God's love.

2) *The Arts.* The arts include novels, poems, paintings, photographs, sculpture, architecture, dance, drama, movies, concerts, and the like.[24] We do not need to live in large cultural centers to have access to art. Art is a part of every community, books of art can be found in every public library, and art reviews are given in newspapers, journals, and on television.

We tell stories from the arts in sermons for at least three reasons. First and most obvious, we need all the relevant stories we can find. Second, art is valuable as another person's perception of reality. Third, in an age of increasing fragmentation, we at least share some of the arts (and news) in common, and as a community are familiar with many of the same characters and people in them.

When we contemplate a work of art, as preachers, we are like journalists on the prowl. Or we are like postmodern literary critics who view their own work as art. We may find our story:

a) In the artwork itself. Robert P. Waznak, S.S., in a Christmas homily, relates a story by Truman Capote of a boy named Buddy (Capote himself) and his best friend, a woman in her sixties who lives with the family. On Christmas they are most pleased with the two kites they give each other as presents. They rush outside to fly them, and the woman ends up surveying the countryside and Buddy, and saying,

My how foolish I am! You know what I've always thought? I've always thought a body would have to be sick and dying before they saw the Lord. And I imagined that when He came it would be like looking at a Baptist window: pretty as colored glass with the sun pouring through . . . such a shine you don't know it's getting dark. And it's been a comfort to me to think of that shine—taking away all the spooky feeling. But I'll wager it never happens. I'll wager at the very end a body realizes the Lord has already shown Himself. . . . As for me, I could leave the world with today in my eyes.[25]

b) In the events that took place around the artwork. Charles L. Rice preached a sermon that was as much about the people around him in the movie theater as it was about the people in the movie, *Ordinary People.*

Sitting next to us were two young people, fashionably dressed—in fact, downright chic. They supplied a second sound track; it was like seeing two movies, one on the screen and one filtered through their eyes. . . . "Boy, look at those cars, color coordinated brown and black. And all that loot!" In another scene. . . . "Look at those pants . . ." And so it went. All the superficial stuff was the story for my neighbors, as if this successful lawyer and his two-years grieving wife and his sleepless lean son had it made. . . . But they need God.[26]

c) In some other artwork or memory that is evoked. In this case we may not even mention the art before us. In fact, if a story is too dated, such that listeners might

> *It matters less whether people in a story recognize God than that we name God in acts of justice, mercy, peace, etc., wherever we see God.*

wonder whether we are out of touch with the contemporary world, we can take the plot of the story and retell it for our time.

We do not need to be looking for stories that are explicitly religious, such as the one by Capote. If all our stories are mainly of religious people, God's relevance for the rest of humanity is diminished. In fact, surprising though it may sound at first, it does not matter whether the people in the story are Christian or even recognize God. It matters that we name God where we see God. (We spoke of this in relation to the story of Eric Clapton in chapter 1.) Part of the purpose in relating any experience is to help people in the congregation to name God in their lives. Preaching can enable the congregation to see God anywhere, not as an uncommon experience but as a common experience of uncommon grace.

Nor do we need to look for stories with positive endings, particularly if we can find a theological way of bringing perspective to the story at hand. Thomas G. Long did this with an account of August Wilson's play, *Ma Rainey's Black Bottom*. This heart-wrenching story of racial humiliation ends with a prayer of desperation: "Where the hell is God? Come down, O God! Let justice roll down like the waters. Save us, O God! Come, quickly, Lord Jesus!" Long takes this plea to his biblical text concerning the wrath of God, and in effect, turns it around, such that the words we have just heard echo God's own anger: "The problem," says Long, "with our understanding of the wrath of God is not that we have made too much of it, but precisely that we have made too little of it."[27] In other words, Long develops the story as an extended metaphor of God's judgment.

In telling any story, as noted it is strongly advisable to start with the action having already begun. Leading with the title of the movie or book, can diminish attention, rather than capture it, for titles may say something the opposite of our intent—they can seem to say, "This is not real life! You do not have to pay attention now." Instead, just begin your excerpt as though it is real life:

Hard-hearted, fast-living Charlie was watching his Lamborghini business in Los Angeles go down the tubes when he received news that his father had died in Ohio. He flew there expecting to inherit the large estate, only to discover that he had a brother, Raymond, who had been living in institutional care all these years. Raymond had inherited the wealth.

Charlie had no love for Raymond. He only took him on his trip back to Los Angeles to try to keep a hand on the wealth. But something happened along the way. We don't know whether it was that Raymond wouldn't fly, or that he had to stop at exact intervals for cheese balls and apple juice snacks, or that he would only wear K-Mart underwear. We don't know if it was because they had to stay in a motel an extra day since Raymond, the Rain Man, wouldn't go out in the rain. Whatever it was, it became apparent as they were driving across the Nevada desert, the sunset a blazing orange. Music was being sung a cappella in the background: "The hip bone connected to the thigh bone / The thigh bone connected to the knee bone / The knee bone connected to . . ."—and we knew before we got to the end of the song that it could only be the work of the Lord. For it was not just bone connected to bone, it was blood connected to blood, and flesh connected to flesh, and brother connected to brother. "Now hear the name of the Lord!"

Homiletical Analysis

Conflict: greed + the need for love
Plot: reconciliation
Metaphor: God acting through Raymond
Central idea of the sermon: God gives peace.

Remember, usually one episode, or one small aspect of the plot or subplot, is what we pursue. Steven Spielberg's Academy Award–winning movie, *Schindler's List*, could conceivably be used in a sermon by focusing on shades of the color red: As the color of the opening scene fades to black and white, pink is the last color of the dying flame of the sabbath candle. Red becomes the color of righteousness, the only color we see in a black-and-white movie. The little girl in the red coat is seen in the streets, then from above as Schindler watches in horror the massacre in the ghetto, then hiding under the bed. When the corpses are dug up, we glimpse the red coat wheeled by on a cart. Like a symbol of God in the movie, the color could not quite be snuffed out. And by the end of the movie, thanks largely to Schindler's efforts, survivors of Schindler's list, dressed in brilliant colors against a summer sky, place stones on his monument.[28]

The same "treat as though real-life" principle can be followed for a photograph. I remember a black-and-white photograph of the interior of the Chartres Cathedral, on exhibit in Pittsburgh some years ago. It was taken by Eugene Smith, the photographer who covered World War II for *Life* magazine:

Some of you may know that during World War II, Chartres Cathedral in France was converted to a hospital ward. Now if a church has to be converted to something else, a hospital is a good choice. I saw a photograph of it recently.

There were no pews. Instead there were cots, rows and rows of cots, on either side of the central aisle. You could almost hear the quick, echoing footsteps of the smartly starched nurse, in apparent haste as she passed one of the stone pillars. In the foreground, apart from the other patients, was a lone soldier, lying on a lone cot, with his head wrapped in cotton bandages. Just above his head, if he had been able to see, he would have seen the fresh roll of bandages that had been placed in the big dry well of the stone baptismal font. The amazing thing about this picture is that the soldier probably did not even know from where his healing was coming.

Homiletical Analysis

Conflict: in this story, internal conflict is not the source of the plot
Plot: healing
Metaphor: God overturning the world
Central idea of the sermon: God is the healer.

In recalling architecture, or other art, where the story may not be so apparent as in some photographs, we can imagine the artist who created the work. Ask yourself, What would I have to be feeling to create this? (i.e., What might have just happened to the artist?) Who would respond well to this? How would this make different people feel? (e.g., someone without a friend, someone hungry). Might I tell their imagined stories as they respond to the art? Or again, could this story be a metaphor of experience in one of our six theological categories?

3) The News. Too often sermons portray a small God. If we portray God acting only with regard to ourselves, or the church, or our local region, or even our nation, we portray a small God, too small in fact to be of help to most Christians who work or travel in the world, see it on television, and are concerned for it. Moreover, a small God encourages a small faith. If God is not interested in the suffering of a woman whose family was killed in a flood in India, how may we trust that same God to be concerned about us in our time of trouble?

God, we may affirm, is concerned for all creation; thus, we look for a balanced range of experience and issues to bring into our sermons. Be sure to balance stories of men and women, young and old. Test sermons to see that you include stories in these categories: *personal, local, church, and world.* God's love knows no national borders; thus, we lean into the pain of the world and discover a grace, says William K. McElvaney, "that restores us as we are 'restoried' in the larger vision and work of God."[29] By taking preaching onto the global stage, we discover the largeness of God's mercy and, amazingly, many new ways to sing God's praise.

A preacher not long ago said that he had stopped reading the newspaper and had sold his television in adopting a simpler life-style. I believe his actions may themselves be a luxury preachers can ill afford. What Barth told preachers needs updating: Have the Bible in one hand, the newspaper in the other, and the TV on in the background. The lives of our congregation's members are shaped by media. How they think is affected by media. What they talk about is in part provided by media. In addition to good local newspapers, try at least once a week to read a leading newspaper, like the *New York Times,* partly because the high quality of reporting can be a source of excellent stories.

The stories we can look for in the newspapers and on television news usually include direct quotations from someone involved. It might be the son's words as he left home. It might be the mother's words when asked about loss of the village's drinking water. It might be the child's words about the coming of the soldiers. Build the story around that person's actual words.

The goal in using stories from the news is to hold up individuals near and far as God's loved ones, to interpret their situations in light of God's truth, to help us recognize God in the midst of even the worst situations, and to restore humanity to the events that threaten to harden us to our neighbors. The purpose is not to turn the sermon into a newscast, or to go into any detail about violence (never do this), or merely to repeat a story we already know too well. Again we are the reporter, looking for a fresh angle and human interest. We use empathetic imagination, which allows the congregation to feel something of what might be the suffering or joy of others.[30]

We use the same test for stories from the news as we have used elsewhere. To repeat, we ask ourselves, Might I use this story as a metaphor of God's judgment; the human condition; Christ's present suffering and crucifixion; God's forgiveness; God's overturning the world; or God using people?

I offer two brief examples, along with one longer one, all from the international scene. In the first I take preacher's license in creating a metaphor of God's judgment from the crushing of the democracy movement in Tiananmen Square, Beijing, China, on June 4, 1989:

One scene from last month's carnage in Tiananmen Square may never be erased from the minds of those who watched its many replays on television.

We only had to see it once to remember it. It was as though we were there. As far as one could see on this vast open square, there were thousands of people who had been supporting democracy. The army was holding them back, making a kind of street for a row of rolling military tanks. As we watched, suddenly a man in a white shirt broke loose from the crowd and ran directly into the path of an oncoming tank and stood there. We watched in horror, sure that as in other reported instances, the tank would crush him. But in this case the tank first slowed, then stopped. The man still stood there. His head was moving back and forth. We could not hear him. But we knew he was saying something and we knew what he was saying. He was saying the only words he could be saying, "Not by might, nor by power, but by my Spirit, says the Lord!"

The scene does not have to be dramatic, however, as in this metaphor of Christ's suffering:

It is the same kind of wonderful faith that was shown by Mary Robinson, the President of the Republic of Ireland. She was the first head of state of a Western country to visit Somalia. She was deeply, profoundly moved by what she saw. "I smelt, felt, touched the suffering. In Ireland we still carry with us the memory of starvation in the 1800s. I found it unacceptable as a mother to see other mothers having their children die beside them. I feel ashamed for our humanity. I feel ashamed as a European head of state. I am personally shamed and offended to sit with women and watch children die. What does it do to us as humans to have this going on?" She said on the "MacNeil/Lehrer Report" that she is on a crusade in faith that things can be different. She is calling for people to be committed and angry and determined to change a world order in which too often men have been found to leave a legacy of war and destruction.

Finally, this example can show how a story from the news may be split, the first portion being told in the first portion of the sermon as a metaphor of life as we experience it, and the second portion as the conclusion to the sermon and as a metaphor of God's love.

How quickly we move from Easter. You could probably each tell a tale of the thief sneaking into the sheepfold. Maybe for you it was a story like Serbian civilian targeting in Bosnia. The TV news showed a mother in a babushka and old winter coat arriving at a hospital with her younger son in tow. They had managed to arrive safely. She was probably around 30, but her hollow eyes, which said she had seen the worst, made her look 60. She had heard that her other son might still be alive, although he had not come home for two days. Sitting in blue flannel pajamas in one of the beds, a bandage wrapped around his head, both eyes now possibly forever blind, sat her son Sayad. "Sayad," she called from the doorway. "Where have you been?" he said in response, his head turning only approximately in her direction. He was not quite sure that he could again trust that she was there, there for him. "Where have you been?"

That may be our question of Jesus, these past weeks. "Where have you been? You said you were the good shepherd, who would keep us safe from the thief." All of the suffering is enough to make one want to rage against the world, to push the resurrection far away, to shut out hope that seems too foolish, impotent, and weak to make a difference in a world awash with despair.

* * * * *

If this morning we could gather around young blind Sayad's bed in Bosnia, as in fact we do this moment in prayer, we would pray with him in the power of the Holy Spirit. We do not know by what name he or his family know God. But we do know that the One we know as Christ was present in Sayad's mother and brother coming to him when he asked, "Where have you been?" And we know that Christ was present even when Sayad thought he was alone. Christ continues to suffer, even as all the power of eternity struggles to bring good out of evil, and justice even out of the pain in your life. And we also know that on this day, when we name people in prayer, ourselves or others like Sayad, that by the power of the Holy Spirit, Christ will attend to their needs, whether or not they recognize who it is that ministers to them.

Exercise 13:3 Write three stories, one personal, one from the arts, and one from the news. Do a homiletical analysis of each including: Conflict, Plot, Metaphor, and possible Central Idea of the sermon, preferably focusing on an action of God.

We can be bold in naming in the sermon situations for which Christ has concern. The situations we name, without limiting Christ, become situations to which Christ is present even as we speak, not by our power but by the power of the Holy Spirit in response to the prayers of the church. Prophetic proclamation of alternative possibilities for this world, conformed to God's will, is not idle dreaming. God can accomplish what God wants, and while God is not ultimately dependent upon us, and does not merely use us as instruments, and is not at our disposal, God nonetheless chooses to use our efforts to facilitate and accomplish God's purpose.

The sermon results in a response of the hearers that becomes Christ's embodied mission in the world. Through preaching, new possibilities unfold. God's purposes take shape in our minds. Even as we lift up these possibilities in prayer, or go forth into the world in the power of the Holy Spirit, they start to happen through our various ministries, as a church that embraces the globe. The event of Christ's encounter in preaching becomes part of the advent of Christ's encounter in the world. And the advent of Christ through our mission to the world becomes part of the event of Christ in the lives of others. What God wills is to be accomplished. Nothing can finally hold out against God.

Perhaps this is the right place to end our tour of the homiletical highlands, listening as we have been to stories, with our focus on God and the world community. This, after all, is part of the purpose of preaching, to send us to our brothers and sisters everywhere, naming God, proclaiming the Good News of Jesus Christ in both word and deed, and ministering to them in the power of the Holy Spirit.

We have been considering four of the great traditions that have informed preaching to the present age. The purpose has been to reunite these important strands of thought that too often have been kept separate in homiletics. If preaching is to be conceived as God's event, we will need to be drawing on the best of our resources, for the task is too important, Christ's mission too urgent, to dally if the Holy Spirit is beckoning. Richard Lischer, who teaches homiletics at Duke University, observes that excessive focus on form has led us astray: "Perhaps . . . preachers will reclaim the center when homiletics reclaims the center, when homiletics grounds the rhetorical act of preaching in God's own speech act." [31]

The Oral Tradition, we have seen, offers us a means of understanding the sermon as relationship with God, and models concrete language about God and clues to oral ways of thought and expression. The Rhetorical Tradition helps us to discover barriers to preaching in our educational approach to it, and underlines the importance: of preaching the cross and resurrection; of theology as a form of persuasion; of listener need; of method in systematic and homiletical theology; and of the necessity for judgment and grace if we are preaching hope. By tracing the Hermeneutical Tradition, we are able to see how preaching has been excluded from the interpretation process, and how both hermeneutics and preaching can benefit from reconceiving the task as a four-stage hermeneutical square. Finally, the Tradition of Poetics allows us to identify the limitations of current homiletics as well as its strengths, with new opportunities for improving the quality of preaching that are coming from attention to metonymy, metaphor, and mission.

In the past we have tended to conceive of the sermon as something less than God's event, and of our outreach narrowly as taking the Good News of Christ out into the world. As long as we conceive of the sermon primarily as an event of God's encounter with us through the reading and interpretation of Scripture and made visible around the table, then it is not primarily information we take with us, for instance that the tomb is empty, but is the gift of God's presence and a firsthand report of an encounter with the risen Christ.

It is the difference between taking to someone a newspaper filled with the facts and coming as a witness who was actually on the scene, able to re-create it. It is also the difference between standing outside a story as a commentator, and standing inside it as a participant. Perhaps this is what Archibald Macleish meant in saying, "A poem should be equal to: / Not true," or "A poem should not mean / But be."

Yet even this sort of comparison falls short. In having been encountered by the risen Christ, we go forth in the knowledge that we are less taking Christ to the world, than we are going forth to encounter Christ already in the world. As the first disciples were told, "He has been raised from the dead, and indeed he is going ahead of you to Galilee; there you will see him" (Matt. 28:7). Moreover, we are going not only as Easter people, but as Pentecost people, in the prayer and knowledge that Christ even goes with us, that he has given us his power, and that some people may glimpse Christ even through our own words and actions in the world.

On the one hand, what we take to the world is a wonderful love that knows no limit, for it is not ours, but is Christ in us. On the other hand we take the grace that enables us to recognize Christ already in the world, and to expect God's approach in any moment. The closing words of the Gospel of John can be constant inspiration for the preacher, for he was pointing to countless resurrection appearances even in his own day: "But there are also many other things that Jesus did; if every one of them were written down, I suppose that the world itself could not contain the books that would be written" (21:25).

To speak of the sermon as God's event, then, is not the end of the story, but another episode in a continuing saga. Our true goal as preachers, through our words, is to facilitate the salvation work the Holy Spirit is actually doing in our midst by making faith an event, salvation a reality, and the encounter of Christ a daily experience upon which we all may count, even to the end of our days.

Review Questions for Chapter Thirteen

1) The primary test of stories for the pulpit is
   a) emotion
   b) imitation of life
   c) action
   d) factuality   [b]

2) Which is incorrect: Truth is an issue in preaching because
   a) our ability to tell it is faulty
   b) we are to proclaim truth boldly
   c) reality is self-evident
   d) reality is a theological issue   [c]

3) According to this chapter, preachers should strive to find
   a) a "preacher's voice"
   b) a natural voice
   c) an "outer" voice
   d) all of the above   [b]

4) Foster-Harris suggests that plot arises out of
   a) events happening to characters
   b) characters acting
   c) conflict in events
   d) conflict within a character   [d]

5) Which word best describes the preacher's appropriate attitude
      to the worst person mentioned in the sermon?
   a) condoning
   b) empathetic
   c) sympathetic
   d) condemning
   e) mocking   [b]

6) Generally in telling a story for the pulpit, start
   a) at the beginning
   b) at the end
   c) with the action already begun
   d) with an introduction   [c]

Questions for Discussion

1) How will you resolve the issue of truth and fiction in your own preaching?
2) We say that the places of mission we name in preaching become places of Christ's presence. How do you understand this? What distinguishes this from magic?

PREACHING AT FUNERALS AND WEDDINGS

The topic of funeral and wedding sermons is too large to be dealt with adequately here, yet too important to be entirely ignored in an introductory textbook. Many students find themselves conducting or assisting in funeral or wedding services shortly after their arrival at church postings.[1]

Funerals

One way of conceiving of the funeral sermon is to identify a number of questions that should be addressed and related needs that must be met. The Christian service is appropriately understood as a celebration of resurrection and is designed less for the deceased than for the living. In any funeral, whatever the age or the manner of death of the one who has died, listeners have questions in at least six subject areas: God and Scripture, God and tradition, the deceased, the family, the congregation, and the preacher. Questions in each of these areas can and often need to be answered in the course of the funeral sermon.

The following sample questions are not intended for appearance in the sermon; they are designed to help the preacher prepare a funeral sermon. Obviously, sensitivity must be exercised in determining which issues to address directly in the course of the sermon. Some of the questions speak of informational (logos) needs, and some speak of emotional and spiritual needs (pathos and ethos):

1) God and Scripture

Informational needs: What does the Bible say about death? this type of death?
What passages speak about death and dying? about life after death?

285

Emotional/spiritual
needs: What comfort is there in the Bible?
                          Do the circumstances of this death resonate
                          positively or negatively with Scripture?

2) God and Tradition

Informational: What does the church say about this type of
                          death?
                          Where is the deceased now?
                          What does the church say about heaven?
                          What comfort does the church offer nonbeliev-
                          ers?

Emotional/spiritual: What Christian doctrines or stories might
                          bring most comfort?
                          Will God love this person whom we have
                          loved?

3) The Deceased

Informational: Who was this person (e.g., family, job, inter-
                          ests)?
                          What was the cause of death?
                          What will people fondly remember?
                          Did this person believe in Jesus Christ?
                          Did this person have a formal relationship
                          with the church?

Emotional/spiritual: What did this person feel about family?
                          What did this person feel about death?
                          God? religion? this service?
                          Was he or she ready to die?

4) The Family

Informational: Who is present? not present?
                          Are there family tensions?
                          What is the family history?
                          Who will care for the family?
                          Did the family have special requests (e.g,
                          things to say or not say)?

Emotional/spiritual: Does the family have a church connection?
                          Were there unresolved issues with the
                          deceased?
                          What will the family miss most?

5) The Congregation

Informational: Who is in attendance?
                          What does the makeup of the congregation say
                          about the dead person?

Emotional/spiritual:	Was this person liked? hated?
	In what ways will this person be missed?
	What are the faith beliefs of those attending?
	How much Christian knowledge can be assumed?

6) The Preacher

Informational:	Did you know this person (how or in what ways)?
	Did you bother to find out about him or her?
	Do you know the family?
	Why were you asked to preach the service?

Emotional/spiritual:	Can we trust you to guide us through this vulnerable time?
	What are your feelings?
	Do you show love or feeling?
	Are you sincere?
	Do you speak out of a deep and confident faith?

The sermon is not primarily a eulogy in praise of the dead, although it is appropriately both personal and specific about the life of the deceased. A few vivid details or brief stories of someone's life, including one or two direct quotations (one perhaps a favorite saying or significant idea expressed during the life of the deceased; the other perhaps a sentiment expressed by a surviving family member), are usually sufficient. If there is to be a repeated non-biblical image used in the sermon, one is enough, and generally let these stories be the source. This image may be placed within the setting of the Christian hope by the end of the sermon. For example, if the deceased was a woman who devoted her life to caring for children, by the end of the sermon we might be speaking of her now being surrounded by children in God's tender care.

The sermon remains, however, first and foremost a proclamation of the gospel of Jesus Christ. Nearly the entire time is appropriately spent developing the heart of the Christian faith from suitable Scripture texts: Through what God has worked in the life, death, and resurrection of Jesus Christ, death no longer has the final say. Since the reality of death is confronting the listeners, our message is largely one of grace and love. If the deceased was a Christian, it is common and appropriate to speak with confidence of that person's being in heaven. If the deceased was a good person outside the church it is still appropriate to express the Christian hope and to speak of him or her as being now with God (i.e. leaving all question of judgment to God). If the deceased was not a good person, it is appropriate nonetheless to extend compassion to the deceased, entrusting that person to God, while realistically and in general ways acknowledging the difficulties survivors may still be experiencing. Let the preaching primarily address these needs. In any case, we consign ourselves, as survivors, as well as the deceased, to God's eternal care, and we extend the continuing love and support of the church to those in attendance.

Funerals, along with weddings, provide excellent opportunity to evangelize, to share the joy and wonder of our faith with others. Funerals are opportunities to express our best theologies—for example of life, death, human suffering, God's purpose in creation, and eternal life. Weddings allow us to speak of the nature of human relationships, Christian marriage, forgiveness and reconciliation, and the importance of relying upon God to make perfect our love. I encourage students while in seminary to develop at least two funeral sermons and one wedding sermon that can later be personalized and adapted to particular needs in the first months of church appointment.

Perhaps because the need of mourners is so immediate, the preacher is wise to pay particular attention to establishing trust either by direct or indirect means in the opening minutes of the funeral sermon. This may be done in answering a variety of the questions just listed.

Finally, a word of caution to preachers may be useful. The funeral service is a time for mourners to receive from God and the community of faith. Many preachers are tempted to conduct the services of their own immediate close family. I believe we thereby deny the function of Christian funerals, and in so doing deny our own physical, emotional, and spiritual needs, possibly to personal and vocational detriment.

Weddings

Wedding sermons also need to answer some questions, for instance concerning God and Scripture, God and tradition, the couple, the congregation, and the preacher. While we need not enumerate these here, students might like to supply these on their own. Here are some basic questions concerning the first two of these categories:

God and Scripture

Informational:	What does the Bible say about marriage? What does the Bible say about love, family life, and relationships? about making covenants with one another? How does Scripture address the marriage vows (e.g., "in sickness and in health")?
Emotional/spiritual:	What kind of emotional issues are raised in marriage? What do we do when marriages fail, or when human love dies? What is the hope for children being reared within a marriage and family?

APPENDIX 1: PREACHING AT FUNERALS AND WEDDINGS

Questions about
God/tradition

Informational: What does culture say about marriage? about
                                  weddings?
                                  What does the church say about marriage?
                                  remarriage? blended families?

Emotional/spiritual: How does the gathered community feel about
                                  responding to the particular history of the cou-
                                  ple?
                                  Was this a long or a short relationship?
                                  Were they previously cohabiting?
                                  Are there any children from previous relation-
                                  ships?
                                  What is the family history of separation and
                                  divorce (including parents)?

Exercise for appendix 1: Supply your own list of questions for a wedding sermon in the categories of the couple, the congregation, and the preacher. (Use
the preceding questions as a guide.)

In spite of our common manner of speaking, the preacher does not marry
the couple. Rather, the preacher presides at their marrying of each other. In
the wedding service they listen to God's Word, they exchange vows before
God and witnesses, they receive God's blessing, and they are given assur-
ances of support from those present on behalf of the church and the larger
community. Thus the sermon is in part an interpretation of the covenants that
are being made in light of God's promises.

However, the wedding service is also an opportunity to share our faith and
to speak to the actual needs of those present. Choice of a church wedding can
be a choice for sharing with guests the faith that offers identity to the couple.
Weddings are a time for Christian proclamation, not romanticism or senti-
mentality. While they are occasions of joy, thanksgiving, and hope for some
people, for others they are also a poignant time often of regret, sorrow, or
repentance over their own relationships. Rather than preach in a manner that
encourages a merely romantic view of what is happening, this is an important time for the church to acknowledge the reality of broken relationships,
the importance of reliance upon God and the community, the need for God in
all human interaction, and God's abiding love and continuing action on
behalf of each one of us. We are not able on our own to fulfill the vows being
made. In other words, even as the funeral sermon appropriately speaks grace
into the midst of grief, the wedding sermon appropriately does not neglect
dimensions of judgment in the midst of apparent grace.

289

GUIDELINES FOR TEACHERS USING THIS BOOK

Homiletics courses often benefit from having most of the workload in the first half of the term. During this time most of the theory that is necessary for composing the first sermon (of a total of perhaps two or three for the course) can be developed. Assuming that students learn best by hearing, reading, speaking, and writing, the following suggestions may help teachers as they design their own courses, if only by way of comparison:

Hearing: The first hour of a two-hour class might be devoted to development of relevant homiletical theory that relates to the assigned readings, following.

The second hour (or perhaps a tutorial session if the class is large) can be devoted to praxis of that theory, using a different biblical text each week, for example, one of the texts from the lectionary. During the first half of the course, a few assigned students might begin these praxis sessions each week, by preaching for only one minute each on the biblical text. The class thus has the opportunity of hearing one another and the teacher (1) work with a different biblical text each week and (2) engage homiletical theory as it develops toward a completed sermon. If students are also organized into small peer groups that meet outside class time, they can preach the completed first long sermon to the small groups and revise it, prior to written submission around midterm.

During the second half of the term, the order of theory and praxis can be reversed. Students might preach a second sermon (after the first is returned) to the entire class (or tutorial group) in the first hour. (For practical purposes, these sermons can be limited to ten or twelve minutes.) During the second hour, students and instructor use the theory of the course to give feedback to the preachers. While something is lost, there is often merit, if numbers are large, in having preachers in turn simply listen to the responses, rather than encouraging defensive countercomments. Many teachers follow an excellent practice, (1) allowing no comparisons among student sermons, and (2) ensur-

290

ing that no suggestions for changes are expressed until sufficient positive feedback has been received.

Readings: If at least six two-hour class sessions are available for developing homiletical theory in the course, prior to hearing any sermons, it may be helpful to structure the readings such that students do not simply read this book from beginning to end. Rather, the chapters can be reordered to assist students week by week with preparation for their first sermon. Thus for the second class (following the introductory session) they might read and do the exercises for chapters 1, 2, and 6; for the third class, chapters 3, 4, and 7; for the fourth class, chapters 5 and 8; for the fifth class, chapters 9, 10, and 13; and for the sixth class, with a view to upcoming final revision of a written sermon, chapters 11 and 12. Alternatively, these latter two chapters might be assigned for private reading after the course is over. Ample endnotes and a bibliography (appendix 3) are provided to assist students in locating additional relevant reading material.

Speaking: Students might be given three formal speaking opportunities. (1) A one-minute presentation can provide experience in speaking before the class; challenge the student to use oral ways of thought; acquaint the student with the opportunities and limitations of one minute; and introduce both the class and the student to an assigned biblical text (on which that student might continue to work to develop the first long sermon for the course). (2) This written sermon, on the same biblical text, can first be preached to a five-member peer group and revised prior to written submission. (3) A second sermon on a second text can be preached to the class, with the class designated as the congregation to which it is addressed. A third sermon, if desired, might be due in written or taped form at the end of term.

Writing: Numbered exercises are provided at various places throughout this book. There are too many exercises here for most teachers to examine closely. Students thus might keep some form of journal or exercise book for occasional submission, with only a few of the assignments designated for marking.

Students often benefit from early engagement of homiletical theory with a biblical text. In the introductory session, students might sign up for two dates: once in what remains of the first six weeks of the course, for the one-minute presentation on a biblical text assigned for that particular week; and once for the class sermon in the remainder of the course on a biblical text assigned for that particular week. Key assignments can be as follows for the first biblical text:

1) For week two: a list of twenty concerns of the text, at least ten from the students' own literary and theological reading of the biblical text, and at least ten from appropriate biblical commentaries (i.e., the class would introduce these).
2) For week three: the same list transposed into concerns of the sermon.
3) For week four: the same list divided according to judgment and grace (if desired), as well as two or three sets chosen for proposed homiletical development. At minimum these sets would be a concern of the text, its concern of the sermon along with a major concern of the text and a major concern of the sermon.

4) For week six or seven: a complete manuscript for the first full sermon already preached to the small group.

By ensuring that students successfully complete (and redo if necessary) each of these assignments, many errors in later sermons can be avoided. After the fourth class, students might begin to develop written paragraphs for some of their concerns of the text and concerns of the sermon, with most of the writing being saved until after the fifth class. Midway through the course, before oral class sermons begin, a test on the homiletical theory might be offered or journals collected to ensure that students have been working on the theory. Ideally, students will have received the teacher's comments on the first written sermon prior to preaching to the class the second sermon, so as to derive the most benefit from experience.

For the class sermons, in addition to oral classroom feedback, students might be asked to supply written evaluations of their peers employing the theory of the course, in addition to oral classroom feedback, on the week following the presentation.

RECOMMENDATIONS FOR THE PREACHER'S LIBRARY

Here are a few resources that may be helpful starters for preachers. Those not currently in print may sometimes be obtained in second-hand bookstores or by direct inquiry of retiring clergy.

I. Basic Resources

Contemporary Homiletical Theory

Allen, Ronald J. *Preaching the Topical Sermon.* Louisville: Westminster/John Knox Press, 1992.
Brueggemann, Walter J. *Finally Comes the Poet: Daring Speech for Proclamation.* Minneapolis: Fortress Press, 1989.
Burghardt, Walter J., S.J. *Preaching: The Art and the Craft.* New York/Mahwah, N.J.: Paulist Press, 1987.
Burke, John, O.P. *A New Look at Preaching.* Wilmington, Del.: Michael Glazier, 1983.
Buttrick, David. *Homiletic: Moves and Structures.* Philadelphia: Fortress Press, 1987.
Craddock, Fred B. *As One Without Authority.* 3rd ed. Nashville: Abingdon Press, 1979.
———. *Overhearing the Gospel.* Nashville: Abingdon Press, 1978.
———. *Preaching.* Nashville: Abingdon Press, 1985.
Duduit, Michael, ed. *Handbook of Contemporary Preaching.* Nashville: Broadman Press, 1992.
Edwards, O. C., Jr. *Elements of Homiletic.* New York: Pueblo, 1982.
Eslinger, Richard L. *A New Hearing: Living Options in Homiletic Method.* Nashville: Abingdon Press, 1987.
Fant, Clyde E. *Preaching for Today.* Rev. ed. San Francisco: Harper & Row, 1987.

Hughes, Robert. *A Trumpet in Darkness: Preaching to Mourners.* Philadelphia: Fortress Press, 1985.

Long, Thomas G. *The Witness of Preaching.* Louisville: Westminster/John Knox Press, 1989.

———. *Preaching and the Literary Forms of the Bible.* Philadelphia: Fortress Press, 1989.

Long, Thomas G., and Meely Dixon McCarter. *Preaching in and out of Season.* Louisville: Westminster/John Knox Press, 1990.

Lowry, Eugene. *The Homiletical Plot: The Sermon as Narrative Art Form.* Atlanta: John Knox, 1980.

Massey, James Earl. *Designing the Sermon: Order and Movement in Preaching.* Nashville: Abingdon, 1980.

Mitchell, Henry H. *Celebration and Experience in Preaching.* Nashville: Abingdon Press, 1991.

Nichols, J. Randall. *The Restoring Word: Preaching as Pastoral Communication.* San Francisco: Harper & Row, 1987.

O'Day, Gail R., and Thomas G. Long. *Listening to the Word: Studies in Honor of Fred B. Craddock.* Nashville: Abingdon Press, 1993.

Rice, Charles L. *Imagination and Interpretation.* Philadelphia: Fortress Press, 1970.

Riegert, Eduard R. *Imaginative Shock: Preaching and Metaphor.* Burlington, Ont.: Trinity Press, 1990.

Schlafer, David J. *Surviving the Sermon: A Guide to Preaching for Those Who Have to Listen.* Boston: Cowley Publications, 1992.

Stapleton, John Mason. *Preaching in Demonstration of the Spirit and Power.* Philadelphia: Fortress Press, 1988.

Stott, John. *I Believe in Preaching.* London: Hodder & Stoughton, 1983.

Troeger, Thomas. *Imagining a Sermon.* Nashville: Abingdon Press, 1990.

Wagley, Laurence A. *Preaching with the Small Congregation.* Nashville: Abingdon Press, 1989.

Wardlaw, Don M., ed. *Preaching Biblically: Creating Sermons in the Shape of Scripture.* Philadelphia: Westminster, 1983.

Willimon, William H. *Preaching About Conflict in the Local Church.* Philadelphia: Westminster Press, 1987.

Wilson, Paul Scott. *Imagination of the Heart: New Understandings in Preaching.* Nashville: Abingdon Press, 1988.

Wilson-Kastner, Patricia. *Imagery for Preaching.* Minneapolis: Fortress Press, 1989.

Biblical Foundations/Hermeneutics

Achtemeier, Elizabeth. *The Old Testament and the Proclamation of the Gospel.* Philadelphia: Westminster Press, 1978.

———. *Preaching from the Old Testament.* Louisville: Westminster Press, 1989.

Allen, Ronald J. *Contemporary Biblical Interpretation for Preaching.* Valley Forge, Pa.: Judson Press, 1984.

Bailey, Raymond, ed. *Hermeneutics for Preaching: Approaches to Contemporary Interpretations of Scripture.* Nashville: Broadman Press, 1992.

Gowan, Donald E. *Preaching the Old Testament.* Atlanta: John Knox Press, 1980.

Greidanus, Sidney. *The Modern Preacher and the Ancient Text: Interpreting and Preaching Biblical Literature*. Grand Rapids: Wm. B. Eerdmans Publishing Co., 1988.

Hauerwas, Stanley. *Unleashing the Scripture: Freeing the Bible from Captivity to America*. Nashville: Abingdon Press, 1993.

Keck, Leander E. *The Bible in the Pulpit: The Renewal of Biblical Preaching*. Nashville: Abingdon Press, 1978.

Klein, George L. *Reclaiming the Prophetic Mantle: Preaching the Old Testament Faithfully*. Nashville: Broadman and Holman Publishers, 1992.

Lowry, Eugene L. *Living with the Lectionary: Preaching the Revised Common Lectionary*. Nashville: Abingdon Press, 1992.

McKim, Donald K. *A Guide to Contemporary Hermeneutics: Major Trends in Biblical Interpretation*. Grand Rapids: Wm. B. Eerdmans Publishing Co., 1986.

Patte, Daniel. *Preaching Paul*. Philadelphia: Fortress Press, 1984.

Reid, Stephen Breck. *Experience and Tradition: A Primer in Black Biblical Hermeneutics*. Nashville: Abingdon Press, 1990.

Seitz, Christopher R. *Reading and Preaching the Book of Isaiah*. Philadelphia: Fortress Press, 1988.

Soards, Marion L., Thomas Dozeman, and Kendall McCabe. *Preaching the Revised Common Lectionary*. Nashville: Abingdon Press, 1992.

Thiselton, Anthony C. *New Horizons in Hermeneutics: The Theory and Practice of Transforming Biblical Reading*. Grand Rapids: Zondervan, 1992.

Bible Commentaries

Preachers are wise to consult at least two commentaries on texts they will preach. Series of commentaries are usually uneven in quality; thus, an entire series may not be a wise investment. Also, those commentaries most tightly focused on historical-critical issues at the expense of theological issues are rarely the most helpful for preachers. One new series that looks promising is *The New Interpreter's Bible* (Nashville: Abingdon Press, 1994–). The following are examples of excellent preaching resources:

Bailey, Kenneth E. *Poet and Peasant; and, Through Peasant Eyes: A Literary-Cultural Approach to the Parables in Luke*. Grand Rapids: Wm. B. Eerdmans Publishing Co., 1983.

Brunner, Frederick Dale. *Matthew*. 2 vols. Dallas: Word, 1987 and 1990.

Brueggemann, Walter. *To Pluck Up and to Tear Down: a Commentary on the Book of Jeremiah 1–25. Vol. 1*. Grand Rapids: Wm. B. Eerdmans Publishing Co., 1988.

———. *To Build, to Plant: a Commentary on Jeremiah 26–52. Vol. 2*. Grand Rapids: Wm. B. Eerdmans Publishing Co., 1991.

———. *Genesis*. Atlanta: John Knox Press, 1982.

———. *1 and 2 Kings*. Atlanta: John Knox Press, 1983, 1982.

———. *1 and 2 Samuel*. Louisville: Westminster/John Knox Press, 1990.

Bultmann, Rudolf. *The Gospel of John: A Commentary*. Trans. G. R. Beasley-Murray, general editor, R. W. N. Hoare, and J. K. Riches. Philadelphia: Westminster Press, 1971.

Campbell, Edward F., Jr. *Ruth: A New Translation with Introduction, Notes, and Commentary*. Garden City, N.Y.: Doubleday & Co., 1975.

THE PRACTICE OF PREACHING

Craddock, Fred B. *Luke. Interpretation: A Bible Commentary for Teaching and Preaching.* Louisville: John Knox Press, 1990.
Luz, Uklrich. *Matthew 1–7: A Commentary.* Trans. Wilhelm C. Linss. Minneapolis: Augsburg Press, 1989.
Schweizer, Eduard. *The Good News According to Matthew.* Trans. David E. Green. Atlanta: John Knox Press, 1975.
———. *The Good News According to Mark.* Trans. Donald Madvig. Atlanta: John Knox Press, 1970.
———. *The Good News According to Luke.* Trans. David E. Green. Atlanta: John Knox Press, 1984.
Talbert, Charles H. *Reading Corinthians: A Literary and Theological Commentary on 1 and 2 Corinthians.* New York: Crossroad, 1987.
———. *Reading Luke: A Literary and Theological Commentary on the Third Gospel.* New York: Crossroad, 1982.
Wenham, Gordon J. *Genesis 1–15.* Waco, Tex.: Word, 1987.
———. *The Book of Leviticus.* Grand Rapids: Wm. B. Eerdmans Publishing Co., 1979.

General Reference

A number of general reference books are useful including a Bible concordance (available in the version of your choice); a Bible atlas (e.g., *The Harper Atlas of the Bible.* New York: Harper and Row, 1987); a Bible dictionary (e.g., *The Interpreter's Dictionary of the Bible.* New York and Nashville: Abingdon Press, 1962; or the *International Standard Bible Encyclopedia.* Grand Rapids: Wm. B. Eerdmans Publishing Co., 1979); a dictionary of theology (e.g., Donald W. Musser and Joseph L. Price, eds. *A New Handbook of Christian Theology.* Nashville: Abingdon Press, 1992; or Alan Richardson and John Bowden. *A New Dictionary of Christian Theology.* Philadelphia: Westminster Press, 1983); and a survey of systematic theology (e.g., Owen C. Thomas, *Introduction to Theology.* Wilton, Conn.: Morehouse, 1983).

Journals

Preachers need to be generalists. Although they cannot read everything, they can select readings in relevant fields through the reviews in the official journal of the Academy of Homiletics, *Homiletic* (Lutheran Theological Seminary, 61 West Confederate Ave., Gettysburg, PA 17325). In addition it is important to subscribe to at least one publication in international news, as well as to a theological journal dealing with current theological events (like *Christianity and Crisis*). Preachers do well occasionally to browse through *Interpretation, A Journal of Bible and Theology* (Union Theological Seminary, Richmond, Va.), and may find useful a weekly homiletical/liturgical resource such as *Word and Witness* (2875 S. James Drive, New Berlin, WI 53151).

II. Special Topics

African American Preaching

There is a need for homiletical research that reflects various cultural backgrounds. To date, African American preaching, though more varied than its literature indicates, has emerged in print with a distinctive homiletic.

Massey, James Earl. *Designing the Sermon: Order and Movement in Preaching.* Nashville: Abingdon, 1980.

Miller, Keith D. *Voice of Deliverance: The Language of Martin Luther King, Jr., and Its Sources* (New York: Macmillan, 1992).

Mitchell, Henry H. *Black Preaching: The Recovery of a Powerful Art.* Nashville: Abingdon Press, 1990.

————. *Celebration and Experience in Preaching.* Nashville: Abingdon Press, 1991.

Proctor, Samuel D. *"How Shall They Hear?": Effective Preaching for Vital Faith.* Valley Forge, Pa.: Judson Press, 1992.

Smith, J. Alfred. *Preach On!* Nashville: Broadman Press, 1984.

Smith, Gerald L. *I Got the Word in Me and I Can Sing It, You Know: Study of the Performed African-American Sermon.* Philadelphia: University of Pennsylvania Press, 1986.

Smith, Warren H., Sr. *Interpreting God's Word in Black Preaching.* Valley Forge, Pa.: Judson Press, 1991.

Taylor, Gardner C. *How Shall They Preach.* Elgin, Ill.: Progressive Baptist Publishing House, 1977.

Homiletical Theology

In addition to what is said about preaching in systematic theology, the following may be consulted:

Barth, Karl. *The Word of God and the Word of Man.* New York: Harper and Brothers, 1957.

The Bishop's Committee on Priestly Life and Ministry. *Fulfilled in Your Hearing: The Homily in the Sunday Assembly.* Washington: U.S.C.C., 1982.

Brown, R. E. C. *The Ministry of the Word.* Philadelphia: Fortress Press, 1976.

Buechner, Frederick. *Telling the Truth: the Gospel as Tragedy, Comedy, and Fairy Tale.* San Francisco: Harper and Row, 1977.

————. *The Clown in the Belfrey: Writing on Faith and Fiction.* San Francisco: Harper & Row, 1992.

Buttrick, David. *Preaching Jesus Christ.* Philadelphia: Fortress Press, 1988.

————. *A Captive Voice: The Liberation of Preaching.* Louisville: Westminster/ John Knox Press, 1994.

Ebeling, Gerhard. *God and Word.* Philadelphia: Fortress Press, 1966.

Fant, Clyde E. *Bonhoeffer: Worldly Preaching.* Nashville: Thomas Nelson, Publishers, 1975.

Forbes, James. *The Holy Spirit and Preaching.* Nashville: Abingdon Press, 1989.

Forde, Gerhard O. *Theology Is for Proclamation.* Minneapolis: Fortress Press, 1990.

Lischer, Richard. *A Theology of Preaching.* Nashville: Abingdon Press, 1981.

Rahner, Karl, ed. *The Renewal of Preaching.* vol. 23, Concilium. Ramsey, N.J.: Paulist Press, 1968.

Willimon, William H. *Peculiar Speech: Preaching to the Baptized.* Grand Rapids: Wm. B. Eerdmans Publishing Co., 1992.

History of Preaching

Brilioth, Yngve. *A Brief History of Preaching.* Philadelphia: Fortress Press, 1965.

Burrows, Mark S., and Paul Rorem. *Biblical Hermeneutics in Historical Perspective.* Grand Rapids, Mich.: Wm. B. Eerdmans Publishing Co., 1991.
Carroll, Thomas K. *Preaching the Word: Message of the Fathers of the Church.* Wilmington, Del.: Michael Glazier, 1984.
Lischer, Richard. *Theories of Preaching: Selected Readings in the Homiletical Tradition.* Durham, N.C.: Labyrinth Press, 1987.
Stout, Harry. *The New England Soul: Preaching and Religious Culture in Colonial New England.* New York: Oxford University Press, 1986.
Wilson, Paul Scott. *A Concise History of Preaching.* Nashville: Abingdon Press, 1992.

Justice

González, Justo L. and Catherine G. *The Liberated Pulpit.* Nashville: Abingdon Press, 1994.
Hessel, Deiter T., ed. *Social Themes of the Christian Year.* Geneva Press, 1983.
———. *For Creation's Sake: Preaching, Ecology, and Justice.* Philadelphia: Geneva Press, 1985.
McElvaney, William K. *Preaching from Camelot to Covenant: Announcing God's Action in the World.* Nashville: Abingdon Press, 1989.
Sider, Ronald J., and Michael A. King, *Preaching About Life in a Threatening World.* Philadelphia: Westminster Press, 1987.
Smith, Christine M. *Preaching as Weeping, Confession, and Resistance: Radical Responses to Radical Evil.* Louisville: Westminster/John Knox Press, 1992.
Smith, Kelly Miller. *Social Crisis Preaching.* Macon, Ga.: Mercer University Press, 1984.
Van Seters, Arthur, ed. *Preaching as a Social Act: Theology and Practice.* Nashville: Abingdon Press, 1988.

Orality

Edwards, Viv, and Thomas J. Sienkewicz. *Oral Cultures Past and Present: Rappin' and Homer.* Cambridge, Mass.: Blackwell, 1990.
Havelock, Eric A. *The Muse Learns to Write: Reflections on Orality and Literacy from Antiquity to Present.* New Haven and London: Yale University Press, 1986.
Lord, Alfred B. *The Singer of Tales.* London and Cambridge, Mass.: Harvard University Press, 1960.
Ong, Walter J. *Orality and Literacy: The Technologizing of the Word.* London and New York: Methuen, 1982.
Rosenberg, Bruce A. *Can These Bones Live?: The Art of the American Folk Preacher.* Urbana: University of Illinois Press, 1988.

Narrative Theory and Practice

Alter, Robert. *The Art of Biblical Narrative.* New York: Basic Books. 1981.
Bonnycastle, Stephen. *In Search of Authority: An Introductory Guide to Literary Criticism.* Rev. ed. Peterborough, Ont.: Broadview Press, 1995.
Chatfield, Don. *Dinner with Jesus and Other Left-handed Story-sermons.* Grand Rapids: Zondervan, 1988.

Hauerwas, Stanley, and L. Gregory Jones. *Why Narrative? Readings in Narrative Theology.* Grand Rapids: Wm. B. Eerdmans Publishing Co., 1989.

Holbert, John C. *Preaching Old Testament: Proclamation and Narrative in the Hebrew Bible.* Nashville: Abingdon Press, 1991.

Lowry, Eugene L. *How to Preach a Parable: Designs for Narrative Sermons.* Nashville: Abingdon Press, 1989.

———. *The Homiletical Plot: The Sermon as Narrative Art Form.* Atlanta: John Knox, 1980.

Robinson, Wayne Bradley, ed., *Journeys Toward Narrative Preaching.* New York: Pilgrim Press, 1990.

Steimle, Edmund, Morris Niedenthal, and Charles L. Rice, *Preaching the Story.* Philadelphia: Fortress Press, 1980.

Thulin, Richard L. *The "I" of the Sermon.* Minneapolis: Fortress Press, 1989.

Troeger, Thomas H. *The Parable of Ten Preachers.* Nashville: Abingdon Press, 1992.

Waznak, Robert P. *Sunday After Sunday: Preaching the Homily as Story.* Mahwah, N.J.: Paulist Press, 1983.

Williams, Michael E., gen. ed. *The Storyteller's Companion to the Bible.* Vols. 1- . Nashville: Abingdon Press, 1991- .

Rhetoric and Literary Criticism

Cunningham, David. *Faithful Persuasion: In Aid of a Rhetoric of Christian Theology.* Notre Dame and London: University of Notre Dame Press, 1991.

Eggleton, Terry. *Literary Theory: An Introduction.* Oxford: Basil Blackwell, 1983.

Hauser, Gerard A. *Introduction to Rhetorical Theory.* Prospect Heights, Ill.: Waveland Press, 1991.

Kennedy, George A. *Classical Rhetoric: and Its Classical and Secular Tradition.* Chapel Hill and London: University of North Carolina Press, 1980.

———. *New Testament Interpretation Through Rhetorical Criticism.* Chapel Hill and London: University of North Carolina Press, 1984.

Loscalzo, Craig A. *Preaching Sermons That Connect: Effective Communication through Identification.* Downers Grove, Ill.: InterVarsity Press, 1992.

McClure, John S. *The Four Codes of Preaching: Rhetorical Strategies.* Minneapolis: Fortress Press, 1991.

McGowan, John, ed. *Postmodernism and Its Critics.* Ithaca and London: Cornell University Press, 1991.

McKnight, Edgar J. *The Bible and the Reader: An Introduction to Literary Criticism.* Philadelphia: Fortress Press, 1985. Meyers, Robin R. *With Ears to Hear: Preaching as Self-Persuasion.* New York: Pilgrim Press, 1993.

Selden, Raman, and Peter Widdowson. *A Reader's Guide to Contemporary Literary Theory.* 3rd ed. Lexington, Ky.: University of Kentucky Press, 1993.

Wilder, Amos. *Early Christian Rhetoric.* Cambridge: Harvard University Press, 1980.

Sermon Anthologies

In order for preachers to find their own voice, it is wise to keep reading excellent sermons by subscribing to some pulpits (e.g., Riverside Church, New York) and by reading anthologies:

Buechner, Frederick. *The Magnificent Defeat.* New York: Seabury, 1979.
Burghardt, Walter J., S.J. *Lovely in Eyes Not His: Homilies for an Imaging of Christ.* New York and Mahwah: Paulist Press, 1988.
Cox, James W., ed. *The Twentieth Century Pulpit.* Vol. 2. Nashville: Abingdon Press, 1981.
Crawford, James W. *Worthy to Raise Issues: Preaching and Public Responsibility.* Cleveland: Pilgrim Press, 1991.
Farmer, David Albert, and Edwina Hunter. *And Blessed Is She: Sermons by Women.* San Francisco: Harper and Row, Publishers, 1990.
Mitchell, Ella Pearson, ed. *Those Preachin' Women: Sermons by Black Women Preachers.* Valley Forge, Pa.: Judson Press, 1985.
Peterson, Eugene. *A Long Obedience in the Same Direction: Discipleship in an Instant Society.* Downers Grove, Ill.: InterVarsity Press, 1980.
Plantinga, Cornelius, and Thomas G. Long. *A Chorus of Witnesses: Model Sermons for Today's Preachers.* Grand Rapids: William B. Eerdmans Publishing Co., 1994.
Rogers, Cornish R., and Joseph R. Jeter, Jr., eds. *Preaching through the Apocalypse: Sermons from Revelation.* St. Louis: Chalice Press, 1990.
Sherry, Paul H. *The Riverside Preachers.* New York: Pilgrim Press, 1978.
Smith, J. Alfred, Sr., ed. *Outstanding Black Sermons.* Valley Forge, Pa.: Judson Press, 1991.
Stewart, James S. *The Wind of the Spirit.* Grand Rapids: Baker Books, 1984.
Theissen, Gerd. *The Open Door: Variations on Biblical Themes.* Trans. John Bowden. Minneapolis: Fortress Press, 1991.
Waznak, Robert P. *Like Fresh Bread: Sunday Homilies in the Parish.* New York/Mahwah, N.J.: Paulist Press, 1993.
Willimon, William H., and Stanley Hauerwas. *Preaching to Strangers: Evangelism in Today's World.* Louisville: Westminster/John Knox, 1992.
Wolff, Hans Walter. *Old Testament and Christian Preaching.* Philadelphia: Fortress Press, 1986.
The Word Is Life: An Anthology of Funeral Meditations. Lima, Ohio: C.S.S. Publishing, 1994.

Women and Preaching

Norén, Carol M. *The Woman in the Pulpit.* Nashville: Abingdon Press, 1991.
Smith, Christine M. *Weaving the Sermon: Preaching in a Feminist Perspective.* Louisville: Westminster/John Knox Press, 1989.
Taylor, Barbara Brown. *The Preaching Life.* Boston and Cambridge, Mass.: Cowley Publications, 1993.
Watley, William D., and Susan D. Johnson Cook. *Preaching in Two Voices: Sermons on the Women in Jesus' Life.* Valley Forge, Pa.: Judson Press, 1992.

Worship

Costen, Melva Wilson. *African American Christian Worship.* Nashville: Abingdon Press, 1993.
Doyle, Stephen C. *The Gospel in Word and Power: The Biblical Liturgical Homily.* Wilmington: Glazier, 1982.

The Revised Common Lectionary: The Consultation on Common Texts. Abingdon Press, 1992.

Rice, Charles L. The Embodied Word: Preaching as Art and Liturgy. Minneapolis: Augsburg Fortress, 1991.

Skudlarek, William. The Word in Worship: Preaching in a Liturgical Context. Nashville: Abingdon, 1981.

Stookey, Laurence L. Eucharist. Nashville: Abingdon Press, 1993.

White, James F. A Brief Introduction to Christian Worship. Nashville: Abingdon Press, 1993.

———. Introduction to Christian Worship. Nashville: Abingdon, 1980.

NOTES

Preface

1. I draw here on a variety of sources, with special debt to Ian Barbour, *Religion in an Age of Science* (San Francisco: HarperCollins, 1990), p. 219; and Ronald L. Grimes, *Ritual Criticism: Case Studies in Its Practice, Essays on Its Theory* (Columbia, S.C.: U. of South Carolina Press, 1990), p. 24.
2. David James Randolph, *The Renewal of Preaching* (Philadelphia: Fortress Press, 1969), pp. 22-23.
3. We do not go beyond a helpful introduction to the significance of classical rhetoric for preaching. Indeed, today's rhetoric defines itself less in terms of persuasion than identification (see Kenneth Burke et al.).

Section I: The Oral Tradition

1. Clyde E. Fant, *Bonhoeffer: Worldly Preaching* (Nashville: Thomas Nelson, 1975), pp. 126-30.
2. Archibald Macleish, *J.B.* (Boston: Houghton Mifflin Co., 1957).
3. Walter Brueggemann, *Finally Comes the Poet: Daring Speech for Proclamation* (Minneapolis: Fortress Press, 1989), p. 4. In fact, Brueggemann draws his title from the poet Walt Whitman: "Finally shall come the poet worthy of that name, / The true son of God shall come singing his songs."

Chapter 1: Preaching as God's Event

1. Jerome Klinkowitz, *Rosenberg/Barthes/Hassan: The Postmodern Habit of Thought* (Athens, Ga.: University of Georgia Press, 1988), p. 8.
2. It might equally be said that throughout the sermon the members of the congregation are also aware of its relationship with others, within and beyond the congregation. I am delaying discussion of these important relationships to others largely to chapters 12 and 13 in the context of mission. It has been common for homiletical literature to speak of three stories (or sets of relationship) of the sermon: the story of God, the congregation, and the preacher. See Edmund A. Steimle, Morris J. Niedenthal, and Charles L. Rice, *Preaching the Story* (Philadelphia: Fortress Press, 1980); and Robert P. Waznak, *Sunday after Sunday: Preaching the Homily as Story* (Mahwah, N.J.: Paulist Press, 1983).
3. See, for instance, Paul Tillich, *Systematic Theology* (Chicago: University of Chicago Press, 1963), I, p. 109; and D. M. Baillie, *God Was in Christ* (London: Faber & Faber, 1948), p. 106.
4. Phillips Brooks, *Lectures on Preaching* (Manchester: James Robinson, 1899), p. 126.

302

5. Thomas G. Long speaks of the listener co-creating the sermon, in *The Witness of Preaching* (Louisville: Westminster/John Knox Press, 1989), p. 131.
6. David James Randolph, *The Renewal of Preaching* (Philadelphia: Fortress Press, 1969), p. 19. From Question 54 of the Methodist Discipline of 1784. German existential theology, promoted the idea that Jesus' living word is an event today through the preaching of the church (thus the movement known as the "new hermeneutic" sought to avoid use of the term "kerygma" or, proclamation of Jesus' victory, because it separated the Jesus of history from the act of preaching). See James M. Robinson, "Hermeneutic Since Barth," in James M. Robinson and John B. Cobb, Jr., eds., *New Frontiers in Theology*, vol. II, *The New Hermeneutic* (New York, Evanston, London: Harper & Row, Publishers, 1964), pp. 49 ff. Other important voices spoke of preaching as God's encounter. See, for instance, Paul Scherer, *The Word God Sent* (Grand Rapids: Baker Books, 1965), p. 24; and Karl Barth, *The Word of God and the Word of Man*, trans. Douglas Horton (New York: Harper & Brothers, Publishers, 1957 [1928]), pp. 107-9, and Karl Barth, *Church Dogmatics*, vol. 1 (Edinburgh: T. & T. Clark, 1936), esp. "God's Language as Act," pp. 162-84.
7. John Claypool, *The Preaching Event* (Waco, Tex.: Word, 1980).
8. Eugene L. Lowry, "The Revolution of Sermonic Shape," in Gail R. O'Day and Thomas G. Long, *Listening to the Word: Studies in Honor of Fred B. Craddock* (Nashville: Abingdon Press, 1993), p. 110.
9. Sallie McFague, *Speaking in Parables* (Philadelphia: Fortress Press, 1975), p. 79.
10. Fred B. Craddock, *Overhearing the Gospel* (Nashville: Abingdon, 1978), p. 83; and *Preaching* (Nashville: Abingdon Press, 1985), p. 47.
11. Don M. Wardlaw, "Preaching as the Interface of Two Social Worlds: The Congregation as Corporate Agent in the Act of Preaching," in Arthur Van Seters, ed., *Preaching as a Social Act: Theology and Practice* (Nashville: Abingdon Press, 1988), p. 54.
12. Eduard R. Riegert, *Imaginative Shock: Preaching and Metaphor* (Burlington, Ont.: Trinity Press, 1990), p. 122.
13. David J. Schlafer, *Surviving the Sermon: A Guide to Preaching for Those Who Have to Listen* (Cambridge and Boston, Mass.: Cowley Publications, 1992), p. 31.
14. Justin Martyr, *The First Apology of Justin, the Martyr*, trans. Edward R. Hardy, *Early Christian Fathers* (vol. 1 in "The Library of Christian Classics," Philadelphia: Westminster, 1953), p. 265.
15. Thomas G. Long, *The Witness of Preaching* (Louisville: Westminster/John Knox Press, 1989), p. 23.
16. See James D. Smart, *The Divided Mind of Modern Theology* (Philadelphia: Westminster Press, 1967), p. 209.
17. Long, *Witness of Preaching*, p. 23.
18. See my forthcoming article, "Paul's Letters as Sermons: A Homiletical Perspective," in *The Toronto Journal of Theology*.
19. Alan of Lille, *The Art of Preaching*, Cistercian Fathers Series, no. 23, trans. Gillian R. Evans (Kalamazoo, Mich.: Cistercian Publications, 1981), p. 20.
20. Karl Barth, *Prayer and Preaching*, trans. B. E. Hooke (London: S.C.M., 1964), p. 69. See also pp. 110-11. He also said, "The Word of God is itself God's act. Thus, directly, it has nothing to do with the general problem of historical understanding." Karl Barth, *Church Dogmatics*, vol. 1 (Edinburgh: T. & T. Clark, 1936), p. 168.
21. Craig A. Loscalzo, *Preaching Sermons That Connect: Effective Communication Through Identification* (Downers Grove, Ill.: InterVarsity Press, 1992), pp. 59-60.
22. An excellent treatment of ethos may be found in Edward P. J. Corbett, *Classical Rhetoric for the Modern Student* (New York and Oxford: Oxford University Press, 1990), pp. 80ff.; and Gerard A. Hauser, *Introduction to Rhetorical Theory* (Prospect Heights, Ill.: Waveland Press, 1986), esp. pp. 91ff. These discussions have informed the one offered here.
23. Aristotle, "Rhetoric," I, 1. 1158b, in *The Complete Works of Aristotle*, vol. 2, Jonathan Barnes, ed. (Princeton and Oxford: Princeton University Press, 1984), p. 2159.

24. Classical rhetoric tends to confine ethos strictly to character as it is communicated through the speech itself, and it thus ignores the realities of a long-term pastoral relationship that Christians cannot appropriately ignore.
25. Craig A. Loscalzo concentrates on this important question of identification, in *Preaching Sermons That Connect*. His chapter on the preacher's integrity (pp. 59-80) is perhaps the best in recent memory.
26. David Buttrick, *Homiletic: Moves and Structures* (Philadelphia: Fortress Press, 1987), pp. 45, 47.
27. Harry Emerson Fosdick, *The Living of These Days* (New York: Harper and Brothers, 1956), p. 99.

Chapter 2: Preaching as an Oral Event

1. T. S. Eliot, "'Rhetoric' and Poetic Drama," in *Selected Essays*, 3rd ed. (London: Faber & Faber, 1951), p. 37.
2. Martin Luther, "Table Talk," Theodore G. Tappert, ed. and trans., *Luther's Works*, vol. 54 (Philadelphia: Fortress Press, 1967), p. 236.
3. Karl Barth, *Prayer and Preaching*, trans. B. E. Hooke (London: S.C.M. Press, 1964), p. 96. The same passage may be found in an awkward translation, in Karl Barth, *Homiletics*, trans. Geoffrey W. Bromily and Donald E. Daniels (Louisville: Westminster/John Knox Press, 1991), p. 83.
4. Gerhard von Rad, "The Prophet's Conception of the Word of God," in *Old Testament Theology*, vol. 2, trans. D. M. G. Stalker (Edinburgh and London: Oliver and Boyd, 1965), p. 80.
5. Sallie McFague, *Metaphorical Theology* (Philadelphia: Fortress Press, 1982), pp. 22-23.
6. Owen C. Thomas, *Introduction to Theology*, rev. ed. (Wilton, Conn.: Morehouse Publishing, 1983), pp. 23-24.
7. Charles L. Rice, *The Embodied Word: Preaching as Art and Liturgy* (Minneapolis: Fortress Press, 1991), pp. 41ff.
8. Kathy Black has argued the inadequacy of this understanding for the deaf, and the need for a new theology of "presence," in "Beyond the Spoken Word: Preaching as Presence," in *Papers of the Annual Meeting of the Academy of Homiletics* (28th meeting, 1993), pp. 79-88.
9. Martin Luther, *D. Martin Luthers Werke*, Kritische Gesamtausgabe (Weimar, 1883–), 12: 259; 37: 207, and 10: I, 2, 48; cited with discussion in Fred W. Meuser and Stanley D. Schneider, eds., *Interpreting Luther's Legacy* (Minneapolis: Augsburg, 1969), pp. 19, 30.
10. Walter J. Ong calls their thinking "residually oral." See Walter J. Ong, *Orality and Literacy: The Technologizing of the Word* (London and New York: Methuen, 1982). See also Jack Goody, *The Domestication of the Savage Mind* (Cambridge, England: Cambridge University Press, 1977); Eric A. Havelock, *The Muse Learns to Write: Reflections on Orality and Literacy from Antiquity to the Present* (New Haven and London: Yale University Press, 1986); and Viv Edwards and Thomas J. Sienkewicz, *Oral Cultures Past and Present: Rappin' and Homer* (Cambridge, Mass.: Blackwell, 1990).
11. In addition to Ong, see Paul Saenger, "Silent Reading: Its Impact on Late Medieval Script and Society," *Viator* 13 (1983): 367-414. See also my *Concise History of Preaching* (Nashville: Abingdon Press, 1992), pp. 17ff.
12. Thomas J. Farrell, "Early Christian Creeds and Controversies in the Light of the Orality-Literacy Hypothesis," in *Oral Tradition* 2/1 (1987): 133.
13. Eduard R. Riegert, *Imaginative Shock: Preaching and Metaphor* (Burlington, Ont.: Trinity Press, 1990), p. 120.
14. Ibid., p. 121.
15. Aleksandr Romanovich Luria, *Cognitive Development: Its Cultural and Social Foundations*, ed. Michael Cole, trans. Martin Lopez-Morillas and Lynn Solotaroff (Cambridge,

NOTES TO PAGES 49-68

Mass., and London: Harvard University Press, 1976). Some of the following examples from Luria are also to be found in Ong's discussion of Luria in *Orality and Literacy.*
16. Luria, *Cognitive Development,* pp. 24ff.
17. Ibid., pp. 34ff.
18. Ibid., p. 38.
19. McFague, *Metaphorical Theology;* David Tracy, *The Analogical Imagination* (New York: Crossroad, 1989).
20. Luria, *Cognitive Development,* p. 55.
21. Horace Bushnell, *Forgiveness and Law, Grounded in Principles Interpreted by Human Analogies* (New York: Scribner, Armstrong, & Co., 1874), pp. 120-33ff.
22. Luria, *Cognitive Development,* p. 57.
23. Ibid., pp. 86-89.
24. Ibid., pp. 102ff.
25. Ibid., pp. 144ff.
26. For instance, Saenger, "Silent Reading," 367-414.
27. See Ong, *Orality and Literacy.* For an understanding of orality that takes issue with Ong, see Angelane Beth Daniell, *Ong's Great Leap: The Poetics of Literacy and Orality,* Ph.D. dissertation (Austin, Tex.: University of Texas, 1986).
28. Laura Sinclair, "Can Your Bones Live?" in *Those Preachin' Women,* Ella Pearson Mitchell, ed. (Valley Forge, Pa.: Judson Press, 1985), pp. 23-24.
29. Fred B. Craddock, "When the Roll Is Called Down Here," *Preaching Today,* tape no. 50.
30. Ronald J. Allen, "The Difference," in Arthur Van Seters, ed., *Preaching as a Social Act: Theology and Practice* (Nashville: Abingdon Press, 1988), p. 191.
31. Ola Irene Harrison, "This Bittersweet Season," in Cornish R. Rogers and Joseph R. Jeter, Jr., eds., *Preaching Through the Apocalypse: Sermons from Revelation* (St. Louis: Chalice Press, 1992), p. 111.
32. Charles G. Adams, "The Power of Prayer," taped sermon (Detroit: Hartford Memorial Baptist Church, Sunday, March 29, 1994).
33. Pamela Moeller, *Kinesthetic Homiletic* (Minneapolis: Fortress Press, 1993).
34. Henry H. Mitchell, *Celebration and Experience in Preaching* (Nashville: Abingdon Press, 1991), esp. chap. 2.

Chapter 3: Theology and Rhetoric

1. I. A. Richards, *The Philosophy of Rhetoric* (New York: Oxford University Press, 1936 [1965]), p. 9.
2. Ibid., pp. 10-11.
3. Amos N. Wilder, *Early Christian Rhetoric: The Language of the Gospel* (Cambridge, Mass.: Harvard University Press, 1980 [1971, 1964]), p. xxx.
4. David S. Cunningham, *Faithful Persuasion: In Aid of a Rhetoric of Christian Theology* (Notre Dame: University of Notre Dame Press, 1992), p. 125.
5. Ibid., p. 5.
6. An excellent account of the rationality of Christian belief and its similarity to scientific reasoning is found in Nancey Murphy, *Theology in the Age of Scientific Reasoning* (Ithaca and London: Cornell University Press, 1990).
7. Rebecca S. Chopp is one who would have us understand theological language as political activity and feminist theology in itself as rhetorical "proclamation" leading to "emancipatory transformation": Rebecca S. Chopp, *The Power to Speak: Feminism, Language, God* (New York: Crossroad, 1989), pp. 3, 22. See Don S. Browning, *A Fundamental Practical Theology: Descriptive and Strategic Proposals* (Minneapolis: Fortress Press, 1991); Cunningham, *Faithful Persuasion,* pp. 41-42.
8. Cunningham, *Faithful Persuasion,* p. 42.
9. By the term "homiletical theology" I mean that rhetorical expression of theology which (1) is appropriate to the pulpit in the first instance or (2) concerns the theology

305

and practice of proclamation. It has a natural overlap with systematic and biblical theology. The term "homiletic theology" was used by David Buttrick in *Preaching Jesus Christ* (Philadelphia: Fortress Press, 1988).

10. Classical rhetoric already recognized this kind of distinction. Aristotle saw that science, metaphysics, and logic primarily functioned using analytical method, particularly when the first principles or highest causes in a line of thought were not in dispute. On the other hand, subjects dealing with opinion, like ethics, politics, and poetics, used a dialectical method of inquiry involving question and answer, point and counterpoint, when dealing with theory; as did rhetoric or persuasion, when dealing with practical issues or applications. Analytic and dialectic methods were complementary, not hierarchical. See Aristotle, "Metaphysics," IV: 1ff., in Jonathan Barnes, ed., *The Complete Works of Aristotle*, vol. 2 (Princeton: Princeton University Press, 1984); and Cunningham, *Faithful Persuasion*, p. 16.

11. This is what Robin R. Meyers calls "self-persuasion" in his, *With Ears to Hear: Preaching as Self-Persuasion* (Cleveland: Pilgrim Press, 1993).

12. Gardner C. Taylor, "Two Words at the End," *How Shall They Preach* (Elgin, Ill.: Progressive Baptist Publishing House, 1977), p. 145. The early Christians sought to make sense of their experience of the resurrected Christ and read the Old Testament with this in mind, thereby determining its function in Christian tradition. Students seeking further reading should consult, for example, Brevard Childs, *Biblical Theology of the Old and New Testaments: Theological Reflections on the Christian Bible* (Minneapolis: Fortress Press, 1992), pp. 452-84; and Frances Young, *Virtuoso Theology* (Cleveland: Pilgrim Press, 1993), pp. 66-87.

13. Clark M. Williamson and Ronald J. Allen, *Interpreting Difficult Texts: Anti-Judaism and Christian Preaching* (London and Philadelphia: S.C.M. Press and Trinity Press International), 1989.

14. Richard Lischer, *A Theology of Preaching: The Dynamics of the Gospel* (Nashville: Abingdon Press, 1981), p. 52.

15. Gerard A. Hauser, *Introduction to Rhetorical Theory* (Prospect Heights, Ill.: Waveland Press, 1991), p. 71.

16. "Rhetoric," *The Complete Works of Aristotle*, Jonathan Barnes, ed. (Princeton: Princeton University Press, 1984), vol. 2, p. 2155.

17. Phillips Brooks, *Lectures on Preaching: Delivered before the Divinity School of Yale College in January and February, 1877* (Manchester, England: James Robinson, 1889), p. 5. Brooks is more frequently cited as saying, "Truth through Personality is our description of real preaching"—a less dynamic understanding.

18. See, e.g., Ronald E. Sleeth, *Persuasive Preaching* (Berrien Springs, Mich.: Andrews University Press, 1981); Craig A. Loscalzo, *Preaching Sermons That Connect: Effective Communication Through Identification* (Downers Grove, Ill.: InterVarsity Press, 1992); John S. McClure, *The Four Codes of Preaching: Rhetorical Strategies* (Minneapolis: Fortress Press, 1991); Meyers, *With Ears to Hear*.

19. Henry H. Mitchell, *Celebration and Experience in Preaching* (Nashville: Abingdon Press, 1990), esp. pp. 23-35. See also his *Recovery of Preaching* (San Francisco: Harper & Row, 1977), pp. 54-73.

20. Meyers, *With Ears to Hear*, p. 14.

21. Ibid., p. 118. Persuasive effect becomes located for Meyers (I suspect too much) in listener-generated response, without sufficient acknowledgment either of the sermon as message, or of the role of the Holy Spirit.

22. Dorothee Soelle sees the debate between God as "beyond us" and God as "relationship" to be "one of the most important arguments between male-patriarchal and feminist theology." Dorothee Soelle, *Thinking About God: An Introduction to Theology*, trans. John Bowden (London and Philadelphia: S.C.M. Press and Trinity Press International, 1990), p. 181.

Chapter 4: Theology in the Sermon

1. These guidelines are adapted from Owen C. Thomas, *Introduction to Theology* (Wilton, Conn.: Morehouse Publishing, 1983), p. 16.
2. Methodological suggestions in systematics have taken a different approach. See, e.g., Friedrich Schleiermacher, who gave guidelines for the division of theology into philosophical, historical, and practical, in his *Brief Outline on the Study of Theology*, trans. Terrence N. Tice (Richmond: John Knox Press, 1966 [1830]). Gerhard Ebeling stood in a long tradition from Schleiermacher in suggesting three possible methodologies for theology in our pluralistic age: apologetic (i.e. developing a supporting foundation for theological inquiry that can withstand challenges put to it); encyclopedic; or foundational (examining the ground rules for the disciplines); see his *Study of Theology*, trans. Duane A. Priebe (Philadelphia: Fortress Press, 1978), pp. 154-55.
3. David H. Kelsey, *The Uses of Scripture in Recent Theology* (Philadelphia: Fortress Press, 1975), p. 134.
4. Richard Grigg, *Theology as a Way of Thinking* (Atlanta: Scholars Press, 1990), pp. 35, 103. Grigg offers four positions in relation to the plurality of theological positions available, and suggests ways in which each might be held responsibly: (1) No theology can provide knowledge of the divine—the position of the skeptic; (2) one theology can provide knowledge of the divine—one chooses the most coherent; (3) many theologies can provide knowledge of the divine—if one admits that everyone has some knowledge of God (i.e. the position of Karl Rahner); and (4) although no theology can provide knowledge of the divine, the task of theology can be reformulated in which the concept of God as a symbol or ideal (that does not correspond to a theological reality) becomes the foundation for exploration. See pp. 103ff.
5. George A. Lindbeck, *The Nature of Doctrine: Religion and Theology in a Postliberal Age* (Philadelphia: Westminster Press, 1984).
6. Thomas C. Oden, *After Modernity . . . What? Agenda for Theology* (Grand Rapids: Zondervan, 1990), pp. 160-61.
7. David Tracy, *The Analogical Imagination* (New York: Crossroad, 1981).
8. James H. Cone, *A Black Theology of Liberation* (Maryknoll, N.Y.: Orbis Books, 1990 [1986]), esp. pp. 63ff.
9. Rebecca S. Chopp, *The Power to Speak: Feminism, Language, God* (New York: Crossroad, 1989), p. 127.
10. Pamela Dickey Young, *Feminist Theology/Christian Theology: In Search of a Method* (Minneapolis: Fortress Press, 1990), pp. 17-21.
11. Students wishing to explore this subject in greater depth should consult Hans W. Frei, *Types of Christian Theology* (New Haven and London: Yale University Press, 1992).
12. This chart is devised with assistance from several sources, including Robert McAfee Brown as cited in Grigg, *Theology as a Way of Thinking*, pp. 75-78; Werner G. Jeanrond, "Theological Method," in Donald W. Musser and Joseph L. Price, eds., *A New Handbook of Christian Theology* (Nashville: Abingdon Press, 1992), pp. 480-86; Gordon D. Kaufman, *An Essay on Theological Method* (Missoula, Mont.: Scholars Press, 1975); Dorothee Soelle, *Thinking About God: An Introduction to Theology*, trans. John Bowden (London and Philadelphia: S.C.M. Press and Trinity Press International, 1990), esp. p. 65.
13. At a simple level, Luther had three very practical suggestions for preacher-theologians, guidelines that he said "have made a fairly good theologian of me": (1) know that the Scriptures turn "all other books into foolishness," (2) "meditate . . . not only in your heart, but also externally" by saying out loud the words of Scripture many times and comparing them with the written words, and (3) seek not just knowledge but also experience and love of the sweet truth of God's majestic Word. This experience and love he called "*tentatio, Anfechtung*. . . . For as soon as God's Word takes

root and grows in you, the devil will harry you, and will make a real doctor of you, and by his assaults will teach you to seek and love God's Word." Martin Luther, "Luther Concerning the Study of Theology," in Ebeling, *Study of Theology*, pp. 167-68.

14. John Broadus, *The Preparation and Delivery of Sermons*, 10th ed. (New York: A. C. Armstrong and Son, 1887), pp. 89ff.

15. James S. Stewart, *Heralds of God* (New York: Charles Scribner's Sons, 1946), pp. 63-70. See also my *Concise History of Preaching* (Nashville: Abingdon Press, 1992), pp. 164ff.

16. James S. Stewart, *A Faith to Proclaim* (London: Hodder and Stoughton, 1953).

17. Stewart, *Heralds of God*, pp. 110ff.

18. Samuel D. Proctor, *"How Shall They Hear?": Effective Preaching for Vital Faith* (Valley Forge, Pa.: Judson Press, 1992), p. 10.

19. Fred B. Craddock, *Preaching* (Nashville: Abingdon Press, 1985), p. 49.

20. I am particularly grateful to Professor Laurence Hull Stookey at a number of places in this chart.

21. See Edward Farley, "Preaching the Bible and Preaching the Gospel," in *Theology Today* 51/1 (April 1994): 90-103.

22. See the discussion of this in my *Imagination of the Heart: New Understandings in Preaching* (Nashville: Abingdon Press, 1988), pp. 140-43.

Chapter 5: Preaching as an Event of Hope

1. There are a number of excellent treatments of hope, including: Emil Brunner, *Faith, Hope, and Love* (Philadelphia: Westminster Press, 1956); Douglas John Hall, *Hope Against Hope: Towards an Indigenous Theology of the Cross* (Geneva: WSCF Books, 1971); Brian Hebblethwaite, *The Christian Hope* (Grand Rapids: Wm. B. Eerdmans Publishing Co., 1985); John Macquarrie, *Christian Hope* (New York: Seabury Press, 1978); and Jürgen Moltmann, *Theology of Hope*, trans. James W. Leitch (London: S.C.M. Press Ltd., 1967).

2. This corresponds to Calvin's third use of the law as a guide for the redeemed, that like torah, we joyfully observe.

3. Professor Stephen Farris of Knox College in the Toronto School of Theology tells this story from his own experience.

4. Sidney Greidanus has written an excellent essay against anthropocentric preaching, "Preaching the Gospels," in Michael Duduit, ed., *Handbook of Contemporary Preaching* (Nashville: Broadman Press, 1993), pp. 329-43.

5. See David Buttrick's discussion of the biblical theology movement in his *Captive Voice: The Liberation of Preaching* (Louisville: Westminster/John Knox Press, 1994), esp. pp. 5-32.

6. Donna Schaper, *Hard Times: Sermons on Hope* (Nashville: Abingdon Press, 1993), p. 9.

7. See I Cor. 1:22ff. See also, e.g.: Rom. 6:5ff.; I Cor. 15:17-19; Eph. 4:4, 12, 15-16; Heb. 4:16; and I Pet. 3:13.

8. Brevard S. Childs dismisses some recent attempts in this direction in his *Biblical Theology of the Old and New Testaments: Theological Reflection on the Christian Bible* (Minneapolis: Fortress Press, 1992): "It is basic to Christian theology to reckon with an extra-biblical reality, namely with the resurrected Christ who evoked the New Testament witness. When H. Frei, in one of his last essays, spoke of 'midrash' as a text-creating reality, he moved in a direction, in my opinion, which for Christian theology can only end in failure ('The Literal Reading')," p. 20; see also Childs' mistrust that "text" serves for Lindbeck as a substitute for "God," p. 22.

9. Gerhard O. Forde, *Theology Is for Proclamation* (Minneapolis: Fortress Press, 1990), p. 157.

10. Richard Lischer, *A Theology of Preaching* (Nashville: Abingdon Press, 1981), p. 50. See also pp. 46-65.
11. Justo and Catherine González, *The Liberating Pulpit* (Nashville: Abingdon Press, 1994).
12. David Buttrick, *Homiletic: Moves and Structures* (Philadelphia: Fortress Press, 1987), p. 382; and his *Preaching Jesus Christ* (Philadelphia: Fortress Press, 1988), p. 84.
13. Thomas G. Long, "Edmund Steimle and the Shape of Contemporary Homiletics," in *The Princeton Seminary Bulletin,* n.s. 11, no. 3 (1990), p. 263. He disagrees with Steimle's understanding of law and gospel in preaching, which is similar to what I am advocating as the movement of hope: "I am more instructed by Steimle's . . . conviction that the overall character of the biblical witness should shape preaching than I am by the particular law-gospel structure of his sermons" (p. 262). See also Long's *Preaching and the Literary Forms of the Bible* (Philadelphia: Fortress Press, 1989).
14. Long, "Edmund Steimle," p. 263.
15. What is sometimes called "canonical criticism" investigates the biblical text in its accepted places for the faith community; in other words, the meaning of texts is in part determined by the use to which the believing community puts them. This approach allows us to see that determining the rhetorical strategy of a biblical passage is not a matter of simple choice, either this or that, between these historical settings and canonical location.
16. Just as the crucifixion precedes the resurrection, we normally move theologically from judgment to grace. Some biblical texts, like Rom. 6:5-11, move from grace to judgment, and our sermons may also. Such a movement nonetheless represents a theological choice to leave the congregation in the muted grace of teachings. Such choices at times are up to us: If this reading was extended to v. 14, it would end in grace.
17. Stanley Hauerwas, *Unleashing the Scripture: Freeing the Bible from Captivity to America* (Nashville: Abingdon Press, 1993), p. 42.
18. John Wesley in an open letter to "My dear friend" originally published in Wesley's own *Arminian Magazine* in 1779, in Albert C. Outler, ed., *John Wesley* (New York: Oxford University Press, 1964), pp. 232-37, esp. p. 237. Wesley was better than Luther in avoiding a dangerous identification of law with Old Testament and gospel with New Testament, when in fact, each is a dimension of God's word, wherever it is found. See my, "Wesley's Understanding of Law and Gospel for Preaching," *The Toronto Journal of Theology,* forthcoming. Judgment and grace are given explicit treatment by many preachers as diverse as Paul (esp. Rom. 2–9), Augustine (his discussion of the primacy of grace), Luther, John Donne, John Wesley, Horace Bushnell, Phillips Brooks, P. T. Forsyth, James S. Stewart, Karl Barth, Martin Luther King, Jr., and a host of others.
19. Charles Haddon Spurgeon, *Lectures to My Students* (Grand Rapids: Zondervan, 1954), p. 70.
20. I avoid these issues here because of the negative freight they carry for many people. It takes a well-disposed student of Luther, for instance, to get past his identification of law with Old Testament. See my *Imagination of the Heart: New Understandings in Preaching* (Nashville: Abingdon Press, 1988), esp. pp. 90ff., and *A Concise History of Preaching* (Nashville: Abingdon Press, 1992), pp. 92ff.
21. Forde, *Theology Is for Proclamation,* p. 151.
22. David L. Bartlett argues that to preach Paul we "start with good news and move to exhortation," in Gail R. O'Day and Thomas G. Long, eds., *Listening to the Word: Studies in Honor of Fred B. Craddock* (Nashville: Abingdon Press, 1993), p. 159.
23. John Wesley in Albert C. Outler, ed., *John Wesley,* p. 234.
24. Karl Barth, *Prayer and Preaching,* trans. B. E. Hooke (London: S.C.M. Press Ltd., 1964), p. 95. The same passage may be found in a less vivid version that removes some of the judgment and grace vocabulary, in Karl Barth, *Homiletics,* trans. Geoffrey W. Bromily and Donald E. Daniels (Louisville, Ky.: Westminster/John Knox

Press, 1991), p. 82. Barth's 1935 essay, "Gospel and Law," argues that we must first be encountered by the gospel of Jesus Christ, before we can be awakened to the judgment that is upon us; thus, the sequence is gospel-law-gospel.

25. Henry H. Mitchell, *Celebration and Experience in Preaching* (Nashville: Abingdon Press, 1990). See also Henry H. Mitchell, *Black Preaching: The Recovery of a Powerful Art* (Nashville: Abingdon Press, 1990), pp. 110ff., 119ff.

26. Frederick Buechner, *Telling the Truth: The Gospel as Tragedy, Comedy, and Fairy Tale* (San Francisco: Harper & Row, 1977), p. 7.

27. Eugene L. Lowry, *The Homiletical Plot* (Atlanta: John Knox, 1980), p. 25.

28. Fred B. Craddock, *Preaching* (Nashville: Abingdon Press, 1985), pp. 61-64. He also says, "There is no insult more painful than having one's flaws and failures, constant sources of disappointment in oneself, taken lightly or dismissed as nothing in comparison to the grosser evils of the world. Or to have grace poured like syrup over one's life with no diagnosis, no recommendation of surgery, no regimen for recovery" (p. 88).

29. Buttrick, *Homiletic*, pp. 382, 449-52. See also his sermon (and Eslinger's analysis of it) "Abraham and Isaac," in Richard L. Eslinger, *A New Hearing: Living Options in Homiletic Method* (Nashville: Abingdon Press, 1987), esp. pp. 166ff.

30. Herman G. Stuempfle called this "law as Hammer of Judgment," *Preaching Law and Gospel* (Philadelphia: Fortress Press, 1978), pp. 21ff. In my discussion here I am indebted to his delineation of two kinds of law and two kinds of gospel.

31. Forde, *Theology Is for Proclamation*, p. 157.

32. Ibid.

33. Spurgeon, *Lectures to My Students*, p. 134.

34. Buttrick, *Homiletic*, pp. 25-27.

35. Calvin conceived of the third use of the law in this manner, and was echoed by Wesley in his understanding of how the law works as we approach sanctification. John Wesley spoke about the life of the Christian as moving from "preventing grace" (the first "tendency towards life; some degree of salvation") to "convincing grace" or repentance; to salvation by grace through faith, first by justification ("we are saved from the guilt of sin, and restored to the favour of God") and second by sanctification ("we are saved from the power and root of sin, and restored to the image of God"). This salvation, he says, is "both instantaneous and gradual" ("On Working Out Our Own Salvation," *The Works of John Wesley*, vol. 3 [Nashville: Abingdon Press, 1986], p. 204). To those "pressing on to the mark" of sanctification and glorification, the burden of the faith is "not only a command but a privilege also . . . a branch of the glorious liberty of the [children] of God" ("On Preaching Christ," in Albert C. Outler, ed., *John Wesley*, p. 233).

Section III: Hermeneutical Tradition

1. The square is suggestive of the logical square of contraries and contradictions (see Aristotle, *De Interpretatione*, 10, *The Complete Works of Aristotle*, Jonathan Barnes, ed., vol. 1 [Princeton: Princeton University Press, 1984], pp. 31ff.), also known more recently as the semiotic square; and Albert Outler's distillation of the Wesleyan quadrilateral.

Chapter 6: Monday: What the Text Says

1. See Eugene L. Lowry, *Living with the Lectionary: Preaching Through the Revised Common Lectionary* (Nashville: Abingdon Press, 1992); see also esp. the "Introduction" to *The Revised Common Lectionary* produced by the Consultation on Common Texts (Nashville: Abingdon Press, 1992), pp. 9-20; and see Justo L. and Catherine G. González, *The Liberating Pulpit* (Nashville: Abingdon Press, 1994), pp. 38ff.

2. In Lionel Crocker, ed., *Harry Emerson Fosdick's Art of Preaching: An Anthology* (Springfield, Ill.: Charles C. Thomas, Publisher, 1971), p. 30.

3. See Clark M. Williamson and Ronald J. Allen, *A Credible and Timely Word* (St. Louis: Chalice Press, 1991), pp. 91-129, esp. 120-25; and Phyllis Trible, *Texts of Terror: Literary-Feminist Readings of Biblical Narratives* (Philadelphia: Fortress Press, 1984).

4. Thomas H. Troeger, *Imagining a Sermon* (Nashville: Abingdon Press, 1990), p. 15.

5. Lowry, *Living with the Lectionary*, p. 20.

6. Augustine, *On Christian Doctrine*, trans. D. W. Robinson, Jr. (Indianapolis: Bobbs-Merrill Co., 1958), III, 15.

7. David Buttrick, *Homiletic: Moves and Structures* (Philadelphia: Fortress Press, 1987), p. 246.

8. See Anthony C. Thiselton, *The Two Horizons: New Testament Hermeneutics and Philosophical Description* (Grand Rapids: Wm. B. Eerdmans Publishing Co., 1980), p. 5, where he is citing Heinz Kimmerle.

9. Paul Ricoeur understands explanation in an interdisciplinary manner, having to do with scientific method, for instance using Freudian psychoanalysis as it applies to interpretation. Each of these human sciences discloses new texts. As he says, "It is indeed *another text* that psychoanalysis deciphers, *beneath the text of consciousness.* Phenomenology shows that it is another *text*, but not that this text is *other.*" Paul Ricoeur, *Freud and Philosophy: An Essay on Interpretation* (New Haven: Yale University Press, 1970), p. 392. See also Anthony C. Thiselton, *New Horizons in Hermeneutics* (Grand Rapids: Zondervan, 1992), pp. 344-78.

10. Understanding a text, says Ricoeur, is to follow its movement "from what it says to what it talks about." Paul Ricoeur, "The Model of the Text: Meaningful Action Considered as a Text," in Paul Ricoeur, *Hermeneutics and the Social Sciences* (New York: Cambridge University Press, 1981), pp. 210-13.

Chapter 7: Tuesday: What the Text Means

1. For instance: Alan Richardson and John Bowden, eds., *A New Dictionary of Christian Theology* (London: S.C.M. Press, 1983); Donald W. Musser and Joseph L. Price, eds., *A New Handbook of Christian Theology* (Nashville: Abingdon Press, 1992).

2. Robert W. Funk, Roy W. Hoover, and the Jesus Seminar, *The Five Gospels: The Search for the Authentic Words of Jesus* (New York: Macmillan, 1993).

3. Gerald T. Sheppard, "Isaiah 1–39," in James L. Mays, gen. ed., *Harper's Bible Commentary* (San Francisco: Harper & Row, Publishers, 1988), p. 547.

4. Thomas C. Oden, *After Modernity. . . . What? Agenda for Theology* (Grand Rapids: Zondervan, 1990), p. 106.

5. Ibid., p. 107.

6. Walter Wink, *The Bible in Human Transformation: Toward a New Paradigm for Biblical Study* (Philadelphia: Fortress Press, 1973), p. 6.

7. Martin Luther, *Sermons*, in *Luther's Works*, vol. 52, ed. Hans J. Hillerbrand, gen. ed. Helmut T. Lehmann (Philadelphia: Fortress Press, 1974), pp. 8-9.

8. Warren H. Stewart, Sr., *Interpreting God's Word in Black Preaching* (Valley Forge, Pa.: Judson Press, 1984), p. 15.

9. See Vladimir Propp, *Morphology of the Folk Tale*, rev. and ed. Louis A. Wagner, 2nd ed. (Austin, Tex.: University of Texas Press, [1968] 1986), pp. 92ff.: "Morphologically, a tale . . . may be termed any development proceeding from an act of villainy (A) or a lack (a) through intermediary functions to . . . other functions employed as a denouement. . . . This type of development is termed by us a move *(xod).* Each new act of villainy, each new lack creates a new move. One tale may have several moves, and when analyzing a text, one must first of all determine the number of moves of which it consists." See also pp. 124ff.

10. David Buttrick, *Homiletic: Moves and Structures* (Philadelphia: Fortress Press, 1987), pp. 23-69.

11. Ibid., pp. 309-12.
12. Paul Tillich, "The Experience of the Holy," in his *Shaking of the Foundations* (New York: Charles Scribner's Sons, 1948), pp. 87-92. This is an example of what is known as an exegetical sermon; it develops the text line by line.
13. Davie Napier, "The Burning in the Temple," and Allan M. Parrent, "The Humanity of the Call of God," both in James W. Cox, ed., *The Twentieth Century Pulpit*, vol. 2 (Nashville: Abingdon, 1981), pp. 141-50, 151-56.
14. Fred B. Craddock, *Preaching* (Nashville: Abingdon Press, 1985), p. 123.
15. Thomas G. Long, *The Witness of Preaching* (Louisville: Westminster Press/John Knox Press, 1989), pp. 86ff.
16. Ronald J. Allen, *Preaching the Topical Sermon* (Louisville: Westminster Press/John Knox Press, 1992), p. 64.
17. Henry H. Mitchell, *Celebration and Experience in Preaching* (Nashville: Abingdon Press, 1990), p. 39.
18. Buttrick, *Homiletic*, pp. 301, 294.
19. Allen, *Preaching the Topical Sermon*, p. 64.
20. Several places in Luther could be cited here, but the best discussion of this with notes may be found in Gerhard O. Forde, *Theology Is for Proclamation* (Minneapolis: Fortress Press, 1990), esp. pp. 13ff., 87ff.
21. James Forbes speaks of the "attitudes which urge silence or privacy regarding the role of the Spirit in our preaching" as being the same attitudes that "rob us of the full empowerment crucial for all who preach the Word." James Forbes, *The Holy Spirit and Preaching* (Nashville: Abingdon Press, 1989), p. 26.
22. For a further brief discussion of inversion, see my *Imagination of the Heart: New Understandings in Preaching* (Nashville: Abingdon Press, 1988), pp. 137-38.
23. Rudolf Bultmann, "Is Exegesis Without Presuppositions Possible?" in Kurt Mueller-Vollmer, ed., *The Hermeneutics Reader* (New York: Continuum, 1989), p. 242. Paul Ricoeur said that preunderstanding allows the reader to "guess" at a text's meaning. Paul Ricoeur, *Interpretation Theory: Discourse and the Surplus of Meaning* (Fort Worth, Tex.: Texas Christian University Press, 1976), pp. 75ff.
24. Bultmann, "Is Exegesis Without Presuppositions Possible?" pp. 247f. He says that continuity in understanding is nonetheless possible through historical-critical research and what he called the "guidance" that might pass from generation to generation.
25. For Gadamer, "Our starting-point . . . in the linguistic composition of the human experience of the world . . . is what exists, what man recognizes as existent and significant, that is expressed in it. In this—and not in the methodological ideal of rational construction . . . [based in] natural science—can the process of understanding practised in the moral sciences recognize itself." Hans-Georg Gadamer, *Truth and Method* (New York: Crossroad, 1986), pp. 413-14.
26. See Anthony C. Thiselton's discussion of *Horizontverschmelzung* in, *The Two Horizons: New Testament Hermeneutics and Philosophical Description* (Grand Rapids: Wm. B. Eerdmans Publishing Co., 1980), pp. 17, 149-68.
27. For Ricoeur, text is always a written text. He would have difficulty in recognizing experience as a text, although he made a move toward this in arguing the relevance of human sciences for hermeneutics. See Thiselton's discussion of this in *The Two Horizons*, pp. 113-14. Nonetheless, Ricoeur does grant that interpretation of experience (i.e. "meaningful action") was analogous to textual interpretation. See "The Model of the Text: Meaningful Action Considered as a Text," in his *Hermeneutics and the Social Sciences* (New York: Cambridge University Press, 1981), pp. 197-221. Recently Stanley Fish (*Is There a Text in This Class? The Authority of Interpretive Communities*, London and Cambridge, Mass.: Harvard University Press, 1980) has taken another approach that has been embraced, e.g., by Stanley Hauerwas in *Unleashing the Scripture: Freeing the Bible from Captivity to America* (Nashville: Abingdon Press, 1993). They would deny that the text exists with any meaning apart from what the

interpreting community brings to it. Such an approach suppresses the relevance of our first two stages in favor of today's meaning in front of the text, in our response. This direction seems misguided for scriptural texts, because it overlooks revelation on one hand, and on the other denies an understanding that God resides as eternal and objective truth beyond the written texts themselves (even if our access to God is incomplete).

Chapter 8: Wednesday: What Experience Says

1. See Elisabeth Schüssler Fiorenza, "Toward a Feminst Biblical Hermeneutic," in Donald K. McKim, ed., *A Guide to Contemporary Hermeneutics: Major Trends in Biblical Interpretation* (Grand Rapids: Wm. B. Eerdmans Publishing Co., 1986), esp. pp. 364-68.
2. José Miguez Bonino, "Hermeneutics, Truth, and Praxis," in McKim, ed., *A Guide to Contemporary Hermeneutics*, p. 348.
3. Schüssler Fiorenza, "Toward a Feminst Biblical Hermeneutic," p. 381.
4. Don S. Browning, building on the work of Gerhard Ebeling, David Tracy, and others, claims that "the pastoral theologian is interested in the full contextual meaning" and proposes "descriptive research" (*A Fundamental Practical Theology: Descriptive and Strategic Proposals* [Minneapolis: Fortress Press, 1991], p. 48). David Polk speaks of using a "hermeneutic of situations," involving "thick description" (a diverse research combining narrative with identification of appropriate questions, categories and methods, verbatim reports, identification of cultural biases, etc.) as a means of adequately reflecting "the complexity of lived experience." ("Practical Theology," in Donald W. Musser and Joseph L. Price, eds., *A New Handbook of Christian Theology* [Nashville: Abingdon Press, 1992], p. 376.) Theology that does this is what Browning calls "descriptive theology" (Browning, *Fundamental Practical Theology*, pp. 110ff.).
5. Barbara Brown Taylor, *The Preaching Life* (Cambridge and Boston, Mass.: Cowley Publications, 1993), p. 14.
6. David Buttrick, *Homiletic: Moves and Structures* (Philadelphia: Fortress Press, 1987), p. 261.
7. Browning, *A Fundamental Practical Theology*, pp. 48-49.
8. Art Van Seters, ed., *Preaching as a Social Act: Theology and Practice* (Nashville: Abingdon Press, 1988), p. 19.
9. Christine M. Smith, *Preaching as Weeping, Confession, and Resistance: Radical Responses to Radical Evil* (Louisville: Westminster Press/John Knox Press, 1992), p. 6.
10. Ibid., p. 41.
11. William K. McElvaney, *Preaching from Camelot to Covenant: Announcing God's Action in the World* (Nashville: Abingdon Press, 1989), pp. 76ff.
12. Ibid., pp. 28-29.
13. Ibid., p. 59.
14. Ibid., p. 30.
15. Ronald J. Allen, *Preaching the Topical Sermon* (Louisville: Westminster Press/John Knox Press, 1992), pp. 38-71.
16. Buttrick, *Homiletic*, pp. 258ff., 293.
17. See my *Imagination of the Heart: New Understandings in Preaching* (Nashville: Abingdon Press, 1988), pp. 86ff., 115ff.
18. Harry Emerson Fosdick, *The Living of These Days* (New York: Harper and Brothers, 1956), p. 99.
19. Fred B. Craddock, *Preaching* (Nashville: Abingdon Press, 1985), p. 123, italics added.
20. Thomas G. Long, *The Witness of Preaching* (Louisville: Westminster Press/John Knox Press, 1989), pp. 86-91.
21. Henry H. Mitchell, *Celebration and Experience in Preaching* (Nashville: Abingdon Press, 1990), p. 52, italics added.

Chapter 9: Thursday/Friday: What the Preacher Says

1. David Buttrick, *Homiletic: Moves and Structures* (Philadelphia: Fortress Press, 1987), p. 311.
2. Thomas G. Long, *The Witness of Preaching* (Louisville: Westminster Press/John Knox Press, 1989), pp. 138-47.
3. Buttrick, *Homiletic*, pp. 83-109.
4. Ibid., pp. 86-87.
5. Ibid., pp. 92-93.
6. David Schlaffer takes the last three of our suggestions as an approach to the entire sermon in, "'Where Does the Preacher Stand?' Image, Narrative, and Argument as Basic Strategies for Shaping Sermons," in *Homiletic:* xix:1 (summer, 1994): 1-5.
7. See Buttrick, *Homiletic*, esp. pp. 103-8.
8. James S. Stewart, *Heralds of God* (New York: Charles Scribner's Sons, 1946), p. 140.
9. Mitchell adds, "For this we had a number of our own terms, such as 'coming on up at the end,' 'the gravy,' 'the rousements,' 'the whoop,' or just the generic 'climax.'" Henry H. Mitchell, *Celebration and Experience in Preaching* (Nashville: Abingdon Press, 1990), p. 12.
10. Ibid., p. 54.
11. James S. Stewart, "The Challenge of His Coming," in *The Wind of the Spirit* (Nashville: Abingdon Press, 1969), p. 179.
12. Don S. Browning, from the perspective of pastoral theology, may be saying something similar. He advocates that the practical theologian will engage in research that describes the "theory-laden practice" of communities, and, in so doing, will raise questions "that help produce the fusion of meaning between situation and text." Don S. Browning, *A Fundamental Practical Theology* (Minneapolis: Fortress Press, 1991), pp. 48ff. In our terms, the creation of a new text facilitates the community process of interpreting its life before the Scriptures. As long as homiletics is invisible, the hermeneutical process will be incomplete.
13. Nowhere is this seen more than in Europe (and in some individual seminaries like McGill in Montreal) where preaching is not taught as part of the academic program, but is left to a final practical year of work in a church.
14. Roland Barthes, "From Work to Text," in Josue V. Haraei, trans. and ed., *Textual Strategies: Perspectives in Post-Structuralist Criticism* (Ithaca, N.Y.: Cornell University Press, 1979), p. 75.
15. Stanley Hauerwas, *Unleashing the Scripture: Freeing the Bible from Captivity to America* (Nashville: Abingdon Press, 1993), p. 41. Hauerwas seems to go too far, or not far enough, in his brief discussion, adopting the literary model of Stanley Fish and ignoring the difference between literature and Scripture.
16. As Jürgen Habermas said, "The art of interpretation is the counterpart of the art of convincing and persuading in situations where practical questions are brought to decision." Jürgen Habermas, "On Hermeneutics' Claim to Universality," in Kurt Mueller-Vollmer, ed., *The Hermeneutics Reader* (New York: Continuum, 1989), p. 294. Hans-Georg Gadamer has said something similar: "Rhetoric [in its universality] . . . is by its very nature antecedent to hermeneutics in the limited sense . . . which represents something like the positive pole to the negative of textual exposition." (Hans-Georg Gadamer, "Rhetoric, Hermeneutics, and the Critique of Ideology: Metacritical Comments on Truth and Method," in Mueller-Vollmer, ed., *Hermeneutics Reader*, p. 276). Charles S. Peirce (c. 1900) argued that there were three divisions to semiotics: grammar (the rules of a language that allow for meaning); logic (the science of determining the truth of what was said); and rhetoric (the task of identifying new laws which govern meaning in language). (See Charles S. Peirce, "Logic as Semiotics: the Theory of Signs," in *Semiotics: An Introductory Anthology*, ed. Robert E. Innis [Bloomington: Indiana University Press, 1985], pp. 5-6.)

Chapter 10: Arranging the Sermon: Unity and Form

1. James S. Stewart, *Heralds of God* (New York: Charles Scribner's Sons, 1946), p. 31.
2. Henry Grady Davis, *Design for Preaching* (Philadelphia: Fortress Press, 1958), pp. v-vi.
3. David James Randolph, *The Renewal of Preaching* (Philadelphia: Fortress Press, 1969), pp. 23, 97ff.
4. Romantic artists include poets (e.g., Wordsworth, Coleridge, Keats); painters (Delacroix); and musicians (Beethoven, Berlioz, and Schubert).
5. Friedrich Schleiermacher, *On Religion: Addresses in Response to Its Cultured Critics,* Terrence N. Tice, trans. (Richmond: John Knox Press, 1969), pp. 139-40.
6. There are affinities for instance with postmodernism in architecture. Modern architecture, seen in most office buildings from the 1960s to the 1980s, was designed to a predetermined ideal that minimized history, ornament, symbol, and metaphor; box shapes and exterior reflective glass maximized uniformity and minimized the human element. Postmodern architecture, by contrast, is eclectic—it draws on a variety of traditions—is representational in its depiction of life, is pro-history, pro-ornament, pro-humor, and relishes the human. See, e.g., Thomas C. Oden, *After Modernity. . . . What? Agenda for Theology* (Grand Rapids: Zondervan, 1990), esp. pp. 73-74, citing Charles Jencks.
7. Horace Bushnell, "Our Gospel, a Gift to the Imagination," in Conrad Cherry, ed., *Horace Bushnell: Sermons* (New York: Paulist Press, 1985), p. 100. See also Horace Bushnell, "Preliminary Dissertation on the Nature of Language as Related to Thought and Spirit," in *God in Christ* (Hartford: Brown and Parsons, 1849). His theory of education was entitled *Christian Nurture* (1847; rev. 1861).
8. Tillich said of his "method of correlation," that it was "a way of uniting message and situation. It tries to correlate the questions implied in the situation with the answers implied in the message." Paul Tillich, *Systematic Theology* (Chicago: University of Chicago Press, 1967 [1951]), I, p. 8; see also p. 66.
9. Davis's image may also be compared to the dominant medieval understanding of the "ladder of spirituality" (Jacob's ladder with seven rungs) required of the preacher. See Alan of Lille, *The Art of Preaching,* Cistercian Fathers Series, No. 23, trans. Gillian R. Evans (Kalamazoo, Mich.: Cistercian Publications, 1981), p. 15. An even earlier precedent is Augustine's five spiritual steps for interpretation of scripture in *On Christian Doctrine* (II:7).
10. Davis, *Design for Preaching,* pp. 15-16.
11. Henry H. Mitchell, *Celebration and Experience in Preaching* (Nashville: Abingdon Press, 1990), p. 55.
12. Several social factors lay behind the revolution in homiletics around 1200, including: growth of urban centers and demand for instruction from the church; increased emphasis on educated clergy; and the need for simple guidelines for local clergy. Point-form structure was simple for priests and abbesses to learn and use and was easy for hearers to follow and recall.
13. Robert of Basevorn, *The Form of Preaching,* trans. Leopold Krul O.S.B., in James J. Murphy, ed., *Three Medieval Rhetorical Arts* (Berkeley: University of California Press, 1971), p. 138.
14. See Craig A. Loscalzo, *Preaching Sermons That Connect: Effective Communication Through Identification* (Downer's Grove, Ill.: InterVarsity Press, 1992), esp. pp. 25ff. He draws on the work of Kenneth Burke in exploring the importance of identification in the sermon.
15. Charles L. Rice, *Interpretation and Imagination* (Philadelphia: Fortress Press, 1970), p. 58.
16. Stephen Crites, "The Narrative Quality of Experience," *JAAR* 39 (1971), pp. 291ff. Reprinted in Stanley Hauerwas and L. Gregory Jones, *Why Narrative? Readings in Narrative Theology* (Grand Rapids: Wm. B. Eerdmans Publishing Co., 1989), pp. 65-88.
17. Fred B. Craddock, *As One Without Authority* (Nashville: Abingdon Press, 1971).

H. Grady Davis spoke of sermons composed with "inductive continuity" as an "organizing principle." See Davis, *Design for Preaching*, pp. 177-80.

18. See my "Beyond Narrative: Imagination in the Sermon," in Gail R. O'Day and Thomas G. Long, eds., *Listening to the Word: Studies in Honor of Fred B. Craddock* (Nashville: Abingdon Press, 1993), pp. 131-46, esp. pp. 136ff.

19. This example was found in Gwyn Walters, *Towards Healthy Preaching: A Manual for Students, Pastors, and Laypersons*, published by Gwyn Walters (n.p., 1987), p. 81.

20. *The Storyteller's Companion to the Bible*, ed. Michael Williams (Nashville: Abingdon Press, 1991–), is devoted to helping its readers primarily with this form, although it does much more than this.

21. Davis, *Design for Preaching*, pp. 177-80.

22. Rice, *Interpretation and Imagination*, esp. pp. 110-55.

23. Eugene L. Lowry speaks of three hybrid forms (although he uses story as a synonym for biblical text): (1) delaying the story—the story entry delayed, possibly until midway; (2) suspending the story—start with story and later return to it; (3) alternating the story—there is a movement into and away from the biblical text. See Eugene L. Lowry, *How to Preach a Parable: Designs for Narrative Sermons* (Nashville: Abingdon Press, 1989). John Holbert identifies a fourth option, (4) a "frame narrative"—the narrative is "framed" with commentary or by a nonbiblical story to help listeners discern the narrator's intent. John Holbert, *Preaching Old Testament: Proclamation and Narrative in the Hebrew Bible* (Nashville: Abingdon Press, 1991), pp. 42ff.

24. Eugene L. Lowry, *The Homiletical Plot: The Sermon as Narrative Art Form* (Atlanta: John Knox, 1980).

25. Ella P. Mitchell, "For Such a Time," in Henry H. Mitchell, *Celebration and Experience in Preaching*, pp. 96-100.

26. Thomas H. Troeger, *Imagining a Sermon* (Nashville: Abingdon Press, 1990), pp. 44-47.

27. Fred B. Craddock, "Praying Through Clenched Teeth," in James W. Cox, ed., *The Twentieth Century Pulpit*, Vol. 2 (Nashville: Abingdon Press, 1981), pp. 47-52.

28. Reuel Howe, *Partners in Preaching* (New York: Seabury Press, 1967).

29. See, for instance, the sermons in Wayne Bradley Robinson, ed., *Journeys Toward Narrative Preaching* (New York: Pilgrim Press, 1990).

30. David Buttrick makes a similar point: "Nevertheless, though storytelling from the pulpit may entertain, excite, and inform, it does not necessarily shape faith-consciousness." *Homiletic: Moves and Structures* (Philadelphia: Fortress Press, 1987), p. 335.

31. Buttrick, *Homiletic*, pp. 321-90.

32. Steimle taught preaching at Union Seminary in New York and though he did not publish much, one book published by him and his students includes three of his essays. See Edmund A. Steimle, Morris J. Niedenthal, and Charles L. Rice, *Preaching the Story* (Philadelphia: Fortress Press, 1980).

33. Eugene L. Lowry, *How to Preach a Parable: Designs for Narrative Sermons* (Nashville: Abingdon Press, 1989).

34. Christine M. Smith, *Weaving the Sermon: Preaching in a Feminist Perspective* (Louisville: Westminster Press/John Knox Press, 1989); Carol M. Norén, *The Woman in the Pulpit* (Nashville: Abingdon Press, 1991).

35. Thomas G. Long, *Preaching and the Literary Forms of the Bible* (Philadelphia: Fortress Press, 1989), pp. 24-34.

36. Ronald J. Allen, *Preaching the Topical Sermon* (Louisville: Westminster Press/John Knox Press, 1992), pp. 75ff.

37. Buttrick, *Homiletic*, p. 23.

38. For a practical demonstration of this, see David Buttrick, "Abraham and Isaac," in Richard L. Eslinger, *A New Hearing: Living Options in Homiletic Method* (Nashville: Abingdon Press, 1987), pp. 166-69.

39. Buttrick, *Homiletic*, p. 338.

Chapter 11: Linear Thought and Homiletical Movement

1. James S. Stewart, *The Wind of the Spirit* (Nashville: Abingdon Press, 1969), p. 9.
2. A sermon that proceeds by listing causes, or consequences, or requirements, or instances is often called a faceting sermon.
3. Within some parts of the African American tradition, this emotional-theological movement to a peak of celebration is given various names: " 'coming on up at the end,' 'the gravy,' 'the rousements,' 'the whoop,' or just the generic 'climax.' " See Henry H. Mitchell, *Celebration and Experience in Preaching* (Nashville: Abingdon Press, 1990), p. 12.
4. Gwyn Walters, *Towards Healthy Preaching: A Manual for Students, Pastors, and Laypersons* (published by the author, 1987), p. 68.
5. Roman Jacobson, "The Metaphoric and Metonymic Poles," in Roman Jacobson and Morris Halle, *Fundamentals of Language* (The Hague: Mouton, 1956), pp. 34ff. He studied aphasia, a medical disorder in which patients suffer language loss and the inability to use or understand certain kinds of familiar language. He determined that some patients lost the ability to combine thought in sequential ways, ways that he connected with the figure of speech known as metonymy. Other patients lost the ability to recognize similarities or to connect thought in associative ways, which he connected with metaphor. The two seemed to be polar opposites. He concluded that these two modes of language, which he did not detail, are two interrelated ways of thought that we all normally use. In other words, metonymy and metaphor are how language works. (This contrasts with Sallie McFague's claim that metaphor is how thought works. See Sallie McFague, *Metaphorical Theology* [Philadelphia: Fortress Press, 1982], pp. 38ff.)

    Jacobson connected his understanding with a similar kind of polarity identified by the Geneva linguist Ferdinand de Sausseure, *Course in General Linguistics,* trans. Roy Harris (La Salle, Ill.: Open Court Publishers, 1991), Parts 2 and 3. (Originally, *Cours de Linguistique Generale,* 1915.) See the distinction between the diachronic (i.e., progressing "through time") mode of language (metonymy) and the synchronic (i.e., existing "at the same time") mode (metaphor). Although countless scholars in diverse disciplines have endorsed Jacobson's view of language, his basic distinction has tended to be lost or obscured by Sausseurean thought, with the exception of David Lodge, *The Modes of Modern Writing: Metaphor, Metonymy, and the Typology of Modern Literature* (London: Edward Arnold Ltd., 1977), esp. pp. 73-124.

    Students interested in pursuing the subject of metonymy may find helpful discussions in books of literary or rhetorical theory, and especially in the following: Claude Levi-Strauss, *The Savage Mind* (London: Weidenfeld & Nicolson, 1966), pp. 204-5; Jacques Lacan, "The insistence of the Letter in the Unconscious," in *Structuralism,* ed. Jacques Ehrmann (New York: Doubleday & Co., 1970); Paul Ricoeur also uses metonymy and metaphor in his *Rule of Metaphor: Multi-disciplinary Studies of the Creation of Meaning in Language* (Toronto, Buffalo, and London: University of Toronto Press, 1977), pp. 55ff.; Giambattista Vico, *The New Science,* trans. of the 3rd ed. (1744) by Thomas Goddard Bergin and Max Harold Fisch (Ithaca, N.Y.: Cornell University Press, 1968); Hayden White, *Metahistory: Historical Imagination in Nineteenth-Century Europe* (Baltimore: Johns Hopkins University Press, 1973), esp. pp. 31ff., 281ff.; George Lakoff and Mark Johnson, *Metaphors We Live By* (Chicago: University of Chicago Press, 1980), esp. pp. 35-41; George Lakoff and Mark Turner, *More Than Cool Reason: A Field Guide to Poetic Metaphor* (Chicago: University of Chicago Press, 1989), esp. pp. 100-106; David Lodge, "Modernism, Antimodernism, Postmodernism," in *Working with Structuralism* (London: Routledge and Kegan Paul, 1981), pp. 3-16; Don Cupitt, *What Is a Story?* (London: S.C.M. Press, 1991), pp. 12ff.; and Stephen Bonnycastle, *In Search of Authority: An Introductory Guide to Literary Theory* (Peterborough, Ont.: Broadview Press, 1991), pp. 75-118. Metonymy is also broadly misunderstood: "Metonymy and synecdoche function as oblique refer-

ence and as such they, if any of the tropes, fit the bill for being primarily ornamental ways of naming." Janet Martin Soskice, *Metaphor and Religious Language* (Oxford: Clarendon Press, 1985), p. 57.
6. Lodge, *Modes of Modern Writing*.
7. In synecdoche, a subform of metonymy, a part stands for a whole or a whole for a part; thus, in common conversation we may say, "Tickets are five dollars per head," rather than "per person"; or "She went for her wheels" when we mean "car." The difference between metonymy and synecdoche is structurally so minimal that I follow Jacobson and many sources here in largely ignoring any distinction. (In fact, the difference is that instead of a part being substituted for a whole, or vice versa, substitution is based on contiguity—proximity in time or space.) Thus metonymy, broadly understood, includes this synecdoche in Dylan Thomas's poem, "The hand that signed the paper felled the city," in which "hand" stands for "king."
8. Lucy Rose, "Body Broken, Blood Spilled," in Wayne Bradley Robinson, ed., *Journeys Toward Narrative Preaching* (New York: Pilgrim Press, 1990), p. 42 (italics added).
9. Robert F. Smith, *Word and Witness*, Palm/Passion Sunday, vol. 93:3 (April 4, 1993), p. 104. Metonymy accounts for the primary strength of this closing. A case could also be made for the metaphoric connection between the face of Jon Sobrino and the face of Christ being its secondary strength.
10. Thomas G. Long, *The Witness of Preaching* (Louisville: Westminster Press/John Knox Press, 1989), p. 166.
11. Ibid., p. 168.

Chapter 12: Polar Thought and Homiletical Relevance

1. Kevin Trudeau, *Mega Memory* (Chicago: Nightingale-Conant Corporation, 1991).
2. If I continued with yet another story or thought that also did not connect, and another after that, we would have a set of unlinked thoughts and images that would function neither in a linear nor a polar fashion, though our minds would keep searching in both modes for some link.
3. Samuel D. Proctor, "The Recovery of Human Compassion," in Samuel D. Proctor and William C. Watley, *Sermons from the Black Pulpit* (Valley Forge, Pa.: Judson Press, 1984), p. 13.
4. An important historical precedent for the dominance of analogy in the post-Reformation period was the *via negativa*, a method of theological speech that constantly emphasized the necessity and inadequacy of terms based in human relationships to deal with God's encounter with us.
5. Martin Luther, *Sermons, Luther's Works*, vol. 52, ed. Hans. J. Hillebrand, general ed. Helmut T. Lehman (Philadelphia: Fortress Press, 1974), pp. 9-10. Both Horace Bushnell and James S. Stewart preached using similar comparisons on the Christmas theme. See my *Concise History of Preaching* (Nashville: Abingdon Press, 1992), pp. 144, 166-67.
6. "Hence, if that, than which nothing greater can be conceived, can be conceived not to exist, it is not that, than which nothing greater can be conceived. But this is an irreconcilable contradiction. There is, then, so truly a being than which nothing greater can be conceived to exist, that it cannot even be conceived not to exist; and this being thou art, O Lord, our God." Anselm, *Proslogium*, III, in *Saint Anselm: Basic Writings*, trans. S. N. Deane (LaSalle, Ill.: Open Court Publishing Company, 1968), pp. 8-9. Simone Weil wrote a chapter on contradiction in her *Grace and Gravity* (1947), in which she says: "All true good carries with it conditions which are contradictory and as a consequence is impossible. He who keeps his attention really fixed on this impossibility and acts will do what is good. In the same way all truth contains a contradiction." Simone Weil, *Grace and Gravity*, trans. Emma Craufurd (London: Routledge and Kegan Paul, 1952 [Fr. 1947]), p. 89.
7. Samuel Taylor Coleridge, *Biographia Literaria*, ed. James Engell and Walter Jackson

Bate (Princeton: Princeton University Press, 1983), p. 156. For an explanation of Coleridge on this subject, see my *"Biographia's* Coherence: God, Self, and Coleridge's 'Seminal Principle,'" in *Philological Quarterly* 72/4 (Fall 1993): 451-69.
8. Gerhard Ebeling, *The Study of Theology,* trans. Duane A. Priebe (Philadelphia: Fortress Press, 1978), p. 156.
9. Henri de Lubac, *Paradoxes of Faith,* trans. Paule Simon and Sadie Kreilkamp (San Francisco: Ignatius Press, 1987 [Fr. 1945]), p. 12.
10. D. M. Baillie, *God Was in Christ* (London: Faber and Faber, 1948), p. 109.
11. Horace Bushnell, "Preliminary Dissertation on the Nature of Language as Related to Thought and Spirit," in *God in Christ* (Hartford: Brown and Parsons, 1849), p. 55.
12. Horace Bushnell, "Free to Amusements, and too Free to Want Them," in *Sermons on Living Subjects* (New York: Charles Scribner's Sons, 1897), pp. 378-79.
13. Aristotle, "Poetics," *The Complete Works of Aristotle,* Jonathan Barnes, ed., vol. 2 (Princeton and Oxford: Princeton University Press, 1984), pp. 2334-35.
14. Aristotle, "Rhetoric," *Complete Works of Aristotle,* p. 2250.
15. Roman Jacobson, "The Metaphoric and Metonymic Poles," in Roman Jacobson and Morris Halle, *Fundamentals of Language* (The Hague: Mouton, 1956), pp. 34ff.
16. See my *Imagination of the Heart: New Understandings in Preaching* (Nashville: Abingdon Press, 1988), esp. pp. 32ff.; see also my "Beyond Narrative: Imagination in the Sermon," in Gail R. O'Day and Thomas G. Long, *Listening to the Word: Studies in Honor of Fred B. Craddock* (Nashville: Abingdon Press, 1993), pp. 131-46; see also my "Biographia's Coherence: God, Self, and Coleridge's 'Seminal Principle,'" in *Philological Quarterly,* 72/4 (Fall 1993): 451-69; see also Richard Kearney, *Poetics of Imagining: From Husserl to Lyotard* (London: HarperCollins Academic, 1991), p. 4.; Eduard R. Riegert, *Imaginative Shock: Preaching and Metaphor* (Burlington, Ont.: Trinity Press, 1990), and Thomas H. Troeger, *Imagining a Sermon* (Nashville: Abingdon Press, 1990).
17. We may say that insofar as there is a natural flow of thought in theology from Scripture to our life, there is a natural metonymic link between the text and our situation. While true and important, this link takes on secondary importance in relation to the primary polar, or metaphoric back-and-forth energy between text and our situation.
18. Gardner C. Taylor, "From Our Own Awful Dignity," in Henry H. Mitchell, *Black Preaching: The Recovery of a Powerful Art* (Nashville: Abingdon Press, 1990), p. 69.
19. I. A. Richards, *The Philosophy of Rhetoric* (New York: Oxford University Press, 1936 [1965]), pp. 118ff.
20. Those students wanting to read more on imagery should consult Patricia Wilson-Kastner, *Imagery for Preaching* (Minneapolis: Fortress Press, 1989).
21. Eugene L. Lowry, *Living with the Lectionary: Preaching through the Revised Common Lectionary* (Nashville: Abingdon Press, 1992), p. 11.
22. I am indebted to Roger Mitchell for this exercise entitled, "Getting at Metaphor," in an excellent book of writing exercises, Robin Behn and Chase Twichell, eds., *The Practice of Poetry: Writing Exercises from Poets Who Teach* (New York: HarperCollins, 1992), pp. 46-47.

Chapter 13: Mission, Truth, and Stories

1. Fred B. Craddock, *Preaching* (Nashville: Abingdon Press, 1993), p. 207.
2. Julian N. Hartt, *Theological Method and Imagination* (New York: Seabury Press, 1977), p. 237.
3. Elizabeth Achtemeier, *Preaching as Theology and Art* (Nashville: Abingdon Press, 1984), p. 51.
4. Don Chatfield, *Dinner with Jesus and Other Left-handed Story-sermons* (Grand Rapids: Zondervan, 1988), p. 27.
5. Craddock, *Preaching,* p. 123.
6. Julian N. Hartt made the distinction between the "verisimilitude" of William

Faulkner's *Absalom, Absalom!* and the "fact-confirmation" of Gibbon's *Decline and Fall of the Roman Empire.* He distinguishes between the novelist and the historian, the latter of whom is concerned with the "first-order facts"; is familiar with the "second-order facts" (the interpretations in the field) and able to assess these with discriminatory judgment; and is able to use "imagination to give proper shape to the facts." Hartt, *Theological Method and Imagination,* pp. 227-29.

7. On the question of the preacher's integrity, see Craig A. Loscalzo, *Preaching Sermons That Connect: Effective Communication Through Identification* (Downers Grove, Ill.: InterVarsity Press, 1992), pp. 81-122.

8. James Forbes, *The Holy Spirit and Preaching* (Nashville: Abingdon Press, 1989), p. 70.

9. Richard F. Ward, *Speaking from the Heart: Preaching and Passion* (Nashville: Abingdon Press, 1992), p. 39.

10. John Mason Stapleton, *Preaching in Demonstration of the Spirit and Power* (Philadelphia: Fortress Press, 1988), p. 45. See also pp. 41-57.

11. Robin R. Meyers, *With Ears to Hear: Preaching as Self-Persuasion* (Cleveland: Pilgrim Press, 1993), pp. 117-18.

12. Augustine, *On Christian Doctrine,* trans. D. W. Robinson, Jr. (Indianapolis: Bobbs-Merrill Co., 1958), IV:17. See also Cicero, *Orator,* sec. 69.

13. Jini Robinson, "What's Your Story," in J. Alfred Smith, *Preach On!* (Nashville: Broadman Press, 1984), p. 101.

14. Paul Ricoeur speaks of all texts having a surplus of meaning in *Interpretation Theory: Discourse and the Surplus of Meaning* (Fort Worth: Texas Christian University Press, 1976). By this he meant that any text has more meanings than we are able to extract, both correct and incorrect. When we create prose in the manner mentioned, we are being intentional about creating a surplus of meaning with pathos and ethos.

15. Victor Jones, *Creative Writing* (London: English Universities Press, 1974), p. 46.

16. Aristotle said, for instance, "The life and soul, so to speak, of tragedy is the plot; and . . . the characters come second," in "Poetics," *The Complete Works of Aristotle,* vol. 2 (Princeton: Princeton University Press, 1984), p. 2321.

17. Foster-Harris, *The Basic Formulas of Fiction* (Norman, Okla.: University of Oklahoma Press, 1963 [1944]), p. 60.

18. Ibid., pp. 9-10.

19. Ibid., p. 32.

20. Ibid., pp. 77-92. It is interesting to compare these steps with those suggested by Eugene Lowry in chapter 12, concerning the "homiletical plot."

21. L. Susan May, "Starting a Fire," in Ronald J. Allen, *Preaching the Topical Sermon* (Louisville: Westminster Press/John Knox Press, 1992), p. 122.

22. Peter Vaught, "Within Reach of the Dragon," in Cornish R. Rogers and Joseph R. Jeter, Jr., eds., *Preaching Through the Apocalypse: Sermons from Revelation* (St. Louis: Chalice Press, 1992), pp. 122-23.

23. Ibid., p. 124.

24. Charles Rice includes a helpful section on use of the arts in sermons in *The Embodied Word* (Minneapolis: Fortress Press, 1991), pp. 93-124.

25. From Truman Capote and Eleanor Perry, "A Christmas Memory," in Truman Capote, Eleanor Perry, Frank Perry, *Trilogy: an Experiment in Multimedia* (New York: Collier Books, 1969), pp. 248-52; as cited by Robert P. Waznak, S.S., "Christmas Is for Seeing," in his *Like Fresh Bread: Sunday Homilies in the Parish* (New York/Mahwah: Paulist Press, 1993), p. 39.

26. Charles L. Rice, "Ordinary People," in Don M. Wardlaw, ed., *Preaching Biblically: Creating Sermons in the Shape of Scripture* (Philadelphia: Westminster Press, 1983), pp. 113-14.

27. Thomas G. Long, "Praying for the Wrath of God," in Rogers and Jeter, eds., *Preaching Through the Apocalypse,* p. 137.

28. George Mayers made this observation in a graduate class.

29. William K. McElvaney, *Preaching from Camelot to Covenant: Announcing God's Action*

in the World (Nashville: Abingdon Press, 1989), p. 26. This is an excellent book on globalization and preaching. See also Arthur Van Seters, ed., *Preaching as a Social Act: Theology and Practice* (Nashville: Abingdon Press, 1988).

30. See my "Beyond Narrative: Imagination in the Sermon," in Gail R. O'Day and Thomas G. Long, eds., *Listening to the Word: Studies in Honor of Fred B. Craddock* (Nashville: Abingdon Press, 1993), esp. pp. 141-43.
31. Richard Lischer, "Preaching and the Rhetoric of Promise," *Word and World* 8 (Winter 1988): 70.

Appendix 1

1. Two of the best funeral resources are Perry H. Biddle, Jr., *Abingdon Funeral Manual* (Nashville: Abingdon Press, 1991) and, specifically on the funeral sermon, Robert Hughes, *A Trumpet in Darkness: Preaching to Mourners* (Philadelphia: Fortress Press, 1985).

INDEX OF NAMES
AND SUBJECTS

INDEX OF NAMES AND SUBJECTS

INDEX OF NAMES AND SUBJECTS

Jesus Christ as, 98
law as, 100
preaching, 106-8

Identification, 28, 30, 64, 79, 133, 135, 186-87, 208, 215, 285-89, 302n. 3
Image/s, 136, 246-47, 253-55
Imagination, 49, 130, 239, 245, 265, 279
Inductive approach, 151, 214-15, 217, 259
Introduction, sermon, 182-84

Jacobson, Roman, 228, 244
Jesus Christ
in Christology, 71-75, 94, 98
church and, 25
confession of, 86
event of, 118, 281
hope and, 98-100
new order and, 23, 104
as poet, 18
preaching on, 71-73, 89
relationship with, 24, 71-75
speaking, 263
Jesus Seminar, the, 144
Jones, Victor, 270
Judgment and grace, 106, 118, 154-55, 162, 186
Justice, social, 77, 111, 143, 161-63, 278-83
Justin Martyr, 25

Keillor, Garrison, 265
Kelsey, David, 85
Kierkegaard, Søren, 241
Klinkowitz, Jerome, 302n. 1

Language, theological
abstract/concrete, 39-41, 235
faith and, 172
homiletics and, 15, 218
performative, 260
structure of, 15
See also Logic; Words
Law and gospel, 104, 108
See also Judgment and grace
Lectionary, 12, 129
Levi-Strauss, 51
Liberal theology, 88, 204

Liberation theology, 88, 159
Lindbeck, George, 85
Linear thought, 220-22
Linguistics, 317n. 5
Lischer, Richard L., 75, 104, 282
Listener
captive audience as, 207
categories of experience, 248
ethos and, 27-35
experience of, 14, 29, 30, 77, 105-6, 109-10, 113, 164, 246
identification, 28, 30, 64, 79, 133, 135, 186-87, 208, 215, 285-89, 302n. 3
needs, 31-32, 102-3, 174, 181-84, 200, 214-15, 217, 218, 285-89
reception/response and, 23, 24, 102, 128, 151, 178, 186, 281
Literary criticism, 130-36
Lodge, David, 228
Logic, 66-67, 76, 205, 206, 208, 214, 222, 224-27, 233, 236, 241-42, 244, 260, 306n. 10
Logos, 76, 78-80, 118-20, 159, 213, 217, 269, 270
Long, Thomas G., 25, 104, 150, 173, 216, 231-32, 246, 276, 303n. 5, 319n. 16
Loscalzo, Craig A., 303n. 21, 304n. 25, 306n. 18, 320n. 7
Lowry, Eugene L., 24, 109, 136, 179, 211, 216, 259, 316n. 22, 320n. 20
Luria, Aleksandr, 49-51
Luther, Martin, 25, 39, 47, 76, 145, 152-53, 240-41, 244, 307n. 13

McClure, John S., 306n. 18
McElvaney, William K., 162, 278
McFague, Sallie, 24, 39, 50, 317n. 5
Macleish, Archibald, 6, 14, 17, 18, 283
McLuhan, Marshall, 51
Macquarrie, John, 308n. 1
Major concern of the sermon.
See Concern of the sermon
Major concern of the text.
See Concern of the text
Mandela, Nelson, 113
Marxist criticism, 159
May, Susan, 273

325

INDEX OF NAMES AND SUBJECTS

Robinson, Jini, 269
Rodenburg, Patsy, 268
Romantics, 200, 202, 245
Rose, Lucy, 229

Schaper, Donna, 103
Scherer, Paul, 303n. 6
Schlafer, David J., 24, 314n. 6
Schleiermacher, Friedrich, 126, 139-
    40, 202, 307n. 2
Schüssler Fiorenza, Elisabeth, 159
Scripture
    authority of, 40, 125, 137
    canon as, 130, 144
    centrality of, 125, 225
    distorting the text, 132
    God's voice as, 17, 125
    interpretation of, correct, 125, 130,
        136-37
    oral tradition and, 19
    See also Bible; Hermeneutics
Segundo, Luis, 111
Sequence, 222, 224-27, 228
Sermon
    aspects of, 24
    body of, 178-82
    composition, 178-80, 198-200
    conclusion, 184-86
    deductive, 214-15, 216, 259-60
    essay and, 22
    event as, 20-22, 82, 145-46
    exegetical, 209
    expository, 209
    faceting, 317n. 2
    form as theology, 105
    funeral, 285-88
    God's action as, 22, 23, 102-3, 112,
        150-52
    inductive, 151, 214-15, 217, 259-60
    as interpretation, 126
    introduction, 182-84
    movement in, 64, 92, 115-16
    moves, 146, 217
    as movie-making, 112, 132, 183,
        255, 264
    narrative, 205-7
    outlines, 203, 226
    points in a, 151, 201-2, 205, 207, 224
    preparation time, 128-30

propositional, 205-7
reception, 102-3
as text production, 191
thematic, 209
theological structure of, 83, 98-124
time of parts of, 113-14, 117, 171,
    174, 225, 254, 259
topical, 209
truth and, 264-67
two-part structure for, 112-18
unity, 136, 199-205
varieties, 12-13
verisimilitude in the, 265-67
views of the, 25-27
violence and, 250-51, 279
wedding, 288-89
See also Poetics; Preacher;
    Preaching
Sheppard, Gerald T., 144
Simile, 222, 244
Sin, 22, 27, 103, 107, 110, 153, 161,
    187, 225, 242, 243, 264
Sinclair, Laura, 52
Sleeth, Ronald E., 306n. 18
Smart, James D., 303n. 16
Smith, Christine M., 161, 216
Smith, Eugene, 277
Smith, Robert F., 230, 246
Sola Scriptura, 137
Spielberg, Steven, 277
Spurgeon, Charles H., 107, 116
Stapleton, John Mason, 269
Steimle, Edmund A., 216, 302n. 2,
    316n. 32
Stewart, James S., 89, 185, 188, 199,
    223, 318n. 5
Stewart, Warren H., 145
Stookey, Laurence Hull, 308n. 20
Story, 270-81
    art as source of, 274-76
    autobiographical, 272
    character and, 270-71
    conflict, 270, 273, 277
    global, 278
    joyous, 270
    metaphor and, 247-49
    news as source of, 278-81
    personal, 272
    plot and, 270-71

328